An Activist's
Foreign Policy
Toolkit

For Sue

America's Foreign Policy Toolkit

Key Institutions and Processes

Charles A. Stevenson
Johns Hopkins University, SAIS

Los Angeles | London | New Delhi
Singapore | Washington DC

Los Angeles | London | New Delhi
Singapore | Washington DC

FOR INFORMATION:

CQ Press
An Imprint of SAGE Publications, Inc.
2455 Teller Road
Thousand Oaks, California 91320
E-mail: order@sagepub.com

SAGE Publications Ltd.
1 Oliver's Yard
55 City Road
London, EC1Y 1SP
United Kingdom

SAGE Publications India Pvt. Ltd.
B 1/I 1 Mohan Cooperative
Industrial Area
Mathura Road, New Delhi 110 044
India

SAGE Publications Asia-Pacific Pte. Ltd.
3 Church Street
#10–04 Samsung Hub
Singapore 049483

Acquisitions Editor: Elise Frasier
Developmental Editor: Nancy Matuszak
Production Editor: Astrid Virding
Copy Editor: Pam Schroeder
Typesetter: Hurix Systems Pvt. Ltd.
Proofreader: Dennis W. Webb
Indexer: Ellen Slavitz
Cover Designer: Edgar Abarca
Marketing Manager: Jonathan Mason
Permissions Editor: Adele Hutchinson

Copyright © 2013 by CQ Press, an Imprint of SAGE Publications, Inc. CQ Press is a registered trademark of Congressional Quarterly Inc.

All rights reserved. No part of this book may be reproduced or utilized in any form or by any means, electronic or mechanical, including photocopying, recording, or by any information storage and retrieval system, without permission in writing from the publisher.

Printed in the United States of America

Library of Congress Cataloging-in-Publication Data

Stevenson, Charles A.
  America's foreign policy toolkit: key institutions and processes / Charles Stevenson.

       p. cm.

  Includes bibliographical references and index.

  ISBN 978–1–60871–985–3 (pbk.)

  1. United States—Foreign relations—Textbooks. 2. United States—Foreign relations administration—Textbooks. I. Title.

JZ1480.S79 2013

327.73—dc23
                                2012012485

This book is printed on acid-free paper.

12 13 14 15 16 10 9 8 7 6 5 4 3 2 1

Brief Contents

Tables, Figures, and Boxes   xv
Preface   xix
About the Author   xxiii

Introduction: Tools and Tool Users   1

Part I: Assembling the Tools

1. The Framers' Design   7
2. Following the Blueprint   27
3. The President's Toolkit   54
4. Congress's Toolkit   86
5. Shared Tools of the Budgetary Process   119

Part II: Using the Tools

6. The Diplomatic Instrument   141
7. The Economic Instruments   170
8. The Military Instrument   200
9. The Secret Intelligence Instruments   231
10. The Homeland Security Instruments   255
11. The International Institutions Instrument   274

Part III: Constraints and Limitations on the U.S. Toolkit

12. Elephants in the Workshop 301

13. Missing Tools 324

Notes 343
Index 365

Detailed Contents

Tables, Figures, and Boxes xv
Preface xix
    The Purpose of This Book xix
    Organization of the Book xx
    Acknowledgments xxi
About the Author xxiii

Introduction: Tools and Tool Users 1

    U.S. Foreign Policy in Action 2
    How Foreign Policy Is Made 3
    The Foreign Policy Toolkit 4
    How This Book Is Organized 5

Part I: Assembling the Tools

1. The Framers' Design 7

    America Under the Articles of Confederation 8
    Behind Closed Doors in Philadelphia 13
    The New Framework 16
    The Battles for Ratification 20
    First Congress and First Precedents 22
    Selected Resources 26

2. Following the Blueprint 27

    The Washington Administration, 1789–1797 27
    John Adams and the Quasi-War With France, 1797–1801 30
    Republican Government, 1800–1828 30
    The Slavery Factor 32
    James Polk, Master Strategist, 1845–1849 34
    America and the World, 1850–1861 35
    Foreign Policy in the Civil War, 1861–1865 36
    Congressional Dominance in the Gilded Age, 1865–1898 37
    Imperial Ambitions, 1898–1913 39
    Woodrow Wilson's Militant Idealism, 1913–1921 43
    Retrenchment in the Jazz Age, 1920–1939 45
    Franklin D. Roosevelt in Peace and War, 1933–1945 47

The Cold War and After, 1946– 49
Selected Resources 52

3. The President's Toolkit 54

Presidential Power 55
   Legal Constraints 57
   Political Constraints 58
   Other Constraints on Presidential Choice 59
Historical Consensus and Dissensus 60
Presidential Management Styles 61
Sources of Information 62
Creation of the White House–Centered National Security Council System 65
The National Security Council and Staff 67
   Role of the National Security Adviser 71
   Other White House Operatives 72
National Security Council System: The Scowcroft Model 74
National Security Council Culture 76
The Paper Flow 76
Crisis Management 78
Process Matters 78
Foreign Policy Is a Never-Ending Process 81
Critiques of the Current National Security Council System 82
Case Study: Obama's Review of Afghanistan Policy 83
Selected Resources 85

4. Congress's Toolkit 86

How Congress Acts 87
   The Legal Tool 88
   Substantive Versus Procedural Laws 89
   The Money Tool 91
   The Treaty Tool 92
   The Nomination Tool 94
   Oversight Tools 97
   Informal Tools 98
Congressional Culture 99
   House Culture 101
   Senate Culture 101
   Committee Cultures and Dynamics 102
Why Congress Acts That Way 103
   Member Motivations 104
   Public Opinion 105

  *Congressional Inputs to the National Security
  Council System 106*
  The Effort to Legislate War Powers 107
  Inconsistency in Practice on War Powers 110
  Tying the President's Hands 111
 Should Politics Stop at Water's Edge? 111
 Case Study: Congress and Cuban Independence, 1898 112
 Case Study: Congress Struggles With Apartheid
 and South Africa 115
 Selected Resources 117

5. Shared Tools of the Budgetary Process 119

 Making Policy by Making Budgets 120
 Evolution of the Budget Process 122
  Role and Culture of the Office of Management and Budget 124
  The Official Budget Process in the Executive Branch 124
  The Official Budget Process in Congress 126
  The Money Committees and Their Cultures 128
 The Usual, Real Budget Process 130
  Playing Games With the Budget Tool 131
  Linking Money to Policy 133
  Contingency Funds 133
  Transfers and Reprogramming 134
  Secret Spending 136
 Causes and Cures for Dysfunction 136
 Case Study: Budget Enforcement Act of 1990 137
 Selected Resources 140

Part II: Using the Tools
6. The Diplomatic Instrument 141

 The Nature of Diplomacy and the Diplomatic Mission 141
 Growth and Professionalization of the State Department 143
 Organization 145
  The Country Team 148
  Leadership 150
 The Changing Foreign Service 153
 State Department Culture 155
 Representation and Engagement 156
  Negotiations 158
  Analyzing and Reporting 158
  Public Diplomacy 159
  Citizen Services 159
  Other Operations 160
  Policy Making 160

Bureaucratic Rivalries Among State, Defense, and the
National Security Council   162
Congress and the State Department   163
Case Study: Building the Gulf War Coalition, 1990   166
Selected Resources   168

7. The Economic Instruments   170

Carrots and Sticks   173
A Disorganized Toolkit   173
The Globalized Economy   174
Key Institutions   175
National Economic Council   177
Federal Reserve   178
Department of the Treasury   178
United States Trade Representative   179
Department of Commerce   180
Department of State   180
United States Agency for International Development   181
Department of Defense   181
Department of Agriculture   182
Other Organizations   182
Key Processes   182
Sanctions   183
Trade   185
Exports   186
Imports   188
Foreign Assistance   189
Financial Flows   192
Foreign Direct Investment   195
Case Study: The Korean–U.S. Free Trade Agreement   197
Selected Resources   199

8. The Military Instrument   200

Nature of the Military Instrument   200
Growth and Professionalization of the Military   204
Consolidation, Nuclear Weapons, and Jointness   206
Leadership   210
People in Many Uniforms   214
Organization   216
The Culture of the Pentagon   219
Use of the Military Instrument   220
Warfighting   221
Engaging With Foreign Governments and Militaries   222

The 911 Force 223
Planning and Policy Making 223
Recurring Tensions 224
The Pentagon in the Interagency Process 225
Congress and the Pentagon 226
Case Study: Planning for the 2003 Iraq Invasion 227
Selected Resources 230

9. The Secret Intelligence Instruments 231

Secret Tools 232
The Long History of Secret Programs 233
Major Institutions 234
Office of the Director of National Intelligence 234
Central Intelligence Agency 236
Pentagon Management 237
Other Intelligence Community Components 238
Major Processes 239
Collection 239
Analysis 240
Operations 244
What Presidents Want 249
Congressional Oversight 251
Selected Resources 254

10. The Homeland Security Instruments 255

A Brief History of United States Homeland Security 255
Creation of the Homeland Security System 257
The Defense Mission 260
Intelligence Collection and Integration Mission 261
Critical Infrastructure Mission 262
Cybersecurity Mission 263
Biological Protection Mission 264
Border Security and Immigration Missions 265
Transportation Security Mission 265
Emergency Preparedness and Response Missions 266
The Anomaly of the Secret Service 267
Culture of the Department of Homeland Security 267
Homeland Security Council 268
Strengths and Weaknesses of the Homeland Security System 268
Congress and Homeland Security 269
International Aspects of Homeland Security 270
Areas of Presidential Choice 271

Case Study: U.S.–Mexican Collaboration on Security   272
Selected Resources   273

11. The International Institutions Instrument   274

The Role of International Institutions   275
Ad Hoc Versus Institutional Multilateralism   277
International Institutions   278
    United Nations   278
    Congress and the United Nations   283
    International Atomic Energy Agency   284
Regional Institutions   285
    North Atlantic Treaty Organization   285
    Organization for Security and Co-operation in Europe   287
    Organization of American States   288
    Association of Southeast Asian Nations, the Association of Southeast Asian Nations Regional Forum, and Asia–Pacific Economic Cooperation   289
Economic Institutions   290
    G-8 and G-20   291
    The International Monetary Fund and Other International Financial Institutions   292
    World Trade Organization   294
International Courts   295
Major Nonstate Actors   296
Case Study: Using the North Atlantic Treaty Organization as an Instrument of Foreign Policy in Libya, 2011   297
Selected Resources   300

Part III: Constraints and Limitations on the U.S. Toolkit
12. Elephants in the Workshop   301

Public Opinion   302
    The Elite, Attentive, and Mass Publics   303
    Polling Opinions   304
    Presidential Message and Public Support   305
    The Bully Pulpit and Framing   306
Media   306
    Shaping the Media   307
    Leaks as a Policy Making Tool   308
    The Media as the Shaper   309
    Shrinking Coverage and Shrinking Audience   310
Advocacy Groups   311
    Stakeholders   312
    Ethnic Identity or Affinity Groups   313

Lobbyists   316
Contributors   318
Impact of Lobbyists and Contributors   320
Think Tanks   321
Selected Resources   323

13. Missing Tools   324

Legacy of Reform Proposals   324
Recommended New Tools   328
  New Organizations and Capabilities   329
  New Processes   332
  New Emphases and Priorities   333
Impediments to Reform   335
  Mistakes   335
  Entrenched Interests   336
  Genuine Dilemmas   337
  Lack of Resources   338
  Warning Lessons   338
The Changing Foreign Policy Toolkit   339

Notes   343
Index   365

Tables, Figures, and Boxes

Tables

1.1 Independence From Tyranny
1.2 Problems Under the Articles of Confederation and Solutions in the Constitution
1.3 Separated Institutions Sharing Powers Over National Security
2.1 U.S. Diplomatic and Consular Missions, 1790–1950
2.2 U.S. Active Duty Military Personnel, 1789–1950
3.1 The Presidential Toolkit Brief
4.1 The Congressional Toolkit Brief
4.2 Congressional Authorizations of the Use of Force, 1798–2011
5.1 The Budget Toolkit Brief
6.1 The Diplomatic Instrument Brief
6.2 Department of State Personnel and Foreign Missions, 1950–2010
7.1 The Economic Instruments Brief
7.2 U.S. Net Economic Engagement With Developing Countries, 2009
7.3 Key Institutions in U.S. Economic Foreign Policy
7.4 Top Recipients of U.S. Foreign Assistance, 1980–2010
8.1 The Military Instrument Brief
8.2 Major U.S. Military Operations and U.S. Battle Deaths, 1775–2011
8.3 U.S. Armed Forces, 1950–2010
9.1 The Secret Intelligence Instrument Brief
10.1 The Homeland Security Instrument Brief
11.1 International Institutions as U.S. Instruments Brief
11.2 Major United Nations Military Operations, 1948–2011
11.3 Membership of Asian Regional Organizations
11.4 G-8 and G-20 Members With 2010 Gross Domestic Product in Billions
12.1 External Influences on Uses of the Toolkit

Figures

3.1 Average Size of the National Security Council Staff, 1961–2008
3.2 National Security Staff Organizational Chart
5.1 The Budget: Where the Money Comes From and Where It Goes
6.1 U.S. Department of State Organizational Chart
6.2 Funding for International Affairs, 1950–2010

8.1   U.S. Department of Defense Organizational Chart
8.2   U.S. Defense Spending, 1960–2012
9.1   Intelligence Community Organizational Chart
10.1 U.S. Department of Homeland Security Organizational Chart

Boxes

1.1   Threats to America in 1786
3.1   Inside View: Henry Kissinger on How Presidents Decide
3.2   The White House Situation Room
3.3   Who Makes Foreign Policy: The Special Role of the Vice President
3.4   Inside View: Keep Memos to the President Short
3.5   How Foreign Policy Is Made: Crisis Day at the National Security Center
4.1   Who Makes Foreign Policy: George Washington Gives Up on Advice and Consent
4.2   Inside View: Senators Are Human; Not All Are Trustworthy
4.3   Additional Examples of Congressional Impact on National Security
5.1   Inside View: The Office of Management and Budget Micromanages the Pentagon
5.2   Inside View: Budgetary Cooperation
6.1   Secretary of State . . . and President?
6.2   Who Makes Foreign Policy: The Busy Secretary of State
6.3   Who Makes Foreign Policy: A Day in the Life of the State Department
6.4   Inside View: The State Department Outnumbered
6.5   Inside View: The Clearance Process
7.1   Inside View: Treasury Versus State During the Asian Financial Crisis
8.1   How Foreign Policy Is Made: Types of Military Operations
8.2   Secretary of Defense: A Hard Job to Keep
8.3   Who Makes Foreign Policy: The Very Busy Secretary of Defense and Chairman of the Joint Chiefs of Staff
8.4   Inside View: Joint Chiefs of Staff Meet in the Kitchen
8.5   Inside View: Rumsfeld's Assertive Style
9.1   How Foreign Policy Is Made: Examining the President's Daily Brief, April 1, 1968
9.2   Inside View: The President's Daily Intelligence Briefing
9.3   How Foreign Policy Is Made: Key Judgments From a National Intelligence Estimate, Saddam Hussein, June 18, 1992
9.4   How Foreign Policy Is Made: Presidential Finding for Covert Action: Nicaragua, September 19, 1983
11.1 International Instruments and Entities
12.1 A Long History of Leaking

12.2 How Foreign Policy Is Made: Why the American Israel Public Affairs Committee Is So Effective
12.3 Inside View: Fund-Raising by Lobbyists
13.1 Bureaucratic Power Ladder

Preface

I'm not much of a handyman, but I recognize the value of having just the right tool for a particular task. I also know, from embarrassing experiences, the wisdom of carpenters, who say, "Measure twice; cut once." To do a job right, you need the right tool and the knowledge of how to use it.

I have a heavy, cast-iron, 14-inch adjustable wrench that is ideal for plumbing work but not much else. I have an ingenious right-angle screwdriver that can reach where a long stem won't fit and where I can't even see the screw, such as on curtain rods. I also have a Leatherman multi-tool that can do almost anything except pound nails. I used to live in a small town that had a tool library, where I could borrow that rarely needed item like a wood plane or floor sander.

The U.S. government has its own tool library for foreign policy activities. And, policy makers would do well to heed the advice about picking the right tool and calculating twice before using it. America has the State Department for diplomacy, the Defense Department for military activities, the Treasury Department and numerous other organizations for foreign economic policy, and the intelligence community for spying, analyses, and covert actions. The president and Congress get to decide how much to spend on these tools, which types and how many to buy, how to keep them well oiled and sharpened, and when and where to use them. *America's Foreign Policy Toolkit: Key Institutions and Processes* is about those tools and the processes for using them.

The Purpose of This Book

The book's title refers to foreign policy, a commonplace term, but its subject is more accurately national security in the broadest sense of that term. U.S. officials now recognize that America's survival and success in the world require dealing with nontraditional issues like climate change, environmental degradation, disease, and human rights along with the traditional topics of defense, trade, and diplomacy. This requires the exercise of numerous instruments from a broad reach of agencies, from the Department of State to the Department of Agriculture but does not always result in a consistent policy.

In the course of my professional life, I have had the opportunity to work, at least for a time, in several of the institutions described in this book—the U.S. Senate, Department of State, Department of the Treasury, and the Department of the Navy. I have also worked closely with people in the White House and National Security Council (NSC), the Office of the

Secretary of Defense and the Joint Chiefs of Staff, the Central Intelligence Agency, and the U.S. House of Representatives. More recently, I spent two years on the Project on National Security Reform, studying ways to improve the structures and processes of the U.S. government for more effective policy development and execution. From these experiences, I learned that, while officials understand their own agencies quite well, they often do not appreciate the strengths and weaknesses or quirks and capabilities of other institutions. I wrote this book to give students, analysts, and practitioners a better sense of how the different agencies think and operate, the pressures they respond to, and when and how they work together. I also wanted to show how the different institutions can be integrated into a coherent policy and yet why it is so hard to maintain a consistent foreign policy strategy.

For many years I was director of the core course on "The Interagency Process" at the National War College. My students—colonels and navy captains, foreign service officers, and career civilians—had two decades' worth of professional experience in their home institutions and knew very well how to plan military operations, run an embassy, or analyze foreign threats. But, they often weren't really sure what the other government institutions did or could do. Believing quite properly that all the instruments of national power should be coordinated as part of a national security strategy, the military officers would say, "We need to do some diplomacy and do some economics."

What did that mean? Send a foreign service officer to a reception or to talk tough to a foreign minister? Send somebody with bags of money that could be given or withheld from a foreign official depending on his or her response to the courier's demands? Those notions were vague and different from how those tools are in fact used.

My course, and this book, are designed to tell students and practitioners what's in America's foreign policy toolkit and how the instruments work. The focus is on institutions and processes rather than the substance of foreign policy, but there is ample evidence that process can affect substance: Who sits at the table and what they are best at doing matters greatly.

Besides rounding up the usual suspects—in the White House, the State Department, the Pentagon, and the intelligence community—I wanted to make sure that this book also explains the role of Congress, the crucial budget process, the diverse but increasingly important tools of foreign economic policy, the role of outsiders, and more recently, the role of the organizations concerned with homeland security.

I have continued to find this framework a useful way to teach my current students at the Nitze School of Advanced International Studies of Johns Hopkins University.

Organization of the Book

America's Foreign Policy Toolkit is organized into three parts: Assembling the Tools, Using the Tools, and Constraints and Limitations on the United States Toolkit. This design allows students to build their understanding of how U.S. foreign policy developed, the tools available today to make policy, and the limitations that exist between what policy makers may want to do and what they're actually able to achieve. Each chapter discusses a discrete tool for foreign policy, including its legal authorities, capabilities, and organizational culture. While the focus is on how the president might choose to use the instrument, I include analysis of the often-ignored role of Congress in writing laws and voting funds that affect its use. Important factors outside the current structure of government that constrain or push how the tools are used are also examined. These include the power of public opinion, the media, and interest groups.

Case studies in most chapters allow readers to connect the theory of the toolkit with real-world examples focused primarily on events since the end of the Cold War. Most chapters have additional sidebars, such as Who Makes Foreign Policy, describing the key leaders of the institutions; How Foreign Policy Is Made, spotlighting key activities; and Inside View, providing quotes from practitioners who know these foreign policy tools intimately. Data in tables and figures also complement the discussion.

Acknowledgments

I would like to thank Patrick Altdorfer, University of Pittsburgh; David Bearce, University of Colorado; and Yoav Gortzak, University of Washington–Tacoma, for their helpful feedback on the proposal for this book. My thanks also to reviewers Gary Donato, Bentley University; David Forsythe, University of Nebraska; and Richard Nolan, University of Florida. Their thoughtful comments on the manuscript were of great assistance in crafting the final product.

I especially wish to thank Kay King and Gordon Adams for encouraging me to develop this book proposal, as well as several of my colleagues at the National War College, who helped to shape this framework for teaching national security strategy: Ron Tammen, Janet Breslin Smith, Mike Mazarr, and David Auerswald. I am also grateful for the opportunity to broaden and deepen my knowledge of the executive branch while working with Jim Locher and Chris Lamb at PNSR. Most of all, I am indebted to my students over the years at the National War College and SAIS for helping me to understand what we all really need to know about foreign policy institutions and processes.

I am also grateful for the encouragement and guidance from acquisitions editor Elise Frasier and development editor Nancy Matuszak at CQ Press, as well as from production editor Astrid Virding.

Last but not least, I want to thank—and dedicate this volume to—the person who endured my long hours and many months at the computer, away from yard work and other household tasks, and my middle-of-the-night inspirations and still provided love, suggestions, and support—my wife Sue. I hope I proved that the boxes of books filling the basement still could be put to good use.

About the Author

Dr. Charles A. Stevenson teaches courses in American foreign policy at the Nitze School of Advanced International Studies (SAIS), Johns Hopkins University. Previously, he was a longtime professor at the National War College, where he was director of the core course on the interagency process for national security policy. He has executive branch experience, including service on the secretary of state's policy planning staff, and served for 22 years as a Senate staffer on defense and foreign policy. He is the author of a study of the congressional role in major military operations, *Congress at War* (2007); a historical survey of U.S. civil–military relations, *Warriors and Politicians* (2006); and a comparative analysis of U.S. secretaries of defense, *SecDef* (2006). He was a member of the Project on National Security Reform (PNSR) and headed its working group on Congress. He has an AB and PhD from Harvard.

Introduction: Tools and Tool Users

"When word of a crisis breaks out in Washington, it's no accident that the first question that comes to everyone's lips is: 'Where's the nearest carrier?'"
—President Bill Clinton, March 12, 1993, aboard *USS Theodore Roosevelt*

"They don't hit an outhouse [in North Vietnam] without my approval."
—President Lyndon B. Johnson[1]

"There is hereby established a council to be known as the National Security Council . . ."
—The National Security Act of 1947, Public Law 80–253, sect. 101

"None of the funds financed by this Act shall be used to finance the introduction of American ground combat troops into Laos or Thailand."
—Defense Appropriations Act for fiscal year 1970, Public Law 91–171

U.S. foreign policy institutions and processes clicked into action immediately after the 9/11 attacks, just as they were designed to do. The morning of September 12, 2001, President George W. Bush convened what he called his "war council" in the cabinet room of the White House. He had rejected a proposal by Dick Cheney that the vice president head a group to develop response options and report to the president. Bush believed that only he could exercise the commander in chief role. In the meeting, the president told his advisors that America was at war with a new and different kind of enemy. He asked them to develop a strategy to eliminate terrorists and punish those who support them.[2]

The meeting began with intelligence reports that identified al Qaeda as the group responsible for the attacks and Federal Bureau of Investigation (FBI) reports on efforts to obtain information on the attackers and those in league with them. Having been told by Defense Secretary Donald Rumsfeld that any military operation might take months to assemble, the president

1

turned first to his other advisors. "We will get to the military options soon, but before we do, let's look at the political, economic, diplomatic, and all the other sources and tools that we've got and see what we can do with those as well."³ In turn, each official offered his or her preliminary advice.

Further meetings were held over the next several days, including a weekend session at Camp David. By Monday, September 17, the president issued formal written orders:

- The attorney general, FBI director, and director of Central Intelligence were tasked to develop a plan for homeland defense.

- The secretary of state was ordered to deliver an ultimatum to the Taliban and to develop a plan to stabilize Pakistan.

- The president signed broad new authorities for Central Intelligence Agency (CIA) operations.

- The secretary of defense and chairman of the Joint Chiefs of Staff (JCS) were tasked to develop a more detailed plan to attack the Taliban and al Qaeda. They were also ordered to institute measures to protect U.S. forces against terrorist attacks worldwide.

- The secretary of the treasury was ordered to target al Qaeda's funding and seize its assets.⁴

Over the days, months, and years to follow, U.S. officials acted to carry out those orders, held meetings to coordinate their efforts, and gained additional orders, guidance, and resources to pursue what became called the Global War on Terror (GWOT). All of the means of hard and soft power, all the instruments in the foreign policy toolkit, were mobilized and utilized in that effort.

U.S. Foreign Policy in Action

Congress responded to the 9/11 attacks with three significant actions. On September 18, 2001, it approved a joint resolution authorizing the use of force against al Qaeda, the Taliban, and their supporters.⁵ On October 25, lawmakers sent to the president the final version of the USA PATRIOT Act (formally the Uniting and Strengthening America by Providing the Appropriate Tools Required to Intercept and Obstruct Terrorism Act), giving the government broader investigative tools and tougher sanctions against possible terrorists.⁶ A bipartisan group of senators and representatives launched what turned out to be a nine-month campaign to persuade the president to approve creation of a Department of Homeland Security (DHS). In each instance, Congress fashioned a response somewhat different from what the president proposed.

In approving the use of force, the functional equivalent of a declaration of war, Congress rejected the blank-check language sought by the Bush administration authorizing actions "to deter and preempt any future acts of terrorism" and instead approved language limited to those nations and persons who "planned, authorized, committed, or aided" the 9/11 attacks.[7] In approving the USA PATRIOT Act, lawmakers included sunset provisions on several of the law's far-reaching powers so that future congresses would have to review and decide whether to extend them.

Even before the 9/11 attacks, many lawmakers had urged the creation of DHS, a recommendation of the 1999 Hart-Rudman Commission. When President Bush resisted and tried to organize domestic defense efforts using only a special assistant with a small staff, lawmakers responded with demands for a consolidated agency. Eventually, the president agreed to accept a new department, which Congress formed by moving 22 government organizations with about 170,000 people into a single entity with the primary mission of preventing terrorist attacks within the United States.[8]

How Foreign Policy Is Made

People make United States foreign policy. People generate the ideas and make the decisions, and people carry them out. Policy makers and their advisers bring to their tasks their own life experiences, ideas and ideologies, prejudices and preferences, and their own ambitions. Individuals can make big differences—through the persuasiveness of their ideas, the force of their personalities, and the power of their offices.

But, the men and women who shape and implement U.S. foreign policy work in organizations and institutions, each of which has its own authorities and responsibilities and cultures and capabilities. Each operates under a set of rules or laws based on actions by Congress and subject to resources provided by Congress.

The organizations and institutions used to make U.S. foreign policy are linked by processes—also called *action channels*.[9] They are the ways that policies are framed, debated, decided, and carried out. They bring key stakeholders to the table and offer the prospect of integrating and coordinating governmental action. Those processes may be complex or simple, transparent or opaque, regular or ad hoc, efficient or cumbersome.

America's Foreign Policy Toolkit is about those people, the institutions where they work, and the processes that make U.S. foreign policy. It is less concerned with the substance of policy—what presidents decide, what strategy if any the nation pursues abroad, why Congress may be supportive or antagonistic toward administration foreign policies—than it is with how senior officials formulate their policies and carry them out. Instead of recommending what to do to strengthen national security, this volume is intended to be a ready reference book on how to do what is decided and who is best suited for particular tasks.

We look at the development of foreign policy from the perspective of the Oval Office. Time and again throughout history, presidents have faced problems and crises with the same series of questions: What should we do? What can we do? How can we pay for it? Who can do what? How do we make it happen? A frequent subordinate question, as mentioned by President Bill Clinton at the beginning of this chapter, is where the aircraft carriers are that might be used in a military operation. Presidents also like to believe, as Lyndon Johnson obviously did, that they control even the smallest details of policy execution whether or not that is true in fact.

The following chapters lay out not only the key details of bureaucratic organization, personnel, and funding but also a discussion of each institution's culture and operating style and sense of core missions. Internal tensions and perennial conflicts, such as among the various military services, between regional and functional bureaus in the State Department, between intelligence analysts and operatives, and between career and political appointees in most institutions, are highlighted, and each institution's strengths and weaknesses are discussed.

We also describe the perspective of lawmakers on Capitol Hill. When advocating their own preferred policies or when responding to presidential requests, they ask, individually and collectively, their own sets of questions: What should America do? Have we in Congress provided the executive branch with the right tools, sufficient authority, and adequate resources for those tasks? Should we provide our own guidance, either mandates or restrictions? And, where's the money coming from? As the quotations at the start of this chapter demonstrate, Congress often decides to create organizations and processes where lawmakers feel they are inadequate and sometimes imposes severe restrictions on the president's possible choices.

These questions may not always be asked explicitly, or answered definitively, but they are embedded in the normal processes of policy making. When the president and Congress consider foreign policy matters, they have established processes for gathering information, weighing choices, deciding and acting, and then overseeing the results. They can short-circuit those processes or even evade them, but such actions carry additional risks and possible benefits. This book explains the major processes used to fashion and implement U.S. foreign policy in the executive and legislative branches.

The Foreign Policy Toolkit

The idea for this book is based on a simple metaphor: that making foreign policy involves picking the right tools from the government's toolkit. For the president to act, the chief executive must assign and task relevant parts of the executive branch to do what they were designed to do. Congress, of course, has a hand in the design of government organizations with its laws and appropriations. Officials at both ends of Pennsylvania Avenue would like to have a large and diverse toolkit to select from—especially to avoid the consequences of the old aphorism, "If all you have is a hammer, every problem starts looking like a nail."

While simple and useful, the toolkit metaphor is, of course, somewhat misleading. Government departments and agencies are rarely as small or simple as a wrench or a saw. Often, they are big and complex like a military weapon system—for example, a multirole aircraft or an aircraft carrier and its battle fleet. The tools may also have minds of their own, allowing discretion and flexibility and resistance. Another metaphor for policy making is architecture—designing something for particular purposes using standard materials but often in creative ways. This notion is a useful contrast to the engineering approach often favored by outside analysts who think there is a simple, self-evident national interest and one best way of pursuing it. Architects can choose beauty over simplicity, effectiveness of use over efficiency of construction, and maybe even pay a higher cost for a special effect. But, the metaphor falls short when one realizes that policy making never ends, unlike the way a building can be completed and opened for use. And, the blueprint may not be followed as intended by the architect. In foreign policy, review and redesign are part of the process. As former Secretary of State George Shultz complained, "Nothing is ever finished in this town."

Another alternate metaphor is that of an orchestra, with the president as conductor trying to bring together in a harmonious whole the various instruments. This, too, is misleading. The president is not the only conductor, for department heads and others lead their own sections. Government players are rarely in a single place but scattered around the globe and facing different conditions as they try to perform, nor is there likely to be a single, finished score. Instead, bits and pieces are being composed or improvised as the performance proceeds.

Given the limitations of other metaphors, we find continued value in the notion of a toolkit created and funded by Congress and directed by the president and senior officials.

How This Book Is Organized

A government can only do what it is organized, trained, equipped, and possesses the resources to do. The U.S. government has many organizations with ample funding to carry out its chosen policies abroad, but its capabilities are not infinite, and all of its instruments need to be used with planning and coordination for maximum effectiveness. A president needs to know which tools are best for which tasks and what their strengths and weaknesses are. Congress needs to judge what mix of powers and restraints to put in the hands of the president. Together, both branches shape and empower the instruments America has for its defense, foreign policy, and national security. *America's Foreign Policy Toolkit* is organized into three parts to explain the challenges of integrating and coordinating policy among so many disparate actors. Case studies in most chapters, focusing primarily on post-Cold War events from 1993 to the present, display foreign policy actors and tools in action, allowing the reader to connect the theory of the toolkit with real-world examples.

Part I of the book, Assembling the Tools, looks at the primary means the president and Congress have in controlling and influencing the creation of foreign policy, including via the budget. It also provides context on how foreign policy instruments evolved and how they were used in the 19th and 20th centuries. A sidebar feature, the Toolkit Brief, appears in most chapters in this section as a quick reference to the primary tools—including people, processes, and actions—available as resources in foreign policy making and the advantages and disadvantages of their use.

Part II, Using the Tools, describes the various policy instruments in greater detail to explore how they're used—from diplomacy, the economy, and the military to intelligence agencies, homeland security, and international organizations. Each chapter in this section contains an Instrument Brief feature box that follows the same model as the Toolkit Brief, identifying who is involved and how policy may be carried out using the instrument in question, noting the advantages and disadvantages of each as well as what role Congress might play.

Finally, in Part III, Constraints and Limitations on the U.S. Toolkit, we look at important factors outside the current structure of government that have major influences on American policy, including the power of public opinion, the media, and interest groups to shape policy. While important elements in policy making, these are not tools. They are influential factors that constrain or push how the tools are used. This section also discusses the many suggestions for changes in U.S. institutions and processes designed to craft better policy formulation and implementation, and the numerous impediments to reform that exist.

That's the layout of the toolkit as it is today and how it might be improved. It's not exactly what the framers had in mind in 1787, but it is derived from the rules and structure they laid down. Throughout these pages, you'll learn the basic details about the key institutions and processes for foreign policy. You'll come to understand the tools at hand for the president, Congress, and other foreign policy actors to use in crafting and implementing policy; review case studies showcasing foreign policy making in action; and get firsthand insights via the Inside View feature from people who were there. In the end, you'll come away with a clear understanding of how the United States crafts and carries out foreign policies and who does the work.

1 The Framers' Design

> "Foreign troops remained on American soil [in 1786]; ships in its ports flew other flags while U.S. vessels rotted at their moorings. Congress could not enforce treaties. Unpaid debts had destroyed U.S. credit abroad. The lack of respect with which the nation was treated provided the most compelling sign of U.S. weakness."
>
> —Historian George Herring[1]

> "[W]hen I saw this Constitution, I found that it was a cure for these disorders. I got a copy and read it over and over. I had been a member of the Convention to form our own state constitution, and had learnt something of the checks and balances of power, and I found them all there. I did not go to any lawyer to ask his opinion. . . . But I don't think worse of the Constitution because lawyers and men of learning, and moneyed men, are fond of it."
>
> —Massachusetts farmer Jonathan Smith[2]

The instruments for U.S. foreign policy making have their roots in the nation's early history. The foundations first developed under the Articles of Confederation for governing the new nation created an ineffective central government that states routinely ignored. How then could foreign powers be expected to show it any more regard? This led to numerous problems addressed several years later with the drafting and ratification of the U.S. Constitution. The new document strengthened the central government, providing it with tools to wield its power and checks to keep that power in balance. Many of the institutions and processes used to create and carry out U.S. foreign policy today stem from the Constitution. Understanding how they developed provides key context to the foreign policy making process.

In 1786, the United States was weak, vulnerable, and nearly bankrupt, on the brink of becoming a failed state. As George Washington wrote to James Madison, "We are fast verging to anarchy and confusion."[3] These problems weighed heavily on the minds of the delegates who met in Philadelphia the following spring to design a stronger and more durable structure for the young government. To protect the new nation from both domestic and foreign threats, they crafted the Constitution with its various policy tools.

The colonies had declared their independence a decade earlier and, with crucial foreign support, had won enough military encounters to persuade the British to conclude a peace treaty, although 15 months passed after the decisive battle at Yorktown before the preliminary treaty was signed in January 1783. Even then, both sides failed to comply with some of its provisions for another dozen years, leaving America boxed in by hostile forces, including Britain, Spain, and Native American tribes.

The Continental Congress served as the central authority for the Revolutionary War effort, establishing committees to manage the functions of government, such as supplying the army and sending emissaries abroad. The newly independent states agreed upon a framework for a national government called the Articles of Confederation. Drafted in 1777, it was not ratified until 1781, when Maryland, the lone holdout, was satisfied by Virginia's cession of western land claims to the national government.

The Articles established a "confederacy," a "league of friendship" among the 13 states, each of which explicitly retained "sovereignty, freedom and independence, and every Power, Jurisdiction and right which is not . . . expressly delegated to the United States, in Congress assembled." Each state had a single vote in the Congress, and nine votes were required to borrow or appropriate money, to engage in war or approve treaties, to build land or sea forces, or to name the top commanders. The government had a common treasury, but taxes had to be voted on and supplied by the state legislatures after receiving requests from Congress. Delegates were chosen by the states each year, and no person could serve more than three years in any six-year period.

America Under the Articles of Confederation

The Articles of Confederation were designed to preserve strong state governments and create a weak central government, and they achieved that purpose. The Articles lacked most of the features and powers that drove the rebels away from the British Crown. (See Table 1.1.) The states continued to have their own armies and navies, to make trade and other arrangements with their neighbors, and even to deal on their own with foreign governments. When asked by Congress for taxes to pay for the national government's activities, states were often slow or delinquent in providing their shares. They named their delegates each year, but Congress often went for long periods without a quorum to do business. This left the central government ineffective in carrying out policy and enforcing laws.

The blessings of liberty did not include a strong economy, however, and the United States fell into a severe depression immediately after the war. The new government was saddled with wartime debts and repayments of foreign loans. Its paper currency was nearly worthless, and specie (coin money) was in short supply. Britain saw no need to grant its former colonies special trade benefits. Instead, Britain refused to sign a commercial treaty and barred U.S. ships from its lucrative West Indies trade as well as from Newfoundland

Table 1.1 Independence From Tyranny

GRIEVANCE AGAINST KING GEORGE III	PROVISION IN ARTICLES OF CONFEDERATION
Refused to agree to laws for public good	Congress decides on war, peace, spending, and requisitions from states
Harassed and fatigued legislative bodies and dissolved them repeatedly	Freedom of speech and debate in Congress; annual meetings
Refused to call new elections, leaving people exposed to "dangers of invasion and convulsions"	Annual appointment of delegates; right of recall by legislatures; three-year term limit
Obstructed laws for naturalization	Free inhabitants are free citizens who have freedom of movement
Obstructed justice; made justices dependent on his will	Full faith and credit for judicial proceedings in other states
"Sent swarms of officers to harass our people"	Very limited national government
Kept standing armies without consent	Every state shall have a well-regulated and disciplined militia but no separate navy or army
Made military independent of and superior to civil power	Congress alone decides questions of peace and war
Quartered large bodies of armed troops, "protected them from murders of our people"	No war, treaty, or appropriations unless 9 of 13 states agree in Congress
Cut off trade with the rest of the world	Congress regulates trade
Imposed taxes without consent	States shall contribute to the common treasury
Deprived people of trial by jury	Congress names commissioners for disputes
Took away charters; suspended legislatures	Each state has "sovereignty, freedom, and independence"
Has waged war, "ravaged our coasts, burnt our towns"	Firm league of friendship for common defense
Sent foreign mercenaries for "death, desolation, and tyranny"	Every state shall have a "well regulated and disciplined militia"
Excited domestic insurrections and urged on "merciless Indian savages"	Congress manages relations with Indians

The Declaration of Independence makes 27 specific complaints against King George III—"repeated Injuries and Usurpations"—that separation was meant to overcome. In 1777, the Continental Congress adopted a framework for the new nation, the Articles of Confederation. While most of the former colonies had ratified the Articles by 1779, Maryland held out until 1781 in a dispute over claims to western lands. Before considering how the Constitution of 1787 solved problems inherent in the Articles, it is useful to compare how that initial framework dealt with the grievances against King George III.

and Nova Scotia. U.S. ships could no longer trade freely in British home ports, where Americans faced higher fees and duties on permitted goods but could not ship fish, whale oil, or salted meats at all. All these restrictions devastated the New England shipping and fishing industries. Britain refused to allow exports of manufacturing items that might promote the creation of infant U.S. industries, but it flooded the American market with other goods, and the Confederation Congress lacked the power to pass import duties. In the years before 1789, America imported two to three times as much from Britain as it exported to the former motherland. State governments contributed to the economic decline by voting for debt relief and issuing paper currency that quickly lost value.[4] The Continental Congress had the exclusive authority to negotiate with foreign powers, subject to a supermajority of nine states to approve any agreements, but there were no takers.

In addition to these severe economic problems, the new nation faced several direct threats to its security, as detailed in Box 1.1. Britain, Spain, and even former ally France took hostile actions against the new nation. As the New York chamber of commerce declared in 1787, "All Europe did indeed desire to see us independent; but now that we are become so, each separate power is desirous of rendering our interests subservient to their commercial policy."[5]

Box 1.1

Threats to America in 1786

The United States faced many national security threats in its early years, including challenges from other countries seeking land in North America and those wishing to take advantage of the young nation's lack of a strong central government. The following lists security threats to the United States in 1786, when the Articles of Confederation offered little means for the country to combat them. Note that not all of the threats are foreign. The Constitutional Convention gathered in Philadelphia that same year to draft a Constitution that would allow the federal government to deal with such problems.

- Britain and Spain block the United States from taking control of newly awarded territory and support Indian land claims.
- Britain bars the United States from West Indies trade and refuses to sign a commercial treaty.
- Britain backs the Mohawk confederacy to oppose U.S. expansion.
- Britain refuses to vacate five forts on the Great Lakes as promised in a 1783 treaty, reinforcing troops there and adding ships; 6,000 to 7,000 armed loyalists camp along the border.
- Britain bars imports of U.S. whale oil and whale bone, leaving Nantucket virtually ruined.
- Spain denies the United States access to the Mississippi River and to the ports of New Orleans and Havana, posting garrisons at Natchez and Vicksburg.

(Continued)

(Continued)
- Spain regains Florida in 1783, claiming some territories in Georgia, North Carolina, and Virginia as far north as the Ohio River.
- Spain recognizes Creek independence and promises guns and gunpowder.
- Spain negotiates treaties with the Creek, Choctaw, and Cherokee and gives arms to resist American settlement.
- Indians conduct ongoing wars on the western frontier, raiding settlements on the Cumberland and Tennessee rivers.
- Seven to eight thousand Creek Indians threaten Savannah.
- France imposes taxes on American tobacco and closes the French West Indies to U.S. exports.
- The Barbary States seize U.S. ships for ransom; Algiers declares open war on U.S. ships.
- U.S. ships are often seized near the West Indies, even when not smuggling.
- Secessionist spirit grows in New England and the West.
- Shays's rebels discuss with Britain possible separation from the Union.
- Vermont sends an emissary to London regarding a possible treaty.

The national government could do little to fight back. It lacked the power to raise taxes or to build a national army and had no centralized executive authority to carry out a national strategy. Seven hundred U.S. troops raised in 1785 to secure the Ohio River had gone unpaid and turned to mutiny and desertion. In June 1786, Secretary of War Henry Knox told Congress that the troops already in the West were "utterly incompetent to protect a frontier" along the Ohio. In October, he warned of "a general combination among the southern and western Indians . . . to levy war on the frontier." Congress voted to expand the army from 700 to more than 2,000 soldiers, but within a few months, the plan was dropped because of a lack of funds. The Treasury told Knox that it could not even afford the $1,000 requested for ammunition for troops already in place. By the summer of 1787, while delegates met in Philadelphia, Knox warned that, unless America built up its military power, "a general Indian war may be expected."[6]

With most of its ships sold, the U.S. navy had pretty much ceased to exist by 1786. Yet, U.S. merchant ships no longer had British protection when sailing in the Mediterranean. Each year, 80 to 100 U.S. ships traded along the North African coast. But, without protection after 1783, several ships were seized by Barbary pirates and their crews imprisoned or sold as slaves. America's only recourse was to pay ransom and then tribute. The Rhode Island delegation in Congress sent a message to its governor in September, 1786, expressing alarm at the pirate raids and warning that "an enemy on our frontiers stands prepared to take every advantage of our prostrate situation."[7]

These military threats could not be countered without money, and the central government did not have the proper tools to raise it. Several times during 1786, the Treasury Board told Congress how desperate the situation was, listing the failures of states to provide the requested revenues and the bills and loan repayments coming due, and warning that the fiscal crisis could "hazard . . . the existence of the Union."[8] Congress tried three times in the 1780s to amend the Articles to allow import duties of up to 5%, but one state and then another vetoed the change.

After Shays's Rebellion—when groups of several hundred men in western Massachusetts blocked courthouses to prevent property seizures—broke out in September–October 1786, Secretary Knox told Congress "that unless the present commotions are checked with a strong hand, that an armed tyranny may be established on the ruins of the present constitutions."[9] George Washington was also alarmed and saw the possibility that London was behind the trouble. He wrote to a friend in October 1786. "For God's sake, tell me what is the cause of all these commotions? Do they proceed from licentiousness, British-influence disseminated by the Tories, or real grievances which admit of redress?"[10]

Faced with these foreign and internal threats, with a government lacking the power to raise money, settle disputes, or field a larger army, American political leaders coalesced for reform. A group meeting in Annapolis in September 1786, spearheaded by James Madison and Alexander Hamilton, approved a call for a new convention "to render the Constitution of the Federal Government *adequate to the exigencies of the Union.*" They called the "situation of the United States delicate and critical," mentioning both foreign and domestic "embarrassments."[11] Congress finally agreed to the proposal in February 1787 and summoned delegates to Philadelphia in May.

Some historians see the Constitution as a response to mainly domestic problems, notably Shays's Rebellion and interstate trade disputes, coupled with a vision of national expansion and greatness.[12] It is almost as if the advocates of a strong central government had been waiting in the wings until enough problems accumulated and created a mood of great despair, then they stepped forward with their master plan.

This narrative fits some of the historical facts but overlooks several others. Some present and former officials at the state and national levels—the politically engaged elite—acknowledged the weaknesses and inefficiencies of the government under the Articles but, remembering why they had rebelled in 1776, feared the remedy of a stronger central government even more. Others saw the defects as existential threats, rendering the new nation vulnerable to invasion and dismemberment from without and to dissension and fragmentation from within. As historian George Herring, whose description of U.S. weakness begins this chapter, concluded, "Foreign policy concerns drove nationalist demands to revise the nation's form of government."[13]

Numerous significant indicators support this analysis. Many of the delegates to the Constitutional Convention made specific mention of those existential threats. Of the 18 powers specifically granted to Congress, 11 involved security. Of the first 36 Federalist Papers—before the authors turned to explaining procedural issues of the new government—25 concerned national insecurity. The question of a standing army was one of the strongest objections raised by opponents of ratification of the completed document, and the victories for the Federalists reflected their persuasiveness on security issues.[14]

In fact, security questions were linked to domestic flaws and remedies. Compelling the states to provide revenues required the same kind of central authority as needed to enforce other national laws. Taxes to fund the army and navy also funded the post offices and collection of customs. Enforcement of trade laws helped to enforce international treaties. Negotiation missions to the Indians paralleled those to the European powers. A government strong enough to provide security against invasion was also strong enough to suppress domestic rebellion. In this way, the Federalists tied together state and national interests, illustrating how a stronger central government could aid the states.

Behind Closed Doors in Philadelphia

Many locally prominent men were named to represent their states at the Constitutional Convention. Of the 74 men chosen as delegates, only 55 actually showed up in Philadelphia. Eight had signed the Declaration of Independence. Seven were governors, either currently or previously. All had held some kind of public office. Among the delegates, 30 had served in uniform in the Revolutionary War, and half of those saw major action. They were all white and mostly Protestant but with two Catholics and a few Quakers. Over half were lawyers, and another quarter owned large farms or plantations. Only two were small farmers. And, 25 owned slaves.[15]

These men were knowledgeable about government and experienced in public affairs. They were practical, not wishful dreamers. Some were gregarious, others withdrawn. Some were loud and boorish, others dignified gentlemen. They all had personal and local interests to protect, but many recognized the need to adopt a national vision. The visionaries foresaw a growing nation that needed a new system of government for its prosperity and security.

Despite the summer heat, the delegates decided to keep the windows closed in order to preserve secrecy over their deliberations. When the clerk gave Washington a draft document that someone had apparently dropped just outside the chamber, the former general sharply reprimanded the delegates and warned them of the dangers of "disturb[ing] the public repose by premature speculations."[16] In fact, few notes were taken, the most copious by James Madison, and they were not made public until a half century later after his death. The brief, disorganized journal of the convention's secretary was publicly released by order of Congress only in 1819.

The convention functioned like a legislature, with debates and motions, speeches and votes, shifting alliances and outcomes often determined by the chance of attendance on a particular day. The delegates even adopted a special rule, different from standard parliamentary procedure, allowing anyone to make a motion to reconsider an earlier vote. This rule, coupled with the secrecy provision, made it easier for members to change their minds or form new alliances. And in fact, this happened notably in the unlikely collaboration between Connecticut's Roger Sherman and the Pinckneys of South Carolina. Connecticut supported the South on slavery and in return received support for its position on shipping and trade.[17]

Slavery loomed as a background issue for the convention and the fulcrum on which the Convention ultimately turned from dissent to consensus. At one point in late June, Madison pointed out the great divide between Northern and Southern interests. "Look to the votes in congress, and most of them are divided by the geography of the country, not according to the size of the states." He went on to suggest that one house of the legislature be represented according to free inhabitants only and the other counting everyone, including slaves. "By this arrangement the Southern scale would have the advantage in one house and the Northern in the other."[18]

The eventual decision on equal representation in the Senate and postponement of any laws on slavery achieved the same result of protecting Southern interests and allowed the convention to reach agreement on the framework of the government. In recognition of the sensitivity of the issue, however, the final text never used the word *slave*. Southern interests were also helped by the decision to count slaves as three fifths of a person, which gave the South greater representation in the House than if only "free inhabitants" were counted.[19] This metric had been chosen in 1783 for the allocation of proposed taxes under the Articles, so it was easy to use it again in the Constitution.

As the convention went on, moods changed, outbursts occurred, and in the final weeks, there was a momentum toward consensus and agreement. At this distance in time, and with the final product venerated as if carved in stone, it is hard to realize that the delegates were ordinary human beings, and their document in truth was a patchwork of compromises, narrow decisions, and sometimes artfully ambiguous wording. Nevertheless, their creation, the U.S. Constitution, established a distribution of power and checks and balances that have endured into the modern day, and it is from this document and the process of its creation that many of the tools in the foreign policy toolkit are derived.

Madison and the Virginia delegation came to the convention prepared. On the third day, after officers had been elected and rules adopted, they offered the Virginia Plan. It called for a bicameral legislature, one popularly elected and the other chosen from nominees by state legislatures. Both chambers were to be proportionate either to the "contributions" of the states (the value of property, including slaves) or to the "number of free inhabitants." There were also executive and judicial branches, but details were lacking. The legislature would have the power to nullify state laws deemed contrary to the new articles.

Virginia Governor Edmund Randolph gave the keynote address. He said that the government under the Articles failed in five ways, three of which were security matters. "It does not provide against foreign invasion.... It cannot preserve the particular States against seditions.... It cannot defend itself against encroachments." He went on to detail the Virginia Plan, the first plank of which was that the Articles needed to be "corrected and enlarged" in order to achieve "common defense, security of liberty, and general welfare."[20]

The delegates soon set to work addressing these matters. They agreed to have a national government with three branches and a bicameral legislature, with one body elected by the people. They then stalled on the means of election of the second body and set it aside to address later. When they took up the executive, they initially agreed on allowing a single seven-year term and rejected the idea of a plural executive. The delegates also agreed on the judicial branch and on selection of senators by state legislatures. The composition of the Senate, however, still needed to be resolved.

At the start of the third week, several alternate proposals to the Virginia Plan were considered, from giving each state one vote in the Senate to creating a unicameral legislature. The debate and defeat of these plans left many small-state delegates angry and frustrated and drove the convention to the verge of collapse. Many considered leaving the convention if their rights were not protected. Delegates on both sides became more heated and intransigent.

The small states had a point. The three largest states of Virginia, Pennsylvania, and Massachusetts had 45% of the U.S. population and would need only one other state to have a working majority over all other states. On many issues, the three most southern states—Georgia and the Carolinas—sided with the big three. Though small at the time, they all expected to grow much larger and saw such an informal alliance as helpful to their other interests.[21]

On July 2, Oliver Ellsworth of Connecticut pressed his resolution for equal representation in the Senate, but with some absentees and some still unexplained vote switches, the delegates tied on the question. That was a parliamentary defeat for the small states but a game-changing, emotional victory because it kept alive their alternative. On reflection, other delegates realized that this issue of Senate composition could destroy any chance at government reform. They agreed to turn the question over to a committee, and three days later, the committee recommended equal votes in the Senate. At the end of the tumultuous week, the delegates approved the plan.

Although the large states tried later to reverse this decision, they ultimately went along with it. This broke the logjam on other issues as well. With small-state rights protected, their delegates were more willing to strengthen the executive and the central government. By mid-July, delegates agreed on a single executive and gave him veto power. They debated and voted inconclusively on how to elect the executive before turning matters over to a committee of detail. With the executive and legislature now largely determined, the delegates turned their attention to the powers each branch would wield, and their voting shifted from close or tied to overwhelming majorities for or against the various proposals. The delegates agreed unanimously to give Congress the power to impose taxes and regulate interstate and foreign commerce.

Taking up the war power issue, arguably one of the most important foreign policy powers in the executive's arsenal, several delegates argued that the legislature was too slow to "make war," as the draft provided. Madison and Elbridge Gerry proposed changing the language to "declare war," thus allowing the executive to repel sudden attacks. Roger Sherman agreed that the executive should be able to repel and not commence war. The delegates voted 8–1 for the change.

The convention next debated the idea of a standing army in peacetime. Most of the delegates had strong fears of such a force. Madison had said, "Throughout all Europe, the armies kept under the pretext of defending, have enslaved the people." George Mason argued for only a "few garrisons," and suggested limiting the time for military funds. Elbridge Gerry, however, went even farther. He proposed permanently limiting the size of the peacetime force to 2,000 or 3,000 men. George Washington reportedly whispered to a colleague that he hoped the enemy would do likewise. Gerry's proposal was soundly defeated, and Mason's was adopted, setting a two-year limit on army appropriations.[22]

On September 7, delegates agreed to require presidential nomination and Senate concurrence on federal officials and a two-thirds Senate vote on treaties. Remaining matters were turned over to a committee of style. Delegates continued to wrangle over details of elections and representation and the ratification process, but no further changes were made to the defense and foreign policy provisions.

How to organize the executive branch and its processes was debated but left vague in the text. Delegates presumed that there would be departments under the president because they gave him power to demand reports from them. But, they repeatedly rejected proposals to create a formal council of advisors, drawing on the model of the English Privy Council and similar bodies under the royal governors of the colonies. Although the framers failed to provide explicitly for government departments and an advisory panel for the chief executive, they did not forbid such arrangements. George Washington and the First Congress saw the need for specific instruments to handle defense and foreign policy, and the first president regularly used his small cabinet as the institution to consider policy questions. The Convention's final product included many provisions specifically designed to correct the flaws of the Articles. (See Table 1.2.)

The New Framework

The document signed on September 17, 1787, was a compromise. Large states and small had each sacrificed important goals. The Constitution provided for a strong Congress, but the legislative branch was split between a chamber based on population and one based on equal representation of

Table 1.2 Problems Under the Articles of Confederation and Solutions in the Constitution

ARTICLES OF CONFEDERATION	CONSTITUTION
Weak, limited central government	Stronger central government
Taxes requested from states	Power to levy taxes
Unitary government in Congress	Three branches, separately chosen
Weak, subordinate executive	Strong executive with veto and nomination power
Appropriations, taxes, borrowing, war, and peace by a vote of nine out of thirteen	Supermajority only for treaties and amendments to the Constitution
No amendment except by unanimity	Amend by two thirds of Congress, three fourths of the states
Each state one vote	Equal in Senate, proportionate in House
Armies in state militia	Two-year limit on standing army
Congress last appeal on legal disputes	Separate Supreme Court
Congress names officials	President proposes; Senate must consent
Term limits of three years	No limits
Discriminatory pacts among states	Congress regulates interstate commerce
States violate treaties	Treaties supreme law of the land
No federal power against internal violence	Guarantee of Republican form of government
No enforcement power, relied on trust	Federal enforcement power
Demagogues prevail, tyranny of the majority	Two legislative chambers, differently chosen
Nullification or noncompliance with federal laws	All federal and state officials must take an oath to support the Constitution
Spanish, British, Indian threats	National army and navy, no state treaties or alliances
Insurrection and secession threats	Guarantee republican form of government and protect against domestic violence
State economic laws, including import duties	Regulate commerce; no state customs duties
Spendthrift, populist state legislatures issuing worthless paper currencies	Coin money with regulated value, decisions by two chambers

The Constitutional Convention in Philadelphia developed several provisions that specifically aimed to eliminate weaknesses in the government under the Articles of Confederation. Among them were provisions that significantly bolstered the new nation's foreign policy powers, giving it the authority and ability to, for instance, counteract threats from Spain and England.

the states. The count of population did not exclude slaves but calculated them as only three fifths of a person. Senators, representatives, and the president each had terms of different lengths, reducing the chances of a tyrannical majority government. The president was chosen by a strange, special-purpose electoral college. If it deadlocked, as many expected, the decision on the president would go to the House of Representatives, but each state was only allowed one vote on the matter. The chief executive was supposed to implement the laws passed by Congress, but he had a few independent powers, such as the pardon and the right to receive foreign ambassadors. The legislature's powers were carefully listed, followed by a very general *necessary and proper* clause.

The new U.S. government was designed to act slowly and deliberately, for there were many hurdles to be crossed and many veto points along the way. The legislature was made parochial, with each member beholden only to the voters of a specified geographical area. Election of senators by state legislatures made them in effect ambassadors from their states.

It was a system of checks and balances. As Madison later described it in *Federalist* 51, "But the great security against a gradual concentration of the several powers in the same department, consists in giving to those who administer each department the necessary constitutional means and personal motives to resist encroachments of the others. The provision for defense must in this, as in all other cases, be made commensurate to the danger of attack. Ambition must be made to counteract ambition." In the same paper, Madison famously explained the need for restraints on governmental power. "It may be a reflection on human nature, that such devices should be necessary to control the abuses of government. But what is government itself, but the greatest of all reflections on human nature? If men were angels, no government would be necessary."[23]

One of the key checks on government was the requirement that two of the three branches agree on most federal actions. The institutions were separated, but they shared basic powers. One branch could propose, but the other had to concur, or there was stalemate. (See Table 1.3.)

In national security and foreign affairs, the framers gave Congress the power to declare war, regulate trade, and approve treaties but left initiative and discretion with the president for conducting relations with other nations. While the president was designated commander-in-chief of the armed forces, Congress retained the power of the purse as well as the explicit power to make rules governing those forces. The president also had implicit emergency powers to fulfill the guarantee of protection against invasion and domestic violence. This mix of separate and overlapping powers led historian Edward Corwin to conclude that the Constitution was "an invitation to struggle for the privilege of directing American foreign policy."[24]

Two important provisions sought to provide long-term stability of the new government. One was a requirement that every federal and state official take an oath to support the Constitution once ratified. Without such

Table 1.3 Separated Institutions Sharing Powers Over National Security

PRESIDENT	POWER	CONGRESS
Negotiate	Treaties	Two thirds of Senate must consent
Propose	Nominations	Senate must consent
Commander-in-chief	War	Declare war; make rules for armed forces
Can veto	Appropriations	Required before spending
Propose agreements	Trade	Sets rules and tariffs
Can receive envoys and recognize governments	Foreign envoys	Funds missions
Direct	Intelligence	Funds; must be informed

While some people like to speak about the separation of powers in the U.S. government because of the three distinct branches and the two houses of the legislature, a more accurate description is *separated institutions sharing power* because both must consent for the government to act, as this table of national security powers indicates.

an oath, they could not hold any public office. Because oaths were taken seriously in 18th-century America, this provision sharply limited dissent over the new framework of government. The second provision spelled out the only parts of the Constitution that could not be amended. No law could be passed before 1808 limiting slavery or how slaves were counted for tax purposes, and no state could be denied equal representation in the Senate without its consent. The slavery provision merely postponed the clash that would culminate in the Civil War. The Senate provision reassured small states that the Great Compromise, as it was called, could not be overturned. To this day, the provision makes it difficult to overcome problems in the Senate, like filibusters and the overrepresentation of small states.

Benjamin Franklin offered comments on the closing day of the convention that probably reflected the views of most delegates. "I confess that there are several parts of this constitution which I do not approve, but I am not sure I shall never approve them. . . . I doubt too whether any other convention we can obtain may be able to make a better constitution. . . . Thus I consent, Sir, to this constitution because I expect no better, and because I am not sure that it is not the best."[25]

To some delegates, these compromises were not enough—or were too much. Edmund Randolph of Virginia refused to sign because the final document failed to reflect the Virginia Plan. George Mason of Virginia objected because there was no bill of rights. Elbridge Gerry of Massachusetts believed too much power was given to the national government and opposed the provisions allowing a standing army. Unquestioned patriots like Patrick

Henry and James Monroe, though not delegates, joined the opposition to ratification.

The Battles for Ratification

Adoption of the new Constitution came only after long and bitter fight, for each state had to make its own decision. The process was similar to the way the United States reaches decisions on major questions of domestic and foreign policy today—with media campaigns and well-organized interest groups and individual arm-twisting. Several states approved the Constitution only after creative compromises, such as including demands for revisions as part of their acceptance.

The framers wisely required that ratification would be decided by special conventions in each state rather than by the legislatures, which were going to lose power to the national government. Those 13 separate fights, staggered over two and a half years, included many close-run victories for the federalists.

When the document reached the Confederation Congress on September 26, the members quickly decided to forward it, without recommendation or other comment, to the respective state legislatures. That was probably unavoidable, despite the fact that the Philadelphia convention had gone beyond its official mandate and had proposed replacing the government then in power. Congress saw no need to debate the new framework itself, and the prospects for ratification were far from certain.

Supporters of the new framework began calling themselves Federalists and labeling their opponents Anti-Federalists. Supporters had numerous advantages: prestigious advocates, momentum, a common set of arguments, and the known alternative of continuing to struggle with the Articles of Confederation. They also had the overwhelming majority of newspapers on their side. Opponents tended to make populist arguments and forecast the growth of aristocratic power under the new arrangements, but they had a hard time defending the existing system and sometimes made contradictory arguments.[26]

Among the most needed, and thorough, defenses of the new framework came in the *Federalist Papers,* which ran in New York newspapers between October 1787 and June 1788. Authored by James Madison, Alexander Hamilton, and John Jay, but appearing under the pseudonym *Publius,* the 85 essays made the case for the Constitution and answered the vigorous attacks from New York opponents. They were reprinted widely, as were other key pamphlets in the debates.

Although security concerns were significant in establishing the Philadelphia convention and in shaping many features of the Constitution, they were less noticeable in the debates over ratification, except in Georgia. Instead of a security focus, the Anti-Federalists stressed the danger of a tyrannical government and the threats of a standing army, while the Federalists argued the commercial benefits of union more than the military advantages.[27]

Delaware earned bragging rights as the first state by ratifying the Constitution unanimously on December 7 after a quick election of delegates and five days of debate. Pennsylvania and New Jersey followed a few weeks later. Georgia voted for ratification on January 2, 1788, also with a unanimous vote, driven in part because of fears of Spanish and Indian threats. Connecticut approved it a week later.

On January 9, Massachusetts convened a large and raucous group of 355 delegates elected from town meetings. Two of its most prominent citizens—John Hancock and Samuel Adams—had not been in Philadelphia and were known to be skeptical of the Constitution. Backdoor discussions ultimately persuaded them to support ratification. Delegates like farmer Jonathan Smith, quoted in the epigraph to this chapter, made up their own minds after a careful reading of the document.

What also helped the Federalists win the final 187–168 Massachusetts vote was a tactical decision to allow discussion of possible future amendments to the Constitution. Surprisingly, the Anti-Federalists insisted on an up or down vote, fearing correctly that the prospect of changes would allow skeptics to agree to support ratification. The Massachusetts convention recommended nine amendments when it voted on February 6, saying they would "remove the fears and quiet the apprehensions" of the people "and more effectually guard against an undue administration of the Federal Government." Among the provisions urged by Massachusetts and also endorsed by several subsequent conventions were a ban on direct taxes, freedom for states to establish their own election rules, and a reservation of powers not expressly delegated to the new government—what became the Tenth Amendment.[28]

Opponents then gained ground in other states. The New Hampshire convention, meeting soon after Boston's debates, adjourned after 10 days of spirited argument because the Federalists feared a defeat if they pushed to a final vote. Rhode Island then rejected the Constitution in a popular referendum 2,708 to only 235 in favor—but the towns of Providence and Newport mostly boycotted the vote. Rhode Island would not ratify the Constitution until May 1790, more than a year after the new government began operating in New York and only two weeks after the new U.S. Senate had passed a bill prohibiting all trade with Rhode Island by land or sea. Even then, the vote was stubbornly close, 34–32.[29]

After strident opposition by Luther Martin, who had left Philadelphia early, Maryland delegates voted 63–11 for ratification on April 28. They considered 13 possible amendments, most of which had unanimous support, but did not include them as conditions. The measures included jury trial guarantees, protections against search and seizure, and various provisions to limit the raising of standing armies.

South Carolina followed suit with ratification on May 23 by a 149–73 vote, including recommendations for four amendments on reserved powers and against direct taxes. Nearly half the favorable votes came from men related by blood or marriage to the Rutledges or Pinckneys, who had been delegates to Philadelphia, thus confirming the political power of the planter elite.[30]

That made the count eight of the nine states required for the Constitution to go into effect. The honor of the ninth state fell to New Hampshire, where confusion in February turned into civil debate and a close 57–46 vote on June 21, made possible by an agreement to recommend a dozen amendments.

At the time, Virginia was in the third week of debating its action, with the outcome uncertain. George Mason and Patrick Henry stood in vehement opposition. Henry made frequent and impassioned speeches against anything like the new Constitution. Mason engaged James Madison in a line-by-line discussion of its provisions. The key vote turned on the question of making amendments advisory or a precondition for ratification. On that point, Madison prevailed 88–80 in favor of advisory amendments, and the convention then voted ratification 89–79 on June 25. Among Virginia's proposed amendments were a lengthy bill of rights and a two-thirds vote requirement for raising a standing army in peacetime and for passing navigation acts and commercial treaties. Delegates also favored a two-term limit on the president.[31]

Despite the ten favorable votes elsewhere, New York's accession was not a foregone conclusion. Alexander Hamilton was the only New Yorker to sign the Constitution and Governor George Clinton had been actively organizing opposition. In fact, 46 of the 65 convention delegates opposed ratification to some degree. After two weeks of thorough debate, news came of Virginia's approval, thus forcing opponents to explain why it was to New York's advantage to stay out of the now inevitable union. Ultimately, the Anti-Federalists agreed to the idea of amendments, and the convention voted 30–27 for ratification, along with a list of anticipatory rather than conditional amendments. These included a two-thirds vote requirement to declare war or to borrow money and a ban on the president "command[ing] an Army in the Field in person" without a prior vote by Congress permitting it.[32]

North Carolina's convention did not meet until July, and the Anti-Federalists had a 2–1 majority, which they deployed with withering criticism. In August, they voted 184–83 against ratification but still proposed 46 amendments. More than a year later, on November 21, 1789, with Washington installed as president and a bill of rights moving toward adoption, a new North Carolina convention voted 194–77 for ratification. The union was formed.

First Congress and First Precedents

The Confederation Congress voted a schedule for the selection of the president starting the first Wednesday in January 1789, and state legislatures established rules for choosing the First Congress. George Washington won unanimously, and Federalists gained 48 of the 59 seats in the House of Representatives.[33]

Delays in the arrival of new members prevented Congress from beginning work until April 1, nearly a month late. Members quickly counted the votes for president and sent a rider to inform Washington of his victory. He was inaugurated in New York on April 30. The House elected a speaker, but the driving force in the chamber, the unofficial floor leader, was James Madison. He was ready with ideas and actual legislation, including bills to create the executive departments and amendments to the Constitution.

The members of the new government were acutely aware that they were setting precedents for their successors, that they were completing the design framed in Philadelphia. Soon after his inauguration, Washington wrote to Madison, "As the first of every thing, in *our situation* will serve to establish a Precedent, it is devoutly wished on my part, that these precedents may be fixed on true principles." Another time, he told a friend, "I walk on untrodden ground."[34] Madison also was sensitive to the precedents being set. He wrote to Jefferson, "We are in a wilderness without a single footstep to guide us."[35]

Among the significant precedents set during that First Congress or shortly thereafter were these:

- After taking the oath prescribed by the Constitution, Washington added the words *so help me God*. He then gave a formal inaugural address.

- The Senate, before voting on its first treaty, a consular convention with France, summoned the still-serving secretary of foreign affairs under the Confederation, John Jay, to answer questions and provide documents about the treaty.

- The Senate rejected a nomination for the first time—of a naval officer to serve in the port of Savannah—greatly angering Washington but leading to a process of consultations on appointments.

- Washington personally came to the Senate to discuss treaties with the southern Indians but stormed out when Senators raised numerous questions and postponed consideration. He never again sought "advice" in that manner.

- The Senate adopted a resolution consenting to two Indian treaties and authorizing the president to ratify them, codifying the process that is still followed today.

- Congress established the first three executive departments—Foreign Affairs [renamed State two months later], War, and Treasury—and gave the president power to remove appointed officers but defeated proposals to require Senate concurrence in such removals.

- Washington established the practice of consulting his senior officials as a group in what is now called the cabinet.

- Congress voted its first appropriations for the new government, giving lump-sum appropriations to the departments in most cases.

- Washington named a special envoy, Gouverneur Morris, to explore the possibility of a commercial treaty with Great Britain but did not seek Senate confirmation of the appointment.
- Without seeking a declaration of war or other authorizing legislation but relying instead on vague language authorizing use of the militia to protect against Indians on the frontier, Washington sent troops against the Wabash Indians "to punish them for their depredations."
- When two such missions ended in military disasters, Congress established the precedent of oversight investigations by summoning the senior general and demanding personal testimony and background documents.
- After consulting his cabinet, Washington complied with the requests.
- In 1793, the Supreme Court denied a request from Washington to issue an advisory legal opinion on separation of powers grounds, thus establishing the principle that the Court hears only actual cases where the parties have tangible interests.

These precedents set the ground rules for legislative–executive–judicial interactions and filled in the otherwise blank spaces in the Constitution. The new Congress also added to that document by approving 12 amendments, 10 of which were approved by three quarters of the states within about two years and are now called the Bill of Rights. Several of them deal directly with security issues: the right to keep and bear arms, the ban on the quartering of soldiers in peacetime, protections against searches and seizures, and arguably even the amendments relating to judicial proceedings.

Congress set another precedent in those early months by engaging in lengthy debates and petty disputes. James Madison complained that lawmakers tended toward a "prolixity of discussion," and that lengthy delays occurred because of "incorrect draughts of Committees" as well as the "novelty and complexity" of creating a new system of government.[36] Madison lamented that Congress spent so long wrangling over other legislation that he could not get lawmakers to turn to constitutional amendments until midsummer. Even today, and even on major foreign policy questions, Congress has a tendency to engage in lengthy debates and petty disputes. In 2011, for example, the House and Senate took several votes on Libya but could not agree on a common approach. Foreign aid bills were not even scheduled for floor debate because of previous experience involving numerous, time-consuming amendments. And, the entire defense authorization bill was held up by a dispute over where enemy detainees could be tried.

The institutions for defense and foreign policy were also created by statute during the First Congress. The law creating the Department of Foreign Affairs was enacted in July 1789, and its secretary was empowered only as an agent of the president. In September, the department was renamed

State and was given additional duties in order to avoid having to create a separate home affairs department. In the early years, State was in charge of the mint, the census, patents, and the management of federal attorneys and marshals. Thomas Jefferson was nominated as first secretary, and he took office, along with three clerks, in March 1790.

The War Department was created in September 1789, and Henry Knox remained as its head, as he had been under the Confederation, along with one clerk. The main purpose remained protection of the frontier areas, but the law contained no specified missions. Seven months later, Congress wrote a more detailed law and increased the army from about 700 to 1,200 "able-bodied men, not under five feet six inches in height" and between 18 and 46 years of age. The measure authorized musicians as well as soldiers. There was no navy to speak of until Congress authorized building six frigates in 1794 and created a separate navy department in 1798. After the failure of the campaigns against the Wabash Indians, Washington and Knox decided that the militia was inadequate for fighting the Indians and never again used them. In 1792, Congress reorganized the army and increased its size to 5,000 to counter the Indians.[37]

The Treasury Department was a different creation, more an arm of Congress than of the president. The secretary was in part an agent of Congress in that he was to make estimates of public revenues and expenditures and to report directly to lawmakers in response to their requests.[38] Alexander Hamilton, the first secretary, took full advantage of this unusual arrangement by making several major proposals regarding public finances and economic development.

***

The framers of the American Constitution gave the new government special tools and powers to deal with the significant security threats—from within and from abroad—facing the new republic. They provided for a standing army and navy, gave the president power to deal with foreign nations, and created a system for making trade and security treaties. After sharp debates, they compromised on the new design—a system of separated institutions sharing powers, with a strong Congress and a potentially strong president. The new government established precedents during Washington's administration for handling nominations and treaties, consultations with Congress, and foreign diplomacy that remain in place to today. The institutions for American defense and foreign policy grew larger in later years and evolved in their capabilities and processes, as Chapter 2 describes. But, the basic design—the assignment of authorities and responsibilities as well as the checks and balances against abuses of power—remain as the framers planned.

Selected Resources

The journals of the Constitutional Convention and the records of the early years of the Republic are at the Library of Congress's website, A Century of Lawmaking for a New Nation at http://memory.loc.gov/ammem/amlaw/lawhome.html.

The story of the convention appears in these lively accounts: Richard Beeman, *Plain, Honest Men: The Making of the American Constitution* (New York: Random House, 2009); Christopher Collier and James Lincoln Collier, *Decision in Philadelphia* (New York: Ballantine Books, 1986); David O. Stewart, *The Summer of 1787: The Men Who Invented the Constitution* (New York: Simon & Schuster, 2007).

The fight over ratification is told by: Pauline Maier, *Ratification: The People Debate the Constitution, 1787–1788* (New York: Simon & Schuster, 2010).

An analysis of the provisions of the Constitution is provided by Akhil Reed Amar, *America's Constitution* (New York: Random House, 2005).

Washington's presidency and the actions of the early Congresses are well described in: Stanley Elkins and Eric McKitrick, *The Age of Federalism* (New York: Oxford University Press, 1993) and David P. Currie, *The Constitution in Congress: The Federalist Period, 1789–1801* (University of Chicago Press, 1997).

2 Following the Blueprint

I have much doubted whether, in case of a war, Congress would find it practicable to do their part of the business. That a body containing 100 lawyers in it, should direct the measures of a war is, I fear, impossible.

—Thomas Jefferson to James Madison, February 19, 1812[1]

I intend to be, myself, president of the United States.

—James K. Polk, 1845[2]

Would it impose too much labor on General Scott to make short, comprehensive daily reports to me on what occurs in his Department?

—Abraham Lincoln, March 30, 1861[3]

As the United States grew in population and expanded in territory, the government grew as well in size, capabilities, and complexity. The executive and legislative branches sometimes cooperated and sometimes fought over whether and how to use the diplomatic, economic, and military instruments of foreign policy. The balance of power between branches shifted at times, often because of external events but also because of the impact of powerful personalities. While these tools have always been part of America's toolkit, they have changed in size and utility over the years, and each use set precedents and taught lessons for later presidents. Reviewing this history can help you understand elements of continuity and change in the conduct of U.S. foreign policy.

The Washington Administration, 1789–1797

The first president and the First Congress established processes for performing their duties that served as models for subsequent decades. Executive branch decision making and congressional handling of foreign policy matters involving nominations, treaties, and investigations still follow those early precedents.

George Washington took his responsibilities as chief executive quite seriously and acted carefully as he established precedents in his roles as commander-in-chief and chief diplomat. He had no models to follow for relations with the two separated branches of government because presidential powers were quite different from those of a monarch. But, he did use his senior appointees—what came to be called the cabinet—as an advisory group, like the British Privy Council and similar bodies in some of the colonial governments.

The first cabinet was small: only Thomas Jefferson, secretary of state; Alexander Hamilton, secretary of the treasury; Henry Knox, secretary of war; and Edmund Randolph, attorney general (who had no department to administer). The president regularly sought reports from them and handled with dispatch the various papers sent to him for clearance. Before leaving the capital, Washington made a point of asking his cabinet officers if there was any business they needed to take up with him. He even insisted on approving requests for leaves of absence by senior officials. He paid attention to the details of federal contracts and especially to the people he appointed to federal jobs. As Leonard White reported, "Appointments, great and small, were of direct concern to Washington, and no collector of customs, captain of a cutter, keeper of a lighthouse, or surveyor of revenue was appointed except after specific consideration by the president."[4] Later presidents realized that their appointment power was crucial to their control of government for both domestic and foreign policy.

Major policy matters were discussed by the cabinet, often following letters with questions from the president. A revealing example was Washington's handling of the American response to the outbreak of war in Europe between revolutionary France and George III's Britain early in 1793. The president circulated a list of 13 questions to his advisors on April 18 and convened a cabinet meeting the next day. The first question was whether the government should issue a declaration of neutrality. Jefferson, an ardent Francophile, urged a neutral position but no formal declaration, hoping that the two sides would bid for American support by offering generous terms of neutrality and that France would be more generous than Britain. Hamilton, an Anglophile who wanted to preserve trade ties, argued for neutrality and for not honoring the 1778 treaty that could have required the United States to help defend French interests in the West Indies. Washington decided to split the differences between his top advisors. He issued a declaration that did not use the specific term *neutrality,* and he balanced the bureaucratic roles in the implementation of his decree by ordering Attorney General Randolph (rather than the secretary of state, the normal channel) to instruct the district attorneys to require reports of possible violations from Hamilton's customs collectors and to have those reports come directly to the president. Washington also sided with Jefferson on the validity of the 1778 treaty but did not believe it required U.S. military action.[5]

Two years later, Washington deftly handled the commercial treaty with Britain negotiated by John Jay, which had stirred domestic passions and led to the creation of pro-British and pro-French clubs that became the basis for the organization of America's first two political parties, the Federalists and the Republicans. The Senate confirmed Jay as envoy while he remained the chief justice but could not agree on instructions for his mission, thus giving full discretion to the president. Washington was unhappy with the treaty Jay negotiated but decided to submit it to the Senate. The debate was held in secret, and the final vote, 20–10, barely met the two-thirds requirement. During consideration, the Senate began a practice that continued throughout the 19th century of voting for an amendment to the treaty language that had to be accepted by the other party before ratification could take place. The text was leaked to the press, prompting widespread public anger because the terms seemed insufficiently favorable to U.S. interests. The opposition-controlled House of Representatives delayed ratification for a year by demanding access to the secret negotiation documents, which Washington denied as a "dangerous precedent" in the first use of what is called *executive privilege*.[6] Later presidents would claim the right to withhold government documents either to preserve executive branch prerogatives and internal secrecy or to prevent Congress from seeing materials that might prove embarrassing.

Congress exercised its power to build an army and a navy in response to continuing frontier problems with the Indians and overseas problems with Barbary pirates. Lawmakers had hoped to rely upon the militia to handle problems like the Whiskey Rebellion—the refusal of farmers in western Pennsylvania to pay the 1791 federal tax on stills and distilled spirits (and also on snuff, loaf sugar, and carriages). Some 15,000 troops were mobilized in September 1794, and Washington rode west to take personal command of the force. Opposition melted away, but the performance of the militia was beset with problems. Congress voted in 1795 to bring the army to full strength of about 4,000 men, demonstrating lawmakers' reliance on a standing army rather than the states' militias.

Commerce raiding by pirates from Algiers as well as harassment by British ships in the West Indies led Congress in early 1794 to pass a law authorizing the purchase or construction of six frigates, but it included a provision cancelling the program in case of peace with Algiers. Secretary Knox, seeking public support for the reestablished navy, contracted for each ship to be built in a different shipyard and arranged for supplies from neighboring states. When an agreement was reached with Algiers in 1796, Congress, at Washington's urging, still allowed the completion of three of the original six ships.[7] Shipping interests outweighed any peace dividend.

Washington concluded his eight years as chief executive by laying down markers for future foreign policy in what was called his "Farewell Address." Drawing on earlier suggestions from Madison and extensive drafts from Hamilton, the president urged the new nation to seek commercial rather than political relations with other nations and to "steer clear of permanent alliances." (Jefferson, in his first inaugural address in 1801, used a slightly different formulation of the same idea. He called for "peace, commerce, and honest friendship with all nations, entangling alliances with none.") To this day, one senator is recruited to read Washington's address each year on the anniversary of the first president's birthday.

John Adams and the Quasi-War With France, 1797–1801

John Adams was no George Washington, but he continued the practice of executive control of foreign policy, and Congress continued to have fiercely partisan fights over foreign policy and military preparedness. His biggest mistake was to keep Washington's cabinet intact—until forced to fire two officials for back-channel dealings with Alexander Hamilton, then a New York lawyer and formerly secretary of the treasury, whom he greatly distrusted. His cabinet was a nest of rivals, not a team.

With relations with Britain friendly after the Jay Treaty, Adams had problems with France, which had openly endorsed his rival Thomas Jefferson in the 1796 elections and which refused to accept Adams's minister to Paris. Early in 1798, France imposed new restrictions on American shipping, and French officials (referred to in secret dispatches as *XYZ*) demanded substantial bribes even to conduct meetings. Adams considered asking for a declaration of war but held off, simply reporting to Congress that he had "no ground of expectation" of a settlement with France. Republicans denounced Adams's criticism of France and demanded publication of the secret dispatches, not realizing what they contained. Adams complied, setting off virulent criticism of France and quick passage of measures to quadruple the size of the army and increase the navy tenfold. To pay for the military buildup, Congress passed the nation's first direct tax on land, houses, and slaves. Lawmakers, frustrated by delays in shipbuilding then managed by the War Department, created a separate Navy Department and reestablished the Marine Corps to go along with the expanded fleet.[8]

War fever also prompted Congress to enact the Alien and Sedition Acts to punish criticism of the U.S. government and allow registration and deportation of noncitizens. By 1799, Adams feared he was losing control of the government to Hamilton, who was helping Washington organize the newly expanded army and was purging its ranks of Republicans. Without consulting his cabinet or Congress, Adams named a new envoy to Paris, who eventually negotiated a treaty that allowed both sides to back away from their "quasi-war."[9] By then, Adams had been voted out of office. He had set important precedents of using war fever to win passage of a military buildup but also taking executive actions to avoid a full-scale war.

Republican Government, 1800–1828

As president from 1801 to 1809, Thomas Jefferson displayed an ambivalent and conflicted view toward several of the instruments for foreign policy. He was philosophically antimilitarist and determined to slash government expenditures, and though a former diplomat, he viewed professional diplomats as elitist and undemocratic. Jefferson cut the number of foreign diplomatic posts from six to three—Britain, France, and Spain—and stopped the practice of career service overseas. He cut the army's budget in half and cashiered the most partisan Federalist officers, but he did approve the creation of a military academy at West Point, an institution designed as an engineering school rather than one for war fighters. Instead of blue-water warships, Jefferson forced the navy to build only shallow-draft gunboats for harbor defense.[10]

He continued his predecessors' practice of using his cabinet for discussions and advice but insisted on routing all documents through his office. He dominated the Republican-controlled Congress by appointing particular members as floor leaders for the administration and by indirect, informal consultations with members. Congress itself created more standing committees and began using the party caucus for business, including the selection of presidential nominees.[11]

His strict reading of the Constitution led Jefferson to agonize over the purchase of Louisiana before finally proceeding in 1803. The purchase encouraged American leaders to envision a continent-spanning nation. Jefferson also sent a four-ship naval squadron to the Barbary Coast with strictly defensive orders soon after he entered the White House and asked Congress, when it next convened in December, for authorization for aggressive action. This action—the first such instance—showed his willingness to order a military operation while still seeking congressional approval as soon as lawmakers met in regular session. A few weeks later, Congress approved the first of several laws for "warlike operations" against pirates.[12] As relations with Britain grew more hostile toward the end of his second administration, with the harassment of U.S. ships and British impressments of several thousand American seamen, Jefferson refrained from further combat actions and got Congress to pass an embargo act that cut all U.S. trade with Europe—a dismal failure diplomatically and an economic disaster for the young nation.

Jefferson's successor, James Madison, led the nation in its first declared war—the War of 1812 (1812–1814), a mishandled conflict that saw the burning of the nation's capital, a bungled invasion of Canada, and just enough naval victories to soothe the national psyche. From the start of his presidency in 1809, Madison was a weak and ineffective leader. The Senate refused to confirm his nominee Albert Gallatin as secretary of state and later forced him to remove Gallatin as secretary of the treasury. When Madison urged preparedness measures, including a 10,000-man increase in the standing army, Congress raised the figure to 25,000. In one of his few decisive actions, Madison fired his secretary of war just after British troops burned Washington, DC, and installed James Monroe in that post for six months while Monroe continued to serve as secretary of state. Monroe was elected president in 1816 and served two terms as a strong executive, particularly in foreign affairs.[13]

James Monroe and his able secretary of state, John Quincy Adams, used economic and diplomatic instruments to set America on course for two decades of economic growth and territorial expansion. There were heavy postwar cuts in the army and navy, but the army had the benefit of energetic leadership and far-reaching reforms by Secretary of War John C. Calhoun.[14]

In keeping with the vision of a country stretching from sea to sea, Secretary of State John Quincy Adams told the British minister to Washington, "Keep what is yours and leave the rest of the continent to us." An 1817 agreement with Britain established an unfortified northern border with British Canada and left the Oregon Territory open to both nations. Andrew Jackson took care of the southeast corner a year later by seizing Florida from Spain under the guise of "pacifying" the Seminole tribes.[15]

Monroe and Adams concluded a dozen commercial agreements with other nations but were unsuccessful in extending that approach to Latin America. As secretary of state, Adams nearly doubled the number of U.S. consuls abroad. He also wrote most dispatches himself and devised a filing system that would be used until 1915. Another innovation by Adams was the practice of issuing each envoy formal letters of instruction, one on administrative duties and a second personal one setting forth objectives for that particular post. This practice continues today with formal letters from the president to each U.S. chief of mission.[16]

Adams also played a crucial role in crafting the section of the president's annual message in 1823 that became known as the Monroe Doctrine. The message called for a "non-colonization principle" in the Western hemisphere and said the United States would not interfere in the "internal affairs" of Europe but warned against European effort to "extend their system" to the Western hemisphere.[17] The doctrine did not foreclose U.S. claims to additional territory. It served as a guiding policy in U.S. foreign affairs throughout the 19th century and remained an emotional lodestar in the 20th century as U.S. leaders opposed Nazi and communist penetration of the Western hemisphere.

Congress conducted more vigorous oversight of the executive, greatly increasing the number of required departmental reports and launching numerous investigations during the Monroe and Adams administrations.[18] John Quincy Adams, elected president by the House of Representatives after a bitter fight in 1824, then confronted a Congress with both houses controlled by the opposition for his last two years in office, the first time that had happened, but not the last.

The Slavery Factor

The Missouri Compromise of 1820—admitting one slave state and one non-slave state to the Union at the same time and dividing the Louisiana Purchase territory into free and slave areas—postponed a more violent national conflict over slavery but left the issue as the backdrop for economic and foreign policy for another 40 years. While the (largely white male) citizenry agreed on American exceptionalism and the mission of extending the blessings of U.S. liberty to benighted races and places, they disagreed on the urgency of expansion westward. Southerners did not want anything to threaten their political power and their "peculiar institution" of slavery. The political heirs of Jefferson and Jackson, now called Democrats, favored opening lands for rural development. A new party, called the Whigs, preferred consolidating growth and promoting industrialization and commerce in established areas as a higher priority.[19]

The economies of the South, North, and West developed differently in the following decades, leading to a sectionalization in thinking about foreign policy. The South's cotton became the major export crop, and two thirds of it went to Britain. Northern states especially imported manufactured goods from Europe and received significant foreign capital investment. Shipping also offset the trade deficit and provided money for domestic investment. Southern planters wanted free trade. They were frequently aligned with western farmers and entrepreneurs who opposed protectionism and the dominance of northeastern financial institutions. Northern manufacturers wanted protection of U.S. industries and government support for transportation. Democrats, dominated by southerners, favored strong commercial diplomacy, seeking strategic ports and territory in the Caribbean and Latin America as well as in Asia. They favored expansion into Texas for slavery reasons and into Oregon and California to facilitate trade with Asia. Whigs, strongest in the North, were less urgent on territorial expansion and hesitant regarding support for colonies seeking independence in the Western hemisphere because they feared it would lead to European retaliation against U.S. trade.[20]

Where and when to expand the United States also got caught up in the slavery factor. Southerners welcomed the acquisition of Texas, where Americans had been settling and had established independence from Mexico in 1836, but they were opposed acquiring more of Mexico because of racial concerns. Foreign policy issues were tested by what they might mean for slavery. For example, slaveholders were nervous about U.S. recognition of Haiti, fearing a contagion of slave revolts. The growing abolitionist movement was also reluctant to endorse expansion that allowed slavery and more slave states in Congress.[21]

President Andrew Jackson recognized the Republic of Texas but deferred the issue of annexation, fearing a divisive impact on his party. Meanwhile, he continued the foreign policy approach of his predecessors by seeking additional trade agreements, concluding 10 in all, but he was preoccupied with domestic policy controversies. His cabinet met infrequently and only rarely discussed foreign policy matters. Jackson ran through four secretaries of state in his eight years in office, but he also reformed the department and the foreign service by creating eight bureaus and a senior subordinate to the secretary as well as by paying consular officers salaries for the first time. The army was temporarily boosted from about 7,000 to over 12,000 between 1836 and 37 to fight Indians and continue the Indian removal policy to western lands.[22] America's overseas presence expanded steadily, beginning with the Jackson years. (See Table 2.1.) The size of the armed forces, however, fluctuated greatly, with only temporary increases to deal with major conflicts. (See Table 2.2.) The United States was expanding its reach and interaction with other countries diplomatically, while the armed forces increased and shrank in response to internal and external threats.

President John Tyler submitted a treaty annexing Texas in 1844, but it was overwhelmingly rejected by the Senate, 16–35. This issue was the most prominent one in the sharply contested presidential election of 1844, where dark-horse candidate James Knox Polk defeated Henry Clay by just 1% of the popular vote. Just before Tyler left office, he won congressional approval by majority votes of a joint resolution admitting Texas to the Union.

James Polk, Master Strategist, 1845–1849

James K. Polk was a political protégé of Andrew Jackson and a seven-term congressman, serving as speaker for his last four years. Even before he took the oath of office in 1845, he vowed to a friend, "I intend to be, *myself*, [italics added] president of the United States." In that regard, he would follow the precedent set by his predecessors in wartime, taking an active leadership role and maintaining a close cabinet. Polk set four specific goals for his administration: settlement of the Oregon question; acquisition of California; reduction of the tariff; and the establishment of what he called a *constitutional treasury*, which meant keeping government funds away from private banks.[23] He achieved all four goals and dramatically expanded the United States in the process.

Polk practiced what today would be called *brinkmanship*. To settle Oregon, he got Congress to pass a measure revoking the 1827 treaty with Britain allowing joint occupation then quietly informed London of his willingness to compromise. He secured prompt approval of the British proposal, which extended the 1818 border along the 49th parallel to the Pacific Ocean and gave the United States the Columbia River basin.[24]

Polk then turned his attention to California, which was then a part of Mexico. He ordered a series of actions to pressure Mexico and make acquisition of California easier. He sent navy ships off of Veracruz in the Gulf of Mexico and deployed troops along the Rio Grande River. Under Polk's orders, agents tried to bribe Mexican officials in the northern provincial capital in Santa Fe to accept U.S. rule. The president gave secret orders to the navy's Pacific squadron to occupy major California ports in case of war. When word arrived that a U.S. border patrol had been attacked, Polk sent his already-prepared war message to Congress. Congress voted overwhelmingly but not enthusiastically for war; many members opposed expansion but said they could not deny additional weapons to American soldiers under attack.[25]

Unlike most presidents—Abraham Lincoln and Franklin D. Roosevelt are the exceptions—Polk was a hands-on commander-in-chief. He had explained his military campaign plan to the cabinet nearly a year before the war broke out, then gave the military the necessary instructions. He became coordinator-in-chief of the army and navy and their respective supply organizations. He would rewrite proposed orders and confer frequently with subordinate officials.[26]

The war did not go as smoothly as Polk expected. While he was a strong and assertive wartime president, Polk was confronted by a Congress displaying the divisions and disruptions feared by Jefferson, as quoted at the start of this chapter. Polk had trouble with his generals, whom he distrusted because they were Whigs, and he faced increased political opposition when the Whigs won a majority in the House in the 1846 elections and later established a special investigating committee and even passed an amendment declaring the war "unnecessarily and unconstitutionally begun."[27] Nor could Congress ever agree on war aims because Southerners filibustered the Wilmot Proviso, which would have denied the extension of slavery into newly acquired territories. Even the treaty ending the war and giving the United States land from Texas to the Pacific Ocean was wrapped in confusion, negotiated contrary to Polk's instructions by an agent he had recalled, but submitted to the Senate anyway.

Polk used all the instruments of foreign policy—diplomacy, trade, secret operations, and military force—to achieve his goals and set a standard of executive activism not seen again in the 19th century except under Abraham Lincoln and William McKinley. Polk ran his presidency as he had run the war, with mind-numbing attention to detail, with regular use of his cabinet for political management rather than administration, including using the cabinet to lobby Congress, and by frequent interaction with subcabinet officials.[28]

America and the World, 1850–1861

In the decade before the Civil War, the government worked with and for private interests in crafting U.S. foreign policy, and sometimes those private interests acted on their own initiatives. Interest in building a canal linking the two great oceans of the Atlantic and Pacific led American officials and businessmen to seek political and economic influence in Central America, and the U.S. established a naval presence there. Southerners sought to acquire Cuba and, with it, several new slave states. Private military expeditions, called *filibusters,* intervened in Mexico, Cuba, Honduras, Nicaragua, and Ecuador to try to take over the governments and secure economic benefits for themselves.[29]

In East Asia, America followed British openings to China with its own trade agreements. The United States then sent warships to Japan to open that country to American trade. President James Buchanan, weak and indecisive in dealing with the slavery question at home, practiced vigorous gunboat diplomacy abroad. He sent 19 warships to Paraguay to avenge the death of a single American seaman and got Congress to approve a law authorizing his use of force against that nation. He also pressured Mexico on financial claims and sought to annex Cuba.[30]

As trade expanded across the Atlantic and Pacific, and to Central and South America, so did the U.S. diplomatic presence. As Table 2.1 shows, the State Department grew in size and scope in this period, giving testament to the country's increasing involvement in and engagement with the rest of the world. In Washington, D.C., the secretary of state had a staff of 44, with 27 diplomatic and 197 consular posts abroad. America was increasing the

Table 2.1 U.S. Diplomatic and Consular Missions, 1790–1950

YEAR	DIPLOMATIC POSTS	CONSULAR POSTS
1790	2	10
1800	6	52
1810	4	60
1820	7	83
1830	15	141
1840	20	152
1850	27	197
1860	33	480
1870	36	612
1880	36	673
1890	41	760
1900	42	713
1910	49	566
1920	47	412
1930	58	362
1940	59	293
1950	74	207

Since its inception, the United States has increased the size and scope of its diplomatic instrument via more diplomatic and consular posts around the world. This increased presence has historically allowed the United States to engage more actively with the rest of the world. See Chapters 6 and 8 for data after 1950.

Source: William Barnes and John Heath Morgan, *The Foreign Service of the United States* (Washington, DC: Department of State Historical Office, 1961): 349–350.

size and scope of its diplomatic instrument in order to engage more actively with the rest of the world.

Foreign Policy in the Civil War, 1861–1865

To fight the Civil War, the U.S. government created not only a large army and navy but also an administrative state that became quite adept at collecting taxes, supplying troops, administering contracts, building infrastructure, conducting espionage, and managing a global foreign policy in support of the war effort. An inexperienced, small-town lawyer from Illinois, Abraham Lincoln, was in charge of these many activities, and he was ably assisted by several men with political, leadership, and managerial skills.

Lincoln's biggest foreign policy challenge was to prevent European recognition of the Confederate government and outside efforts to negotiate a peace that would leave the Union divided. While keeping a close rein on military operations, the president generally left Secretary of State William H. Seward in charge of diplomacy. Initially, only tsarist Russia supported the Union. Britain declared neutrality a month after the fall of Fort Sumter in 1861. The British were torn between their antipathy toward slavery and their dependence on southern cotton for their textile mills. The U.S. minister in London, Charles Frances Adams, the son and grandson of presidents, skillfully raised moral and other arguments in support of the Union. The Confederacy mishandled its cotton leverage by establishing an embargo on shipments in hope that Europeans would provide their support out of desire to have the embargo lifted. Instead, Britain developed other sources for its cotton while simultaneously becoming more dependent on the Union for wheat.[31]

The turning point came in late summer of 1862. Britain and France were suffering economically because of the cotton shortages and thought that Confederate victories and Union defeats on the battlefield required a negotiated settlement. Napoleon III had sent troops to Mexico in 1861 ostensibly to collect debts but in fact to establish an imperial foothold that would be aided by the existence of a Confederate buffer state. The British cabinet was divided but tilting toward diplomatic intervention to force an armistice. A French proposal for Franco–British–Russian mediation fell apart, mainly because of distractions over unrest in Poland and Mexico but also thanks to U.S. policies. Despite U.S. sympathy for the Poles, Lincoln and Seward sided with Russia as the tsar suppressed an uprising in his empire. That secured Russian support for the Union. Confederate general Robert E. Lee's retreat from the bloody battlefield at Antietam was viewed as enough of a Union victory for Lincoln to announce his plan to issue an Emancipation Proclamation at the start of 1863, giving the Union the high moral ground against slavery and making it harder for the British especially to intercede.[32]

Lincoln had his own troubles with his generals until he finally gave command to General Ulysses S. Grant; with his first secretary of war until he replaced him with Edwin Stanton; and with the Congress, which established an intrusive oversight committee that demanded papers and summoned generals to testify on why military operations were going so badly. But, Lincoln remained an active commander in chief, asserting civilian control as intended by the Constitution. After his first plaintive efforts to gain information from his generals, as in his note to General Winfield Scott quoted in the epigraph to this chapter, Lincoln was more assertive, intrusive, and directive. He monitored the war closely by telegraph and sometimes gave operational orders while denying that he intended to interfere.[33]

Congressional Dominance in the Gilded Age, 1865–1898

Politics turned bitter after the Civil War. Presidential foreign policy initiatives were repeatedly rebuffed by Congress, where lawmakers pandered to local ethnic and economic interests. President Andrew Johnson was impeached by the House of Representatives in 1868 and narrowly acquitted by the Senate. Congress imposed its own reconstruction laws on the South and tried to limit the president's authority over his subordinates. Only one of the five treaties Johnson submitted to the Senate—the purchase of Alaska—was approved.

Weak presidents confronted a domineering Congress and an especially assertive Senate. President Ulysses S. Grant and his cabinet lobbied extensively for a treaty annexing the Dominican Republic, the first big step toward guarding approaches to the train route across Panama and the anticipated isthmian canal. A tie vote defeated that agreement. In fact, between 1869 and 1898, 134 treaties were submitted to the Senate and 20 were lost, some by defeat, some by indefinite delay, and some by amendments unacceptable to the other parties. Others were withdrawn when the White House changed hands and the new president didn't want to support what his predecessor had negotiated.[34]

Grant, a Republican president, had problems even with an overwhelmingly Republican Congress. They worsened when the Democrats won the House in the 1874 elections. In the subsequent two decades, party control switched back and forth. There were only three congresses (six years) in which one party controlled both houses at the same time and only two congresses (four years) when the majority party also held the presidency.[35] Divided government meant divisive politics on foreign as well as domestic affairs.

Relations with Britain regularly got entangled with partisan politics as each party fought for the growing Irish vote. An 1886 extradition treaty, which would have required the United States to surrender Irish nationalists for trial in Britain, languished before the Senate for two years before a flood of petitions from Irish clubs led to a final debate and defeat. A more important treaty with London, an 1888 agreement settling an angry dispute over northeastern fisheries, became the first treaty ever to be debated in open session. A party-line vote set the precedent for public debate, which went on for nearly three months before the treaty was defeated by another party-line vote. As one Republican senator confided, "We cannot allow the Democrats to take credit for settling so important a dispute."[36]

Tariffs were the main domestic political controversy, but they of course had foreign policy consequences. Democrats sought to lower tariffs, Republicans to raise them. Three major, and differing, tariff laws were enacted in the 1890s alone. Many political leaders came to believe that America needed to expand into overseas markets in order to avoid a glut from overproduction. And, America was growing: Its population doubled between 1865 and 1898, and gross national product more than tripled. But, the growth was uneven. Two deep recessions in the 1870s and early 1890s added to domestic unrest. Foreign trade surged, with exports quadrupling and imports tripling in the last third of the century. Iron, steel, and petroleum became big export items along with cotton and wheat. By 1898, 79% of the exports and 50% of the imports were to or from Europe. These changes increased the pressures for favorable commercial agreements with other nations, but what the Americans wanted was bilateral reciprocity treaties rather than most-favored nation agreements that would grant the same tariffs to all other nations. Reciprocity agreements were only available outside Europe.[37]

The United States courted Latin America for trade and also for an isthmian canal, which was seen as having enormous commercial and military benefits. Americans also sought to increase their presence in the Pacific Ocean by dominating and trying to annex Hawaii and by acquiring joint control of Samoa. These interests led to a new interest in a modern navy. By this time, the Civil War fleet had been mostly sold or dismantled. U.S. admirals then had wanted wooden ships. General orders into the 1870s continued to call for ships to have "full sail power" and to use steam only when absolutely necessary.[38] Beginning in 1882, Congress began authorizing new, big, steel ships that moved America up the ranks to a global power. Naval expansion received bipartisan support and coincided with ideas about naval power serving as the basis of national power. By 1898, the United States had a blue-water, or ocean-going, navy led by half a dozen battleships, and the number of navy personnel had more than doubled the rate from eight years earlier. (See Table 2.2.)

Imperial Ambitions, 1898–1913

By 1898, the United States had an appetite for conquest and an eagerness to play on a world stage. Within 20 years, America would acquire colonies in Asia and Latin America, would send troops to several countries in the Western hemisphere, and would join the fighting in a world war. There would be a backlash to this growing U.S. involvement, including the rise of anti-imperial groups in the 1900 elections and later. But at the start, Democrats vied with Republicans to promote Cuban independence, as the case study in Chapter 4 makes clear. The Republican platform in 1896 was expansionist, calling for annexation of Hawaii, acquisition of the Virgin Islands, a U.S.-controlled canal across the isthmus of Panama, independence for Cuba, and a voluntary union with Canada.[39]

Cuba served as a pretext for war. It offered America a chance to oppose colonialism and support independence of a downtrodden people while benefitting economically. Spain was losing its grip to rebels fighting for their independence. The island's economy was dominated by the United States, which took 87% of its exports, and U.S.-owned businesses wanted an end to the fighting to preserve their profits. Cuban expatriates in Florida and New York raised funds and smuggled arms in support of the rebels.[40]

President William McKinley proved as skilled a diplomat and warrior as Polk and Lincoln. He tried for over a year to achieve Cuban independence via diplomatic maneuvering, always backed by the threat of force. After the explosion of the U.S. battleship *Maine* in Havana harbor, Congress voted $50 million in unrestricted funds for defense. On April 20, 1898, with McKinley still resisting a declaration of war, Congress took the lead and

Table 2.2 — U.S. Active Duty Military Personnel, 1789–1950

YEAR	ARMY	NAVY	MARINE CORPS
1789	718	...	...
1795	3,440	1,856	...
1801	4,051	2,700	357
1810	5,956	5,149	449
1814	38,186	8,024	648
1820	10,554	3,988	571
1830	6,122	4,929	891
1840	12,330	8,017	1,269
1848	47,319	11,238	1,751
1850	10,929	8,794	1,101
1860	16,215	9,942	1,801
1865	1,000,692	58,296	3,860
1870	37,240	10,562	2,546
1880	26,594	9,361	1,939
1890	27,373	9,246	2,047
1898	209,714	22,492	3,579
1900	101,713	18,796	5,414
1910	81,251	48,533	9,560
1918	2,395,742	448,606	52,819
1920	204,292	121,845	17,165
1930	139,378	96,890	19,380
1940	269,023	160,997	28,345
1945	8,267,958	3,380,817	474,680
1950*	593,167	381,538	74,279

*The Air Force, separated from the Army in 1947, had 411,277 personnel in 1950.

Throughout much of its history, the United States expanded its army and navy only when it engaged in wars and then cut back deeply afterwards. The army, for instance, saw drastically increased numbers in 1898, when the United States engaged in war with Spain, and again in 1918 and 1945 during the two world wars.

Source: *Historical Statistics of the United States* (U.S. Department of Commerce, 1961) 736–737.

passed a measure declaring Cuba independent and directing and empowering the president to use U.S. land and naval forces to achieve that result. Five days later, after Spain rejected an ultimatum for Cuban independence, McKinley asked for a formal declaration of war, which Congress promptly passed by voice votes. This marked the start of the Spanish-American War, which would grow beyond the conflict over Cuba to involve Spanish imperial holdings as far away as Southeast Asia. Congress then proceeded to add two artillery regiments and greatly increased the navy's resources, tripling McKinley's request for battleships, doubling the number of torpedo boats, and almost tripling the number of destroyers.[41]

As commander-in-chief, McKinley created a war room on the second floor of the White House and installed 15 telephone lines and telegraphs to communicate with U.S. forces and federal officials. He held daily sessions with his secretaries of war and navy and the adjutant general. McKinley reviewed all orders and sometimes rewrote them. He did not hesitate to reverse the judgment of field commanders.[42]

McKinley did not stop with liberating Cuba. While the war there continued, he acted to annex Hawaii and seize the Philippines and other Pacific islands. Because McKinley lacked the votes to annex Hawaii by treaty, which would have required a two-thirds vote, he obtained congressional approval of a simple law, just as John Tyler had done to bring Texas into the Union. McKinley ordered troops to seize Puerto Rico before Spain asked for peace. He also ordered the navy to take control of Guam and Wake Island in the Pacific and sent 20,000 troops to occupy the Philippines before learning of the Spanish surrender.[43]

The Spanish-American War lasted only four months. McKinley tried to pave the way for Senate approval of the peace treaty by naming three senators to the peace delegation. A major constraint on the negotiations was the Teller Amendment added to the declaration of war that prevented the annexation of Cuba. Domestic sugar producers did not want Cuba to be able to export its sugar tariff free. The peace treaty gave Cuba independence and the United States control of the Philippines, Guam, and Puerto Rico in return for $20 million. Despite the three senators in the peace delegation, the administration was not confident of victory in the Senate, so it reportedly offered several promises of patronage appointments. Democratic leader William Jennings Bryan also urged ratification, limiting Democratic opposition. When the final vote came, the treaty was approved with two votes to spare.[44]

Seemingly overnight, the United States became an imperial power, with overseas territories to administer and an expanding navy to police the oceans. Troops in the Philippines took four brutal years to suppress the insurgency there. In 1900, 6,000 soldiers were sent to China as part of a multinational force to end the siege of Beijing and put down the Boxer Rebellion. America continued to play great power politics with China, Japan, and Korea. Despite the Teller Amendment, Congress in 1901 approved the Platt Amendment, essentially establishing a protectorate over Cuba. It gave America two bases on the island and allowed U.S. intervention in Cuban internal affairs. Cuba was coerced into incorporating the Platt provisions into its own constitution. Secretary of War Elihu Root called the new system of colonial government *patrician tutelage*. He also quipped that the Constitution "follows the flag but doesn't quite catch up with it."[45]

Taking the oath of office after McKinley's assassination in 1901, Theodore Roosevelt was an energetic president, both in using the powers of his office and in reforming the instruments he had for foreign policy. He was an active diplomat, an enthusiastic militarist, and a defender of U.S. economic interests. Many of his successors, starting with Woodrow Wilson and Franklin Roosevelt, followed his precedents of assertive leadership. "I believe in a strong executive," he said. "I believe in power." When Colombia rejected a treaty giving America rights to build a canal across the isthmus of Panama, Roosevelt gave a green light to Panamanian rebels and sent warships to prevent Colombia from sending troops. He then concluded a quick treaty with the rebel government in Panama. To secure U.S. dominance of the route to the canal, Roosevelt also proclaimed the Roosevelt Corollary to the Monroe Doctrine, declaring the United States had the right to intervene against weak, brutal, or incompetent governments in the Western hemisphere. He followed that announcement with intervention in the Dominican Republic to control the customs house and secure funds for foreign creditors.[46]

Roosevelt enjoyed diplomacy and even won the Nobel Peace Prize for his efforts to achieve a peace treaty ending the Russo-Japanese War of 1905. To get around likely Senate opposition to treaties, he expanded the practice of using executive agreements, some kept secret, as key tools of his diplomacy. An early supporter of career public service, Roosevelt pushed for the professionalization of the foreign service. During the 19th century, U.S. diplomats were poorly paid and forced to rotate from office to provide patronage under the spoils system. Prior to the 20th century, only seven envoys served abroad longer than 10 years. Roosevelt changed the practice on appointments and established a merit promotion system by executive order, and Congress eventually changed the law to create a career system for U.S. diplomats. These changes made the diplomatic instrument a more professional institution, just as the State Department was doubling in personnel strength between 1898 and 1908 and expanding the number of overseas posts.[47]

Secretary of State Elihu Root served as the chief administrator of foreign service reform. He had instituted similar far-reaching changes a few years earlier while Secretary of the Army. Root took over the War Department just after the Spanish-American War, which had been a military success but a logistical nightmare. He created a general staff headed by an army chief of staff, established the Army War College, and centralized control of the various army bureaus under the secretary. Roosevelt himself ordered tough new physical standards for soldiers. When officers complained publicly, Roosevelt, with the press in tow, completed the three-day test in a single day.[48]

Roosevelt also pushed the services to adopt new technologies. He urged creation of machine-gun units in the army and added funds for aircraft development. He endorsed the idea of an all big-gun battleship even before the British *Dreadnought* showed the value of such a design in 1906, and he secretly boarded one of the navy's new submarines for a firsthand look at underwater operations. During Roosevelt's presidency, the navy rose to third largest in the world, and personnel more than doubled. With the Philippine insurgency controlled, the army declined in strength from 84,000 to 64,000 over the same period.[49]

William Howard Taft followed Roosevelt in the White House and continued his policies. Taft's approach, especially in Central America, has been called *colonialism by contract* or *dollar diplomacy*. Whatever the label, the United States felt free to send in troops to force governments to deal favorably with private interests. This was the practice in Honduras, Nicaragua, the Dominican Republic, and even Liberia.[50]

Public opinion during this growing imperial age came to have a stronger influence on U.S. foreign policy as well. The press had stirred public support for Cuban independence in the 1890s, and civic groups pressed for international peace agreements in the following decade, based on the notion of arbitration of disagreements instead of resorting to war. The United States negotiated 35 arbitration agreements with all major powers except Russia and Germany.[51]

Ethnic groups also became more active, as the Irish had been earlier. Russian persecution of Jews prompted American Jews to organize and press Washington for action. Eventually, they demanded abrogation of the 1832 commercial treaty with Russia, which the House of Representatives urged in a 300–1 vote. The Taft administration acquiesced and revoked the treaty. Less admirably, Congress and the White House went along with domestic pressures to restrict or exclude immigrants from Asia and to limit their civil rights in the United States.[52]

Woodrow Wilson's Militant Idealism, 1913–1921

Though labeled an idealist for supporting democratic governance and national self-determination over traditional power politics and for recommending the rule of law and moral principles over national interests, Woodrow Wilson was no pacifist. He was quite willing to use military force to impose his vision, to force foreigners to "elect good men." A racist at home, Wilson had little regard for nonwhite peoples abroad.

In contrast, Wilson's Secretary of State William Jennings Bryan, who served from 1913 to 1915, was a pacifist. He proudly negotiated *cooling off treaties* with 20 nations that supposedly required nations to submit disputes to an international commission and refrain from war until the commission reported.[53] Bryan also supported Wilson's numerous interventions in Central America, most of which were bloodless.

Wilson was a hands-on chief executive. He distrusted the State Department and criticized poor English in dispatches. Often, he would correct and return them. At other times, he composed diplomatic correspondence on his own typewriter and handled major issues without consulting others. Other presidents were at times micromanagers of some issues, but America's only chief executive with a PhD was a special case. Having declared, "I want to teach the South American republics to elect good men," Wilson set out to do so through military action. He sent troops to Cuba once, Panama twice, and Honduras five times. He added Nicaragua as a U.S. protectorate and sent troops into the Dominican Republic and Haiti. He did not seek to replace the local governments with U.S. soldiers but to ensure that those governments followed policies favorable to U.S. economic and political interests. As Mexico was coping with revolution and unrest, Wilson ordered troops to occupy Veracruz for several months. Wilson's action was ostensibly to force Mexico to apologize for an incident in which some U.S. sailors were briefly detained but, in fact, was aimed at forcing the ouster of the Mexican leader. As civil conflict continued in Mexico, Pancho Villa, the military leader in the north, who had been friendly toward U.S. interests, turned hostile and began confiscating U.S.-owned property. After Villa attacked Columbus, New Mexico, in 1916, Wilson sent 10,000 troops in an unsuccessful nine-month search for Villa. He also mobilized the National Guard, and ordered 30,000 troops to the Mexican border, but stopped short of seeking a formal authorization to invade.[54]

War in Europe in 1914 led Wilson to declare neutrality "in fact as well as in name." He also admitted, "We have to be neutral, since otherwise our mixed populations would wage war on each other." The U.S. position favored the Allies, since the British blockade of Germany left most U.S. trade going to them. By 1915, Wilson allowed U.S. banks to extend credit to the Allies and eventually loans. By the time the United States entered the war in 1917, American bankers held over $2 billion in Allied debts and only $27 million from Germany and Austria–Hungary.[55]

Germany fought the British blockade with submarine warfare, largely via U-boats, but the sinking of passenger ships carrying Americans turned American public opinion against the kaiser. After an incident in March 1916, in which several Americans died when the Germans torpedoed a British ship and the United States threatened to break diplomatic relations, Germany temporarily halted its U-boat campaign. Meanwhile, Wilson campaigned for reelection on a peace platform and sought congressional approval of preparedness measures in the event the United States joined World War I. Congress, aroused by the latest U-boat attack and Pancho Villa's raid into U.S. territory, responded vigorously, passing a law to increase the regular army from about 100,000 to 175,000 and to increase the strength of the National Guard from about 100,000 to 400,000. The law also imposed tighter standards on the Guard. Congress also voted the largest naval expansion in history, accelerating the navy's five-year plan to a three-year program and aiming for Wilson's new goal of a navy second to none.[56]

A Senate filibuster defeated a bill to arm merchant ships as the term of the 64th Congress expired in March 1917. Public outrage and senatorial feelings of guilt led the Senate a few days later to adopt its first-ever rule allowing debate to be cut off by a two-thirds vote. That action immediately preceded Wilson's call for a declaration of war against Germany, which was overwhelmingly approved. Soon thereafter, Congress enacted laws creating a draft of soldiers, imposing highly progressive income taxes and a corporate excess profits tax and giving the president power to fix prices on some goods.[57]

Wilson kept close watch and control over the diplomatic aspects of the war but left the military operations to the generals. He didn't even study the war maps posted in the cabinet room. When an armistice was declared 18 months later, Wilson decided to head the U.S. delegation to the peace talks in France, remaining abroad for six months—an unprecedented presidential absence from Washington. He did not want any interference, however, and chose not to include any senators on his delegation. Wilson, however, was not very engaged with the major urgent issues of the peace talks—how the boundaries were drawn to allow self-determination for new countries and the economic and political consequences of decisions on reparations. He focused most of his energies on creating an international organization to maintain peace. When the Treaty of Versailles, including the blueprint for the League of Nations, was signed on June 28, 1919, Wilson determined to return to America and campaign vigorously for its approval. He even broke precedent and personally answered questions from the Senate Foreign Relations Committee for three hours.[58]

Senator Henry Cabot Lodge (R-MA) used his chairmanship of the Foreign Relations Committee to build opposition to the treaty first by stacking the membership with critics and then by delaying action with lengthy hearings, mainly on the flaws of the treaty, and also by crafting amendments that altered the agreement. Wilson was stubbornly opposed to any amendments, even if they might have allowed a favorable Senate vote for ratification. In the course of the lengthy debate, Wilson suffered a debilitating stroke while campaigning across the country, leaving him even less capable of managing the treaty fight. The Senate voted down the treaty three times, once without and twice with reservations proposed by Lodge.[59]

Wilson had fully exploited America's diplomatic, economic, and military instruments to pursue his chosen foreign policy. He also demonstrated skill at what we now call public diplomacy, so entrancing people in Western Europe that there are still major boulevards named after him. Though successful abroad, he ultimately failed at home, and his immediate successors worked to reverse many of his foreign policies.

Retrenchment in the Jazz Age, 1920–1939

America after World War I was not isolationist. The United States was actively engaged in Latin America and East Asia, with trade in most places and troops in some. U.S. diplomats took the lead in international conferences limiting naval armaments and trying to outlaw war by a treaty. But, the United States remained outside the League of Nations and followed Thomas Jefferson's warning against "entangling alliances." Historian George Henning's apt phrase for the period is "involvement without commitment."[60]

The Republican Congress in 1920 tried to end the war by passing a law rather than approving the Versailles Treaty, but Wilson vetoed the measure. The next year, President Warren Harding signed the law. Congress also pushed for reductions in the armed forces and their deployment abroad. A contingent of 1,000 U.S. troops was part of the occupation force in Germany, but in 1923, when Congress was on the verge of passing binding withdrawal legislation, Harding agreed to bring them home. Congress also cut the regular army to 140,000 from the wartime peak of 2.4 million and adopted a measure calling for the United States, Britain, and Japan to reduce their navies by 50%.[61]

Secretary of State Charles Evans Hughes consulted with U.S. admirals, Senator Lodge, and others in developing an American proposal for naval disarmament that was codified in nine treaties in the 1921–1922 Washington Armament Conference. The agreements limited nations' capital fleets, restricted submarine warfare, and guaranteed China's independence and territorial integrity. President Calvin Coolidge proposed additional restrictions on naval cruisers in 1927, but that conference failed to reach agreement. The United States then proposed a wildly popular treaty to outlaw war as an instrument of national policy that came to be known by the names of the American and French foreign ministers, the Kellogg–Briand Pact. Eventually, 62 nations signed on, including Germany, Italy, and Japan. Though it failed to prevent the wars of the 1930s, one tangible effect of the treaty was the Stimson Doctrine, announced under President Herbert Hoover, declaring that the United States would not recognize territorial changes brought about by use of force in violation of Kellogg–Briand.[62]

Disarmament fever continued into the 1930s, with additional naval limits approved at a 1930 London conference and an unsuccessful 1932 proposal by President Hoover to abolish all offensive armaments. Franklin Roosevelt repeated the idea soon after he took office. These proposals reflected the strong domestic antiwar pressure from Republicans and Democrats alike. In a dramatic example, two years of hearings (1934–1936) by a special Senate committee investigating the armaments industry tried to demonstrate that the United States was drawn into World War I by "merchants of death." An immediate outcome was the passage of the first of several neutrality acts banning arms shipments and loans to nations at war.[63]

The Republican administrations of the 1920s also backed away from the gunboat diplomacy of their predecessors. They withdrew U.S. troops from the Dominican Republic and Nicaragua, leaving in place U.S.-trained constabulary forces. They used private financial advisers to work out arrangements with Latin American governments that satisfied U.S. bankers. In Europe and Asia as well, the United States used the private sector to pursue many of its foreign policy goals, especially trade promotion. Hoover himself came close to apologizing for earlier U.S. interventions in Latin America and explicitly disavowed military interventions to protect U.S. investments. He also first used the phrase *good neighbor,* which Franklin Roosevelt later applied to his own hemispheric policy.[64]

Although the United States reduced its military forces in the interwar period, it greatly strengthened its diplomatic instrument by merging the diplomatic and consular corps into a single career foreign service, with entrance exams and merit promotions, in 1924. The State Department tried to coordinate foreign economic policy through various interdepartmental committees but failed to make much headway. It lacked the resources, and other departments, notably Hoover's Commerce Department, wanted to run their own foreign policies.[65]

Franklin D. Roosevelt in Peace and War, 1933–1945

With a mostly willing Congress and only a handful of aides, President Franklin D. Roosevelt (FDR) amassed enormous executive power that allowed him to fight the Great Depression, put America on the road to rearmament, and then fight a global, two-front war. In one of the first emergency relief bills, FDR got Congress to add 7% for navy shipbuilding, enough for two aircraft carriers, four cruisers, 20 destroyers, and four submarines that later proved vital after the Japanese attack on Pearl Harbor. A proposal to create jobs making munitions for the army, however, was defeated by pacifist sentiment.[66]

Along with the alphabet soup of domestic agencies, FDR created the Export-Import Bank (Ex-Im) to promote U.S. exports. He persuaded Congress to surrender much of its trade policy power by allowing presidential negotiation of reciprocal trade agreements that no longer required a subsequent congressional vote and then turned that job over to the long-serving Secretary of State Cordell Hull. That practice has continued in recent decades when Congress has granted the president Trade Promotion Authority (TPA), subjecting trade deals to a single up-or-down vote in each house. FDR, however, kept tight control over security issues and other foreign policy matters.

Although FDR often consulted his cabinet and close advisors, he made up his mind independent of advice. He did, however, take several steps that greatly aided interagency coordination of national security policy and that set the precedents for postwar creation of the National Security Council (NSC) system. A few days after war broke out in Europe, FDR declared a "limited national emergency" and brought into the new Executive Office of the President (EOP) the Joint Board of the Army and Navy and its Joint Planning Committee.

The Joint Board, created in 1903 by Theodore Roosevelt, served as the first effort to bring the two services together for policy coordination and future planning. It had no staff and met infrequently. After World War I, the Joint Board was strengthened, and the State Department was invited to sit in on meetings. The secretary of state, however, brushed off the suggestion, objecting to military involvement in foreign policy. It was not until 1936 that Franklin Roosevelt's Secretary of State Cordell Hull suggested a regular coordinating body be established. The Standing Liaison Committee was comprised of the undersecretary of state and the two service chiefs. It met off and on until 1943 but focused mainly on hemisphere defense and the good neighbor policy.[67]

FDR himself preferred to deal directly with the senior military officers. He created a war council of the military chiefs and the departmental secretaries in the autumn of 1941 but stopped inviting the secretary of state after Pearl Harbor. Like many other leaders of that era, he felt that diplomats were not needed when military strategy was being planned. FDR turned the Joint Board into the Joint Chiefs of Staff (JCS) in 1942 in order to parallel the British system in wartime conferences. He later brought State back in for postwar planning under the State War Navy Coordinating Committee. While many senior officials were unhappy with FDR's administrative style—Henry Stimson called him "the poorest administrator I have ever worked under"—the interagency panels were deemed valuable and worth maintaining after the war. In fact, many viewed creation of the NSC in 1947 as a way of preventing future presidents from avoiding a broad range of civilian and military advice, as FDR had done.[68]

While constrained by law, especially the Neutrality Acts, and public opinion, FDR worked deftly to bring the country along with him in preparing for war. He used worsening events in Europe to justify revisions in the neutrality laws and to win congressional support for increased defense expenditures. He ordered secret naval talks with Britain starting in 1937. FDR also let the Army Chief of Staff General George C. Marshall take the lead in fighting for the first peacetime draft, and he browbeat his chief of naval operations into agreeing to the destroyers-for-bases deal with Britain. FDR fought for and won congressional approval of military aid to Britain, called Lend-Lease, by comparing the provision of military hardware in wartime to letting a neighbor borrow a hose to fight a fire.[69]

In 1941, FDR maneuvered America into an undeclared naval war with Germany in keeping with a private comment he had made in 1937: "After all, if Italy and Japan have developed a technique of fighting without declaring war, why can't we develop a similar one?" To get around a restriction in the draft law forbidding sending conscripts outside the Western hemisphere, FDR declared Iceland inside the hemisphere and sent troops there in July. By September, he issued shoot-on-sight orders to the navy. War came first with Japan, but FDR insisted the United States take a Europe-first strategy.[70]

The United States fought World War II with all of the instruments of national power. Congress, while willing to criticize the administration on domestic issues and defense program management, wrote blank checks for the war effort. Diplomats cajoled and reassured allies and neutrals. The armed forces expanded to 12 million men and women and fought on five continents. The Office of Strategic Services, a forerunner of the Central Intelligence Agency (CIA), gathered and analyzed intelligence and conducted covert operations. Scientists and engineers pushed the limits of technology and developed radar, jet airplanes, and atomic weapons. Propaganda operations were active inside the United States, which had censorship rules, and overseas. The United States used military aid and advisors in Latin America to combat Axis influence. FDR himself managed the key relations with British Prime Minister Winston Churchill and Russian leader Joseph Stalin as well as directly overseeing military operations.[71] Theodore Roosevelt and Woodrow Wilson had exploited the traditional diplomatic, military, and economic tools for foreign policy. FDR went further, with a robust intelligence instrument and with massive programs using science and technology for military purposes.

The Cold War and After, 1946–

As this book's later chapters will show in greater detail, the basic arrangement and design of the instruments in America's foreign policy toolkit were set during the years just after 1945. The end of the war found Harry S. Truman in the White House, Europe and Japan in ruins, and the Soviet Union ready to defend its new empire. While Truman and Congress wanted rapid demobilization, they soon agreed to maintain a much larger standing armed force than before the war. They put the military under somewhat tighter central control under a secretary of defense, created the CIA, expanded the State Department, and began a larger-scale foreign aid program aimed first at combating communism in Greece and Turkey and later at rebuilding war-torn Europe. Truman's diverse approach to fighting the Cold War with all the instruments of national power reached its height in 1950, when the State Department budget equaled half that of the Pentagon.

Meanwhile, the United Nations (UN), established after World War II, was growing in size and adding specialized agencies, despite its weakness in dealing with U.S.-Soviet problems. The Bretton Woods system of the World Bank, the International Monetary Fund (IMF), and the General Agreement on Tariffs and Trade rejuvenated the global economic system in ways helpful to the American economy.

The American public was also accepting of the United States' global interests and anticommunist mission, as it showed by supporting, at least initially, the war in Korea (1950–1953), the foreign aid program, and the permanent stationing of troops in Europe and Asia.

Nuclear weapons were a dramatic addition to America's military capabilities, but once the American nuclear monopoly ended in 1949, the weapons became the basis for deterrence rather than warfighting. The U.S.-Soviet arms race during the Cold War was driven less by worries of imminent attack than by concerns about future capabilities. Each side made worst-case calculations about its adversary, even as leaders came to understand that a nuclear exchange would be an unimaginable catastrophe for all involved. Eventually, Washington and Moscow found a stable balance of terror, and they turned their attention to other nations that still expected to reap political benefits from nuclear weapons capabilities.

Dwight Eisenhower made significant changes in many of the instruments and processes of foreign policy. He institutionalized the NSC system with a large staff, regular meetings, and careful processes of policy formulation and oversight. Eisenhower reshaped the military by deemphasizing conventional warfare capabilities and increasing reliance on nuclear deterrence. He revived summit diplomacy to engage with the post-Stalin Soviet Union. Eisenhower's administration negotiated a series of mutual defense treaties with nations in Southeast Asia and the Middle East. He gave public diplomacy a strong institutional basis in the new U.S. Information Agency. Eisenhower also broadened foreign aid programs, defending them vigorously against political opposition, and he used the CIA to counter communist influences abroad and to overthrow unfriendly governments in Iran and Guatemala.

John F. Kennedy dismantled the NSC system but enhanced White House control of foreign policy by establishing the Situation Room, with its immediate access to classified reports that previously had to come through the regular government departments. From 1961 to 1963, he gave Secretary of Defense Robert McNamara free rein to reshape the military establishment and bring it under tight civilian control. Kennedy negotiated the first major arms control agreement with the Soviet Union—the nuclear test ban treaty—and launched the first round of global trade negotiations. He also used military advisors to help the struggling South Vietnamese government fight its communist opponents but stopped short of sending U.S. combat troops.

Kennedy's successor, Lyndon B. Johnson (LBJ), sent troops to Vietnam, more than half a million of them, and fought an increasingly unpopular war. Johnson tried several diplomatic efforts to negotiate limits, but they all failed, probably because the sides were too far apart. Congress, realizing and not liking that the presidency had become so imperial, began passing legislation to limit presidential power in foreign policy and force disclosure of secret executive agreements.

From 1969 to 1974, President Richard Nixon colluded with Henry Kissinger, his national security adviser, to centralize foreign policy in the White House, even to the point of excluding the secretaries of state and defense on key matters. Nixon achieved major diplomatic successes—a negotiated end to U.S. military combat in Vietnam, an opening to China, and major arms control agreements with the Soviet Union. Nixon and Kissinger faced several conflicts involving Israel and its neighbors and managed to contain them. The Democratic-controlled Congress challenged Nixon even more than it had challenged Johnson, limiting military operations in Southeast Asia and enacting, over his veto, the War Powers Resolution. Nixon used his economic instruments boldly, shocking the Japanese and the world community in 1971 by suddenly abandoning the gold standard and imposing a 10% surcharge on imports in order to gain new trade concessions.

Gerald Ford's two-year presidency had to cope with several problems not of its own making. Disclosures of CIA dirty tricks and questionable operations over the years led to embarrassing revelations and tighter limits on the intelligence community (IC). The end of the Vietnam War prompted political calls for a *peace dividend* through cuts in military spending. A bipartisan backlash against the policy of détente with the Soviet Union thwarted further diplomatic accomplishments.

With his 1976 election, Jimmy Carter injected moralism into U.S. foreign policy and achieved several major diplomatic milestones. Carter established formal diplomatic relations with China, concluded another far-reaching arms control pact with the Soviet Union, pressured Israel and Egypt to reach a peace agreement, and signed a treaty returning control of the Panama Canal to Panama, which won, just barely, Senate approval by a two-thirds vote. Despite these successes, Carter and his administration were distracted and ultimately defeated for reelection by domestic economic problems—double-digit inflation and unemployment—and the failure to rescue Americans held hostage in Tehran, Iran, by the new Islamic theocracy there.

Ronald Reagan's foreign policy efforts were not as encumbered as his predecessor's. Reagan downgraded his NSC adviser and staff, sending them to the White House basement, where they proceeded to launch the illegal Iran-Contra affair. He fired his first secretary of state and tolerated his second, without resolving the nasty disagreements between the chief diplomat and the secretary of defense. After first denouncing the Soviet Union as an "evil empire," Reagan decided to negotiate major arms limitation agreements with Moscow. He used military assistance, approved but with limits and conditions by Congress, to fight leftist groups in Central America and sent troops to combat a leftist government in Grenada. Reagan won congressional approval to send U.S. troops to Lebanon to participate in a UN peacekeeping mission, despite the opposition of his military advisers, but then withdrew them after 240 marines were killed in an attack. He also used covert operations to support democracy-seeking Poles and anti-Soviet *mujahedin* in Afghanistan.

George H. W. Bush (*the elder* or *Bush 41*) established the NSC system that continues to this day, a layered, regular process that includes all major stakeholders. His senior advisers were an unusually collegial group that kept its disagreements secret and achieved notable diplomatic and military successes, especially the nonviolent dismantling of the Soviet empire and the Gulf War coalition that fought Operation Desert Storm in 1991.

From 1993 to 2001, Bill Clinton made few changes to his foreign policy toolkit, though he elevated economic issues both within the White House, through the creation of the National Economic Council (NEC, modeled on the NSC), and overseas, with regular economic summits among developed nations. Clinton also backed diplomacy with the threat of force and, in fact, authorized force to resolve conflicts in Somalia, Haiti, Bosnia, and Kosovo. He targeted the IC on terrorist threats but was unable to neutralize the threat of al-Qaeda before his term ended.

George W. Bush (*the younger* or *Bush 43*) maintained the NSC system but empowered his vice president, Dick Cheney, who used his own large, separate security staff and back-channel means to shape policy. Bush 43 tolerated the ongoing disputes between Secretary of Defense Donald Rumsfeld and his two secretaries of state, Colin Powell and Condoleezza Rice, and let Rumsfeld create additional Department of Defense (DOD)-run instruments for foreign aid, such as the Commanders' Emergency Response Fund. Following the 9/11 attacks, Congress eagerly supported the war on terror with new domestic legislation and authorization for military operations abroad.

After taking office in 2009, Barack Obama kept the existing NSC system and staff but merged the Homeland Security Council into it. He gave his vice president, Joe Biden, important foreign policy missions, notably the withdrawal of U.S. armed forces from Iraq, and named special envoys for Afghanistan and Pakistan and for Middle East peace talks. Obama expanded the size and scope of intelligence operations, especially the use of unmanned aerial drone strikes. He was deeply and personally involved in the review of Afghan policy in 2009 and in planning the raid that killed al-Qaeda leader Osama bin Laden in 2011.

* * *

The framers would probably have viewed this history as a reasonable application of the system they created, with excesses of power eventually checked and with constraints imposed by popular sovereignty. The tools of foreign policy helped the nation grow in size and strength and remain secure against existential threats. Sometimes, the executive branch was dominant, sometimes the legislative. Sometimes, foreign policy promoted the national interest; sometimes, it protected special interests. The test of a democracy, after all, is not whether its decisions are wise and just but only whether its processes are fair. The framers' design assured that.

Selected Resources

A comprehensive, one-volume history is George C. Herring's *From Colony to Superpower: U.S. Foreign Relations Since 1776* (New York: Oxford University Press, 2008).

The growth of the presidency and the federal departments for war and diplomacy are well explained in Leonard D. White's several studies: *The Federalists: A Study in Administrative History, 1789–1801* (New York: Free Press, 1948); *The Jeffersonians: A Study in Administrative History, 1801–1829* (New York: Free Press, 1951); *The Jacksonians: A Study in Administrative History, 1829–1861* (New York: Free Press, 1954); and *The Republican Era: A Study in Administrative History, 1869–1901* (New York: Free Press, 1958).

A history of presidents in wartime can be found in Ernest R. May (ed.), *The Ultimate Decision: The President as Commander in Chief* (New York: George Braziller, 1960) and is detailed further in individual presidential biographies.

The congressional role in major military operations is summarized in Charles A. Stevenson, *Congress at War: The Politics of Conflict Since 1789* (Washington, DC: Potomac Books, 2007).

The creation and development of three key national security institutions is analyzed by Amy B. Zegart, *Flawed by Design: The Evolution of the CIA, JCS, and NSC* (Palo Alto, CA: Stanford University Press, 1999). Additional materials on other policy instruments are listed in later chapters.

3 The President's Toolkit

The real organization of government at higher echelons [is] how confidence flows down from the President.

—Secretary of State Dean Rusk[1]

"Not this one, Mr. President, your helicopter is over there," said the Army sergeant.

Replied Lyndon Johnson, *"Son, they're all my helicopters."*

The Framers took only 223 words to describe the powers of the president:

> The President shall be Commander in Chief of the Army and Navy of the United States, and of the Militia of the several States, when called into the actual Service of the United States; he may require the Opinion, in writing, of the principal Officer in each of the executive Departments, upon any Subject relating to the Duties of their respective Offices, and he shall have Power to grant Reprieves and Pardons for Offences against the United States, except in Cases of Impeachment.
>
> He shall have Power, by and with the Advice and Consent of the Senate, to make Treaties, provided two thirds of the Senators present concur; and he shall nominate, and by and with the Advice and Consent of the Senate, shall appoint Ambassadors, other public Ministers and Consuls, Judges of the supreme Court, and all other Officers of the United States, whose Appointments are not herein otherwise provided for, and which shall be established by Law: but the Congress may by Law vest the Appointment of such inferior Officers, as they think proper, in the President alone, in the Courts of Law, or in the Heads of Departments.
>
> The President shall have Power to fill up all Vacancies that may happen during the Recess of the Senate, by granting Commissions which shall expire at the End of their next Session. (Art. I, Sect. 2)

They added a requirement for the president "from time to time" to give Congress "Information on the State of the Union" and permission to recommend measures for consideration. They also made him the point of contact for foreign governments by saying "he shall receive Ambassadors and other public Ministers." They saw little need to elaborate on the "Executive Power" that they "vested" in the president in part because they saw him as the agent of the legislative branch, implementing their laws, and in part because they trusted the likely first president, George Washington.

Presidents have built on these formal powers a strong and flexible set of tools to shape and carry out foreign policy. Several tools are centered in the White House: the President, the staff, the National Security Council (NSC) system. These tools can be used at the president's discretion and in numerous ways, from informal conversations to formal executive orders. (See Table 3.1.) The president can also order use of the key institutions for foreign policy making that are discussed in later chapters. The president may choose to use any or all of government's capabilities—the diplomatic instrument managed by the State Department, the economic instruments available to several other government agencies, the military instrument operated by the Defense Department (DOD), the secret intelligence instruments, the homeland security instrument, or even international organizations. But first, it is important to understand the way the president as a person and the presidency as an institution use their powers.

Presidential Power

Many laws passed by Congress over the past two centuries have added specific requirements and authorities for the president. Even when lawmakers expect a cabinet officer to use the authority, they often assign it to the president to establish the highest level of accountability. For example, the basic foreign aid law stipulates the following: "The President shall withhold assistance under this Act to the government of any country that provides assistance to the government of any other country" on the list of terrorist supporters. Another section of that law demands that "the President shall assist American small business to participate equitably in the furnishing of commodities, defense articles, and services (including defense services) financed with funds made available under this Act."[2]

Longstanding law requires a cutoff of aid when U.S. property abroad is nationalized or seized by the local government and adequate compensation is not promptly provided. Laws also may assign authority to the president. For instance, a 1998 law imposing sanctions on individuals found trying to circumvent the Chemical Weapons Convention says, "The President shall take all steps necessary to block any transactions in any property subject to the jurisdiction of the United States" of such individuals.[3] Congress wanted the ball in the president's court even if he chose to pass it to a cabinet department.

Laws without enforcement mechanisms may not be effectively implemented. The War Powers Resolution, PL 93–148, tried to force an end to military operations not specifically authorized by Congress. Section 5(b)

Table 3.1 The Presidential Toolkit Brief

TOOL	ADVANTAGES	DISADVANTAGES
People	**Greater credibility because of closeness to the president**	**Enormous time constraints on senior leaders**
President	No higher authority	Limited time and focus
Vice president	High authority if seen as close to the president	Spread thinly over domestic and foreign policy
National security adviser	Authoritative conduit	More time but still limited
NSC staff	Loyal, attuned to White House moods	May have own agendas
Special envoys	Manage major issues across agencies	Actual power limited if not Senate-confirmed
Processes	**Allows issue resolution at the lowest possible level**	**Time-consuming, not usable in crises**
Principals Committee (PC)	Avoids overreaction to presidential signals	Requires president to resolve conflicts
Deputies Committee (DC)	Workhorse of NSC process	Overburdened from above and below
Interagency Policy Committees (IPC)	Venue for interagency coordination	Leader may lack clout with bureaucratic equals
Presidential actions	**Greater authority from White House actions**	**Legal and political limitations often apply**
Personal contact	Conveys presidential views directly; gets responses	Personal chemistry may hurt as well as help
Public statement	Clarity and transparency	Hard to satisfy multiple audiences
Executive order	Force of law; hard to change	Needs careful drafting; hard to change
International agreement	Many models: private understanding, agreed statements, executive agreements, treaties; the more formal, the more binding	The more formal, the more time-consuming for senior leaders
Allocation of funds	Gives specific resources for policy actions	Many funding actions require notification or approval by Congress
Order to departmental instruments	Delegates action to presumed experts with authority to act	Reduces White House supervision and control; agencies may pursue separate agendas

There are numerous resources available to the president in making foreign policy, including people, processes, and actions. The president relies on people he trusts to serve as his advisers and bring high-level issues to him with their recommendations. Through the process of delegation, the president allows committees to resolve low-level issues. The actions the president takes, from signing international agreements to making public statements, have the weight of authority, though they may still be constrained by political and legal limitations.

required: "Within sixty calendar days after a report is submitted or is required to be submitted pursuant to section 4(a)(1), whichever is earlier, the President shall terminate any use of United States Armed Forces with respect to which such report was submitted (or required to be submitted), unless the Congress" has acted. This mandate left action up to Congress. It had no teeth other than the willingness of Congress to punish noncompliance with a cutoff of funds—something Congress historically has been unwilling to do during ground combat.

The chief executive also has discretion over carrying out the laws because of their inherent vagueness or generality. For example, one of the laws passed by the First Congress in 1789 authorized the president to summon militia from the several states "for the purpose of protecting the inhabitants of the frontiers of the United States from the hostile incursions of the Indians." The lawmakers left the decisions on how to do this up to President Washington. In 1798, Congress empowered the president "to instruct and direct the commanders of the armed vessels belonging to the United States to seize, take, and bring into any port . . . any such armed vessel which . . . shall be found hovering on the coasts" that threaten U.S. merchant ships.[4]

Even today, the law often gives broad discretion to the president. A 1996 law, noting the threat from terrorists using weapons of mass destruction, contained this order to the chief executive: "In light of the potential for terrorist use of weapons of mass destruction against the United States, the President shall take immediate action . . . to enhance the capability of the Federal Government to prevent and respond to terrorist incidents involving weapons of mass destruction."[5]

In practice, presidential power and influence are derived from more than those legal authorities. As Richard Neustadt argued, presidents ultimately have only the power to persuade others to do what he asks because they conclude it is in their own interests. In addition to their formal authorities, presidents have certain levels of public prestige, measured in approval ratings by opinion polls, that strengthen or weaken their persuasiveness. They also develop professional reputations within the Beltway among the political and media elites that attract or repel allies and potential adversaries.[6]

Legal Constraints

The chief executive is, of course, bound to follow the law and stay within the limits set by the Constitution, but he can also hire lawyers. Lyndon Johnson (LBJ) reportedly once asked a new staff member whether he was "a yes lawyer or a no lawyer." The president obviously wanted permissive legal advice rather than obstruction. Franklin Roosevelt (FDR) worried about how to help British Prime Minister Winston Churchill by transferring 50 older U.S. destroyers until his attorney general provided a legal opinion blessing the deal—notwithstanding some obvious obstacles in existing law. Dwight Eisenhower twice sought prior congressional approval of military commitments to Formosa (now called Taiwan) and Lebanon in part because of legal doubts but also to secure congressional support for the policy.

In recent decades, conservative legal scholars have elaborated a theory of the *unitary executive*. They argue that the Constitution permits full presidential control of the executive branch, including over appointees and so-called independent agencies and regulatory commissions. They supplement this notion of executive power with a very broad reading of presidential power over national security. This view, most strongly expressed in Justice Department opinions after the 9/11 attacks, admits virtually no limits on presidential actions in wartime or in defense of the United States.[7]

Congress passed the War Powers Resolution of 1973 over Richard Nixon's veto, but no subsequent president has acknowledged its constitutionality or binding validity. Instead, presidents have sidestepped the law's conditions by reporting military deployments consistent with the law but never pursuant to its requirements. Despite much bluster, lawmakers failed to make presidents comply fully with the act. In practice, there have been notifications and consultations as envisioned by the law, and until the 9/11 attacks, most military operations were designed to be completed within the law's 90-day time limit.

Leaving aside the legal questions surrounding war powers, it is clear that presidents feel some constraints on their ability to employ the military instrument and on their freedom of action on other foreign policy matters. No White House counsel would likely recommend actions to diminish executive power, such as accepting the validity of the War Powers Resolution. Even if a new president previously criticized an earlier president's behavior, most would be reluctant to toss away a tool that might be useful to him as well. For example, Senator Obama criticized the George W. Bush administration's use of *signing statements,* indicating a refusal to abide by a provision of law deemed unconstitutional, but as president, Obama has found it useful to issue a few such statements himself.

Political Constraints

Most presidents treat legal constraints as political ones, raising the costs of taking controversial actions but not preventing choices that can be popularly defended. Political constraints can limit a president's actions. They can be imposed by the president's political party or come from opposition parties. They can be molded by public opinion as well as international influences. The Reagan executive order prohibiting assassinations of foreign officials remains on the books, for example, but the post-9/11 determination to attack terrorists has made targeted drone strikes politically legitimate.

The more significant political constraints are those imposed by public opinion and by the strength and motivations of the president's adversaries and supporters. As Kennedy aide Theodore Sorensen once stated, or perhaps understated, "Politics pervades the White House without seeming to prevail." He called it an "ever-present influence—counterbalancing the unrealistic, checking the unreasonable, sometimes preventing the desirable, but always testing what is acceptable."[8] Presidents and their White House staffs always follow public opinion polls closely in part as a barometer of the success of their messaging and in part to learn of warning flags regarding particular policy choices. They know that to go against solid public opinion on a matter has high risks, while framing a policy in terms of public preferences has benefits.

The domestic political context usually imposes significant constraints on presidential foreign policy actions unless they can be carried out in secret. The president's political supporters need to be consulted and persuaded to fall in line. Meanwhile, his political adversaries stand ready to pounce on unpopular or unsuccessful moves. Even if they support the announced policy, they feel free to criticize the way it is implemented. When the opposition party controls one or both houses of Congress, the incentives to criticize and investigate and even obstruct presidential policies are usually too attractive. Presidents can ignore such opposition, at least for a while, but they need to work to reassure the public and to achieve some examples of progress.

Other Constraints on Presidential Choice

Newly elected presidents do not enter office with a blank slate for foreign policy. They have to deal with the world as it is, not as they might prefer. They face geopolitical contexts that often have long histories and numerous precedents in U.S. policy. Accordingly, their ability to change existing policies is limited. For example, in 1992, three weeks before leaving office, President George H. W. Bush gave Serbian president Slobodan Milosevic the "Christmas warning" that Serb military action against the ethnic Albanian majority in Kosovo would lead to an American military response against Serbia. In stating its position, the incoming Clinton administration reiterated the warning. The response was reflexive, not based on a calculated policy review, but it locked Clinton into a policy that made the 1999 bombing of Serbia practically inevitable.

Campaign themes also limit presidential flexibility, even if they were chosen for competitive advantages or in search of favorable publicity rather than as part of a planned international strategy. For example, George W. Bush's criticism of nation building by the Clinton administration made it harder for his administration to embrace nation-building programs when they were required to stabilize Afghanistan and Iraq. Similarly, Bill Clinton's campaign attacks on President Bush the elder for coddling the "Butchers of Beijing" made it difficult for him to decouple human rights concerns from broader economic and strategic interests when dealing with China, a change that took more than 18 months and was met with predictable sharp criticism. Ronald Reagan also spent several years as president criticizing the Soviet Union as an "evil empire" before changing his approach in response to changed leadership in the Kremlin and their promising initiatives.

Personnel choices also have a powerful influence in predetermining future policies. Woodrow Wilson chose a three-time Democratic presidential nominee and party luminary as his secretary of state only to discover that William Jennings Bryan had his own Christian pacifist views of what

American foreign policy should be. Dwight Eisenhower admired John Foster Dulles's diplomatic skills, but he also had to work around the Presbyterian moralism that made Dulles inflexible in dealing with some Cold War issues. Ronald Reagan fired his first Secretary of State, Alexander Haig—one of the few such officials to be ousted in modern times—because of the secretary's differing views and abrasive style on foreign policy issues.

Presidents select their national security teams only partly with regard to compatibility of views. They also may want symbolism from the nominee's prior roles, political base, or race or gender. President Truman chose Louis Johnson as his second secretary of defense because of personal friendship, recognition of Johnson's well-regarded earlier service in the War Department, and his political standing as former head of the American Legion. But, Johnson's budget-cutting zeal became a political liability when Truman had to change course in his military policy and rearm troops to fight in the Korean War. Lyndon Johnson expected that longtime friend and adviser Clark Clifford would be a loyal defender of the Vietnam War when he was named to replace Robert McNamara as secretary of defense, but Clifford soon became a critic and the architect of a radical change in policy.

Senior officials often have their own agendas—personal or political—that may conflict with the president's or drive policy along unintended paths. Madeleine Albright's Czech background made her especially concerned about Eastern Europe. Caspar Weinberger's romanticizing of Winston Churchill made him uncompromising on defense issues either with congressional leaders or his Reagan administration colleagues. Faced with a cabinet officer's separate agenda, the president usually acquiesces unless or until the policy becomes a political problem because the consequences of firing the person would likely be more harmful as that would call into question the president's judgment in nominating the official in the first place.

Historical Consensus and Dissensus

There are other important givens that limit presidential flexibility on national security policy, especially patterns of historical consensus and dissensus that have existed for several decades. For example, U.S. political leaders almost without exception strongly support Israel diplomatically and financially. Many feel it would be political suicide to be seen as critical of Israeli policies. There have, of course, been occasions when U.S. officials have openly opposed some Israeli positions, such as on control of West Bank territories captured in 1967 and the expansion of settlements there, but on many occasions, pro-Israeli members of Congress rejected executive branch policies seen as adversely affecting Israel.

Another area of broad consensus has been on policy toward Europe. Support for the North Atlantic Treaty Organization (NATO) as an institution and for NATO expansion by adding nations formerly under the domination of the Soviet Union have been bipartisan policies since the 1950s. This favorable attitude still allows criticism of particular European policies and insistence that Europeans do more burden sharing with the United States, but it is unlikely that any president could easily withdraw from NATO or America's European commitments.

There are also areas of shared antipathy, such as bipartisan demonization of certain regimes, that limit presidential flexibility to engage with them. This has been the case with Castro's Cuba since 1961 and with the Islamic regime in Iran since 1979. The same hostility dominated U.S. policies toward Libya until that nation openly showed a willingness to make amends for its pariah behavior. The few friendly gestures tried by recent presidents toward Cuba or Iran have been quite limited and still politically painful.

On the other hand, certain policy areas have long been shackled with dissensus and caught up in perennial debates. One of the most significant was policy toward the Soviet Union and now toward Russia. Some U.S. political leaders favored steadfast hostility, while others sought engagement on matters that seemed reasonable and resolvable. This dissensus also affected arms control issues, with anti-Soviet advocates doubting the wisdom of any agreement with Moscow and pro-arms control advocates fighting an uphill battle to obtain limits on Soviet capabilities, which arguably were more significant than those on U.S. forces. The same black–white divide has existed since the 1970s on programs for national missile defense, with one group embracing successive technological approaches and the other doubting the need, the effectiveness, or the cost estimates.

China policy has also often been politically contested since the 1940s. Richard Nixon changed his own views and, as president, changed China policy—and was praised for it. His successors, however, have been sharply criticized when they seemed to move closer to Beijing. In the 21st century, a new faction has emerged in U.S. policy making, linking those who want to contain China as basic strategy with U.S. critics of China's economic policies and human rights practices.

While there is strategic consensus on opposing China's neighbor North Korea and especially its nuclear weapons programs, there is sharp tactical disagreement on what can and should be done to thwart the hermit kingdom. Presidents who campaign and govern as opponents of dealing with major adversaries find it hard to make exceptions when that seems opportune, and those who campaign and govern in support of engagement find it hard to shift gears when the engagee acts nasty.

The prospects of political disagreement, either by going against established consensus or by trumpeting a firm position where there is dissensus, tend to limit presidential choice, usually to baby steps, symbolic measures, or reversible policies.

Presidential Management Styles

How presidents organize the White House and the national security system of the government depends a lot on their individual personalities and management styles. If the president chooses a compatible design for the system to make use of foreign policy tools, the system should function well. If not, flawed processes are likely to lead to flawed policies. Most advisers want to fit the system to the president rather than trying, and probably failing, to fit the president to an existing system. A talented executive can overcome a poorly organized system at least on some important issues, and a good system can reduce the number of errors by an inexperienced or unskilled manager. There are always trade-offs.

One analytic approach identified three organizations models used by recent presidents: competitive, formalistic, and collegial. Alexander George acknowledged trade-off dilemmas with each system but recommended a process of "multiple advocacy" to obtain the best decisions.[9] Thomas Preston developed a typology based on two personality characteristics—presidential need for control and involvement in the policy process and prior policy experience or expertise. In terms of the need to control the policy, he built a matrix of four types: director, magistrate, administrator, and delegator. In terms of prior experience and need for information, his matrix included navigator, observer, sentinel, and maverick.[10] While these scholarly insights are illuminating, most presidents blur the lines in practice, depending on the particular issue and its political context as well as their basic personalities and managerial tendencies. Moreover, these typologies are better used for retrospective analyses than for implementation by an incoming administration, where so many personal, political, and organizational factors need to be weighed and balanced and there is so much uncertainty about each of them.

Some presidents want some advisers to advise, others to debate, and still others to simply validate their own predilections. Some encourage disagreement; others want to avoid it. Bill Clinton enjoyed debate in front of him; Richard Nixon hated it. Some presidents want to feel that they alone are making decisions; others want to ensure group support. George W. Bush proudly called himself "the Decider." McGeorge Bundy, national security advisers to Presidents Kennedy and Johnson, said that LBJ treated his senior officials as if they were senators whose votes he needed.[11] Each approach has its pluses and minuses. Demanding consensus can result in the president's receiving a single option, perhaps including ambiguous compromises. Demanding options can force the president to choose among advisers, perhaps undermining their morale, as Henry Kissinger suggests. (See Box 3.1.)

Sources of Information

Presidents need information and a system for obtaining it, especially once they enter the security bubble that surrounds them in order to protect the chief executive. Normal human contact is highly restricted. White House lawyers don't want presidents to have private e-mail accounts or diaries because of legal requirements that all official actions be documented and subject to possible subpoena.

> **Box 3.1**
>
> ## Inside View: Henry Kissinger on How Presidents Decide
>
> Presidents get a lot of advice on what to do, often conflicting. Their advisers are bright people who can be very persuasive and thus are influential in the decision-making process. In choosing among alternatives for policy or action, presidents have to recognize that they are leading teams where morale is also an important factor.
>
> Henry Kissinger aptly described how presidents make up their minds when they are confronted by so many supplicants with reasonable-sounding ideas.
>
> *Before I served [in government], I had believed, like most academicians, that the process of decision-making was largely intellectual and that all one had to do was to walk into the President's office and convince him of the correctness of one's views. This perspective I soon realized is as dangerously immature as it is widely held. . . .*
>
> *A President's schedule is so hectic that he has little time for abstract reflection. Almost all of his callers are supplicants or advocates, and most of their cases are extremely plausible—which is what got them into the Oval Office in the first place. As a result, one of the President's most difficult tasks is to choose among endless arguments that sound equally convincing. The easy decisions do not come to him; they are taken care of at lower levels.*
>
> *As his term in office progresses, therefore, except in extreme crisis a President comes to base his choices more and more on the confidence he has in his advisers.*
>
> *A Presidential decision is always an amalgam of judgment, confidence in his associates, and also concern about their morale.*
>
> Source: Henry A. Kissinger, *White House Years* (New York: Little, Brown, 1979), 39–40.

To gauge public opinion, presidents used to rely on newspaper editorials and letters to the White House. Now, they can draw on instant public polls as well as privately commissioned ones. Nevertheless, each White House monitors carefully the volume and tone of incoming letters and messages and provides frequent reports to the president and senior officials.

In order to get "unvarnished" advice, especially on things that a president doesn't really want to hear but needs to be told, they rely on old friends outside the White House as well as longtime colleagues who get appointed to the staff. Each president builds a core staff of people he can trust with the most sensitive matters, often those who were in the campaign trenches, suffering the political highs and lows and learning how to deal with the boss. This reciprocal trust and loyalty explain why presidents tend to ignore their cabinet officials and work with and through their inner circles. Too much use of people not in the chain of command, however, can undermine the processes of government and limit the necessary sharing of information. When Henry Kissinger and Richard Nixon conspired to exclude the secretary of state from key decisions, the whole State Department was less effective as a consequence.

Presidents also need official information, reports on government activities for which he is ultimately responsible as well as secret information developed by the intelligence community (IC). For that, there are regular channels that ultimately funnel into the Situation Room. (See Box 3.2.)

> **Box 3.2**
>
> ## The White House Situation Room
>
> The president receives information from sources far and wide. This information contributes to how foreign policy gets made. In the old days, before personal computers, video conferences, or even fax machines, couriers would bring paper copies of a selection of overseas cables and intelligence reports to the White House, where they could be distributed to the president and his senior aides. After the failed Bay of Pigs operations in 1961, President Kennedy asked his national security adviser, McGeorge Bundy, to get simultaneous copies of these messages in the White House. He wanted to know what State, Defense, and the CIA knew as soon as they knew it. An old White House bowling alley was replaced with the Situation Room.
>
> In fact, the "room" is a set of rooms in the basement of the White House, including work stations for the staff, secure telephone booths, video facilities, and the main conference room where the president can meet with his advisers during crises. The situation room is a communications, intelligence, and operations complex, staffed around the clock by about 30 people organized into 5-person watch teams. They gather classified and unclassified reports and prepare morning and evening summaries of the most significant items. They also provide breaking news information to senior officials, serving as a constantly streaming source of information. Another major duty is arranging for secure presidential calls to foreign leaders. The staff also maintains constant communication with Air Force One when the president is traveling.
>
> Movie sets intended to show the situation room usually have more high-tech gear and a larger facility than the real thing. The main conference room seats only a dozen people around its table, and there's room for only another dozen against the walls. Only in 2007 were the cathode ray video displays replaced with six flat screens, along with other upgrades of the 1985-era computers, phones, and faxes.
>
> The real impact of having the situation room was not that it was more secure and better wired for meetings than the Oval Office or the cabinet room. Its communications capabilities and access to reports to State, Defense, and the CIA gave NSC staff the ability to centralize real-time control over national security information and operations inside the White House. The Situation Room complex increased the power of the president's staff, who were no longer dependent on what those couriers brought them, eventually, from distant buildings. They could get the president to act immediately without waiting for advice from subordinate officials and their departments.
>
> *Sources:* "Situation Room," www.whitehousemuseum.org/west-wing/situation-room.htm; Michael K. Bohn, Nerve Center (Washington, DC: Brassey's, 2003).

A president's most valuable, and inevitably limited, resource is time. He needs time to think, to read, to talk with others, to sleep, and to get away from the pressures of the Oval Office. Those who serve him, therefore, are sensitive to the time constraints as they decide what information to provide, when, and in what form. George W. Bush was famously told in August 2001 that Osama Bin Laden was likely to strike in the United States, but the information wasn't specific enough to be actionable. Bush himself reportedly congratulated the intelligence briefer for protecting his own backside by conveying the warning.

Some presidents seek out information, occasionally by calling experts in the bowels of the bureaucracy. But normally, they are passive recipients of what subordinates choose to share with them. Just as they rely on certain people to cover certain policy areas, the rest of the government relies on those same people to keep the boss informed and, if the circumstances require it, advised regarding possible courses of action. Advisers, however, can offer conflicting advice, and in the end, the president must face difficult choices for high-level decisions. (See Box 3.1.)

Creation of the White House-Centered National Security Council System

Presidential personalities and management styles can make big differences on all aspects of government, but in foreign policy, there is now a regular, proven system for advice and decision making. The modern president relies on a system of national security advisers not available to his early predecessors. The NSC evolved out of the need to close or minimize gaps in information—necessary for the best presidential decision making nationally and internationally. Roosevelt's successors built on the foundations of his Joint Board of the Army and Navy to create the NSC system in place today.

Franklin Roosevelt came to office in 1933 to lead a government much larger than the one originating with George Washington, yet Roosevelt's immediate resources were in many ways similar to the first president's. Despite the increased responsibilities of the job, Roosevelt ran his ever-growing executive branch with just a handful of aides. Only in 1939, in response to a commission saying "the president needs help," did Congress approve funds for six assistants, who formed the core of the new Executive Office of the President (EOP). They were sufficient, however, because Roosevelt empowered them by supporting their actions when challenged by others. His management style of dealing one-on-one with his aides and giving them sometimes overlapping areas of responsibility greatly frustrated many senior officials. Even a loyal admirer like Secretary of War Henry Stimson confided to his diary in 1943, "But the President is the poorest administrator I have ever worked under in respect to the orderly procedure and routine of his performance. He is not a good chooser of men and he does not know how to use them in coordination."[12]

Despite Stimson's impressions, Roosevelt strengthened his ability to manage national security affairs by bringing into the EOP—two months before the start of war in Europe—the only body in use that forced the military services to work together, the Joint Board of the Army and Navy. The Joint Board provided staff for what later became the Joint Chiefs of Staff (JCS). Two months before Japan attacked Pearl Harbor, FDR began regular meetings with a new war council, composed of the chiefs of staff and the secretaries of war, navy, and state. After Pearl Harbor, however, he stopped inviting the secretary of state to the meetings and ran the war without formal diplomatic input. He tended to deal directly with the military chiefs, taking them and personal aides like Harry Hopkins, but no other civilian officials, to the key wartime conferences with Churchill and Stalin.

Those conferences exposed U.S. military leaders to the well-oiled British chiefs of staff system and the cabinet-level coordinating body, the Committee on Imperial Defence. A senior American army planner complained that "we lost our shirts" at the 1943 Casablanca conference because the U.S. delegation had not developed coordinated proposals.[13] Out of necessity, therefore, the JCS adopted the British structure and improved their own coordination as a result.

After the war, many officials wanted to codify the best practices, such as a permanent JCS supported by a joint staff. They also wanted to overcome what a major study for the navy called "serious weaknesses in coordination," which had occurred during the war. That study cited "gaps between foreign and military policy—between the State Department and the Military Establishments. Gaps between strategic planning and its logistical implementation—between the Joint Chiefs of Staff and the military and civilian agencies responsible for industrial mobilization. Gaps between and within the military services . . ."[14] To narrow these gaps, many officials wanted to try to force the president to listen to alternative views and to give clear strategic guidance. While the idea of creating an NSC was broadly supported, its strongest advocate, Navy Secretary James Forrestal, viewed it as a substitute for what he vehemently opposed—unifying control of the armed services under a single secretary of defense.

The end result in the landmark National Security Act of 1947 was a compromise. The post of secretary of defense was created, but he had little real power and had to work through the separately managed army, navy, and air force departments. The law also created the NSC as a group "to advise the President with respect to the integration of domestic, foreign, and military policies relating to the national security."[15]

FDR's successor Harry Truman distrusted Forrestal's intentions, thinking he wanted to create a British-style cabinet government and fearing that the NSC could undermine the authority of the president. As a result, Truman remained aloof from the NSC for the first few years. But, when the Korean War broke out in June 1950, he saw the value of a formal advisory group and began regular meetings.

Dwight Eisenhower was even more comfortable with a strong staff system given his army experience, so he turned the NSC and its staff into the primary body for developing and implementing basic national security policy. Despite the differences in their specific structures and utilization, each president since the 1930s has seen the value of some mechanisms under White House control that would provide the chief executive with information and advice and channels for implementing decisions.

The National Security Council and Staff

Several major distinctions need to be kept in mind while studying presidential control of foreign policy. First is the difference between the NSC as a list of key stakeholders in national security matters and the NSC as a formal advisory body. Second is the difference between NSC meetings and the numerous other sessions the president has with key officials and those they have among themselves. Third is the difference between the NSC group and the supporting NSC staff.

The membership of the NSC was intended to include those officials most knowledgeable and most responsible for national security matters and those most necessary for coordinating policy implementation. For nearly 60 years, the formal membership remained unchanged despite its inclusion of some officials whose posts were eliminated in the 1950s, such as the mutual security director and national security resources board chairman. The current members include: the president, the vice president, the secretary of state, and the secretary of defense. The chairman of the JCS and the director of national intelligence (formerly the director of central intelligence) are statutory advisers to the council. In 2007, Congress added a little-noticed provision making the secretary of energy a formal member.

Membership confers status and prestige, hence the desire to add particular officials as formal members. Recent presidents have issued formal orders conferring standing invitations to attend NSC meetings for several other cabinet-level officials and some senior White House staff. The secretary of the treasury has been a regular participant most of the time since the 1950s. Other White House aides handling economic and trade issues have been included when their issues were under review. Often, the attorney general or FBI director has been included as well as the U.S. ambassador to the United Nations and the director of the Office of Management and Budget (OMB). Recent presidents have added their chiefs of staff and even their political advisers to the list. These lists signify prestige but not power. Power depends, as Dean Rusk noted at the start of this chapter, on the official's personal relationship with the president and the confidence the chief executive has in his subordinate.

Despite its legal mandate, the NSC doesn't really function as an advisory body. It doesn't decide matters; only the president decides. It doesn't vote on policy questions; only the president's vote matters. It's also hard to see how the president as chairman of the NSC can advise himself. All presidents need a process to give them time-urgent information and at least partially considered and vetted policy recommendations. They tend to seek information and advice from people they trust, whether those individuals are part of the formal system or not.

Being on the attendee list does not even guarantee access to the president or attendance at key policy meetings because they may not be formal NSC meetings. Presidents have frequent meetings with their secretaries of state and defense and other key officials where they can discuss and maybe resolve policy matters. Calling a formal NSC meeting, however, has broader consequences. It may be done as a signal to the press and public that major issues are being seriously reviewed at the highest level of government. It may be done to give officials a formal opportunity to express their views on a pending crisis. But, it also raises the bureaucratic need for formal documentation, both for guidance to the rest of the executive branch and for the historical record.

In fact, other than President Eisenhower, most presidents have held few formal NSC meetings. Even if they start off with a burst of activity, the tendency is to drop off thereafter. President Nixon held 27 during his first six months, but only 10 during the following six months. President Carter held only 10 during his four years in office. President George H. W. Bush held only six during his last two years in the White House. President Clinton held only eight during his first year.[16]

A major reason for the decline in formal NSC meetings is the fear of leaks. After some news reports in the summer of 1969, Richard Nixon told his chief of staff, "No more NSC meetings. Result of leak. Can't trust to papers. Will make decisions privately with K[issinger]."[17] In fact, Nixon did not halt all NSC meetings, but he relied more frequently on his single channel to Henry Kissinger. A similar incident early in the Clinton administration led to an end to formal NSC meetings for several months, as a staffer explained, "So we wouldn't have to do a memo that might be leaked."

Instead, each administration has established multiple, regular, informal meetings of the president with key advisers and among those advisers. LBJ had *Tuesday lunches* with his national security adviser and the secretaries of state and defense. He added the chairman of the JCS only in 1967 when Congress began exposing military criticism of his Vietnam strategy. Jimmy Carter had *Friday breakfasts* with the same troika of civilian officials. Ronald Reagan had *family group* lunches with the same group plus the Central Intelligence Agency (CIA) director, his longtime friend William Casey. George Bush the elder convened the traditional three officials in inner circle meetings and occasionally broadened them to *Big Eight* meetings, adding the vice president, JCS chairman, White House counsel, and deputy national security adviser. Bill Clinton had informal meetings with varied sets of advisers, and the three senior officials—state, defense, and national security adviser—convened in regular lunches and breakfasts. George W. Bush had some informal meetings, and his key officials often had daily phone calls for coordination.[18] The Obama administration also had frequent meetings among senior officials and between them and the president in addition to

The President's Toolkit

the regularly scheduled sessions. These numerous informal channels demonstrate why one must look outside the formal NSC box to understand how U.S. foreign policy is made.

Although the NSC as an institution is mostly symbolic, its staff is a powerful instrument for the president. That staff grew significantly during the Nixon administration and then again under Clinton and Bush the younger. The hundred or so professional staff members are backed by another hundred support personnel. (See Figure 3.1.)

The NSC staff is its own small bureaucracy divided into directorates with specific portfolios. For issue management, George W. Bush divided his NSC apparatus into 6 regional and 11 functional interagency committees. The Obama administration had a similar arrangement of 8 regional and 11 functional groups. Obama also merged the Bush administration's Homeland Security Council staff with the NSC staff. (See Figure 3.2.)

These staff members are the president's issue experts for the huge variety of national security policy matters. They get the same field reports as their departmental counterparts. They are responsible for convening meetings of stakeholders to discuss developments in their domains and to prepare

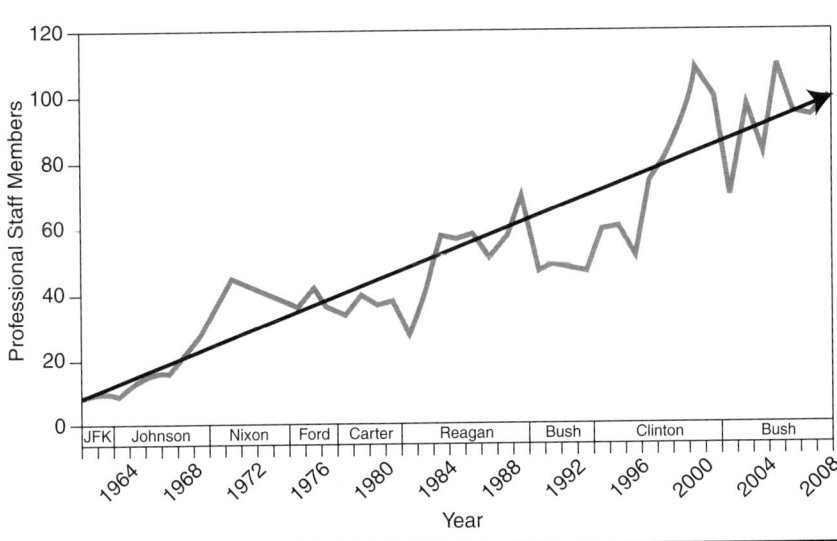

Figure 3.1 Average Size of the National Security Council Staff, 1961–2008

The NSC staff, with the resources and information it has access to, is a powerful tool for the president. The growing importance of the NSC staff to the president is evident in its growth over time. The larger numbers allow the White House to cover more policy areas and convene interagency meetings regularly and frequently.

Source: From Jeffrey Gelman, Ivo Saalder, and I. M. Destler, Brookings Institution NSC Project, in *Project on National Security Reform*, "Forging a New Shield," November 2008, 142, fig. 9. Reprinted with permission of the Brookings Institution Press.

Figure 3.2 National Security Staff Organizational Chart

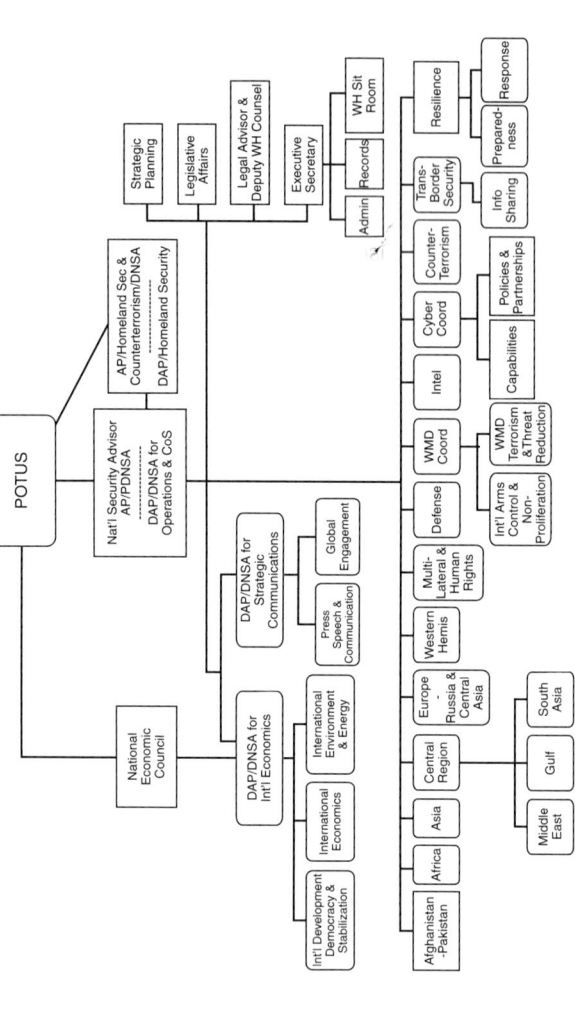

Though the formal NSC is comprised of a small number of advisers, the NSC staff has grown extensively over the years to gather information and report on a number of areas, from geographic regions to terrorism to human rights. Each of these units is supposed to be the coordinator for interagency planning in its area. In addition to the regional units, note the large number of offices dealing with various new threats like terrorism, cybersecurity, and homeland security ("resilience").

Source: Alan G. Whittaker, Shannon A. Brown, Frederick C. Smith, and Ambassador Elizabeth McCune, "The National Security Policy Process: The National Security Council and Interagency System, Appendix D," National Defense University, Industrial College of the Armed Forces, August 15, 2011, 69, at www.ndu.edu/icaf/outreach/publications/nspp/docs/icaf-nsc-policy-process-report-08-2011.pdf.

materials for meetings of higher-level officials. They head the assistant secretary-level Interagency Policy Committees (IPCs) that form the lowest rung of the interagency policy process. Most are detailees from their home agencies sent to work in the White House for a grueling couple of years, bringing their knowledge of their own departments and their capabilities as well as a roster of contacts to get information and pass along informal guidance.

Role of the National Security Adviser

In charge of the NSC staff is the national security adviser, now often abbreviated as the NSA, although the official title is assistant to the president for national security affairs. Since 1953, the NSA has usually been seen as the most important foreign policy adviser to the president, usually given cabinet rank, although the position does not require Senate confirmation or confer directive authority over departmental officials. Their offices are traditionally in the West Wing not far from the Oval Office, and that proximity gives power. The adviser is also influential because he or she is often the first and last to discuss any policy matter with the president and can put a cover memo on documents from cabinet secretaries that colors the president's own reading.

NSAs tend to follow one of two basic models for the position. One is that of policy advocate, using NSC-level meetings and other devices to push for attendees to adhere to a particular policy that is encountering some resistance. This could be the NSA's own preferred approach or what he or she believes the president wants the rest of his foreign policy team to accept. The second model, more widely praised by outside observers, is that of *honest broker*, the person who makes sure that the president hears all relevant views and who conducts the policy process in a collegial and transparent way. Brent Scowcroft articulated this model and practiced it when he was NSA for President Bush the elder.[19]

Most NSAs develop close relationships with their presidents and succeed when they adapt the NSC staff to the president's operating style. McGeorge Bundy gave John F. Kennedy the small, informal, fast acting policy team Kennedy favored; he found it hard to adjust to LBJ's more demanding and demeaning style. Henry Kissinger was the skilled consigliere who gave Richard Nixon a tightly controlled operation, filled with secrecy and surprises, that allowed the pair to craft grand strategy, often deliberately excluding the secretaries of state and defense. Zbigniew Brzezinski gave Jimmy Carter the assertive, moralistic policies he favored. Ronald Reagan subordinated his NSA and the NSC staff, not even granting the NSA routine direct access to the Oval Office. He wound up with a rogue staff that got him into the Iran-Contra scandal. Brent Scowcroft gave George Bush the elder the smooth-running and collegial process both men strongly favored, while Tony Lake and Sandy Berger worked diligently to keep the interagency process in tune with Bill Clinton's changing priorities and enthusiasms. Condoleezza Rice and Steve Hadley gave George W. Bush opportunities to set bold goals in the way he favored. Jim Jones gave Barack Obama a well-organized system in keeping with his pragmatic style. Tom Donilon proved himself as an energetic deputy NSA for Obama and was rewarded with the top spot.

Other White House Operatives

The NSA and NSC staff are not the only ones working with and for the president on national security matters. The vice president often has the stature and experience to play a major role, as George Bush the elder, Al Gore, Dick Cheney, and Joe Biden have done. (See Box 3.3.) The president's chief of staff can also be a major player, both in giving advice with a political perspective and in enforcing the president's wishes on a recalcitrant administration. Many presidents hate to disagree with their loyal appointees and find it even harder to discipline them. Those tasks are often left to the chief of staff. For example, Richard Nixon had a recurrent pattern when someone got into the Oval Office and got him to agree to take some action that the president later regretted. He would call in Chief of Staff Bob Haldeman, tell him he had no intention of doing what he had agreed to, and insist that the subordinate never be allowed to see him alone again.[20]

Box 3.3

Who Makes Foreign Policy: The Special Role of the Vice President

As the only prescribed duties for the vice president are to preside over the Senate and cast tie-breaking votes, he has lots of time for other things if the president wants to give him work. For much of U.S. history, vice presidents were political hacks, chosen for their electoral help and then banished from the White House. Richard Nixon, for instance, was allowed only a peripheral role in the Eisenhower administration, which he later avenged by treating his own vice presidents the same way. Vice presidents often traveled abroad on the principle of "You die, I fly" but rarely other than to show the flag.

Starting with the Carter administration, however, presidents chose running mates with congressional and foreign policy experience and gave them fuller access to the national security policy process, thus making them more influential in the foreign policy-making process. Walter Mondale asked for and received from Jimmy Carter several opportunities to be a much more substantive player in both domestic and foreign policy. He had on office in the West Wing and weekly private lunches with the president. He got to see the paperwork going to and from the president. And, he got a budget for his own staff. Later vice presidents were also granted such access, thus allowing them to partially institutionalize the office.

Some vice presidents preferred to be close advisers, often reserving their personal views for private meetings with the president. Others took on delegated tasks, such as Al Gore's supervisory role over U.S. policy with Russia, which became formalized in twice yearly meetings between him and the Russian premier. They all knew that their influence depended on maintaining close, personal relationships

(Continued)

(Continued)

with the president and that they might see their clout wax and wane depending on other political developments.

George H. W. Bush as vice president had a staff for foreign policy of about 10 professionals. Gore had about eight, but his own national security adviser was an active member of the DC. Dick Cheney greatly expanded and changed the vice presidential national security operation by hiring at least 14 professionals, many of whom were political appointees rather than agency detailees, as in previous administrations. Other estimates, including consultants and other seconded individuals, put the Cheney foreign policy staff at an unprecedented 35.

With so many people, Cheney was able to send agents to almost any interagency meeting that might be convened and thus monitor closely any issue he chose. He personally also was actively involved, such as by attending Principals Committee (PC) meetings and by meeting with CIA analysts to discuss their findings prior to the Iraq war.

Cheney would have had enormous influence in the Bush administration simply because of his broad experience—former White House chief of staff, secretary of defense, and deputy Republican leader in the House of Representatives—but he was even more powerful because of his staff support. News reports tended to call him *Bush's CEO* or *prime minister*.

President Obama chose Joe Biden as his vice president with full knowledge of the Delaware senator's long background and interest in foreign policy matters. He also delegated some key issues to him, including supervision of Iraq policy. And, insider reports suggest that Biden was willing to speak up with differing views in interagency meetings rather than reserving them for private sessions with the president. He appeared to make full use of the tools of the vice presidency to shape policy.

Sources: Jack Lechelt, *The Vice President in Foreign Policy: From Mondale to Cheney* (El Paso, TX: LFB Scholarly Publishing, 2009); Rothkopf, 421–422.

Because White House aides have predetermined loyalty to the president and the proximity that makes them easily accessible, they can be called on for a variety of tasks, domestic and international. In recent years, presidents have given special portfolios to some of these aides or have named officials to report directly to them, although they are based elsewhere. Harry Hopkins was in effect the deputy president for foreign affairs during World War II. L. Paul "Jerry" Bremer headed the U.S.-run Coalition Provisional Authority in Iraq and dealt frequently with President Bush, though he was nominally under Secretary Rumsfeld. President Obama made Richard Holbrooke his special representative for Afghanistan and Pakistan and former Senator George Mitchell as special representative for Middle East peace issues. While such appointments allow the president more direct control over particular policy matters, they also can undermine the interagency process by circumventing its normal procedures and protections.

As economic policy matters have gained in priority for presidential attention, White House economic advisers have been drawn into the NSC process. Bill Clinton created a separate, NSC-like National Economic Council (NEC) to coordinate administration economic policy, a body continued by his successors, though with varying effectiveness. Often, the NEC personnel for international economic issues including trade were dual-hatted with the NSC staff assigned those subjects.

As the Presidential Toolkit Brief (Table 3.1) shows, the chief executive has a number of people in the EOP to use for foreign policy missions as well as a number of possible actions even before turning matters over to one of the established departments or agencies. The president can engage in personal diplomacy by phone calls or face-to-face meetings with foreign leaders, or he can use people seen as close to him—especially the vice president, NSA, or special envoys—as instruments to convey messages and seek mutual agreements. While such actions have important advantages, they must be used sparingly because of the enormous demands on the limited time of senior officials.

Presidents also can use the White House *bully pulpit* to promote their foreign policies, though they must recognize that everyone can hear what they say, and not all overseas audiences will react the same. Presidents have legal powers to implement some policies by the stroke of a pen, such as by signing an executive order forbidding assassinations or authorizing a CIA covert operation. And within some limits, depending on the purpose and size of the sums involved, they can allocate funds to special activities without further action by Congress.

As chief diplomat, the president can conclude international agreements directly, ranging from agreed statements to formal documents to treaties that require Senate approval. More often, of course, the negotiations are delegated to other government officials, subject to presidential review and endorsement.

While America's foreign policy instruments are numerous and diverse, as later chapters will detail, presidents may choose to keep the action close to the White House either for secrecy or urgency.

National Security Council System: The Scowcroft Model

Former Air Force Lt. Gen. Brent Scowcroft was promoted by President Ford to be NSA and then was brought back to that post by President Bush the elder. In 1987, he was one of three members of the Tower Commission investigating the Iran-Contra scandal for President Reagan, where he learned how dysfunctional the NSC staff had become in the Reagan years. Scowcroft and Bush formed a solid team of shared views and created the NSC system that remains essentially unchanged to this day. Some features had been used by earlier administrations, but Scowcroft organized and codified them into an elegant whole.

At the top is the formal NSC, used sparingly. Scowcroft added a venue—called the Principals Committee or PC—for senior officials to meet without the president. The PC could be used to develop recommendations or options for the president, and their deliberations could occur without the jockeying that might take place as members reacted to presidential comments or body language. This can work for several different operating styles—those presidents who want an agreed consensus as well as those who want discrete options to decide on.

Beneath the PC, the real workhorse for the interagency process was the DC, the Deputies Committee, consisting of the number two officials in most departments. They would meet frequently to "tee up" matters for the PC and the president.

Below them would be the issue groups at the assistant secretary level, called variously Policy Coordinating Committees (Bush) or Interagency Policy Committees (Obama). These would be the standing panels to meet and prepare materials for meetings at higher levels. The key political issue for members was who had the authority to convene a meeting, that is, to elevate a particular matter for interagency consideration. In some administrations, that power rested solely with the NSC staff; in others, some groups were chaired by departmental assistant secretaries.

Scowcroft also argued that the NSA should play the honest broker role and that the NSC staff should avoid getting involved in operational activities. That approach worked well in the first Bush administration because of the extraordinary collegiality of the senior officials. Secretary of State Baker and Defense Secretary Cheney had known and worked well with Bush and Scowcroft in earlier administrations, and they remained determined to keep their deliberations out of the newspapers and their staffs collaborative. Those conditions did not prevail in subsequent administrations.

Despite broad agreement that the Scowcroft model was best, his successors have failed to recreate it. Bill Clinton had a more fluid if not undisciplined management style, and he broadened the number of members of advisory groups, thus sacrificing efficiency for inclusion. George W. Bush named NSAs that were unable to corral the vice president and defense secretary. One high-level participant said that "the Pentagon had their thumb on the scales" and that the vice president created his own parallel system that short-circuited the regular process.[21]

On taking office, President Obama's NSA, retired Marine Corps General Jim Jones, issued a formal memorandum to national security policy makers that implicitly overturned many Bush administration practices. Jones declared that the president wanted an interagency process that was "strategic, agile, transparent, and predictable." He also promised that policy papers would be circulated 48 hours in advance of meetings, that there would be a "regular announced schedule" of meetings; an agreed agenda; and that "every meeting will end with clear agreement on what was decided and *what may not have been decided*. Such an ending will also include the delegation of responsibilities for implementation." Jones also insisted that "agency representatives must be able to speak for their agency."[22] The extent to which the Obama administration met these standards is unclear.

National Security Council Culture

Whether there is a distinctive NSC staff culture is a matter of debate. One scholar says no organization culture develops because most NSC staff stay no longer than a president's term of office, that the staff consists of "an ever-changing mix of officials" of diverse backgrounds, and that detailees from other agencies are chosen carefully but asked to set aside their bureaucratic loyalties for the duration.[23] On the other hand, former staff report that they become immersed in the rhythms of the White House and are acutely sensitive to the personal and political moods of the president. In short, their culture is that of the White House, where political considerations are omnipresent, and policy success often depends on presidential success. Condoleezza Rice underscored the same point by telling her staff, "Your first responsibility is to staff the president." Their second responsibility, she said, was "to make sure that when he wants to move an agenda in a particular direction that you can get this huge ship of state turned around and moved in the direction he wants to go."[24]

This psychological as well as physical proximity to the president and other senior White House officials sets norms of responsiveness as well as a kind of authority to command others in the interagency process. *The president wants this* is about as close to a command as any bureaucrat would expect to hear, and it implicitly demands compliance and warns of punishment of resistance. NSC staff are loyal to the president as a man and to the presidency, rarely in a partisan way but in an institutional way.

The Paper Flow[25]

Disappointing as it may be to acknowledge, even the biggest national security issues get resolved through a mundane process of meetings and policy papers. In the George W. Bush administration, the PC, with cabinet members and maybe the vice president but excluding the president, met once or twice a week. In the first year or so of the Obama administration, there were often several meetings in a week. These formal sessions were supplemented in both administrations by regular informal lunches or breakfasts as well as telephone and video conferences. The role of the PCs is to develop coordinated consensus recommendations for the president or at least to highlight options when the principals disagree.

The DC is supposed to review issues papers and policy options provided by the subordinate IPCs and decide what should go forward to the PC. During the Bush administration, at least two DC meetings were scheduled each week, and sometimes more were held. In the first year or so of the Obama administration, the DC met almost daily, sometimes in person but also via teleconferences. In addition, some issues get handled without formal meetings but through a *paper PC* or *paper DC* process of circulating documents for review and approval. There are often four or five paper DC documents circulating at any one time.

The IPCs are organized regionally and functionally. They meet at the call of the chair. NSC staff directors often oversee three to five IPCs at the same time. The committees are supposed to do the heavy lifting of policy analysis and the formulation of viable options, which then go forward to the deputies. Sometimes agreement is easy, as on routine matters. At other times, however, differing ideas or departmental equities lead to sharp clashes, the most likely result of which is indecision and delay—doing nothing for now. When they act, the IPC is supposed to draft integrated policy options papers including the basic strategy, assignment of responsibilities among agencies, the resources and mechanisms to be used, and metrics for evaluating the policy.

All of this work must be highly condensed into crisp prose. The typical paper submitted for presidential decision is only a couple of pages in length. Integrated policy options papers are only a few pages longer, no matter how complex the issue. (See Box 3.4.)

Box 3.4

Inside View: Keep Memos to the President Short

Robert Gates worked on the NSC staff in several administrations before he became CIA director and later secretary of defense. He describes his actions as deputy national security adviser in the G. H. W. Bush administration. His role as a senior adviser to the president gives an inside view into how someone in this position serves as an intermediary and gatekeeper for the president and aids in the policy-making process.

More than sometimes, I frequently would send it [the memos] back. One of the common faults, even at the NSC level, is that experts think that Presidents cannot conceivably understand an issue unless it covers several pages. One of our jobs in that front office was to protect the President. So one of my tasks was to make sure not only that the stuff was clear, but that it was concise. And I've been doing this my whole career, chopping things down to a page or a page and a half for senior officials, and that's what I did. Sometimes I'd make them do it, sometimes I'd do it myself. But also it was questions of clarity, questions of whether it had been properly coordinated, whether other affected members of the NSC had seen a piece of paper.

Everybody tries to slip their stuff through without having to share it with anybody else and play these games and we, I think, put a discipline in the process that after a few months became less and less necessary because they understood it wasn't going through if it hadn't been properly coordinated. So all the paper came through me. A lot of it went back to be worked on or re-worked. A lot of drafts would come over. And I spent a lot of time just sitting with NSC staffers. They would just come in and talk.

Source: From the oral history for the G. H. W. Bush administration, interview with Robert Gates at http://millercenter.org/president/bush/oralhistory/robert-gates.

Crisis Management

The process is often different in short-fuse crises. (See Box 3.5.) The news report of a military incident or a sudden change of government abroad forces the government into crisis mode. That means urgent meetings that may drag on for hours and subordinates drafting options papers in another room with little guidance from their bosses. It may mean seat-of-the-pants judgments without fuller consideration of alternatives. Critics of groupthink point to the tendency of policy makers under stress to agree to the first reasonable-sounding proposal. Critics of reasoning by analogies point to the habit of policy makers to try to compare one situation to a past event despite the inevitable differences. Many officials looking at Vietnam saw "another Munich," while only a few said "it's another Korea, an unwinnable ground war." On the other hand, rapid agreement may be better than prolonged debate while the situation deteriorates. And, the right analogy can expedite a selection of good choices. The Kennedy administration reached a better decision by taking time for deliberation in the Cuban missile crisis instead of immediately launching air strikes, as some recommended. And, international support to drive Iraqi forces from Kuwait in 1991 was stronger because there was a clear invasion across an internationally recognized border, a stop-Hitler-now situation.

In such crises, presidents usually turn to informal processes to handle the issue. They usually rely on a very small circle of key advisers both because of the urgency of the situation and the need for secrecy, especially if use of force could be involved.[26] They have to decide whether or when to include congressional leaders in the discussion. Bringing them in raises the risks of leaks and political opposition; excluding them raises the risks of anger and fractured unity in the face of threats.

Process Matters

Does the process really matter? Can it shape the substance of policy choices in subtle and perhaps nonrational ways? Yes it can and sometimes does. Part of the policy process is defining the participants—the stakeholders who deserve to have a seat at the table when matters affecting their responsibilities are discussed. When Dwight Eisenhower included his treasury secretary in NSC meetings, he forced all participants to avoid the argument often used in defense discussions: if we need it, we should pay whatever the cost. John F. Kennedy included his brother the attorney general in the Cuban missile crisis discussions, and at other times, he added someone who made significant and influential comments that drove other participants to a different outcome than they otherwise seemed likely to recommend. When Richard Nixon regularly excluded his secretaries of state and defense from key discussions, he avoided their insights and thus felt more confident in his own decisions. When Ronald Reagan subordinated his NSA to other White House staff, he made it easier for them to run their own

Box 3.5

How Foreign Policy Is Made: Crisis Day at the National Security Council

When a crisis erupts, the NSC system goes into a 24/7 mode. Participants are pulled away from their normal activities and forced to focus on a single, major problem. Participants say that such events "suck the oxygen" out of their departments and agencies as lesser matters get postponed and senior officials are preoccupied with crisis matters. A National Defense University study of the NSC during crises such as the 1991 Gulf War, 1999 Kosovo crisis, the aftermath of the terrorist attacks on September 2001, and the conduct of military operations in Afghanistan and Iraq, described how hectic a typical day was for senior policy makers.

- Departmental meetings with Secretaries or Deputy Secretaries in the early morning to review developments, responsibilities, taskings, and policy issues of concern to the mission of each department.
- In mid-morning, the DC (Deputies Committee) meets, sometimes conducted via secure teleconferencing with senior staff and area/functional experts, to develop interagency positions on developments and new policy issues. This DC meeting might be followed immediately by a meeting of the DC senior members (without supporting staff) to discuss sensitive intelligence or policy issues.
- In late morning or early afternoon, the PC (Principals Committee) meets to discuss the results and unresolved issues of the DC, consider strategic policy directions, and determine what issues need to be brought to the attention of the President. PC members may then meet with the President (who usually receives updates on the crisis situation from the National Security Advisor throughout the day).
- In mid or late afternoon, the DC again meets to discuss the implementation of decisions reached by the PC and President, and discuss the results of IPC [Interagency Policy Committees] meetings that have been held throughout the day (individual IPCs may meet more than once a day during crisis periods).
- Individual members of the DC are likely to have a late afternoon meeting with their principals to confer about developments of the day, and a subsequent meeting with their staffs to discuss the day's decisions, developments, and next steps. Depending upon the circumstances of the day, the PC may have an additional evening meeting and subsequent consultation with the President.
- This kind of high operational tempo may persist for several weeks or months, depending upon the duration of the crisis and the need to involve the President and cabinet level officers on a daily basis.

Source: Alan G. Whittaker, PhD, Frederick C. Smith, and Ambassador Elizabeth McKune, "The National Security Policy Process: The National Security Council and Interagency System," Annual Update: October 8, 2010, NDU paper at www.ndu.edu/icaf/outreach/publications/nspp/docs/icaf-nsc-policy-process-report-10–2010.pdf.

unsupervised foreign policies. When NSA Tony Lake deliberately scheduled meetings when Richard Holbrooke could not attend, he avoided whatever wisdom or problems the assertive Holbrooke might have brought to the table. When Vice President Cheney sat in on PC meetings and sent his aides to most lower-level NSC staff meetings, he intimidated discussion, just as he intended to. When Barack Obama skipped General Jones to deal with his longtime aide Denis McDonough, he weakened the presumed influence of his NSA.

The process also establishes who can delay or object to clearance of a proposed statement or policy. Can a subordinate act for his principal? Can a senior NSC staffer override the request of a secretary of state or defense? Protocols have to be established, and whoever truly has veto power gains enormous leverage over the process. Even within the White House, rules have to be established. One frequent area of conflict is between cabinet department heads and presidential speech writers. CIA Director George Tenet objected to President George W. Bush's mention of Iraq seeking uranium from Africa in a State of the Union speech only to be overruled by Condoleezza Rice and the speechwriters.[27] What gives a speech punch may be what the diplomats want to avoid.

The policy process also creates action channels for implementation of presidential decisions. When DOD received formal responsibility for preparing for Phase IV of the Iraq war—the post-hostilities situation after the defeat of Saddam Hussein—State Department experts on those matters were excluded from the minimal planning that took place. When White House speechwriters are making last-minute revisions to a presidential statement, they may not have time or inclination to check with an issue expert in a cabinet department who may have valuable advice.

Another way process can affect substance is when the face of the issue—the apparent matter up for decision—is different from its broader or more appropriate context. A request from the president of Taiwan to visit his college reunion in America became a major foreign policy problem for the Clinton administration when Chinese officials objected to this action as a kind of diplomatic recognition of the Taiwanese government. When the United Nations (UN) Security Council was debating how to respond to an ambush killing 24 Pakistani peacekeepers in Somalia during the Clinton administration, the face of the issue was how to keep the UN operation from falling apart rather than the broader issue of the U.S. military role in Somalia. General Colin Powell learned of the U.S. vote while exercising on his treadmill. Similarly, Rumsfeld's creating the notion of a Global War on Terror (GWOT) automatically redefined issues that might have been treated as minor incidents or criminal matters as part of the GWOT channel, thereby adding some bureaucratic elements and excluding others from policy deliberations.

Secretary of State Powell was also excluded from many important Bush administration meetings because of what his aides deemed a refusal by other officials to follow the "regular order" of interagency policy discussions.

Time and again, Vice President Cheney or Defense Secretary Rumsfeld got the president to agree to some national security matter without involving the State Department.

As the below case study on Obama's Afghanistan Policy Review demonstrates, the president can insist on a thorough process, but that takes time and is subject to leaks intended to influence the ultimate decision. Yet, such a process can also lead to a narrowing of differences and even consensus in support of the policy.

The absence of a regular process satisfactory to the participants leads to one-off deals with the president and only narrowly considered policies. That was what Nixon realized had occurred and which he tried to stop by further isolating himself from many of his advisers. On the other hand, FDR relished conducting policy that way. The value of vetting ideas is that mistakes and unintended consequences are more likely to be avoided. The costs of vetting are delays and possible unwanted disclosures of matters under discussion. There's no way to avoid these dilemmas and trade-offs. The process can shape the substance of policy.

Foreign Policy Is a Never-Ending Process

Despite the finality of announcements that the president has decided on some new policy, the reality is what former Secretary of State George Shultz complained about. "Nothing ever gets settled in this town, a seething debating society in which the debate never stops, in which people never give up, including me. And so that's the atmosphere in which you administer." His comments point to two realities: first, big issues are perennial issues; second, each big decision requires numerous subsequent decisions on implementation. How to deal with a rising China won't be settled by a single policy paper. Whoever loses the policy fight in round one may scheme to win in round two and may even stir up a new issue to provoke a second round. That has been the story, for example, of policy toward North Korea, where new accusations of cheating on earlier agreements resurrects the policy debate. Even when there is a settled policy—like President Obama's December 2009 on Afghanistan—practical questions arise each month afterward that can lead to tweaks or revisions, such as further troop deployments that later occurred. Issues are settled only when no one has any reason to disagree any more. And even those may require additional confirming decisions.

New presidents inherit the NSC process, but they don't inherit the files. In fact, NSC materials are trucked away to the departing chief executive's presidential library on Inauguration Day, leaving the files empty and thus imposing an immediate loss of institutional memory.[28] In fact, of course, some staff serve before and after January 20, and cabinet departments have their own files. But, the system imposes a blank slate event that exaggerates the freedom of maneuver of a new administration.

Critiques of the Current National Security Council System

The president can change the NSC system, and each does to some extent. While the Obama administration was reacting to perceived flaws of the Bush system, it stopped short of adopting changes suggested by outside analysts. Among the frequent recommendations are to have a robust strategic planning cell and to empower issue team leaders by giving them staff, directive power over other agencies, and even some budget authority. While Bush and Obama both endeavored to do more strategic planning, they encountered problems that are probably inherent in trying to get people nearly overwhelmed by immediate problems to think long range.[29]

Empowering issue team leaders, as might have been done for Richard Holbrooke or George Mitchell, requires legislation, which the administration did not request. In fact, the NSA has no legal standing or authority because the post is not Senate confirmed, and thus the NSA cannot be an officer of the United States with any directive authority. Requiring confirmation, of course, would give the Senate a veto over the president's preferred adviser and subject the nominee to testify before Congress, a task now avoided by presidential order and long-standing precedents.

Some analysts consider the NSC staff too large, others too small. That of course depends on what one expects the staff to do. More people creates a larger staff to manage, only a few of whom would ever come in contact with the president. Fewer people might leave some issues unwatched at the White House level, thus freeing the operating agencies to do more smart or dumb things on their own. There are always these trade-offs.

Presidents can learn too. They can change the way they do business if they have incentives to change—either policy failures or new opportunities—and if they can find the right people and an effective mechanism to do the job. Most organizations innovate not by radically changing what everybody does but by empowering a new entity to do the new tasks. There are many ways a president can add to his foreign policy toolkit or find new ways of using the existing ones.

* * *

The president has enormous discretion over which tools to use to carry out his foreign policies and how to use them. There are some legal constraints and often even stronger political constraints from public opinion and Congress. Since the 1960s, the president has had a White House-centered information and advisory system based on the NSC and its staff. But, the president can also make use of the vice president, other White House officials, and special envoys. The process of cabinet-level, deputy secretary-level, and assistant secretary-level committees has been largely the same since 1989, but in crisis situations, most presidents turn to much smaller groups of trusted advisers.

While there is a tendency to focus on specific presidential announcements and actions as definitive, the policy process in fact is ongoing, never ending, and frequently revisiting and changing what had been decided earlier.

Case Study: Obama's Review of Afghanistan Policy

This case shows how one president used his foreign policy advisory system in a lengthy and deliberate way to review a major issue and devise a new strategy. President Obama had the luxury of time in which to conduct his reassessment. He also had a mostly unified national security team—unlike George W. Bush, who in 2006–2007, relied on outside advocates and disagreed with the recommendations of his senior military advisers regarding a U.S. troop surge for Iraq.

Barack Obama campaigned for the presidency as a critic of the war in Iraq, but he supported the fight against the Taliban and al Qaeda in Afghanistan, calling it a *war of necessity*. On January 21, 2009, the day after his inauguration, he held his first NSC meeting and was told of a pending military request to send an additional 30,000 U.S. troops to Afghanistan, nearly doubling the existing 38,000 who were there along with 29,000 from NATO countries. He ordered a 60-day policy review.

His new team included Defense Secretary Robert Gates, who had led the Pentagon for the previous two years under George W. Bush, Secretary of State Hillary Clinton, National Security Adviser General Jim Jones, and his special representative for Afghanistan and Pakistan, former Ambassador Richard Holbrooke.

Sensing resistance, military planners scaled back their request to 27,000 troops. On February 13, with the policy review just starting, Obama held an NSC meeting that considered whether to postpone action on the troop request until completion of the review, or to send 17,000 troops immediately and consider the rest later, or to send the entire 27,000. As often happens, Obama chose the middle option.

The new policy was announced on March 27. The president declared a goal to "disrupt, dismantle, and defeat al Qaeda and its safe havens" and said an additional 4,000 U.S. troops would be sent, along with the 17,000 announced earlier, in order to accelerate the training of Afghan security forces. The classified policy paper included 20 recommendations and 180 subrecommendations for action.

On May 11, Secretary Gates, seeking fresh thinking and new military leadership, replaced the U.S. commander in Afghanistan with Gen. Stanley McChrystal. In his Senate confirmation hearing, McChrystal said he might need more troops than had already been sent.

The troop increase question led to renewed tension between the president and some of his civilian advisers and senior military leaders. People in the White House thought that the troop issue had been settled for the rest of the year and resented the pressure to revisit Obama's decision. The military had meanwhile translated the policy into one of defeating the Taliban as well as al Qaeda and thought the mission was inadequately resourced.

At the end of August, Gen. McChrystal sent a 66-page classified assessment of the problems his command faced and what was needed to carry out the announced policy. He warned that "the status quo will lead to failure" and said much had to be done promptly to avoid "strategic defeat." At Gates's request, there were no troop increase numbers in the report. They were provided on September 25—a three-option proposal for 10,000 or 40,000 or 80,000 more U.S. troops.

Obama began another formal and extensive policy review on September 13. He spent more than 25 hours in 10 meetings over the next three months. Gen. Jones later said that "none of us ended up where we started." The president ran the meetings with a lot of questions. He forced the group to consider what goals were achievable given the bleak military and political situation. By October 9, the group consensus was to change the explicit goal from *defeating* to *degrading* the Taliban, thus prompting suggestions for lower troop numbers.

Vice President Joe Biden was the most vocal opponent of substantial troop increases, calling instead for what he labeled counterterrorism plus. He worked back channel with the vice chairman of the JCS, Gen. James Cartwright, to develop a 20,000-troop plan, but it was opposed by Gates, Clinton, and others. Obama later said that he particularly wanted to be sure that he maintained Gates's support for his strategy.

Obama continued to express frustration in several NSC meetings during October because he didn't feel he had been given real options. "We don't have two options yet," he complained. "We have 40,000 and nothing." On October 30, Gates responded with an Option 2A, calling for 30,000 to 35,000 more troops.

Obama welcomed the sign of flexibility and even told his November 11 meeting that he supported a *surge* of troops into Afghanistan, using the term for a similar policy he had opposed in Iraq. He also began pushing back on the deployment timetable. "Why can't we get them there faster?" he asked. He then seized on Gates's willingness to start troop reductions after 18 to 24 months in order to pressure the Afghan government.

The remaining debates in November focused on the precise troop number, the speed of their deployment, and the possible timetable to start withdrawals. The sizable surge pleased the military, the planned withdrawals pleased the skeptical civilians, and the accelerated deployments pleased everybody.

On November 29, Obama met with his advisers, told them he would approve 30,000 troops plus no more than 10 percent more for trainers. He insisted on a July 2011 deadline to begin withdrawals but agreed that the pace of reductions would depend on conditions. He also told his generals, "Don't clear and hold what you can't transfer [to the Afghans]." He asked for and received formal support for the plan. He even took the unusual step of getting them to endorse a six-page terms sheet that he had drafted, laying out the new strategy.

While not part of the Afghanistan policy review, though it was at the back of everyone's mind, was what to do in Pakistan. In October, the president approved increased secret operations in Pakistan, including more drone strikes against terrorists there.

Obama announced his Afghanistan policy in a nationally televised address delivered to cadets at West Point on December 1.

While other aspects of Afghanistan policy had been considered earlier, this case focuses on the question of how to use the military instrument. The president used his NSC advisory system to discuss and debate policy options. The process was disrupted by press reports of leaked information. Eventually, the president obtained formal assent from his advisers before announcing his policy publicly.

Sources: Peter Baker, "How Obama Came to Plan for 'Surge' in Afghanistan," *The New York Times,* December 5, 2009; Anne E. Kornblut, Scott Wilson, and Karen DeYoung, "Obama Pressed for Faster Surge," *Washington Post,* December 6, 2009; Bob Woodward, *Obama's Wars* (New York: Simon & Schuster, 2010).

Selected Resources

The current White House website is at www.whitehouse.gov/. There are also archived presidential websites for earlier presidents:

George W. Bush—http://georgewbush-whitehouse.archives.gov/

Bill Clinton—www.clintonlibrary.gov/archivesearch.html

The best recent description of the White House staff is in Bradley H. Patterson, Jr., *To Serve the President: Continuity and Innovation in the White House Staff* (Washington, DC: Brookings, 2008).

Historical studies of the NSC and the ways different presidents have used the NSC and its staff can be found in: Peter W. Rodman, *Presidential Command* (New York: Knopf, 2009); David Rothkopf, *Running the World* (New York: Public Affairs, 2005); Ivo M. Saalder and I. M. Destler, *In the Shadow of the Oval Office* (New York: Simon & Schuster, 2009); and John P. Burke, *Honest Broker? The National Security Advisor and Presidential Decision Making* (College Station, TX: Texas A&M University Press, 2009).

Historical collections of presidential documents and other information are available through The American Presidency Project at the University of California, Santa Barbara, www.presidency.ucsb.edu/ and the CB Presidential Research Services site, Presidents of the United States, www.presidentsusa.net/.

4 Congress's Toolkit

If we cannot inquire into the state of the Army, it follows that the Army belongs to the President and not to the nation.

—Nathaniel Macon (D-NC), three-term speaker of the house, 1810

I don't care to be involved in the crash-landing unless I can be in on the take-off.

—Harold Stassen, later frequently repeated by Senator Arthur Vandenberg

We don't need 535 secretaries of state.

—Vice President Dick Cheney, April 13, 2007

Congress is rarely in the driver's seat for U.S. foreign policy, but it fuels the car, sometimes tries to navigate from the front seat, and often complains from the backseat. It also has its own hand brake to use in emergencies. Needless to say, the vehicle goes farthest and fastest when Congress and the president agree on the route forward.

The Constitution gives Congress its own set of powers over foreign policy, including most notably the powers to appropriate funds and to write the laws governing executive departments. The Senate has the additional right to advise and consent to nominations and treaties. These powers can be abused, but they also can be left dormant or delegated. History has examples of each. Sometimes over the course of U.S. history, Congress has been assertive and influential in foreign policy matters. At other times, lawmakers have been deferential toward the executive branch or cowed by strong presidents.

This chapter describes the legislative tools that Congress has—summarized in the Toolkit Brief (See Table 4.1)—and gives examples of how and when lawmakers have used them. While the formal tools of the legislative process are the most powerful, the most influential tools are often the less visible ones—the informal contacts, the framing of issues, and the law of anticipated reactions that often limit presidential options. Congress is a political institution, not only in the sense of being influenced by partisan and electoral considerations but also as it competes with the executive branch for power over domestic and foreign policy.

Table 4.1 The Congressional Toolkit Brief

ACTION	ADVANTAGES	DISADVANTAGES
Substantive legislation	Binding law; limits presidential discretion	Harder to pass; much harder to change
Procedural legislation	Puts onus on president	Can be evaded
Advisory legislation	Easier to pass	Can be ignored
Appropriations	Unchallengeable as grants or denials of funds	Many hurdles to approval; some loopholes to denials
Oversight (hearings, investigations, reports)	Dramatizes issues; gains information	Time-consuming; can be abused
Informal contacts	Easy; less confrontational	Can be ignored
Delay or rejection of nominations	Gains attention and leverage over issue	Limits presidential choice and actions
Delay or rejection of treaties	Gains attention and leverage over issue	Can damage relations with other nations
Framing issues	Rewards for early action	Many potential competitors

Congress has several means at its disposal to use to influence foreign policy making, including the passage of legislation, use of appropriations, oversight, and delaying or rejecting nominations and treaties. While each of these provide advantages to Congress, such as setting limits on presidential actions, they also hold drawbacks, including the potential to damage U.S. relations with other countries through inaction or inconsistency. Congress used its legislative tools in 1947 to provide a new instrument of foreign policy to the executive branch when it created the Central Intelligence Agency (CIA), the National Security Council (NSC), and what became the Department of Defense (DOD).

How Congress Acts

The formal legislative process—how a bill becomes a law—explains only partly how Congress influences U.S. foreign policy. There are occasions when a member introduces a bill, watches a committee hold hearings and report it, debates it on the floor, and succeeds in getting it passed, only to await similar action by the other chamber until the measure is sent to the president for signature. More often, foreign policy legislation is attached to broader bills that are expected to be passed, sometimes with little or no consideration by the relevant committees or foreknowledge by the executive branch. Sometimes, the new law is the product of months of negotiations among interested officials. Other times, it may be a quick response to that day's news.

Congress can also influence presidential actions without actually passing a law. The threat of passage, or even a narrow defeat, can persuade senior policy makers to alter course. Consultations might actually change minds. Suggestions from lawmakers might be adopted by the administration. A scheduled hearing can force a divided executive branch to make up its mind.

A required report on human rights or religious liberty can give U.S. diplomats leverage over another nation that hopes to get a favorable comment.

Simply by drawing attention to a foreign policy issue—the plight of Soviet Jews in the 1970s, starvation in Somalia in 1992, ethnic conflict in the Balkans in the 1990s, genocide in Sudan in the 2000s—Congress can force a reluctant administration to fashion a policy and take action abroad. By their speeches and activities, lawmakers can frame issues for public debate, pushing secondary issues like drug trafficking or terrorism to the front burner. The most powerful tools, however, are the regular ones that are part of the constitutional system.

The Legal Tool

The legislative process can create instruments for the executive branch in foreign policy by creating the agencies and giving them authorities, responsibilities, and capabilities. There was no secretary of defense until Congress created the post in 1947. In fact, there was no DOD until two years later. The first secretary had only coordinating powers over the long-established service bureaucracies. The 1947 law also created the CIA and gave statutory standing to the Joint Chiefs of Staff (JCS).

The Marshall Plan to rebuild war-ravaged Europe required an agency to administer it. Congress created that bureaucracy and later broadened its mandate to other foreign aid programs. Over the decades, lawmakers have frequently changed foreign aid agencies, often by adding new and separate entities like the Millennium Challenge Corporation and by giving new mandates such as combating HIV/AIDS.

Although it stopped short of creating a Department of Trade, Congress did create the post of U.S. trade representative (USTR), the official charged with negotiating trade agreements, located it in the Executive Office of the President (EOP), and made it equal in rank to any cabinet officer. As discussed in Chapter 7, this made the USTR more an arm of Congress than a subordinate to the president.

When Congress wanted to push the executive branch toward greater efforts at nuclear arms control, it created the Arms Control and Disarmament Agency in 1961. Nearly four decades later, Congress reversed course and abolished the agency.

Similarly, to increase military capabilities for special operations and counterterrorism, Congress created a separate combatant organization, the Special Operations Command (SOCOM) and protected its budget by segregating it from the rest of Pentagon spending. After the 9/11 attacks, Congress and President George W. Bush sparred over how to strengthen the government's capacity for homeland security. The president favored informal coordination but was ultimately forced by Congress to accept a full-fledged department for that task.

Once created, these national security organizations depend on financial and human resources to do their assigned jobs. Sometimes that comes easily, as when Congress mandated increases in the army and marine corps in 2004. Other times, there is resistance, as there has been to proposals to increase the civilian capacity of the U.S. government for post-conflict stabilization missions in Iraq and Afghanistan.

Congress can also pass laws changing the rules under which agencies operate. Policies followed in international family planning programs have been reversed and re-reversed by changing congressional provisions related to domestic disputes. Likewise, the nature of military leadership has been changed by legislation like the Goldwater–Nichols Defense Reorganization Bill of 1986, which forced military officers seeking to become generals or admirals to serve an assignment in a so-called joint post that would give them familiarity with other armed services. Congress also wrote new rules into the laws underpinning the foreign aid programs, such as the numerous provisions requiring cuts in assistance to countries that abuse human rights or help terrorist organizations or suffer military coups against democratically elected governments.

Substantive Versus Procedural Laws

There are two basic models of foreign policy laws. One approach, substantive legislation, sets forth policy principles and administrative tasks. The other, procedural legislation, establishes a series of steps the executive branch must take before it has the authority to act abroad. Sometimes, Congress stops short of binding laws and passes *sense of Congress* measures that are merely advisory, however strongly felt.

Laws with teeth include embargos against trade and other relations with Fidel Castro's Cuba, imposed by executive order in 1962 and codified in law in 1992 (PL 102–484). Another example of substantive legislation was the 1986 law, passed over President Reagan's veto, prohibiting new U.S. investment in South Africa as well as trade in agricultural products, steel, and nuclear supplies. As discussed in the accompanying case study, bipartisan majorities demonstrated their opposition to South African apartheid policies. During the early 1980s, Congress also wrote a series of laws trying to constrain Reagan administration policies toward Central America. A ban on aid to the Nicaraguan contras, who sought to overthrow the leftist government there, was passed 10 times during the 1980s.[1] In another example, the Nuclear Non-Proliferation Act of 1978 (NNPA) revised the laws controlling the export of nuclear-related materials and mandated renegotiation of existing cooperative agreements with other countries. It also imposed sanctions on countries that conducted nuclear tests or failed to sign on to the Non-Proliferation Treaty.

On occasion, tough laws have unintended consequences. In 1981, Congress waived provisions of the NNPA that would have required cuts in U.S. aid to Pakistan because lawmakers wanted to help that nation in its efforts to undermine the Soviet invasion of Afghanistan. In 1985, in order to head off even tougher provisions, Congress approved an amendment allowing aid so long as the president could certify that Pakistan did not possess a nuclear device. By 1990, however, the first President Bush could no longer make such a certification, and arms sales were abruptly halted.² What was sold as a way to deter a Pakistani nuclear capability created major diplomatic problems when it failed. Lawmakers granted further exemptions for Pakistan in the mid-1990s, but the experience has had a lasting impact on U.S.–Pakistani relations. Even as Pakistan has been a major recipient of U.S. aid since 2001, both civilian and military leaders in Islamabad have expressed distrust of U.S. motives and anger at U.S. policies in the region.

When President Jimmy Carter established full diplomatic relations with the People's Republic of China and abrogated the 1954 Mutual Defense Treaty with the government on Taiwan, new legislation was required. Conservatives in Congress challenged the legality of Carter's treaty action, which was ultimately upheld by the courts. They also tried to mandate U.S. military support for Taiwan in case of an attack from the mainland. The final version of the bill contained rhetorical provisions sympathetic to Taiwan and declared that the United States would continue to provide defense articles and services "to enable Taiwan to maintain a sufficient self-defense capability." Other provisions established unusual arrangements for unofficial, quasi-diplomatic relations (PL 96–8). This is an instance in which Congress sought to first reverse and then strictly limit the impact of the president's policy change.

The second basic model of foreign policy law, procedural legislation, is commonly used to establish tough principles but then allow the president discretion in implementing the provisions. Most mandatory sanctions carry waivers allowing the president to avoid imposing them by submitting some certification to Congress. Aid to El Salvador in the 1980s, for example, followed this pattern—requiring presidential certification that the Salvadoran government was complying with human rights, making political and economic reforms, and preventing torture by its armed forces. When this was attested by President Reagan, U.S. aid was allowed to be given. Other waivers are tied to presidential declarations that important national security interests require the law to be set aside. Such a waiver allowed President Clinton to suspend a section of the 1996 Helms–Burton law that would have allowed U.S. nationals to sue foreign companies that did business with Cuba.³

Starting during the 1970s, Congress passed a series of major foreign policy laws creating procedures for handling important issues. The War Powers Resolution is a prime example. It allows presidential decisions to use military force but tries to limit the duration of combat operations and allows Congress to revisit the decision later. The Arms Export Control Act sets rules and conditions for arms sales but gives Congress a right to review and veto them. Fast-track provisions allowing the United States to enter into trade negotiations, now called *trade promotion authority (TPA)*, establish procedures leading ultimately to non-amendable bills with guaranteed single up-or-down votes in the Senate and House. These examples illustrate the ways in which Congress can restrain presidential action and help guide policy as well as ways that Congress seeks to allow itself flexibility to change decisions later.

Lawmakers have also built procedural remedies for opponents of certain trade practices. The International Trade Commission is an independent, quasi-judicial agency that has been empowered to administer trade remedy laws. It hears complaints of unfair trade practices by foreigners, such as the *dumping* of commodities at prices below those at home, and makes recommendations for presidential actions. Another trade law created the interagency Committee on Foreign Investment in the United States (CFIUS) to make findings on whether a planned foreign investment in an American company would have adverse national security risks.

Procedural legislation has numerous advantages for the executive and legislative branches. From the president's standpoint, it allows some discretion as he determines whether the specified conditions apply or whether a waiver is justified. Yet, the threat of sanctions gives the administration leverage over foreign nations in pressing for policy changes. The advantage for lawmakers is that they can trumpet their stances on principle yet distance themselves from the consequences and place any blame on the president if things go badly.

The Money Tool

Congress frequently uses its appropriations bills to shape and direct U.S. foreign policy. As Chapter 5 discusses in more detail, lawmakers boost aid to favored nations and restrict it to those that fall out of favor. They also demand that the executive branch seek agreements with others, such as in sharing military burdens and in joining sanctions against misbehaving states. At various times, Congress has used its money tool to forbid certain military operations, as in parts of Southeast Asia during the Vietnam War, or to oppose certain military capabilities desired by the Pentagon, including antisatellite weapons and certain kinds of missile defense systems. Even routine buy-American provisions can cause foreign policy problems for the U.S. government.

Current practice also gives congressional committees leverage over other foreign policy transactions. They must be notified in advance of proposed arms sales and aid disbursements and transfers of funds between accounts above certain thresholds.

America's foreign aid programs are also tightly constrained by earmarks—where lawmakers assign funds for specific countries, thereby limiting executive branch discretion or flexibility in changed circumstances. About three fourths of the Foreign Operations Appropriations Bill has been routinely earmarked in recent years. Theoretically, earmarks in committee reports are not legally binding, though those in law are. Even so, bureaucrats are reluctant to disregard committee wishes, fearing retaliation the following year.

While substantive and procedural legislation may contain ambiguities or loopholes that allow for presidential discretion or even evasion, the money tool is unchallengeable. No president has claimed the right to ignore congressional denial of funds for foreign policy activities. Even Richard

Nixon ended U.S. combat operations in Southeast Asia when Congress cut off funds.

The Treaty Tool

The Senate can influence foreign policy through its special power to advise and consent to treaties with other nations. The president, of course, can decide how closely to consult with senators or whether to accept their advice. George Washington's experience led to a distancing rarely closed in the past two centuries. (See Box 4.1.)

Box 4.1

Who Makes Foreign Policy: George Washington Gives Up on Advice and Consent

The Constitution allows the president to conclude treaties and nominate officials "with the advice and consent" of the Senate. George Washington thought that that provision meant that he was to consult with senators in advance so that he could receive their advice. His first attempts to do so, however, created more problems than they solved.

From the start of his presidency, Washington was scrupulous in following the intent of the framers as he performed his duties. He was greatly offended, however, when the Senate for the first time rejected one of his nominees, Benjamin Fishbourn, to be a naval officer assigned to the port of Savannah, Georgia. Fishbourn was the only one of 102 nominees for various posts to be voted down. On August 5, 1789, the president stormed into the Senate chamber, surprising its members, and demanded an explanation for the rejection. He also suggested that the senators should have told him of their problems with his nominee before actually taking a vote. One of the Georgia senators outlined his own opposition but noted that the Senate was not obligated to give any reasons. This marked the beginning of *Senatorial courtesy*, which allowed lawmakers to block appointments of federal officials in their own state.

Washington calmed down and submitted an alternate nominee, who was quickly approved. Meanwhile, the Senate voted to establish a committee to work out "the mode of communication proper to be pursued between him and the Senate" in appointment and treaty matters. Some members suggested that Senate advice and consent should be given in the presence of the president, but Washington said he preferred written communications as a general rule. He said he didn't want to inhibit free discussion by the lawmakers.

On Saturday, August 22, by prior arrangement, Washington again went to the Senate, accompanied by Secretary of War Henry Knox, this time to seek its advice and consent on plans to negotiate some Indian treaties. He handed the vice president his message and took his seat. Noisy carriages outside drowned out the first reading of the president's message, so it had to be read again. It explained his plans and asked the Senate's advice on a series of seven questions related to the negotiations.

Senators started discussing the first question, then postponed action until the following Monday in order to get more information. They started to discuss the

> (Continued)
> second question, and agreed to postpone it as well, but continued to argue over the issue. Some members favored creation of a special committee to consider the message. Washington then rose "in a violent fret." He complained, "This defeats every purpose of my coming here."
>
> Washington eventually agreed to the delay, returned on Monday, and stayed during the long session while Senators argued and voted on the seven questions. He then left and never again returned in person to seek the Senate's advice and consent, nor did any of his successors.
>
> Washington's troubled experience seeking Senate advice led later presidents to restrict consultation to informal soundings and private conversations. The consultation tool has been used much less frequently than the framers probably expected.
>
> ---
>
> *Sources:* Annals of Congress; David P. Currie, *The Constitution in Congress: The Federalist Period* (Chicago: University of Chicago Press, 1997), 21–26; Ron Chernow, *Washington: A Life* (New York: Penguin Press, 2010), 590–593.

The constitutional requirement for a two-thirds vote for approval makes any treaty an easy hostage for any groups of senators who object to its provisions or want other matters settled to their satisfaction. The historical record misleadingly suggests that treaty ratification is common. In its first 200 years, the Senate voted in favor of more than 1,500 treaties, about 90% of those submitted. Moreover, only 21 treaties were actually rejected by the Senate, and only three of these defeats occurred since the 1930s. (These were the Law of the Sea convention in 1960, the Montreal aviation protocol setting new limits on damage awards in plane crashes in 1983, and the Comprehensive [nuclear] Test Ban Treaty in 1999.)

But, the threat of defeat or of indefinite delay led many presidents to resort to executive agreements that do not require Senate approval. Since the start of World War II, the United States has concluded approximately 16,500 executive agreements and only about 1,100 treaties.[4] When Congress learned of secret agreements concluded in the 1950s and 1960s, it passed the Case Act (1 USC 112b[a]) requiring congressional notification of all such agreements within 60 days.

What's the difference between a treaty and an executive agreement? Basically, if the deal is called a treaty, it requires a two-thirds vote; if it's not called a treaty, no vote is necessary. The State Department has published criteria separating the more technical agreements from the policy-significant matters that could become treaties, including a provision calling for consultations with the Senate on the matter. Sometimes, it's a close call. In 2002, the Russians insisted that the Strategic Offensive Reductions Treaty (SORT) be considered a treaty and sent to the Senate a for approval, a demand probably made to force the Bush administration to defend its Russia policy just six months after the president announced that the United States would withdraw from the 1972 Anti-Ballistic Missile Treaty, which the Russians wanted to preserve.[5] The 2007 security agreement with Iraq became less controversial when it imposed a deadline for U.S. troop withdrawals favored by antiwar congressmen, who dropped their insistence on considering it a treaty.

Treaties need to run the Senate's legislative gauntlet like any other bill. They are all referred to the Foreign Relations Committee, where hearings are usually held. A favorable vote there reports a resolution of ratification, which is what needs the two-thirds vote. During its consideration, the Senate may amend the treaty itself as well as the resolution of ratification, but any treaty amendment has to be accepted by other signatories. Such proposals are often *killer amendments* that can defeat the treaty under the guise of strengthening or clarifying it. If a treaty is not acted on in the first year or so, it goes back on the calendar, where it can languish until there are enough votes for passage. The Genocide Convention stayed on the Senate calendar for 40 years before finally being approved in 1988.

Noncontroversial treaties, like bilateral tax conventions, are often approved by voice vote. Controversial ones, however, can tie up the Senate for weeks and lead to complex maneuvering. The 1977 Panama Canal treaties were debated for six weeks and were ultimately approved only after the Panamanian leader accepted an actual amendment to the treaty text.

The Senate can attach reservations to the resolution of ratification that may or may not require consent by other signatories, depending on their substance. One of the more famous measures was the *Connally Reservation* to the treaty establishing the International Court of Justice to bar the court from having jurisdiction over domestic matters "as determined by the United States." In addition to reservations, the Senate sometimes adds *understandings* that are binding only on the United States, and *declarations* that are rhetorical and advisory. In 2010, action on the new START nuclear arms treaty with Russia, the Senate used a different formulation. Instead of reservations, it attached *conditions* that it said were "binding upon the [U.S.] President." In that case, the conditions included increased spending on programs to maintain the effectiveness of U.S. nuclear weapons capabilities.[6]

During treaty consideration, the Senate leadership often negotiates with the executive branch in order to win acceptance of such additions to the resolution of ratification precisely in order to build bridges for skeptical senators to cross over from opposition to support. The sponsors of amendments can then claim that they improved the treaty and thus justify their votes. This process is another way for the Senate to influence foreign policy.

The Nomination Tool

The Senate takes seriously its *advice and consent* power over nominations. From the earliest days of the republic, Senators told presidents whom they favored for various administration jobs. Proposed nominations are often quietly vetted with key senators, especially the chairman and ranking member of the committee with jurisdiction over the nomination. And senators are quite willing to give advice to nominees during their confirmation hearings on how they should perform their jobs.

The path to Senate confirmation is often long and difficult. The average time from inauguration to confirmation of senior officials has more than tripled since the 1960s, from less than three months in the Kennedy administration to more than eight months for recent presidents. Some of those delays are the fault of the White House, which can be slow to pick people and which requires personal background checks by the FBI and lengthy financial and other reports. The Senate then adds its own delays and a different set of required reports. In order to avoid possible conflicts of interest, the Armed Services Committee has long required senior Pentagon officials to divest themselves of stocks in defense companies and to recuse themselves from decisions involving companies they worked for. Delays in handling Pentagon civilian nominations have become so persistent that about 20% of political appointee posts are vacant at any one time.

The number of officials requiring confirmation has grown in recent years—to the point that there is now a push in the Senate to reduce that number. Currently 115 officials in national security positions—plus more than 120 ambassadors—require Senate confirmation. There are 44 in the State Department, 45 in the Defense Department, 8 at CIA, and 18 in Homeland Security. As recently as 1994, there were 27 in State, and in 1977, there were only 31 in DOD. Several senior members of the White House staff—though not the chief of staff or the national security adviser (NSA)—also require confirmation, including the budget director, the science adviser, the members of the Council of Economic Advisers, and the U.S. trade representative.

Lawmakers look at more than the nominee's qualifications for the job. They also consider the person's views on the programs they will administer and their willingness to support ideas favored by Congress. Since the 1950s, senior military officers have been required to promise to come before Congress and give their personal and professional views on military issues, even if those views are different from the president's.

Sometimes senators abuse their power over nominations by taking hostages, usually by placing a *hold* on a nomination until some demand is met. These holds were completely secret until 2007, but a new law trying to ban anonymous holds has been only partially effective. The demand might be for information, or for a certain policy decision, or for something totally unrelated to the responsibilities of the nominee facing delay. An Alabama senator blocked action on over 70 nominations in several departments in an effort to prevent budget cuts affecting his state. He eventually backed down. A Louisiana senator delayed action on the budget director pending an administration decision on offshore oil drilling. In 2011, the Senate adopted a minor reform to end secret holds on nominations but still allowing acknowledged holds.

> **Box 4.2**
>
> ## Inside View: Senators Are Human; Not All Are Trustworthy
>
> Congress has many means at its disposal to influence foreign policy, and one of its main vehicles for doing so is via the Senate Foreign Relations Committee. Established in 1816, this standing committee has considered a range of issues over the course of U.S. history. Committee members thus play integral roles in the development of U.S. foreign policy, and the committee can be equally influential on other members of Congress, though it is not without its own internal politics. Carl Marcy, chief of staff of the Senator Foreign Relations Committee from 1955 to 1973, describes some of the men he worked with and some of their personality quirks.
>
> *One of the most effective senators on the Committee during the time that I was there was Senator (Jacob) Javits (R-NY). He was effective because he had an organized mind. He could organize the miscellany of conversations that went on. As you will have seen from the transcripts of executive and mark-up sessions, a lot of things are thrown on the table and then usually the discussion would get to the point where the chairman (William Fulbright, D-AK) would turn to me and say, "Well, Carl, write it up," or "include it in the report." And it was very confusing to know what in the dickens the Committee had really done! Often times Senator Fulbright was more considerate of me and would ask Senator Javits to summarize the discussion, put it in a form that could be used. Javits was very good at that. . . .*
>
> *This business of the powerful chairman of the Foreign Relations Committee, implying that the chairman was a tyrant who controlled everything, when would the Committee meet, what subjects would come up, how people would act, what would come out. He wasn't that kind of person at all. He listened, he'd try to educate. At some point I remember Senator (Stuart) Symington (D-MO) coming to me after he had changed his attitude with respect to our involvement in Vietnam and said something to general effect that "Carl, I've changed my position, and the reason was because Bill educated me. I've learned." For a former secretary of the Air Force to have been exposed to the Fulbright school of foreign policy and admit that it had an impact on him, says much about Fulbright-Symington is not the kind of person anyone would be inclined to whip around at all; Senator Al Gore (Sr., D-TN) was very much the same way. What happens in a committee, or happened in that Committee, was that judgments are developed about how particular people, how senators will act in given situations.*
>
> *Senator Fulbright at one point said to me, "You can't count on Frank Church (D-ID). You can count on Senator Gore, you can count on Senator Symington." What he meant was that if Symington or Gore or (Bourke) Hickenlooper (R-IA) said they were going to do so-and-so, they'd do it. They would support him on the floor on an amendment or whatever it might be. Fulbright was never sure of Senator Church. Always the implication being, without his every [sic] having said it, that Senator Church was a bit of an opportunist. If that meant that he had to change his position or create a doubt about something maybe Fulbright had been led to believe he was firm on, he'd shift. I don't think of any others.*
>
> *Source:* Senate oral history, Carl Marcy, SFRC chief of staff 1955–1973, 175, 178 at www.senate.gov/artandhistory/history/resources/pdf/Marcy_interview_5.pdf.

Oversight Tools

Lawmakers also gain leverage over senior officials by their power of oversight. While no committee has jurisdiction over multiagency operations as such, each panel jealously guards its rights to investigate the departments within its purview. The defense committees oversee the Pentagon; the foreign policy committees oversee the State Department and foreign aid agencies; the intelligence committees oversee the intelligence community (IC); and the appropriations subcommittees oversee the spending by their respective agencies.

Since 1946, every congressional committee has had a requirement to "exercise continuous watchfulness" over programs and agencies within their jurisdiction. Oversight is usually defined as the review, monitoring, and supervision of federal agencies, programs, activities, and policy implementation. The ideal, at least to political scientists, is continuous and comprehensive oversight for purposes of better governance and not merely reelection or intimidation of the bureaucracy being overseen. It should be ongoing and thorough, forward-looking (anticipatory) as well as retrospective, with a focus on big, strategic issues and not merely minutiae. Lawmakers should uncover problems and legislate solutions rather than punishments. They should look beyond compliance issues and try to create incentives and rewards for better performance as well as developing organizational capacities to cope with emerging problems. Members should subordinate scoring political points to promoting better governance. And, of course, the executive branch should be fully forthcoming in providing information.

Besides uncovering past misdeeds, checking up on agencies can also help to prevent future ones. As former Congressman Lee Hamilton has said, "Congressional oversight helps keep federal bureaucracies on their toes."[7]

In practice, however, much oversight is of the *fire-alarm* type, responding to scandals and crises, rather than the regularized *police-patrol* variety. Oversight is a political act. Lack of oversight is also a political act. Everything Congress does or chooses not to do is suffused with political considerations and pregnant with political consequences. Political motivations take many forms—personal power and reelection, notably, but also the institutional power of a committee or a legislative chamber as well as partisan, ideological, or regional power. Even when committees investigate programs to determine their efficiency, effectiveness, and compliance with existing law, how and when they act have political consequences.

Studies have found that congressional oversight—especially measured in terms of frequency of hearings—is most active when the congressional body differs politically with the president.[8] Party loyalty, on the other hand, can mute investigative tendencies. During the Vietnam War, for example, the Foreign Relations Committee under Chairman J. William Fulbright (D-AR) held hearings critical of the conflict, while an Armed Services Committee panel gave military officers a chance to criticize restrictions on the air campaign against North Vietnam.

Lawmakers have several tools to conduct oversight. The most notable are committee hearings and investigations. Sometimes, special committees are established for the purpose, such as the joint panel created to review the Iran-Contra scandal during the Reagan administration, the joint hearings held into the firing of General Douglas MacArthur in 1951, and the 1930s hearings into *merchants of death* involvement in World War I. High-profile investigations of the IC by the Church and Pike Committees in 1975 and 1976 led to the establishment of permanent intelligence oversight committees in both the House and Senate.

At other times, the regular committees of jurisdiction investigate waste, fraud, and abuse in programs they authorize. Routine program hearings and crisis briefings by senior officials can all be occasions for productive oversight, even if that is not the formal purpose of the event. Committees can also request formal reviews by the Government Accountability Office (GAO) or other legislative support organizations. Since the 1940s, the House Appropriations Committee has had a surveys and investigations staff for detailed but quiet oversight. Congress has also created independent inspectors general in most departments and is a ready recipient for their reports.

Another tool for Congress, much resented by the executive branch, is a requirement for reports, one-time or regular, on a vast array of topics. The Pentagon complains that it has to submit more than 700 annual reports to Congress. The State Department says that it has to prepare 310 separate reports each year and that there is a lot of overlap, redundancy, and duplication among those reports. From the congressional perspective, such requirements may be a way of focusing attention on a problem area in order to stimulate the department to devise a better approach. Or, it may be an alternative to an immediate change in the law favored by other lawmakers.

For example, since 1986, the president has been required to submit a comprehensive report on national security strategy each year at the same time the presidential budget is submitted. Few presidents met the annual requirement, and Congress has held no hearings specifically on the content of the report in part because the official responsible for the report, just below the president, is the NSA, who by custom, is not allowed to testify before Congress. Nevertheless, the report forces action and policy coordination within the executive branch and provides Congress with a formal policy statement to use in evaluating administration programs.

Informal Tools

While hearings gain the most publicity—and are often designed for that purpose—Congress is also very influential over executive agencies by means of less formal devices, such as contacts by members and staff and the resulting meetings and briefings. Outside of the glare of cameras, legislators and administrators can share ideas and information and sometimes make deals separate from what the White House might want. Some observers see an *iron triangle* linking officials in the two branches of government with outside interest groups in cooperation, or collusion, over policy.

Congress also influences policy by raising issues to public consciousness and thus forcing the executive branch to respond with some kind of policy. What happens in medical research—where celebrities are recruited to publicize diseases and lobby for funds—also occurs on foreign policy issues when other celebrities draw attention to human rights issues in particular countries or to savage conflicts that don't receive daily news coverage.

Raising and framing issues occur in both branches, sometimes collaboratively, sometimes competitively. Members of Congress worked with some allies in the executive branch to focus attention on Soviet Jews in the 1970s, Bosnia and then Kosovo in the 1990s, and on the southern Sudan in the 2000s.

Consultations between senior officials and lawmakers occur all the time. Sometimes, they are used to float trial balloons or to try to obtain advance support for measures to be announced. Members routinely demand consultations prior to decisions, and they complain about being informed after the fact. As former Minnesota Governor Harold Stassen and Senator Arthur Vandenberg repeatedly said regarding Roosevelt and Truman foreign policy, "I don't care to be involved in the crash-landing unless I can be in on the take-off."

Perhaps the greatest congressional influence over executive branch decisions comes by way of the *law of anticipated reactions,* where expectations of opposition on Capitol Hill can sidetrack certain policy options in favor of steps that would not be opposed by lawmakers. In 2007, for example, General Peter Pace was denied a second two-year term as chairman of the JCS because lawmakers indicated that he would be sharply criticized in his confirmation hearing. Bill Clinton ruled out the use of ground troops in the conflict with Serbia over Kosovo because of a fear that ground combat would be strongly opposed on the Hill.

While Congress gets regularly praised—or blamed—for its efforts to influence, or meddling, in U.S. foreign policy, its impact has been broader and more significant than the typical examples of the Vietnam War and Cuba. (See Box 4.3.)

Congressional Culture

Members of Congress are politicians with all that implies. They thrive on confrontation and publicity and so are quite willing to turn minor misunderstandings into major clashes, either among themselves or with the executive branch. Senior members have relatively safe seats, freeing them somewhat from the shifting sands of public opinion but also allowing them to pursue their fixed ideas and bumper-sticker slogans. Seniority is rewarded with power in both chambers, especially committee chairmanships. But, that seniority often reflects issue involvement and familiarity far in excess of what political appointees bring to their positions. Long-serving members and staff are quite willing to remind the new secretaries and assistant secretaries that the big ideas they advocate were actually tried and failed two decades before.[9]

> **Box 4.3**
>
> ## Additional Examples of Congressional Impact on National Security
>
> In addition to the high-visibility actions relating to war and peace and U.S. relations with Russia, China, and the Middle East, Congress has succeeded in influencing U.S. policies on many of the major national security issues since the 1940s:
>
> - Framed the debate and urged the creation of NATO
> - Originated ideas for what became the Peace Corps
> - Provided aid to Franco's Spain to reduce its alienation from the West
> - Created rules for high technology trade with communist nations that led to the creation of the Coordinating Committee for Multilateral Export Controls (COCOM)
> - Elevated the policy priority of human rights issues
> - Banned military assistance to Augusto Pinochet's regime in Chile
> - Aided mujaheddin fighting in Afghanistan
> - Pressured U.S. citizens to stop funding the Irish Republican Army
> - Pressured the administration to intervene to protect Bosnian Muslims
> - Pressured the administration to recognize Vietnam
> - Urged the overthrow of the Saddam Hussein regime in Iraq
> - Banned trade in *conflict diamonds*
>
> Source: Ralph G. Carter and James M. Scott, *Choosing to Lead: Understanding Congressional Foreign Policy Entrepreneurs* (Durham, NC: Duke University Press, 2009), 3–5.

Party identification and loyalty are the basis for congressional organization. The parties decide who sits on which committees and who gets punished for breaking with the leadership on a key vote. In recent decades, the Democratic and Republican members of Congress have become increasingly polarized with fewer centrists and more frequent party-line votes even on relatively minor issues. While there is a tradition of saying that "politics stops at the water's edge," the historical practice has varied widely, from the cooperation in containing communism in the 1940s to the bitter fights over the Vietnam War and relations with Russia in later years. Despite all the incentives for party loyalty, some members, especially the more senior ones, become institutionalists, staunch defenders of congressional prerogatives even against presidents of their own party.

Legislators are deal makers, not managers or decisive executives. Former governors who go to Congress regularly lament their inability to get things done quickly. The default position in a legislature is often to study the matter further, sometimes in a search for more definitive information that would make their choices easier, sometimes in the hope of avoiding an action that may prove unpopular. Politicians may be even more risk averse than the citizenry as a whole. Deal makers thrive on compromise, so they hedge their positions as long as possible and try to avoid outcomes that anger sizable segments of voters. They prefer both/and results to either/or; they enjoy addition more than subtraction, especially when it comes to budgets.

Members are often very jealous of their constitutional powers. As the statement by Speaker Nathaniel Macon quoted at the head of this chapter indicates, Congress believes it is essential to civilian control of the military and of the president's use of force. They also insist on consultation, not just being informed of presidential actions on foreign policy, for they share the view of Harold Stassen and Arthur Vandenberg, also quoted at the start of this chapter, that Congress wants to be in on the policy takeoff and not called only just before a crash-landing.

Congress is torn between assertiveness and deference to the president on foreign policy. As former Congressman Lee Hamilton (D-IN) has said, "Its tendency too often has been either to defer to the president or to engage in foreign policy haphazardly."[10] Humorist Will Rogers, writing in the 1930s, had another explanation: "If you don't scare Congress, they go fishing; if you do scare them, they go crazy."

House Culture

Party differences are especially evident in the House of Representatives, which runs by strict majority rule. The speaker's party almost always gets its way, not least because the Rules Committee can change the rules on any measure by simple majority vote, thereby structuring the legislative process so that the majority party wins.

Representatives are on fewer committees than senators, and they usually become quite knowledgeable on the matters within their jurisdictions. House culture supports cosponsorship of legislation as a means of issue promotion in contrast with the more individualistic Senate.

Their two-year terms also mean that members are continuously in campaign mode, raising money, listening to voters, and trying to appeal to their constituents. Representatives have even greater incentives than senators to be partisan and confrontational.

On national security and other foreign policy matters, the House is more closely attuned to whatever the current public sentiments are regarding those issues—critical of the Pentagon sometimes and quite deferential at other times; ready to endorse the most extreme but popular measures against overseas adversaries; sometimes quite parochial in support of local ethnic interests, such as whether to condemn Turkish genocide of Armenians a century ago.

Senate Culture

Senators have the luxury of six-year terms, giving them more time and political freedom to develop issue expertise in areas they deem important. They also have greater prestige and media attention, especially on foreign policy questions. As a result, every senator hires staff and uses opportunities to express positions on the broad range of national security issues, whether or not they serve on one of the committees with formal jurisdiction.

Senate rules give enormous power to individual members. Most legislative action is based on *unanimous consent* agreements. These understandings do not require agreement on all matters of substance but rather on the process to be followed on a given measure, particularly the offering of amendments and the length of debate. Without prior agreement, bills and nominations can be debated forever unless and until 60 Senators vote to end debate, called *cloture*.

Prolonged debates, called *filibusters*, have been used more frequently in recent years on all kinds of measures. Even the threat of a filibuster can force the leadership to sidetrack a bill or change an amendment. Efforts in 2011 to modify the filibuster rules fell short when the party leaders, each worried about setting precedents that might hurt them after the next election, agreed only to minor rules changes and a nonbinding gentleman's agreement to show more restraint. It is noteworthy that it took a foreign policy dispute to force the Senate into adopting its first rule allowing the cutoff of debate. When a handful of senators successfully blocked a bill to arm U.S. merchant ships threatened by German submarines in 1917 only a few days before the United States declared war on Germany, the outcry was so strong that the Senate adopted the original version of Rule XXII allowing cloture by a two-thirds vote.

Unlike the House, the Senate has no *germaneness rule* except in limited circumstances. What that means in practice is that any subject can be brought up at any time. Foreign policy measures can be offered whenever the proponent gets recognized, even if the pending bill deals with education or agriculture or commerce. That allows the Senate to be responsive to fast-breaking events but also creates legislative confusion.

While the Senate has been less partisan than the House, that seems to be changing with changes in the national parties and the election to the Senate of former House members, who are more comfortable with partisan clashes and less deferential to civility traditions.

Committee Cultures and Dynamics

Most congressional action on foreign policy is handled by committees of jurisdiction, especially the defense, foreign policy, and appropriations committees, plus the intelligence and trade committees for those issues. By long-standing precedents, however, several other committees also have control over other legislation affecting U.S. foreign policy, including agricultural exports, exports of security-related items, foreign direct investment in U.S. firms, the EOP and NSC, and government reorganization and reform.

Whatever their jurisdictions, committee chairs are extraordinarily turf conscious and defensive of their prerogatives. It took an unusual degree of comity for the House Foreign Affairs and Armed Services Committees to work together in overseeing the combined civil–military provincial reconstruction teams in Iraq and Afghanistan in 2007–2009. It was surprising in 2009–2011 to have both Secretary of State Hillary Clinton and Secretary of Defense Robert Gates appear together before committees that nominally have jurisdiction only over one of them. Even though executive branch foreign policy making is done jointly through the interagency NSC process, congressional committees still largely refuse to work together on interagency matters because of their jurisdictional jealousies.

Committees act when the chairs want them to act and thus in response to the chairs' interests and political objectives. Rules do give the minority some say in naming witnesses, but only the chair can decide whether to hold a hearing on a given issue. Senator John Warner (R-VA), chairman of the Senate Armed Services Committee, held six hearings on the Abu Ghraib prison scandal, but his House counterpart held only one, saying he didn't want to undermine public support for the war in Iraq by holding more sessions.

The defense committees frequently fight over particular programs and occasional policies like allowing gays in uniform, but they have united each year since 1961 to produce a defense authorization bill and shepherd it through floor debate and conference with the House. The House Armed Services Committee has long had a combined staff, while most congressional committees have clearly defined majority and minority staff.

Because foreign policy committees have weak records of producing actual legislation—no foreign aid authorization bill has been enacted since 1986, for example—they have less experience with compromising to produce a single major bill. The chairs and ranking members of the Senate Foreign Relations Committee (SFRC), however, have traditions of cooperating on a wide range of issues and trying to minimize their differences on other foreign policy questions.

A major tool of member education and oversight is overseas travel. Congressional delegations (CODELs) are often feared by embassy staff, who worry about catering to the egos and demands of lawmakers, and criticized by the media as *junkets*. While some congressional travel seems wasteful or at least questionable, visits to war zones in recent years have given a great many lawmakers invaluable firsthand knowledge of the conflicts in the Middle East. Congressional visits may also help U.S. diplomacy by letting lawmakers play *bad cop* to foreign governments reluctant to believe the seriousness of American demands for changed policies.

Why Congress Acts That Way

These are the ways Congress acts to shape U.S. foreign policy. The results can be criticized and defended, depending on one's perspective. Lee Hamilton, former congressman and longtime House Foreign Affairs Committee chairman, acknowledges the legislative branch's deficiencies in dealing with foreign policy. "Congress often fails to act in a constructive manner, views foreign policy through domestic political lenses, acts unilaterally or at the instigation of special interest groups, and shirks many of its foreign policy responsibilities."[11] But, he also notes the strengths of Congress in representing the diversity of views and interests of the American people and serving as a prod and check on the president.

In fact, congressional weaknesses in foreign policy mirror those of any democracy, as Alexis de Tocqueville noted in the 1830s. "Foreign politics demand scarcely any of those qualities which are peculiar to a democracy; they require, on the contrary, the perfect use of almost all those in which it is deficient. . . . [A] democracy can only with great difficulty regulate the details of an important undertaking, persevere in a fixed design, and work out its execution in spite of serious obstacles. It cannot combine its measure with secrecy or await their consequences with patience."[12]

Yes, indeed, Congress is shortsighted, erratic, prone to changes of course in the face of problems, congenitally unwilling to keep secrets, and impatient of results. Presidents, except in reelection years, are a little less subject to these pressures. They can have slightly longer time horizons, maintain steady courses despite problems, impose secrecy, and wait more patiently for favorable results.

The fundamental explanation for congressional behavior is politics and the dynamics of the American political system.

Member Motivations

Members of Congress are human beings engaged in the very public realm of politics. (See Box 4.2.) They are diverse in background and experience, but most share an ambition to promote good policies and to be recognized for that work. As scholar David Mayhew has written, "With the member's job goes a license to persuade, connive, hatch ideas, propagandize, assail enemies, vote, build coalitions, shepherd coalitions, and in general cut a figure in public affairs."[13] Most want to be reelected, and they work hard to make that possible and to avoid actions that would make it more difficult. But, electoral motivations are only part of the story, sometimes a misleading part.[14]

Working on foreign policy issues is sometimes hard to justify to the voters back home. Senator Charles Percy (R-IL) attributed his defeat to an opponent who said that Percy was "more interested in the Middle East than the Middle West."[15] But another Midwesterner who served as chairman of the Foreign Relations Committee, Richard Lugar (R-IN), had little trouble winning reelection five times—until his 2012 defeat—in spite of his extensive work on foreign policy issues.

Lawmakers have freedom to choose how to spend their legislative time. They have to raise money, of course, and stay in touch with the voters, but what issues they dig into and what committees they serve on are within their choice. They may be interested in Israel because they are Jewish, or many of their constituents are, or they have visited the area, or they see Israel as a key to U.S. security and Middle East peace—for any or all of these reasons. They may be interested in childhood diseases in Africa because of medical training, or travel there, or membership in a nongovernmental organization

(NGO) that has programs there, or because they know some constituents active in those issues. They may be interested in better equipment to protect troops from improvised explosive devices (IEDs) because of their own prior military service, or because of bases or contractors in their districts, or because they believe the issue deserves more attention.

The nature of contemporary U.S. politics makes them, as Tom Mann and Norm Ornstein say, "independent entrepreneurs, each with an autonomous electoral base, who will not allow other members, even leaders, an excessive degree of control over their careers."[16] Candidates for Congress may receive some money from official party sources, but they largely have to rely on their own efforts. Once in office, they chart their own courses, whether to be party loyalists or mavericks, mirrors or leaders of public opinion.

Public Opinion

With rare exception, the only public views that really matter to any lawmaker are those of the voters back home. And, few of them have much interest in most national security and foreign policy issues. Former Congressman Steve Solarz (D-NY) reported the typical experience when he spoke to a black church group. Afterward, they gently reminded him, "What you said about South Africa was well and good, but we mostly care about what's going on in Coney Island."[17]

War and peace issues are more salient to the public than, say, policy toward Burma or counterdrug programs in South America. But even there, as Bruce Jentleson discovered long ago, Americans are "pretty prudent" in judging military actions in terms of their primary objectives. The U.S. public generally views use of force as a last resort after diplomacy, economic pressure and sanctions, and military aid and arms sales to possible surrogates. Americans also prefer limited operations and air strikes to ground combat forces. They are willing to support use of force to stop aggression and provide humanitarian aid but not to bring about internal political change.[18]

On the other hand, one of the greatest constraints on lawmakers who favor an active, civilian-led foreign policy is the overwhelming public opposition to foreign aid, which many people think consumes up to 20% of the U.S. budget when the actual figure is 1%.

Lawmakers may point to public opinion to justify some of their positions, but legislative activists are more concerned with shaping public views than reacting to them. Only a relatively small number of members tend to be active on foreign policy issues, but they are policy entrepreneurs who really care about their causes and can't wait for the administration to act. Ralph Carter and James Scott say these members are expert and persistent and are not especially driven by constituent pressures. These entrepreneurs tend to be from the party opposite the president, and they tend to serve on the defense, foreign policy, or intelligence committees.[19] It is often easier for senators to be active on foreign policy issues because of the fewer constraints in the Senate rules.

Congressional Inputs to the National Security Council System

Congress created the NSC and the NSC system in 1947 and has continued to try to influence national security policy by legislative action ever since. One key purpose of the original act was to force the executive branch to integrate and coordinate all of its activities—military, diplomatic, and economic—that affected national security. As is often the case, lawmakers thought that was best achieved by giving designated stakeholders seats at the table next to the president so that their points of view would not be overlooked.

That pattern has been followed in recent years as Congress added statutory members to the NSC and to the JCS and created the Homeland Security Council. It was echoed in other advisory panels that Congress created or supported with funding, such as the National Economic Council (NEC), the president's Foreign Intelligence Advisory Board, and second-opinion panels reviewing the Pentagon's Quadrennial Defense Review.

Just as Congress hoped to impose a particular decision process on the president by establishing the NSC, it tried to structure the processes for national security strategy, defense planning, arms sales, treaty commitments, intelligence operations, and even international economic transactions. Some have been followed, others mostly ignored.

Congress also forced structural reforms on the executive branch. First, it created and later disbanded the Arms Control and Disarmament Agency to give bureaucratic voice to arms control proposals. Later, it created SOCOM in order to build a counterterrorist capability that was a low priority for the Pentagon. The reforms of the 1986 Goldwater–Nichols Act were as steadfastly opposed by many in the Pentagon as the original 1947 act was. The navy and its friends especially feared that greater central control would weaken its independence. Lawmakers created the CIA in large part to avoid another Pearl Harbor, and when the CIA failed to prevent the 9/11 attacks, Congress created a superior office, the director of National Intelligence, to prevent another 9/11. Congress also forced a reluctant executive branch to establish a new Department of Homeland Security (DHS) for the same purpose.

In addition to these structural changes, Congress has also tried to reform some of the processes used for particular national security issues. One of the most significant reforms was the 1974 Hughes–Ryan amendment on covert operations by the CIA. Prior to its enactment, presidents could *plausibly deny* that they had any personal knowledge of CIA operations that ranged from dirty tricks to the overthrow of governments. Oversight by Congress was weak, with many lawmakers willing to be kept in the dark. Responding to disclosures of long-secret CIA operations, the Hughes–Ryan amendment required the president personally to approve the activity in what is called a *finding* and to promptly notify the relevant congressional committees. The amendment was recodified in 1990 with provisions for notifying only eight members of the congressional leadership in special circumstances. This basic process has been acceptable to both branches.

The Effort to Legislate War Powers

Despite the clear language of the Constitution giving Congress the power to declare war, lawmakers over the years have varied in their interpretations and assertions of congressional war powers. Congress has actually declared war in only five major conflicts, though it has authorized the use of force an additional 15 times. (See Table 4.2.) Lawmakers also tolerated and funded numerous presidential military operations without raising war powers issues.[20]

Prior to the availability of jet aircraft, ballistic missiles, and nuclear weapons, getting into war was a slow-motion process, requiring the mobilization and dispatch of soldiers and sailors. The United States and other nations felt few restraints on using military force to solve diplomatic and economic problems without triggering major combat. While some lawmakers criticized U.S. military interventions in Central America and the Caribbean in the late 20th century, Congress as an institution went along, as it did with the suppression of rebels in the Philippines at the start of the 20th century.

After 1945, however, lawmakers generally agreed that the president needed to be able to act quickly to defend the nation, perhaps within the half-hour flight time of a nuclear armed missile from the Soviet Union. They supported the development of warning radars and other technologies

Table 4.2 Congressional Authorizations of the Use of Force, 1798–2011

YEAR	ENEMY/OBJECT	PROVISIONS
1798	France	"Subdue, seize, and take any armed French vessel" on the high seas
1802	Tripoli	"Subdue, seize and make prize" of Tripoli's ships and goods
1812	Britain	Declaration of war: The president "authorized to use the whole land and naval force" of the United States
1815	Algeria	Allowed "acts of precaution or hostility"
1846	Mexico	Declaration of war: The president "authorized to employ the militia, naval and military forces" and accept volunteers
1858	Paraguay	Authorized "such measures and use such force" as may be necessary to obtain "just satisfaction" in a dispute
1861	Confederacy	To enforce the laws and suppress rebellion
1898	Spain	1) Authorization of force issued against Spain; 2) Declaration of war: The president "directed and empowered to use the entire land and naval forces" of the United States

(Continued)

Table 4.2	(Continued)	
YEAR	ENEMY/OBJECT	PROVISIONS
1914	Mexico	"President is justified in the employment of the armed forces of the United States to enforce his demands"
1917	Germany, Austria–Hungary	Declaration of war: The president "authorized and directed to employ the entire naval and military forces" and "resources of the government"
1941–1942	Japan, Germany, Bulgaria, Hungary, and Romania	Declaration of war: The president "authorized and directed to employ the entire naval and military forces" and "resources of the government"
1955	Defense of Formosa (Taiwan)	The president authorized to use force "as he deems necessary for protecting the security of Formosa"
1957	Threats to Middle East	To preserve independence and integrity, the United States is "prepared to use armed forces to assist [nations facing] armed aggression from any" communist-controlled country
1962	Cuba	United States is "determined to prevent by whatever means may be necessary, including the use of arms" threats by Cuba
1964	Defense of Southeast Asia Treaty Organization (SEATO) nations	United States is "prepared, as the President determines, to take all necessary steps, including the use of armed force" to assist SEATO members "in defense of freedom"
1983	Defense of Lebanon	Authorized U.S. forces in UN peacekeeping mission for 18 months; they "will not engage in combat" but can take "protective measures"
1991	Iraq	Force authorized to obtain compliance with United Nations Security Council (UNSC) resolutions, but the president must determine that all peaceful means had been used and more would not be successful
2001	9/11 attackers	Authorized "all necessary and appropriate force against those [who] planned, authorized, committed, or aided" the 9/11 attacks
2002	Iraq	The president "authorized to use the [U.S.] armed forces" to "defend [U.S.] national security . . . against the continuing threat posed by Iraq" and to enforce UNSC resolutions

While Congress has declared war in only 5 conflicts, it has authorized the use of force on 15 additional occasions. In most cases, the congressional action was at the request of the president. In some cases, however, Congress took the initiative, and the president acquiesced: the first authorization of force against Spain in 1898 (later followed by a requested declaration of war); Cuba, 1962; and Lebanon, 1983. Many lawmakers felt that Lyndon Johnson (LBJ) had abused his authority under the 1964 Tonkin Gulf resolution, and they fashioned the 1973 War Powers Resolution to create a regular process for congressional involvement in use of force decisions.

Source: Charles A. Stevenson, *Congress at War: The Politics of Conflict Since 1789* (Washington, DC: Potomac Books, 2007), 30–31.

allowing the United States to have a hair-trigger defense capability. They abandoned their reluctance to have a large standing army and put the United States on a permanent war footing with a large army, navy, marine corps, and air force. Congress also created a diverse, if not duplicative, nuclear weapons capability deployed on aircraft, ships, submarines, and underground.

In response to presidential requests, Congress also approved laws authorizing force in certain contingencies. This was done in 1955 for Formosa (Taiwan) and in 1957 for the Middle East, where troops were later sent to Lebanon. Lawmakers also approved contingent force measures against Cuba in 1962 and Vietnam in 1964 (the Tonkin Gulf Resolution).

But, when the Vietnam war involved more than half a million American troops, many of them draftees, Congress began rethinking what it had done in 1964 and searching for a way to avoid a repetition of what by then was considered a mistake. Leading members of the Senate and House drafted bills codifying a new war powers procedure and ultimately approved a compromise, the War Powers Resolution, that became Public Law 93–148 despite President Nixon's veto.

The law insists that "the President in every possible instance shall consult with Congress before introducing United States Armed Forces into hostilities or into situations where imminent involvement in hostilities is clearly indicated by the circumstances." It also requires a report to Congress within 48 hours when U.S. troops "equipped for combat" are sent abroad in large numbers or into hostile situations. Recent presidents have generally followed these provisions, although the reports have been submitted *consistent* with the War Powers Resolution rather than *pursuant* to it, a lawyerly distinction denying that the reports were legally required but suggesting that Congress ought to be happy with receiving them anyway.

A compromise most troubling to some members who felt that Congress should approve any major military operation in advance except time-urgent self-defense was that the War Powers Resolution allowed the president to use force for 60 days pending a congressional vote to authorize the operation. If Congress failed to act, he could still take another 30 days if the president declared an "unavoidable military necessity."

What greatly undermined the act's effectiveness, however, was a Supreme Court decision in 1983 *(INS v. Chadha,* 462 U.S. 919) outlawing the use of legislative vetoes that were not subject to presidential vetoes, thus requiring reliance on a two-thirds vote to override the chief executive. The original War Powers Resolution had provided for a concurrent resolution of both houses, requiring only majority votes, as sufficient to force the withdrawal of combat troops. No sitting president since 1973 has ever declared that he considered the law binding on his administration, further weakening the act. Efforts to amend the law have been unsuccessful, as were proposals to repeal it. The most widely discussed alternative is a new law simply requiring presidential consultation.

It's clear now that the 1973 law was based on a faulty assumption that Congress would be willing to vote to stop an unpopular war, either immediately or after 60 days. While theoretically possible, it has not been true historically. The vote cutting of funds for the Vietnam War applied only to air operations and only after ground combat troops had been withdrawn. The cutoff of funds for operations in Somalia merely codified a presidential commitment to complete withdrawals within six months. The more relevant example is the war with Mexico in 1846. Although both houses voted overwhelmingly for a declaration of war, many members opposed the conflict on strategic grounds but said that they couldn't bring themselves to vote against sending guns and bullets to General Taylor's troops, who were already engaged in battle.

The War Powers Resolution was an effort to limit presidential warmaking while preserving a role for Congress. It tried to balance recognition of some need for immediate military action with the constitutional requirements for congressional authorization. The law, however, was weakened by presidential refusal to concede its force and effect despite the submission of reports and by Congress's own unwillingness to insist on compliance.

Inconsistency in Practice on War Powers

With the law still on the books, Congress has reacted inconsistently to various uses of force in recent decades. As Lee Hamilton explained, "Congress frequently prefers to play Monday morning quarterback, letting the president make the tough military decisions, then criticizing or praising him depending on the results."[21] Put another way, Congress and the American people like short, successful wars but do not like any operation that is prolonged or unsuccessful.

Another variation in congressional behavior is that members of the president's party tend to argue for executive discretion and members of the opposition repeat the arguments about congressional war powers. There have been some exceptions, like Senator Robert C. Byrd (D-WV), who regularly argued that only Congress could authorize major military operations. But, most members tended to defer to the president on substantive and practical grounds or criticized his actions only when problems arose.

The only times Congress has approved the use of force abroad in advance as envisioned by the War Powers Resolution, and with presidential endorsement, were for peacekeepers in Lebanon in 1983, to drive Iraqi forces from Kuwait in 1991, for action against those involved in the 9/11 attacks in 2001, and for war on Iraq in 2002.

Congress failed to pass measures on Somalia in 1993–1994 until it wrote into law President Clinton's pledge to remove U.S. troops by a certain date. It took many votes but failed to enact legislation on Haiti in 1994 or Kosovo in 1999 or Libya in 2011. In 1995, Congress was on the verge of passing a bill supporting military action against Serbia over President Clinton's veto when peace talks were started and proved successful.

In fact, the War Powers Act has had a major impact on presidential behavior despite its uncertain legal standing and inconsistent legislative support.

Almost every major military operation since 1973 has been designed and conducted within the 60-day limits—except for the conflicts specifically authorized by Congress. No president has initiated prolonged combat operations without seeking or at least welcoming congressional support.²²

Tying the President's Hands

Congress has also asserted itself in setting war aims and restrictions on combat in those measures it has passed. The 1983 war powers authorization for Lebanon was limited to 18 months, and troops were allowed only a defensive mission of backstopping the Lebanese army and protecting themselves. After the tragic barracks bombing that killed 241 marines, President Reagan decided to withdraw the troops prematurely.

The 1991 authorization for war against Iraq was limited to enforcing various UNSC resolutions, which only required a withdrawal from Kuwait, not regime change in Baghdad.

In 2001, the White House sought language that would have authorized preventive attacks against any and all terrorists. Congress refused to go along with that blank check and limited the authorization of force to people and nations involved in the 9/11 attacks.

An effort to limit the 2002 authorization for renewed war against Iraq failed, but the final bill did require regular reports as well as a presidential certification that "diplomatic or other peaceful means" had failed.²³

Congress has tried to tie the president's hands on other occasions as well. Lawmakers declared war on Spain in 1898 but prohibited annexation of Cuba, as detailed in the case study for this chapter. They limited U.S. arms sales in the 1930s until Germany's Adolph Hitler launched an all-out war. They barred Franklin Roosevelt (FDR) from sending draftees outside the Western hemisphere—until war was declared after Pearl Harbor. They prohibited U.S. ground combat operations in Laos or Thailand after 1969 but neglected to include Cambodia, which Nixon invaded in 1970 until forced to withdraw by another law. After U.S. combat troops were largely withdrawn from Vietnam, Congress set a deadline for the end of all U.S. bombing raids in Southeast Asia. Congress also prohibited U.S. military operations in Angola in 1975 and tried to ban aid to the Contras in Nicaragua in the 1980s.²⁴

While these examples demonstrate congressional willingness to limit presidential options and otherwise guide U.S. policy, they contrast with the usual practice of allowing presidents broad freedom of action in foreign policy. Only occasionally, and for reasons that may be political rather than substantive, does Congress actively fight what the president wants to do. Of course, it always reserves the right to kibbitz and criticize.

Should Politics Stop at Water's Edge?

Bipartisanship seems to be the last refuge not of scoundrels but of beleaguered presidents and their supporters. Calls for suspending the usual political infighting when it comes to foreign policy are usually made when a policy is under attack, not before it is crafted and announced. In short, saying politics should stop at the water's edge is primarily an argument to suppress dissent.

On the other hand, there is no doubt that a nation is stronger when it speaks with a single voice. The absence of dissent suggests that a policy will be sustainable over time and that corollary actions can follow logically. Unity of purpose and unity of action can lead to successful outcomes.

How to get from disagreement to consensus, from uncertainty to clarity of purpose, from political gamesmanship to genuine collaboration, is an art, not a science. The U.S. political system has more incentives for conflict than for cooperation, especially in Congress. Foreign policy is not exempt from debate, for members remember well Professor Edward Corwin's famous observation, "The Constitution . . . is an invitation to struggle for the privilege of directing American foreign policy."[25]

***

Congress has many tools to shape U.S. foreign policy, most notably the power of the purse through appropriations but also by writing legislation with substantive requirements, procedural rules, or advisory opinions. Lawmakers also influence policy by raising issues for public debate and by investigating U.S. programs. The Senate's special powers over treaties and nominations give it tools to obstruct or delay presidential plans. Congress has been inconsistent in exercising its war power. While formally authorizing the use of force on at least 20 occasions, it has often failed either to support or oppose many military operations in recent decades.

Case Study: Congress and Cuban Independence, 1898

This case tells of a Congress eager for war and a reluctant president. It also shows how Congress can set war aims that affect the conduct of military operations and the ultimate peace settlement. Congress used its formal legislative tools to make war inevitable, to condition how it was fought, and to limit what America gained as a result. The president abided by those conditions as commander-in-chief.

Congress pushed President William McKinley into war with Spain in 1898. He hoped to avoid war until the very last minute but could not resist the public and political pressures to fight.

A rebellion against Spain and for independence began in Cuba in 1895. When the Cleveland administration sided with Spain, congressional Republicans responded by passing nonbinding resolutions urging recognition of the insurgent government. Both Republican and Democratic conventions in 1896 approved platforms favoring the Cubans, with the Republicans calling for U.S. efforts to secure Cuban independence. The popular press had aroused U.S. public opinion in support of the Cuban insurgents and against the repressive acts by Spain. Politicians of both parties echoed a romantic view of the rebels and the virtues of independence from Spain.

McKinley won the White House, and the Republicans retained control of Congress. No action on Cuba occurred for several months, however, because House Speaker Thomas Reed (R-ME) strongly opposed Cuban independence. By early 1898, rioting in Havana and brutal repression by Spanish soldiers brought the issue back onto the front pages of American newspapers. On February 14, both houses of Congress passed resolutions calling on the president to publish the reports of the U.S. consuls in Cuba—reports that the foreign policy committee members already knew depicted the suffering of the Cuban people and the failures of the Spanish military.

Two days later, an explosion on the U.S. battleship *Maine* killed 266 soldiers. The ship had been sent to Havana harbor in case it might be needed to evacuated U.S. citizens. Later analysis determined that the damage came from an internal explosion rather than from a Spanish mine or torpedo, but suspicions at the time put added pressure on McKinley to act. In early March, he told lawmakers that America was not prepared for war and that he needed money and time to get ready.

On March 7 and 8, with great enthusiasm but virtually no debate, Congress voted $50 million for national defense, giving the president full discretion on how to spend it. This was a staggering 60% increase above what had been voted for the army and the navy only a few months before. McKinley's supporters called the funds a *peace measure*.

Still the president hesitated. Though he drafted a message to Congress, he locked it in his safe to allow more time for diplomacy. Meanwhile, backbencher Republicans talked with Democrats about joining to declare war regardless of McKinley's position. This forced the president to send his message on April 11.

The message did not satisfy lawmakers. It criticized the Spanish for their military actions and described the suffering of the Cuban people. But, it did not call for war. It even opposed Cuban independence, arguing that that would limit U.S. freedom of action. Instead, McKinley said, "I ask the Congress to authorize and empower the President to take measures to secure a full and final termination of hostilities between the Government of Spain and the people of Cuba, and to secure in the island the establishment of a stable government, capable of maintaining order and observing its international obligations, insuring peace and tranquillity [sic] and the security of its citizens as well as our own, and to use the military and naval forces of the United States as may be necessary for these purposes."

Democrats in the House responded with a resolution recognizing Cuban independence, but the Republican majority voted to authorize the president to use U.S. forces "to intervene at once to stop the war in Cuba" and seek to establish "a stable and independent government" by the free action of the Cuban people

The Senate took six more days to debate and vote on its alternative, which became, with some minor changes, the final version sent to the president. A key provision added by the Senate was the amendment of the silver Republican from Colorado, Henry Teller, that declared that the United States would not seek to annex Cuba. Although many interventionists, including businessmen eager to protect their investments in Cuba or to import Cuban products tariff free, favored eventual U.S. control, others strongly opposed annexation. Southerners did not want to grant citizenship to the nonwhite, non-English-speaking people of the island. Lawmakers like Teller, from sugar beet growing areas, did not want competition from Cuban sugar, which then was under a stiff tariff. Another argument against annexation was the concern that the United States might incur the obligation to repay the $400 million bond issue Spain used to finance its military efforts, pledging Cuban revenues.

The law signed by McKinley on April 20 called for the recognition of Cuban independence, using language from the Declaration of Independence: "[T]he people of the Island of Cuba are, and of right ought to be, free and independent." The measure demanded an end to the Spanish government and "directed and empowered [the president] to use the entire land and naval forces of the United States . . . to carry these resolutions into effect." It also included the Teller amendment denying any intent to control Cuba after pacification.

Despite his earlier reservations, McKinley signed the joint resolution and notified Madrid. When the Spanish government, as expected, rejected the U.S. demands, Congress voted a formal declaration of war on April 25.

The war ended quickly, with Spanish surrender of Cuba on July 17 and of the Philippines on August 13. The peace treaty, signed on December 10, gave Cuba independence but gave the United States control of Puerto Rico and the Philippines. Many in Congress, especially anti-imperialist Democrats, had second thoughts about the war and its consequences. The peace treaty was approved in the Senate by only a two-vote margin on February 6, 1899. Congress had succeeded in limiting U.S. war aims but had not fully realized that America would now face the burdens of empire.

This case shows Congress taking the initiative on a major foreign policy matter, passing a huge bill for unspecified military expansion, forcing the president to act prematurely, and then limiting the war aims of the conflict. It also shows both parties maneuvering for political advantages with an aroused public. A Congress determined to act, and able to pass binding legislation, can dominate a hesitant president.

Sources: Ernest R. May, *Imperial Democracy* (New York: Harcourt, Brace, 1961); Paul S. Holbo, "Presidential Leadership in Foreign Affairs: William McKinley and the Turpie-Foraker Amendment," *The American Historical Review*, vol. 72, no. 4 (July 1967), 1321–1335; *The Congressional Record*.

Case Study: Congress Struggles With Apartheid and South Africa

In this case, bipartisan majorities in Congress forced a major change in the administration's foreign policy, going so far as to override a presidential veto. Lawmakers chose moral concerns over strategic arguments and insisted on prompt action against a pariah regime rather than sustained pressure and the hope of eventual change.

Starting in 1948, the South African government imposed racial separation—*apartheid* in Afrikaans—in a series of laws. Among other things, those laws imposed official racial identity on all citizens, prohibited mixed-race marriages, set aside geographic zones where designated groups could reside, and segregated schools and public transportation. Later on, separate Bantu Homelands were created, and blacks were allowed into white areas only as temporary guests.

U.S. policy makers largely ignored the racial repression in South Africa because the white minority government was an anticommunist bulwark on a continent where the Soviet Union and its allies were supporting nationalist independence movements. Newly inaugurated President Ronald Reagan reflected this attitude in a 1981 interview: "Can we abandon a country that has stood by us in every war we've ever fought, a country that strategically is essential to the free world in its production of minerals we all must have and so forth?"

Reagan's predecessor Jimmy Carter had condemned apartheid and ordered compliance with the arms embargo voted in 1977 by the UNSC, but his administration resisted efforts by the UN and the U.S. Congress to impose economic sanctions. The only restriction voted into law was a 1978 amendment requiring U.S. firms seeking Export-Import Bank (Ex-Im) financing to demonstrate that they followed "fair employment practices" in South Africa.

The Reagan administration adopted a policy labeled *constructive engagement* that avoided public pressure but sought to encourage reform by the South African government. The U.S. government relaxed the terms of the Carter arms embargo by allowing sales of some nonlethal items like food, clothing, computers, and chemical and transportation equipment. And the P.W. Botha government in South Africa made some modest reforms, such as including colored and Asian representation in a tricameral parliament that still excluded blacks. Protests erupted in black townships starting in September 1984 and were brutally suppressed in full view of the international news media.

Congress had been under pressure from antiapartheid activists for several years, but the uprisings in South Africa and a July 1985 declaration of a state of emergency spurred lawmakers to action. As freshman Senator Mitch McConnell (R-KY) said, "The apartheid issue made civil rights black and white again. It was not complicated." Across the United States, 13 state governments, 11 city governments, and 102 colleges and universities had by 1985 adopted measures divesting themselves of investments linked to South Africa.

In April 1985, the Republican-controlled Senate approved a resolution condemning apartheid by a vote of 89–4. The Democratic-controlled House of Representatives developed and passed on June 5 a different measure that would have banned U.S. bank loans to the South African government and businesses, barred new U.S. business investment there, and prohibited importation of the gold coins called Krugerrands. The vote was a veto-proof 295–127, with 56 Republicans joining 239 Democrats. In July, the Senate adopted (80–11) a more limited measure that banned bank loans to the South African government and barred sales of nuclear and computer equipment. In conference committee, the two sides agreed to the Krugerrand ban but dropped the immediate ban on new investments. The revised version passed the House 380–48 on August 1.

Senate Republicans wanted to support the president, who threatened a veto of the bill, but many also wanted some action on South Africa. They launched a filibuster that delayed action until after the August recess. On September 9, President Reagan tried to preempt legislation by issuing Executive Order 12532, banning most new loans, Krugerrand imports, and computer and nuclear-related sales. This satisfied enough Republicans that they joined the filibuster in order to prevent an embarrassing defeat for the president. When sanctions supporters pressed for another vote to halt debate, Senate Republican leaders then took the extraordinary step of removing the formal copy of the conference report from the Senate chamber and locking it in a safe in the Foreign Relations Committee. Under Senate rules, no consideration of the conference report could occur in the absence of the signed conference report. The document was returned two weeks later, but Senate willingness to push for a final vote had subsided. No further legislative action occurred until 1986.

Racial violence continued in South Africa, leading to another state of emergency in June. That month, the House debated a new and broader sanctions bill. House Republicans, apparently calculating that an extreme measure was doomed to defeat, allowed an amendment to pass by voice vote that would have suspended virtually all trade with South Africa and force U.S. businesses to leave within 180 days. They then allowed the amended bill to pass by voice vote.

Senators now felt under pressure to pass something tough. Foreign Relations Committee Chairman Richard Lugar (R-IN) was no longer willing to defend the administration's position. He had concluded that "the president's normal passion for democracy and freedom seemed to diminish when Africa came into view." Lugar persuaded his committee to pass a bill that rejected the more extreme measures in the House bill and accepted some minor amendments by conservatives. The measure, which ultimately passed the Senate 84–14, banned new U.S. business investment in South Africa as well as trade in agricultural products, steel, and nuclear supplies. It threatened additional sanctions in a year if South Africa failed to make "substantial progress" in eliminating apartheid. The bill also put into permanent law the sanctions in Reagan's executive order the year before. The measure also gave the president authority to lift or modify the sanctions if some of five specified conditions were met, including the release from prison of Nelson Mandela and the repeal of the laws on population registration and residency restrictions. Lugar successfully insisted that the House adopt the Senate version of the bill in order to avoid any filibuster, and representatives did so by a 308–77 vote.

President Reagan vetoed the bill on September 26, arguing that sanctions would be counterproductive, hurting blacks more than the white minority government. But, the large majorities held firm, and the veto was overridden by the House 313–83 (with 81 Republicans joining 232 Democrats in the majority) and by the Senate 78–21 (with 31 Republicans joining all 47 Democrats). This was one of the rare cases in American history when Congress overrode a presidential veto on a major national security issue.

The Comprehensive Anti-Apartheid Act of 1986 (Public Law 99–440) did not lead to an immediate end of apartheid in South Africa, but it put the United States and its economic and moral power on the side of political reform and added to the external pressures on the white minority government, which released Nelson Mandela in 1990 and negotiated power-sharing arrangements and a gradual dismantling of apartheid. Multiracial elections were held in 1994.

As this recounting indicates, there were important policy differences over how to deal with South Africa, but there was also sufficient bipartisan consensus in favor of tough action that many Republicans were willing to oppose their popular president. For several weeks, Republicans tried to support the administration by legislative tactics in the House and Senate, filibustering in the Senate to buy time for the president and in the House allowing passage of a more extreme measure so that a veto might be sustained. But ultimately, they felt compelled to join with Democrats to be sure some law was passed in response to the situation in South Africa. Lawmakers wanted to be on the right side of history.

Sources: Congressional Quarterly Almanacs; Alex Thomson, *U.S. Foreign Policy Towards Apartheid South Africa, 1948–1994* (Palgrave Macmillan, 2008); Peter J. Schraeder, *United States Foreign Policy Toward Africa: Incrementalism, Crisis and Change* (Cambridge University Press, 1994).

Selected Resources

The gateway congressional website is at http://thomas.loc.gov/home/thomas.php.

Valuable books on the history of Congress include: Julian E. Zelizer (ed.), *The American Congress* (Houghton Mifflin, 2004); Julian E. Zelizer, *Arsenal of Democracy* (Basic Books, 2010); Robert David Johnson, *Congress and the Cold War* (Cambridge University Press, 2006); James M. Lindsay,

Congress and the Politics of U.S. Foreign Policy (Johns Hopkins University Press, 1994).

The Center on Congress at Indiana University has a useful website for information on Congress at http://congress.indiana.edu/.

CSPAN, in addition to live coverage of congressional debates and many hearings, has its own website with other links and resources at http://www.c-span.org/.

5 Shared Tools of the Budgetary Process

No Money shall be drawn from the Treasury, but in Consequence of Appropriations made by Law.

—U.S. Constitution, Art. I, sect. 9

"Present them with some margin for the economists in Congress to plume themselves upon paring down. . . . They think they must retrench something from the estimates presented to them; and if some superfluity be not given them to lop off, they will cut into the very flesh of public necessities."

—John Quincy Adams[1]

The president and Congress share the power of the purse. Only Congress can open the purse, but the president has broad discretion in spending the money within. Budgets matter. Spending levels determine the variety and size of the tools the government will have to conduct foreign policy. Conditions on spending can empower or constrain foreign policy instruments. Fights over foreign policy budgets are ultimately contests for control of policy, even if they appear to be disputes over budget deficits or program inefficiencies.

Washington insiders like to speak of the Golden Rule: He who has the gold rules. Those departments and agencies with sufficient budgets can get things done; those that are constantly squeezed of people, equipment, and other resources often fail in their assigned tasks. On the other hand, large spending requirements on time-urgent programs often lead to errors and waste. Close oversight can detect such problems early but at the risk of intimidating creative management. Despite what John Quincy Adams suggested above and what congressional budget cutters seem to believe, there is no line item of waste, fraud, and abuse in each agency's budget.

As the budget toolkit brief indicates (see Table 5.1), the budget is built through a process that entails actions by both the president and Congress. It is a means to build and shape the foreign policy tools, with multiple stages and numerous opportunities for cooperation or conflict.

Table 5.1 The Budget Toolkit Brief

ACTION	PRESIDENTIAL ROLE	CONGRESSIONAL ROLE
Program planning and budget preparation	Sets ceilings and gives guidance to the Office of Management and Budget (OMB)	Sets expectations and demands reports during prior year consideration
Budget submission	Sends to Congress in early February	Receives budget; gets analysis by Congressional Budget Office (CBO)
Budget review	Officials defend and explain budget before Congress	Sets broad limits in budget resolution; holds hearings and markups of specific legislation
Set program goals and organization	Administration proposes	Authorizing committees report bills; may be passed
Enactment and disbursement	Approves bills; OMB disburses	Passes appropriations bills, often with earmarks
Meet unexpected needs	Submits request for emergency or supplemental appropriations	Considers requests; may pass appropriations
Oversight	OMB reviews programs	Committees and Government Accountability Office (GAO) review programs
Transfers between programs	Proposes change, subject to various rules	Committees receive notifications; may have to approve

Budgeting is policy making. Funding levels and restrictions, if any, determine the availability and capability of the foreign policy tools as well as all other activities of the government. Budgeting is often highly political, both in partisan terms and as a struggle between different power centers. While congressional approval of appropriations is the most important result of the budget process, this table shows that each branch has powers before and after appropriations to try to influence the use of foreign policy tools.

Making Policy by Making Budgets

Budgets are a tool, a means of organizing governmental activities around available resources. Once organized, they also reflect priorities, both in terms of current efforts and ongoing trends. The federal government obviously cares a lot about income support and medical care for older people: Medicare and Social Security spending equals 35% of current spending. Defense spending also has a high priority for the U.S. government: 19% of total spending and 52% of the discretionary spending Congress votes on each year. By contrast, the State Department, foreign aid programs, and other international affairs spending together equal 1.5% of the grand total and 4% of the amount Congress has to vote on. (See Figure 5.1.) The ratio between Pentagon and civilian foreign policy spending demonstrates that the United States prefers a much more robust military instrument for its national security activities than its diplomatic and economic instruments.

As a tool, budgets allow policy makers to redirect activities by increasing or decreasing their sizes and scopes. For example, military planners in recent years have greatly expanded their budgets and therefore the capabilities of special operations forces (SOF) and of unmanned aerial vehicles. Similarly, international aid programs have given added funds and therefore emphasis for control of HIV/AIDS. The American system of government, with its separated institutions sharing powers, allows officials to fight over who gets to use the budgetary tools to achieve their preferred policies.

The key point is that money matters. Budget making is policy making. In law, the connection is clear. The president needs authority and appropriated

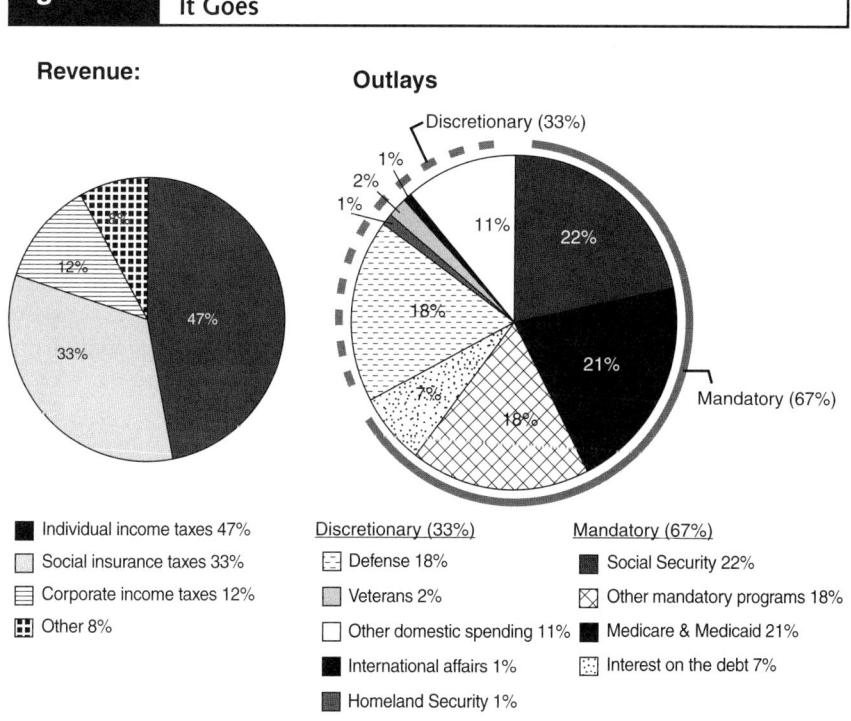

Figure 5.1 The Budget: Where the Money Comes From and Where It Goes

Note: Numbers may not total 100 due to rounding.

Source: Fiscal Year 2013 Estimates, Office of Management and Budget, Congressional Budget Office at www.whitehouse.gov/sites/default/files/omb/budget/fy2013/assets/tables.pdf.

As this figure shows, all spending on national security is double what is spent on domestic discretionary programs, but even that is dwarfed by mandatory spending on health and social security programs. A 2010 World Public Opinion poll showed that Americans thought U.S. foreign aid spending comprised 25% of the federal budget. In actuality, that is a drastic overestimation. The 1% marked for international affairs includes foreign aid and spending on diplomacy.

funds to carry out his preferred programs. In practice, however, national leaders sometimes forget the connection. They think announcing a policy or writing a new law is sufficient without guaranteeing that dollars are needed to make the ideas real.

Budget fights, whether within an agency or between the president and Congress, are necessarily policy fights because their outcomes affect policy, even if the motive for the conflict is a power struggle between branches or political parties. Disputes over spending are easier for the public to understand than, say, ones over the reliability of an ally scheduled to receive aid or the strategic consequences of building an antisatellite weapon.

Not all foreign policy actions require money. A presidential speech declaring opposition to an Iranian nuclear weapons capability costs nothing, nor does a law from Congress demanding pressure on China to revalue its currency. The president can also extend recognition to a new government in the Balkans or cancel a mutual defense treaty with Taiwan without needing appropriated funds. But, if policy makers want to back those words with actions, it often takes money—for intelligence programs to monitor Iranian weapons programs and for Treasury Department investigations of foreign businesses dealings with Iran; for careful analyses of the Chinese economy and the trade balance; for setting up a suitable embassy in the newly recognized country; and for making alternative security arrangements with Taiwan. Ultimately, money matters.

Evolution of the Budget Process

From the earliest days of the republic, government agencies submitted their estimates for the coming year to the Treasury Department, which sent them on to Congress, usually with little or no input from the president. Until 1865, Congress assigned the annual appropriations bill to the same committees that handled the tariffs and taxes to pay for them—House Ways and Means and Senate Finance. After the Civil War, both chambers created separate appropriations committees to consider these bills.

Power struggles in Congress led to a weakening of the appropriations committees from the 1880s until 1920, when they were reconsolidated as the sole venue for spending bills. One reason for the change was that, when authorizing committees also got to report appropriations measures for their programs, they showed little spending restraint.

World War I greatly complicated government financing. Despite a stiff, highly progressive income tax and excess profits corporate taxes, revenues covered only 60% of the cost of the war. The rest had to be borrowed. To fix the problem, Congress assigned responsibility to the president, created a Bureau of the Budget in the Treasury Department, and required for the first time that the president submit an annual budget for Congress to consider. That bureau took on the job of preparing the president's program, dealing with the different departments and coordinating their testimony on the Hill. Franklin Roosevelt (FDR) moved the Budget Bureau into the new Executive Office of the President (EOP) in 1939, where it remains under its current name, Office of Management and Budget (OMB). Different presidents used the budget office in different ways, but all depended on its professional expertise on government programs and its loyal service in enforcing presidential decisions.

In Congress, the appropriations committees grew very popular and very powerful, for they had the ability to *earmark* funds for local projects and other favored activities. Those earmarks over time became political targets, despite the fact that they do not increase spending but only allocate it according to committee rather than agency preferences and despite the fact that most earmarks are in committee reports rather than actual bills and thus are not legally binding on the executive.

In 1973, a political fight between President Nixon and the Democratic-controlled Congress prompted lawmakers to create a new internal budget process. Nixon tried to slash some popular domestic programs by impounding funds, a device used sparingly in previous administrations. Congress retaliated with legal requirements to spend the money unless Congress voted to rescind the funds and—as symbolic proof of its determination to control federal spending—added this new process.

The Budget and Impoundment Control Act of 1974 created budget committees in each chamber but limited their power to setting broad spending limits on about 21 budget functions, such as defense, international affairs, energy, and so forth. They were forbidden to set targets for specific departments or line items. If both houses agreed on a set of limits, the measure was not sent to the president for approval or veto but was controlling on the appropriations committees, whose bills became subject to points of order if they exceeded the limits. The 1974 law also created the Congressional Budget Office to advise Congress and to make cost estimates of proposed bills. The budget committees gradually gained respect and power but were still far less significant than the appropriations panels.

Later, budget battles between Congress and the president led to revisions in the process. A 1985 change—called the Gramm–Rudman–Hollings Amendment—required automatic across-the-board cuts of every government program by an identical percentage in order to reach a specified deficit target. In 1990, that law was changed to set dollar spending limits rather than deficit levels; it also provided that any spending increases or tax cuts had to be offset by increases in revenue. Further spending limits were approved as part of the 1997 balanced budget agreement between President Clinton and congressional Republicans. Those limits expired in 2003, thus setting the stage for the legislative–executive budget battles of recent years.

Despite some expectations that this congressional process would lead to pressure on defense budgets once they were posted side by side with smaller domestic programs, in fact, defense spending stayed steady or growing until 1985 and then came under restraints for deficit reduction until the 9/11 attacks. And though they never bragged about it, lawmakers also quietly protected international affairs programs from amendments transferring funds to domestic programs from 1987 until 2003.

In 2011, in order to resolve a political stalemate over raising the legal limit on the size of the national debt, Congress passed the Budget Control Act (BCA) that combined features of earlier budget legislation and tried to force agreement on a package of long-term deficit reduction measures. The BCA set dollar limits on new spending authority for fiscal years 2012–2021 that were estimated to cut $917 billion below projected spending. The law created a Joint Select Committee on Deficit Reduction that was supposed to develop a package of $1.2 trillion in additional savings and would be subject to a single up-or-down vote in each chamber. The committee failed to reach agreement, thereby triggering an across-the-board spending cut, with half coming from the defense budget, to take place in January 2013. That deadline was chosen so that Congress could consider alternative budget packages before or immediately after the 2012 elections. Some lawmakers argued that the mandatory defense cuts would be so injurious to U.S. national security that Congress would be driven to adopt a different budget plan.

Role and Culture of the Office of Management and Budget

The OMB is small, only about 450 people, but quite powerful. The office's employees serve the president with what is called *neutral competence*, giving their political bosses their best advice and then loyal execution of their decisions. Only the director, the deputy, and top level of associate directors are political appointees; the rest are career civil servants. The core staff of budget examiners, according to a 1999 study, are "young, well-educated, male, and moderate with regard to ideology and party identification."[2] Many become valuable recruits to departmental and congressional staffs after a few years because of their budget expertise and contacts.

A former associate director for national security programs, Gordon Adams, describes OMB's organizational culture as "flat, swift, hard-working, loyal, trustworthy, professional, skeptical, and insular."[3] There is little hierarchy. Staff can prepare major documents and estimates overnight if necessary. They are keen to prove their loyalty and competence to their political superiors. Unlike most government agencies, they don't leak to the press. Their default position is to say "no" to spending request, and to demand persuasive proof of the need for the agency proposals.

Besides its budget preparation role, OMB has the power to review and clear testimony and communications to Congress in order to enforce consistency with administration policies. And, it gathers information to prepare recommendations to the president on whether to sign or veto measures sent from Congress. Administration witnesses in prepared testimony must defend their budgets as adequate, but senior military officers are often asked to list *unfunded requirements* in case Congress wants to make additions. (See Box 5.1.)

The Official Budget Process in the Executive Branch

It takes a bureaucracy with elaborate rules to manage a $3.7 trillion budget. OMB sets the rules and runs that process. One challenge is that OMB

> ### Box 5.1
>
> ### Inside View: The Office of Management and Budget Micromanages the Pentagon
>
> The OMB enforces presidential policies and budget restraints on the executive branch, even on the Pentagon during wartime, but relations can be difficult, as the Pentagon comptroller recounts. While the president can control the Defense Department (DOD) by direct orders to the Secretary, OMB is another instrument to control the military—not so much in terms of strategy as in terms of dollars. This example shows that OMB is a power center in its own right.
>
> *[OMB Director Mitch Daniels] delegated the job of fighting DoD to his associate director for national security, Robin Cleveland. . . . One of her former staffers who later joined my staff (and invariably described himself as a 'refugee from Robin's office') told me that she made it clear that DoD was the enemy. 'She told us, "Don't you understand, we are at war with them?"' he said. . . .*
>
> *OMB, unbidden by anyone, apportioned the [post 9/11] supplemental funds among nine account categories that it created and was not prepared to allow DoD to move funds among these categories without its approval. . . . [As a result,] DoD had to make 'mother may I' requests for funding to the small, understaffed OMB national security office and its strong-willed leader. . . .*
>
> *Source:* Dov S. Zackheim, *A Vulcan's Tale* (Washington, DC: Brookings, 2011), 64, 91–92.

budgeters have to juggle three years of programs simultaneously—the current year, for which they give quarterly disbursements to federal agencies; the coming fiscal year, the president's budget proposals, which are released in early February and then defended in Congress until some action is taken; and the following year, for which they work with agencies to develop the new budget.

Soon after the White House sends the coming year's proposed budget to the Hill, agencies are given guidance for their follow-on budgets. (See Table 5.1.) By midsummer, OMB issues formal planning instructions on what information has to be included in their submissions. Those requests are due to OMB in September, after which the budget examiners conduct hearings into program details. The examiners prepare materials for the director's review in November. By early December, OMB issues a *pass back* to agencies, identifying the approved budget plan, which agencies can then appeal to the president. Needless to say, cabinet officers and presidents tend to be reluctant to make many appeals or changes, although both Secretaries of State Powell and Rice were successful in getting substantial increases after such appeals.[4]

DOD gets slightly different treatment. With most agencies, hearings are held at OMB offices. With DOD, however, OMB staff are located in the Pentagon, working side by side with defense budget personnel throughout the year. This has costs and benefits for both sides but has been the procedure since the 1970s. While budget analysts have fuller knowledge of military programs, they also run the risk of being co-opted by their colleagues.

Budget examiners bring a particular mind-set to their agency hearings. They want to be sure that the president's policy guidance is understood and implemented in their programs. They usually have to enforce budget constraints, often of a no new growth or a flat percentage growth target. And, they need to be convinced that ongoing programs are working as promised the year before. Accordingly, they are skeptical of new programs not previously endorsed by the White House and especially of promises that spending more now will save money in the long run. Agencies have to prepare persuasive information, including metrics for policy evaluation, that they will be held accountable for in later years. Bureaucrats defend their programs in terms of their high-sounding goals; budget examiners scrutinize them over the concrete accomplishments and efficiency. Program managers fear that any cut, even for an understandable and unavoidable reason, will be the new baseline in future years, thus disrupting their long-term plans. Budget examiners, however, see any savings as opportunities to add funds to higher-priority programs.[5]

Once the president has decided any appeals or made any other last-minute changes to the 2,000-page document, the budget is printed for Congress.

The Official Budget Process in Congress

In Congress, the budget is reviewed along three mostly separate tracks—one through the authorizing committees, one through the budget committees, and the one that matters most, through the appropriations committees. Authorizing committees write the basic law governing departments and agencies and their programs. Some programs, like those for agriculture and transportation, are reauthorized every five years. Others are based on permanent law and do not need regular authorizations, although legislation might be necessary to start new programs or change agency organization.

In the national security area, there are profound anomalies. The armed services committees have produced, and gotten presidential signatures on, defense authorization bills for more than 50 years. Although the only real need for such a bill is to set military pay raises, lawmakers use the process to change force size and structure, establish funding levels for weapons programs that they hope the appropriators will follow, and require Pentagon reports on a vast array of topics. The bill now totals more than 900 pages each year. The foreign policy committees used to try to do annual authorizations for international programs, but they haven't been able to enact a foreign aid authorization bill since 1985 because of the political unpopularity of foreign aid programs and the adoption of poison pill amendments on domestic and foreign policy issues. They have occasionally passed a more limited State Department authorization bill dealing with issues like embassy security and internal reorganization. There have also been periodic authorization bills for intelligence programs, including a highly classified annex, but controversies prevented them from achieving a regular annual authorization between 2005 and 2009. Nor have authorizers ever been able to enact a regular authorization bill for the Department of Homeland Security.

The budget committees have a timetable written into law, but it is rarely met in practice, especially in recent years. Following the submission of the president's budget proposals in February, the authorizing committees are supposed to submit their own estimates in March. By April 1, the budget committees are supposed to report a budget resolution that sets spending targets by budget function rather than by department or agency. The measure also sets figures for revenue and public debt, but these largely represent the mathematical outcomes of the aggregate spending limits. By April 15, both chambers are supposed to have passed their budget resolutions and resolved differences in conference. The final agreed concurrent budget resolution may also provide reconciliation instructions requiring authorizing committees to report measures that cut spending further or raise revenues—the process used to get around Senate filibusters on Bush administration tax cuts and the Obama health care bill. One important feature of the 1974 budget process is that Senate debate is strictly limited, thus preventing filibusters on this narrow set of measures.

Once a final budget resolution is adopted, the appropriations chairmen set *302(b) allocations*—spending ceilings on each appropriations subcommittee. They have some flexibility because the budget functions do not line up precisely with government departments. The defense function, for example, contains money for nuclear weapons programs administered by the Energy Department. If any bill exceeds that target, it is subject to a point of order. In the House, waiving such challenges requires only a majority vote, in the Senate, a supermajority of 60 votes.

The official timetable then calls for appropriations bills to be considered in the House starting on May 15 and finishing by June 30. The Senate has until the end of the fiscal year, September 30, to pass its own versions of the appropriations bills and resolve differences with the House. Although the 1974 law even changed the start of the fiscal year to October 1 to allow time for this process, delays are common throughout this timetable.

Any spending bill can get caught up in the megapolitics of the budget, especially large bills like those for defense and domestic social programs. The foreign operations appropriations bill has often been delayed until it could be packaged with more popular measures.

The appropriators funnel the budget requests through 13 bills. Two fund DOD—defense and military construction. One provides money for the State Department and foreign aid programs. Another covers the Department of Homeland Security. The EOP, including the NSC and OMB, is funded by the appropriations bill for the Treasury Department and the postal service, now called Financial Services and General Government. As most funding for the intelligence community (IC) is hidden within the Pentagon budget, the defense subcommittee also covers those agencies.

Defense spending has broad congressional support, so it is one of the few bills that has regularly passed before the end of the fiscal year, at least until recently. Controversial items added to the defense authorization bills, however, may prevent them from passing prior to action on defense appropriations, thus lessening their impact. Foreign aid is the least popular appropriations measure, so it often has to be joined with a more favored bill to ensure passage.

Changes in spending are supposed to be driven by rational considerations, but sometimes political considerations get in the way. Lawmakers and executive branch officials often have different priorities, pet programs, or mantras. They make policy fights look like budget fights by talking about wasteful spending and use budget fights as means to shape policy, such as freezing State Department spending but not that of the Pentagon. The face of the issue seen by outsiders isn't always the real matter in dispute.

Much oversight by Congress is based on the interests of the committee chair, who gets to call hearings with witnesses from a particular agency. If the chair wants to endorse a particular program, he or she can call government and outside witnesses who praise it. If there are newsworthy reports of problems, he or she can browbeat the bureaucrats, often in the bright lights of television cameras. Despite the good government calls for regular (*police patrol*) oversight, Congress more often than not responds with fire-alarm hearings into apparent scandals. The defense authorizing and appropriations panels are exceptions because they regularly give Pentagon officials time to explain and defend their programs, not just the ones that might be controversial.

The wars in Iraq and Afghanistan have posed particular challenges for congressional oversight as important aspects of U.S. policy have been performed by civilian agencies and no one committee has jurisdiction over the broad political-military strategy in the region. Another problem was that most of the funding for these conflicts has come through supplemental appropriations bills that were not subject to review by the armed services committees. Still another complication has been that the Defense Department is now the source of over one fifth of U.S. foreign aid, mainly through programs in Iraq and Afghanistan, but those programs are not in the jurisdiction of the foreign policy committees.

The Money Committees and Their Cultures

Each of the three money committees—for budget, appropriations, and revenue—has a distinctive approach to its responsibilities. The budget committees have a macroeconomic focus and a concern with debt and deficits. They also have a whole-of-government, big-picture mandate that transcends the narrow agency focus of the authorizing committees and appropriations subcommittees. Over the decades since their creation, these committees have repeatedly drawn attention to the rising share of spending for mandatory programs, also called *entitlements,* the ones that escape annual review by the appropriations committees. These programs, like Social Security and Medicare and various government pensions, now account for 56% of annual spending, yet they are not part of annual spending bills. Because they cannot establish spending limits on departments or agencies as such, or even on line-item programs, they tend to adopt simple guidelines: spending freezes; across-the-board cuts of an equal percentage; no more than a certain percentage of real growth above inflation. The committees have expert staffs and can draw on the excellent nonpartisan resources of the CBO. In addition to providing regular economic reports and budget estimates on proposed legislation, CBO also provides Congress every year with a several-hundred-page list of alternatives to consider to cut spending or increase revenues. The budget committees, however, must contend with a basic weakness: They do not pass binding laws signed by the president, and their efforts can be ignored by the rest of Congress.

The appropriations committees, at least until very recently, were at the top in power and prestige in Congress. Lawmakers begged to join, not least because of the opportunities membership offered to direct federal spending to their home areas. The political backlash against earmarks may have diminished the attractiveness and value of appropriations membership, at least in the short run. Although some federal activities are highly controversial, appropriators are practiced deal makers who know they have to pass their bills in order to keep the government in operation. (See Box 5.2.) Compromise is an essential part of their culture. And while they may care about the substance of federal programs, what they care most about, what they focus most on, is money. The staff—and staffs are quite small, such as only about 16 people covering the entire Pentagon budget in each chamber—are the ultimate green eyeshade analysts. They scour the budgets for those dollars they can scoop up and transfer to their members' higher-priority programs. They are adept at locating those dollars that may be ultimately required but for technical or contractual reasons won't actually be spent in the coming fiscal year. They know that $5 million here and $10 million there can easily add up to enough to give a major boost to some favored program. Many nongovernmental organizations (NGOs) with overseas programs that receive government funds—like CARE or Catholic Relief—plead for those extra dollars for their activities.

The revenue committees—House Ways and Means and Senate Finance—have very different approaches to the budget. They have a vested interest in two of the biggest programs, Social Security and Medicare, because they are financed directly by taxes. As a result, these committees are the overseers and authorizers for those programs. They can set the benefits as well as the funding sources. As federal revenues were largely the result of tariffs until early in the 20th century, these committees also write trade legislation and oversees trade negotiations, although these have little direct impact on budgets. What does have an impact, of course, is taxes. The revenue committees get to decide who pays and who gets loopholes. Politically, changes in basic income and corporate tax rates are the most salient, while other revenue measures get less attention. Given the political resistance to raising taxes,

> **Box 5.2**
>
> **Inside View: Budgetary Cooperation**
>
> The Pentagon comptroller during 2001–2004 describes how he accommodated the chairman of the Senate Appropriations Committee and made his own job easier. The scenario he describes illustrates pork spending as well as legislative-executive cooperation.
>
> *Soon after I took office, [Senate Appropriations Staff Director Terry Sauvain] showed me a list of pet West Virginia programs, totaling some $50 million, that [Senator Robert Byrd, D-WV, chairman of Appropriations] wanted pushed through the defense budget. . . . I told Terry I would do what I could but warned him that I might be able to obtain only $20 million or so for him. . . . In the event, I provided some $30 million for projects in the great state of West Virginia. . . . I had much less trouble with my budgets than otherwise would have been the case, and much less grief when I testified before Senator Byrd. . . .*
>
> Source: Dov S. Zackheim, *A Vulcan's Tale* (Washington, DC: Brookings, 2011), 70.

the revenue committees look at other ways to raise necessary funds like user fees and tax expenditures. OMB has long been forced to report each year the cost of the tax expenditures, that is, the revenue foregone by their inclusion in the tax code. For example, allowing homeowners to deduct their mortgage interest costs the government over $104 billion each year; the deduction for business meals and entertainment costs $10 billion; the deduction of charitable contributions other than for education and health costs $44 billion; the tax breaks for 401(k) plans and individual retirement accounts cost more than $80 billion. The more that changes in the basic tax rates are politically off limits, the more likely the revenue committees will be to change some of the many tax expenditures. Some tax expenditures have direct foreign policy consequences, notably the law allowing U.S. businesses to avoid taxation of income earned by foreign subsidiaries so long as the money is kept abroad ($31.5 billion in revenue lost each year).

The Usual, Real Budget Process

In practice, the careful timetable for action on the budget is rarely followed, sometimes with enormous disruptive consequences. No final budget resolution was adopted by Congress for fiscal years 1999, 2003, 2005, 2007, 2011, or 2012. Only four times since 1974 have all appropriations bills been passed by the October 1 deadline, the last time being 1997.

The budget resolution is the primary vehicle for macroeconomic political fights over spending levels, deficits, taxes, and priorities. The struggles are symbolic, however, because the measure itself never becomes law. Appropriations bills then get slowed down by programmatic controversies and then by the other matters fighting for floor time in the House and Senate. When several bills get bogged down at the same time, the leadership bundles them together in *omnibus*—or sometimes smaller *mini-bus*—bills that force lawmakers to vote on complex measures they have no time to study. Foreign assistance has often survived only because it was combined with more popular domestic spending bills.

Even the defense appropriations bill has fallen victim to controversy and delay in recent years. The measure has been signed into law by the start of the fiscal year only four times since the 9/11 attacks. Three times, the measure was delayed until December. The bills for the State Department and for foreign operations fared even worse. Since 9/11, those measures were finally enacted only in December three times, and not until January or February twice, and March or April twice.

These delays force the agencies to rely on a *continuing resolution,* a temporary spending bill passed by Congress that usually limits them to no more than the previous year and forbids any new program starts. This creates enormous uncertainty and forces officials to juggle all of their programs, sometimes delaying contract awards and other actions and sometimes leading to shortfalls that require personnel layoffs. Appropriations for fiscal year 2011 were not signed into law until April 15, 2011, more than halfway through the budget year and only after seven continuing resolutions and numerous budget fights.

When Congress and the president reach a major impasse over budget issues—as happened most notably in 1985, 1990, 1995, and 2011—lawmakers have often devised new rules and processes to resolve the immediate problems while setting the stage for renewed fighting later on. This chapter's case study on the Budget Enforcement Act of 1990 describes the grand bargain that led to declining spending and tougher budget rules and ultimately balanced budgets during the 1990s.

Playing Games With the Budget Tool

Both branches of government have numerous budget games they can play when it is to their advantage.[6] One is to embrace Rosy Scenario and pick economic assumptions that allow both branches to avoid painful choices. Presidents may forecast robust economic growth that lawmakers doubt. Or tax cut advocates may claim that the lost revenues will somehow be offset by economic growth. Other assumptions that can affect budget calculations include the spend-out rate for various programs and the multiyear costs of major programs. The Pentagon has a long history of estimating cost growth in weapons programs that falls far short of reality.

Another tactic is to change the rules when they begin to bite. Senate leaders have literally stopped the clock above the presiding officer's chair in order to stay within some legal deadline for action. On occasion, Congress has shifted the federal payday at the end or start of the fiscal year backward or forward to change the apparent deficit for the year. The due date for corporate taxes was also shifted once for the same purpose.

The original congressional concern with reducing the deficit led to a focus on outlay rates and future economic assumptions. When that didn't seem to work very well, Congress changed the rules to focus on spending authority. Congress also didn't like the painful impact of automatic across-the-board cuts under the 1985 Gramm–Rudman–Hollings amendment. Later on, when the pay-as-you-go (PAYGO) rules requiring revenue-neutral tax bills threatened the Bush tax cuts, they were allowed to expire—and the Republican majority in the House of Representatives started the 112th Congress by dropping the requirement that spending cuts be offset by revenue increases. For two decades, until 2011, both Democrats and Republicans in the House avoided politically embarrassing votes to increase the statutory limit on the national debt by deeming passage of such a measure upon enactment of a budget resolution anticipating it.

And if the rules still bite, they can often be waived. The House rules regularly get waived in the resolution setting terms for debate of bills that might otherwise be jeopardized by their enforcement. The Senate can also waive budget rules, but it takes a 60-vote majority. The rules are more guideposts than fences for lawmakers.

There is a longstanding rule in both chambers forbidding "legislation" on appropriations bills. In practice, this means that only provisions controlling spending are allowed. Thus, Congress could say, "None of the funds appropriated by this act shall be used to finance the introduction of American ground troops into Laos or Thailand" (a provision, by the way, that was enacted in 1969 as part of congressional efforts to limit the Vietnam War), but it could not use an appropriations bill to reorganize the Pentagon to create a combatant command for Southeast Asia. Because the foreign policy committees have repeatedly failed to pass foreign aid authorization bills since 1985, however, they have teamed with the appropriators to have some of their legislation added to the Foreign Operations Appropriations Bill. The House then was to waive the rule on "legislation" so that it will not be ruled out of order.

Another budget game, allowed by the 1990 law, is to evade spending caps by declaring certain expenditures as *emergency* measures. That makes sense for hurricane and other natural disaster relief and for some unexpected military expenditures. But in recent years, it has been used for the census, some drought relief efforts, and some long-term defense programs. The Budget Control Act of 2011 permits such emergency expenditures above the specific spending caps, but House Republicans objected to funding Federal Emergency Management Agency (FEMA) relief and recovery efforts without offsetting program cuts.

Still another ploy is to label some activities *off-budget*. For many years, Congress has forced OMB to submit budget estimates showing Social Security and postal service funding that way, even though both bring in 26% of government receipts and account for 15% of federal expenditures. This budgetary fiction was intended to shield those programs from the budget-cutting frenzy.

Similar treatment is applied to Government Sponsored Enterprises (GSEs) like Fannie Mae and Freddie Mac. Their basic loan operations are excluded from budget calculations, except that their losses are counted as outlays. In fact, by common agreement between the branches, loan guarantees at home or abroad are counted in the budget only in terms of the subsidy cost, not the actual loan amount. Similarly, U.S. contributions to the International Monetary Fund (IMF) are treated as credit financing that does not count toward the deficit.

Bureaucrats have also perfected the use of *Washington Monument cuts*, where they insist that planned reductions, by OMB or Congress, would necessarily affect their most visible or popular activities if implemented. Thus, say, the National Park Service would close the Washington Monument to visitors before it cut back in headquarters personnel or travel costs. The military services have their own cut insurance. Many contracts for major weapons are written in such a way that, after a few years, it would cost more to cancel the program than to complete it.

In short, the real budget process is a lot more varied and interesting than the official one and harder to predict and control.

Linking Money to Policy

The executive branch is also creative when it needs to get money for things the president wants. When Bill Clinton wanted some funds to help stem Mexico's peso crisis in 1995 and congressional leaders suddenly balked, Treasury Secretary Robert Rubin found some obscure authorities in an Exchange Stabilization Fund that allowed him to give $20 billion in credits to Mexico. (It was soon paid back in full.) When George W. Bush announced a plan to broaden educational benefits for military families in his 2008 State of the Union address, budget officials had to scramble to find funds for it because the idea had been added by speechwriters and not included in the president's budget.[7]

A key role for OMB is finding both funds and legal authorities for presidential programs. That may involve shifting spending in their budget plans or legal determinations so that the activity is permitted under existing statutes. This is where it's important to have *yes* lawyers.

One of the flaws in the policy process is that many significant foreign policy decisions are made without consideration of costs or funding authorities. If the decision involves an existing program, then funds can be shifted into it. If it involves a long-term effort, then getting congressional support, although time-consuming, is not necessarily debilitating. The bigger problem occurs when agencies fight over who has the money and the authority to do something the president wants. Insiders report lengthy meetings during the Iraq war as agencies sparred over some small programs everyone favored but wanted someone else to pay for.

Contingency Funds

Over the years, the executive branch has regularly asked Congress for contingency funds to handle unforeseen problems. The only area where lawmakers have been generally supportive is disaster relief, both domestically for FEMA, now part of the Department of Homeland Security (DHS), and abroad, through the State Department's humanitarian assistance program that now receives more than $4 billion annually. In general, however, Congress is reluctant to provide contingency funds for other foreign policy purposes. Some lawmakers fear that the money will be wasted; others want to be sure it is for a purpose Congress otherwise supports.

In fact, there is a broad contingency fund in current law. Section 451 of the Foreign Assistance Act of 1961 (PL 87–195, as amended) allows the president "to use funds made available to carry out any provision of this Act (other than [development assistance]) in order to provide, for any unanticipated contingencies, assistance authorized by this part in accordance with the provisions applicable to the furnishing of such assistance . . ." Congress is to be informed *promptly* of any such use of funds. Current law sets a ceiling for this fund of only $25 million per year. In much of the 1950s, that fund received $100 million per year—equal to $619 million today. The highpoint was in 1961, when the president's contingency fund received $275 million—equal to $1.548 billion today.

Congress reduced this fund—and other contingency funds—when abuses occurred, such as applying the funds to programs cut by Congress or spending on frivolous purposes, such as buying a helicopter as a gift to a foreign leader. A CIA contingency fund was cut after Congress discovered that the Reagan administration was using it to secretly fund the Nicaraguan Contras. The relevant lesson, therefore, is that the way to get Congress to approve contingency funds in larger amounts is to build confidence between branches that the spending flexibility will not be abused—and that takes time, consultation, and full information sharing.

DOD has its own long-standing contingency authority, the 1861 Feed and Forage Act. The act was based on the commonsense judgment that troops in remote areas need to be able to buy provisions in anticipation of normal appropriations that might be many months and hundreds of miles away. Once on the books, it has been a useful tool for the Pentagon. It was used three times to support Vietnam War operations. It was used to fund the military buildup in 1990 for the Gulf War and again in 1994 for operations in Haiti. The George W. Bush administration invoked it in 2001, but appropriations for the war in Afghanistan came quickly, making its use unnecessary.[8]

In 2012, Congress created a new contingency fund of $200 million. The law authorized DOD to transfer funds from its operations and maintenance accounts and required at least 20% of the total to come from State Department funds. Advance notification of Congress was also required.[9]

Transfers and Reprogramming

The more typical situation is when the president wants to transfer money from one program to another during the fiscal year. That's not as easy as it sounds because congressional committees are very jealous of their power of the purse and don't like to see money go for something they haven't approved, especially if it takes away funds from something they strongly favor. There is no common set of rules in current law for shifting funds among national security programs. Some restrictions are set by long-standing law; others change with annual appropriations bills. Many of the rules are based on informal understandings between executive departments and congressional committees.

For example, the committees of jurisdiction over foreign aid programs generally demand notification followed by 15 days in which to decide whether to place a hold on the transfer. In general, there is consultation with the committees prior to formal notification, and failure to reach agreement delays the notification. The Foreign Assistance Act of 1961 (PL 87–195), as amended, has basic transfer authority of up to 15% from any account (section 109) and up to 10% for military aid (section 610). The president is given broad authority (section 614) to furnish assistance without regard to current law provided that he consult in advance with and provide written justification to the foreign policy and appropriations committees. The annual appropriations bills tend to have specific additional restrictions on the use of these and other transfer authorities, often including a 15-day prior notice requirement. As the HELP Commission on foreign aid reported:

> At present, the interpretation, management, and operation of these [reprogramming, congressional notification, and legislative holds on fund shifts and transfers] procedures is at best unwieldy and at times unworkable. . . . Within the legislative branch itself, the authorizers and appropriators follow different procedures, and the House and Senate obey their own distinct processes.[10]

DOD has the most elaborate system governing reprogramming. Prior approval by the defense committees is required for *special interest items* identified by those committees, for new program starts, and for transfers exceeding certain dollar figures, such as $20 million for procurement programs, $10 million for research and development programs, and $15 million for operations and maintenance activities. In recent years, Congress has shown increased flexibility, particularly for operations in Afghanistan and Iraq. The total general transfer authority for DOD funds has been increased from $2 billion in FY 2002 to $3.5 billion in FY 2005 to $5 billion for FY 2008. It is now $4 billion. Congress also allowed broader authority for special programs in Afghanistan and Iraq.

The president has another very effective but seldom-used tool to transfer funds between departments. There is still on the books a provision from the 1933 Economy Act (31 USC 1535) giving the broad authority for one department to pay another department for goods or services for its activities. OMB seems highly reluctant to use this authority, despite suggestions that this would allow the Pentagon to pay for civilian activities by the State Department that even Secretary Robert Gates wanted to fund. As a result, decisions on U.S. civilian capacity for foreign policy activities are left to the weak foreign policy committees and the unpopular Foreign Operations Appropriations Bill.

Secret Spending

Sometimes the president wants to spend money secretly and urgently. While some commentators doubt that this is allowed under the Constitution, which explicitly requires "a regular Statement and Account of the Receipts and Expenditures of all public Money" (Art. I, sect. 9), the very First Congress passed a law in 1790 providing $40,000 for diplomatic agents. In 1793, it was broadened to cover intercourse with other nations. Instead of vouchers, lawmakers said the president merely had to provide certificates that the funds had been expended with no other details. Current law contains the same provision (31 USDC 3526[e]) as well as a specific exemption for the CIA (50 USC 403j[b]).

FDR got confidential spending provisions included in his World War II emergency funds. Secret funding, known only to a handful of congressional leaders, was used to develop the atomic bomb. By the early 1970s, there were 20 different accounts for executive agencies to use confidential funds.[11]

Today, the IC relies on secret funding, although a recent law requires disclosure of the bottom-line total of the budget. Within the defense budget, there are special highly classified activities called *black programs* that are exempt from many of DOD's rules and regulations. Only a few people in Congress receive regular information on such programs. Stealth aircraft, for example, were developed using such secret funding, and DOD today acknowledges that about $50 billion of its programs are in the *black budget*.[12]

Causes and Cures for Dysfunction

The president and Congress could run the budget process better. Delays would be less frequent if the Senate had time limits on appropriations debates. There might be a foreign aid authorization bill, and a thorough revision in the cumbersome 1961 law, if the committee leadership made it a priority and the chamber leadership backed them up. Important bills might be passed instead of sidelined if members refrained from offering unrelated poison-pill amendments to national security legislation.

The most important reform in executive branch handling of national security budgets would be for the president to propose a comprehensive budget for that function, bringing together the defense and international affairs activities as well as some of those for homeland security. This would allow trade-offs among programs and shifts between departments that now are difficult. It might also better protect such programs in Congress by showing that *foreign assistance* is just another way, like military deployments or diplomacy, to defend American interests.

Internally, it would help if the NSC staff had a closer working relationship with OMB so that policies would be developed with the full understanding of the resource issues involved.

Small steps can lead to bigger ones. Both sides could devise confidence-building measures that might make them more willing to grant discretion to each other. For example, better trust could allow Congress to approve larger contingency funds and less onerous transfer authorities, which would add speed and flexibility to executive options. In return, the executive could engage in closer consultation with lawmakers. Better legislative–executive relations could lead to better policies.

This may seem like a pipe dream in our currently polarized political system. But, it has happened in the past, even when emotions were high and political calculations paramount. A Democratic Congress gave a Republican president a $1.5 billion contingency fund for foreign policy operations. Presidents and opposition congressional leaders compromised on effective budget limits and procedures in 1990 and 1997. Differences were set aside even in 2009 to pass a huge aid program for Pakistan in a matter of days. The process doesn't always fail, but there are numerous incentives for conflict rather than collaboration.

* * *

The president and Congress clash over the budget because each wants to set priorities and control spending. While the executive branch follows a detailed process directed by the president's OMB, Congress often fails to follow its prescribed process when political disputes lead to delays and new rules. The budget committees and authorizing committees have far less power than the appropriations committees, whose bills must be enacted in order to fund government operations. Budgets for military purposes tend to be less controversial and less subject to fights over money and policy than the budgets for other foreign policy activities.

Case Study: The Budget Enforcement Act of 1990

This case tells how the existing budget rules created economic and political dilemmas for the president and how Congress forced him into a grand bargain that created a new set of budget rules. Both sides threatened to let the government shut down for lack of spending authority, but both sides ultimately compromised on the new law. During the budget fight, each side used its particular tools over spending. The president proposed a budget that congressional leaders opposed; each side postured for political benefit, but they eventually negotiated a complex deal with good faith and compromise.

President George H. W. Bush had a problem. In 1988, at the Republican Convention, he electrified the crowd with a solemn pledge: "Read my lips. No new taxes." In the spring of 1990, however, that pledge clashed with a soaring deficit and tight budget rules.

His budget for fiscal year 1991 forecast spending of $1.23 trillion and revenues of $1.17 trillion, leaving a deficit of $64 billion, just low enough to avoid the automatic across-the-board cuts mandated by the Gramm–Rudman–Hollings amendment of 1985 that required year-by-year reductions in the deficit levels.

That estimate was flawed, however, in part because it was based on overly optimistic assumptions of economic growth, often labeled *Rosy Scenario*. Budget Director Richard Darman had told Bush in August 1989 that the only way to keep the no-new-taxes pledge was to come up with a "genuinely radical" budget. Darman envisioned either a "big fix" proposal early in the year or a bipartisan deal negotiated at the last minute in September. The president wanted to be sure congressional Republicans would support any such plan, but they proved reluctant.

In late spring 1990, the U.S. economy slipped into a recession, and new estimates put the cost of the federal bailout of failed savings and loan institutions at $45 billion. As a result, the size of the cuts needed to comply with the budget law soared to about $100 billion. In early May, Bush began talks with congressional leaders and said they should be based on "no preconditions." Congressional Democrats wanted Bush to abandon his no-new-taxes pledge, and they were reluctant to support big cuts in domestic spending. Republicans especially wanted a lowering of the capital gains tax as well as domestic cuts.

The negotiators were at an impasse by mid-June, so Bush called a White House meeting on June 26. House Speaker Tom Foley (D-WA) proposed a set of principles for a bipartisan package; Bush agreed, and Darman drafted the statement that was released to the press. It called for entitlement reform cuts in defense and domestic discretionary spending, reform of the budget process, and tax revenue increases. Democrats crowed and Republicans complained that the last phrase meant abandonment of Bush's campaign pledge.

The summer dragged on without agreement. On July 15, Darman announced that the deficit now appeared to be approaching $231 billion. A constitutional amendment requiring a balanced budget, seen by some lawmakers as a preferred solution to the budget impasse, fell seven votes short of the two thirds needed for passage by the House of Representatives on July 17.

On August 2, Iraqi forces invaded Kuwait and seemed to threaten Saudi Arabia, thus raising the specter of disruption in oil supplies and the fear of wider war. Defense Secretary Dick Cheney warned on August 9 that "our existing defense capabilities would be shattered" by the looming automatic budget cuts under Gramm–Rudman–Hollings. Defense spending would have to be cut 13.6% immediately on October 1.

On September 7, following the August congressional recess—it was an election year—White House and congressional negotiators convened at Andrews Air Force Base just outside Washington. For 11 days, largely incommunicado with the outside world, they hammered out a budget deal, finishing just hours before the end of the fiscal year on September 30.

While most congressional leaders grudgingly supported the agreement, Deputy House Republican Leader Newt Gingrich (R-GA) refused to go along. He persuaded a majority of Republicans to oppose the deal, and nervous Democrats felt free to oppose it as well. In the early hours of October 5, the House defeated the measure, 179–254.

Congress passed a short continuing resolution to keep the government funded and to delay the Gramm–Rudman–Hollings automatic cuts, but an angry Bush vetoed the bill on October 6. The impact was minor, however, as the three-day Columbus Day holiday weekend was just starting.

Faced with the prospect of a full-scale government shutdown, the congressional negotiators went back to work. They kept the basic outline of the agreement but eliminated many of the detailed requirements for other committees to find spending cuts. Their revised package was approved by the House on October 8, 250–164, and by the Senate the next day, 66–33. The final technical details, including complicated income and capital gains tax changes and increased excise taxes on items like alcohol and tobacco, passed three weeks later.

The Budget Enforcement Act of 1990 had several notable features. It "held harmless" the large but unknown costs of the war in Kuwait and the continuing costs of the savings and loan bailout, leaving those sums out of the deficit calculation. Both sides realized that agreed defense cuts might have to be reversed if the United States got into war with Iraq, and both sides knew that there would have to be some major expenditures to rescue failed savings and loan institutions. The 1990 law was also notable because lawmakers changed the focus of deficit reduction from the vagaries of outlay estimates to the precise numbers of spending authority. They wrote into law firm caps on discretionary spending totals for each of the following five years. They added PAYGO, the requirement that tax cuts and entitlement increases be revenue neutral.

Although the new law averted the immediate spending crisis, George H. W. Bush was punished electorally for endorsing new taxes. The 1990 budget agreement lasted five years and was followed by a similar package negotiated by President Clinton and congressional Republicans that led to a balanced federal budget as the 20th century ended.

This case shows how action-forcing measures like the deficit reduction target can compel officials to renegotiate both spending details and the budget process. Lawmakers learned that, when existing law bites too hard, it can be changed. Politicians learned that promises like "no new taxes" were painful to break, despite the unforeseen circumstances. The American people learned that, on occasion, the president and Congress can set aside politics and negotiate effective compromises. One reason the 2011 budget dispute turned out differently was that political considerations were deemed more important than economic ones by many of those involved.

This case also demonstrates that budget fights are power struggles—in 1990 between president and Congress and between the two major parties. The budget is a tool to control the activities of government and thus an object to be contested by opposing sides.

Sources: Richard Darman. *Who's in Control?* (New York: Simon & Schuster, 1996); *CQ Almanac 1990* (Washington, DC: Congressional Quarterly, 1991).

Selected Resources

Official websites for the OMB (www.whitehouse.gov/omb/) and the Congressional Budget Office (www.cbo.gov/).

The basic text on U.S. government budgeting is Allen Schick, *The Federal Budget: Politics, Policy, Process, Third Edition* (Washington, DC: Brookings Institution, 2007).

A thorough explanation of budgeting for defense, international affairs, and homeland security is in Gordon Adams and Cindy Williams, *Buying National Security* (New York: Routledge, 2010).

A legal and historical analysis of Congress's power of the purse can be found in William C. Banks and Peter Raven-Hansen, *National Security Law and the Power of the Purse* (New York: Oxford University Press, 1994).

The Congressional Research Service (CRS) issues many reports on the budget and appropriations process as well as on particular government programs and policy issues. Many of them can be found at http://fpc.state.gov/fpc/c18183.htm and www.opencrs.com/.

6 The Diplomatic Instrument

> *The State Department is a bowl of jelly. It's got all those people over there who are constantly smiling.*
>
> —President John F. Kennedy to reporter Hugh Sidey in 1961[1]

> *[My] one legacy is to ruin the foreign service. I mean ruin it—the old foreign service—and to build a new one.*
>
> —Richard Nixon to Henry Kissinger, November 13, 1972[2]

While the president is the chief diplomat because of his constitutional duties to receive foreign ambassadors and appoint American ones, the State Department is the primary tool for U.S. diplomacy. The secretary of state holds the most prestigious cabinet post and is fourth in line of succession to the presidency after the vice president and two congressional leaders. The secretary is also viewed as the primary spokesperson to explain and defend U.S. foreign policy.

Despite the professionalism of the foreign service, presidents of both parties, as quoted at the start of this chapter, have often distrusted the State Department. They often turned instead to White House-based people for key diplomatic missions. Nevertheless, the bulk of U.S. diplomatic activities, and the infrastructure and procedures for them, are handled by the State Department. As with all of the foreign policy instruments, Congress can play a role along with the president. While the president can use officials from anywhere in government and sometimes even private citizens for diplomatic activities, most diplomacy in conducted by or through the State Department, the principal focus of this chapter. (See Table 6.1.)

The Nature of Diplomacy and the Diplomatic Mission

Despite the comment by the English diplomat Sir Henry Wotton (1568–1639) that an ambassador is "an honest man sent to lie abroad for the good of his country," diplomacy is a long-respected profession. Every country uses ambassadors (the highest formal rank) and other envoys to represent its interests in dealing with other governments. Diplomats are protected

Table 6.1 The Diplomatic Instrument Brief

PEOPLE	ADVANTAGES	DISADVANTAGES
Secretary of state	Authoritative, powerful	Limits on time, multiple demands
U.S. ambassadors	Empowered heads of country teams	Uneven in skills and host-country influence
Foreign service	Professionals	Subject to instructions
ACTIONS		
Engagement	Allows broad exchanges of views	Multiple voices, sometimes confusing or discordant
Negotiations	Can achieve definitive agreements	Often time-consuming, subject to domestic pressures
Public diplomacy	Nonthreatening, potential long-term benefits	Slow, hard to judge effectiveness
ROLE OF CONGRESS	Independent voice; can play "bad cop"	Can confuse others regarding U.S. positions
CULTURE	Professional, high value on negotiations, comfortable with ambiguity	Resists ruptures in relations

The diplomatic instrument of foreign policy consists of people—U.S. government officials—and actions they can perform. Those actions can be broadly grouped in the categories of engagement, negotiations, and public diplomacy. Diplomats, however, have a special culture that shapes how they operate.

against local arrest by international conventions, thus allowing them to disregard parking and speeding tickets and to avoid jail for even more serious crimes. Misbehaving diplomats can be declared *persona non grata*, however, thereby forcing recall to their home countries.

Traditionally, diplomacy has been seen as *the art and practice of conducting negotiations between nations*, but scholars now distinguish between formal intergovernmental relations, called *Track One*, and numerous additional tracks for conflict resolution, including nongovernmental contacts by professionals, businesspeople, academics, and religious organizations. While these private organizations may consult and collaborate with governments, our focus here is on the formal channels the president can use to conduct American foreign policy.

Modern American diplomats perform many functions besides negotiating with established governments. They represent the United States to foreign publics. They help U.S. citizens overseas, including Americans in trouble and businesses seeking markets. They analyze and report on developments abroad from grand strategy and economic trends to cultural changes and leadership gossip. They carry out the duties assigned by various laws from assessing the qualifications of people seeking visas to helping Afghans and

Iraqis build new institutions. And, they are the experts who advise in the development of new policies.

The State Department is the lead agency for U.S. diplomacy, but officials from other departments often meet with foreign officials on matters related to their responsibilities. Sometimes, the disparate perspectives and concerns of different U.S. agencies leave outsiders confused about American policy despite the best efforts of the State Department to have Americans speak in a single voice. In foreign capitals, however, the U.S. ambassador heads *the country team* of American personnel and is empowered to enforce a common strategy.

The diplomatic instrument already exists, ready for the president to use. The United States is caught in a web of international agreements and organization memberships. Many of them have regular meetings or prepare regular reports that can be used for discussions, negotiations, and actions—the United Nations Security Council (UNSC) and General Assembly, the North Atlantic Treaty Organization (NATO) Council, ad hoc groups such as those convened to discuss aid to Afghanistan and contact with anti-Qaddafi Libyan rebels.

Deciding to use diplomacy is only the first step, raising further issues of when, with whom, where, and how. Any new initiative has to be put in the mix with ongoing interactions and other issues where there may be agreements or disagreements. The president and subordinate officials need to determine which matters have priority, which have deadlines, and which have the greatest promise of success. Every time the president or secretary of state meets with a foreign official, someone has to decide which handful of the many issues that could be raised for high-level discussion actually will be raised in the limited time available. Diplomacy isn't just talking, much less negotiating, but rather involves pursuing particular goals in the context of overall foreign policy.

Growth and Professionalization of the State Department

In creating the State Department in 1789, Congress made clear that it was an instrument for the president by reiterating four times that it was subordinate to the chief executive. The secretary was to "perform and execute such duties as shall from time to time be enjoined on or entrusted to him by the President" and was required to conduct departmental business as the president "shall from time to time order or instruct." Current law has similar phrasing.[3]

Thomas Jefferson, the first secretary, was paid $3,500 (equivalent to about $85,000 today) and had three clerks, an interpreter, a doorkeeper, and a messenger.[4] In the first few years, the new nation had small diplomatic missions abroad in London, Paris, Lisbon, Madrid, and the Hague. As there were only two other executive departments in the early years of the republic—War for military affairs and Treasury for raising revenue and managing government accounts—State functioned as the department of everything else. State managed the mint and issued patents; it oversaw U.S. marshals and conducted the census; it supervised territorial affairs and collected immigration data. It kept and used the Great Seal of the United States and served as the repository for official documents. These collateral duties explain why the department was named State instead of just Foreign Affairs. As other departments were established in subsequent decades, most of those domestic duties were transferred away from State.

The department grew as the nation grew and expanded as America increased its dealings with the rest of the world. As Tables 2.1 and 6.2 show, personnel figures stayed below 1,000 until the 1890s and surged again only during and after World War II. The number of major diplomatic posts abroad was small until the 1830s, then doubled after the Civil War, and continued to climb with America's rise as a global power. The number of consular posts, however, was large by the middle of the 19th century as America saw the need for agents to promote commerce and protect American ships and crews. After 1945, many of these smaller posts were upgraded to full embassies.

One factor aiding the professionalization of the department and continuity in foreign policy was the presence of long-serving officials. Only three men held the top career post from 1841 to 1924, providing institutional memory and establishing a distinctive style to American diplomacy. And despite the use of political patronage in most presidential appointments, many highly-regarded 19th-century diplomats were retained in their posts through several changes of administration and party.

Grover Cleveland instituted written examinations and language tests for subordinate officials in 1895, and Congress combined the diplomatic and consular services into a single foreign service in 1924, with salaries and benefits creating opportunities for those with less wealthy backgrounds. While no career officers served as chief of mission before 1920, the figure rose to 30% after 1924 and to 55% by World War II.

These changes and subsequent ones gave America a professional foreign service of skilled practitioners diverse in background and well trained to deal with the complexities of modern international affairs. The department also reorganized periodically to cope with the emergence of new states and the rise of new problems.

American foreign policy changed more gradually, with periods of isolation from many of the rest of the world's diplomatic and security controversies even as the United States expanded its overseas economic activities and foreign trade. In the early years, American diplomacy sought to assert and protect its new nationhood, a goal endangered by the European wars after the French Revolution and America's still-unresolved problems with Great Britain. The mid-19th century saw the resolution of America's borders through a combination of threats, proposals, negotiations, and even limited war. The Union won the Civil War in part because of deft diplomacy that limited outside support to the Confederacy.

Table 6.2 — Department of State Personnel and Foreign Missions, 1950–2010

Personnel

1950	1955	1960	1965	1970	1975	1980	1985	1990
24,628	27,495	37,983	40,656	39,753	30,376	23,497	25,254	25,288

1995	2000	2005	2010
24,859	27,983	33,808	39,016

Foreign Missions

Year	1950	1960	1970	1980	1990	2000	2010
Diplomatic Posts	74	99	117	133	145	160	184
Consular Posts	179	166	122	100	97	92	84

This series of tables shows the expansion of the State Department during the 1960s and the reductions following the Vietnam War that were reversed only after the 9/11 attacks. The number of overseas missions has steadily expanded with the creation of new foreign governments and international organizations.

Sources: *Statistical Abstract of the United States;* Department of State, Office of the Historian.

By the start of the 20th century, the United States had acquired overseas territories, which it was unwilling to call colonies, and a sense that it had political, security, and economic interests that required global engagement with other powers. Despite a retrenchment after World War I, President Franklin D. Roosevelt (FDR) pushed and pulled the United States into a leadership role even before Pearl Harbor. Later presidents used diplomacy and other instruments in their foreign policy toolkits to prevail in the Cold War and to cope with the newly emerging major powers and security threats of the 21st century.

The State Department today employs about 12,000 people in the foreign service plus about 9,000 in the civil service. It maintains 260 embassies, consulates, and other posts in 180 countries. Support staff of foreign nationals at these posts totals 37,000. State's operational budget, not counting foreign assistance or contributions to international organizations, was $11.4 billion in 2011. While these figures have been growing in recent years, driven especially by the need for safer embassies and for civilian activities in Iraq and Afghanistan, deficit reduction pressures may limit or reverse these trends.

Organization

The diagram of the State Department (Figure 6.1) is misleading because it shows connections rather than power. Each node is equal-sized on the chart, despite wide variations in personnel, resources, and influence in practice. Nevertheless, it demonstrates that State has a section for every major issue

Figure 6.1 U.S. Department of State Organizational Chart

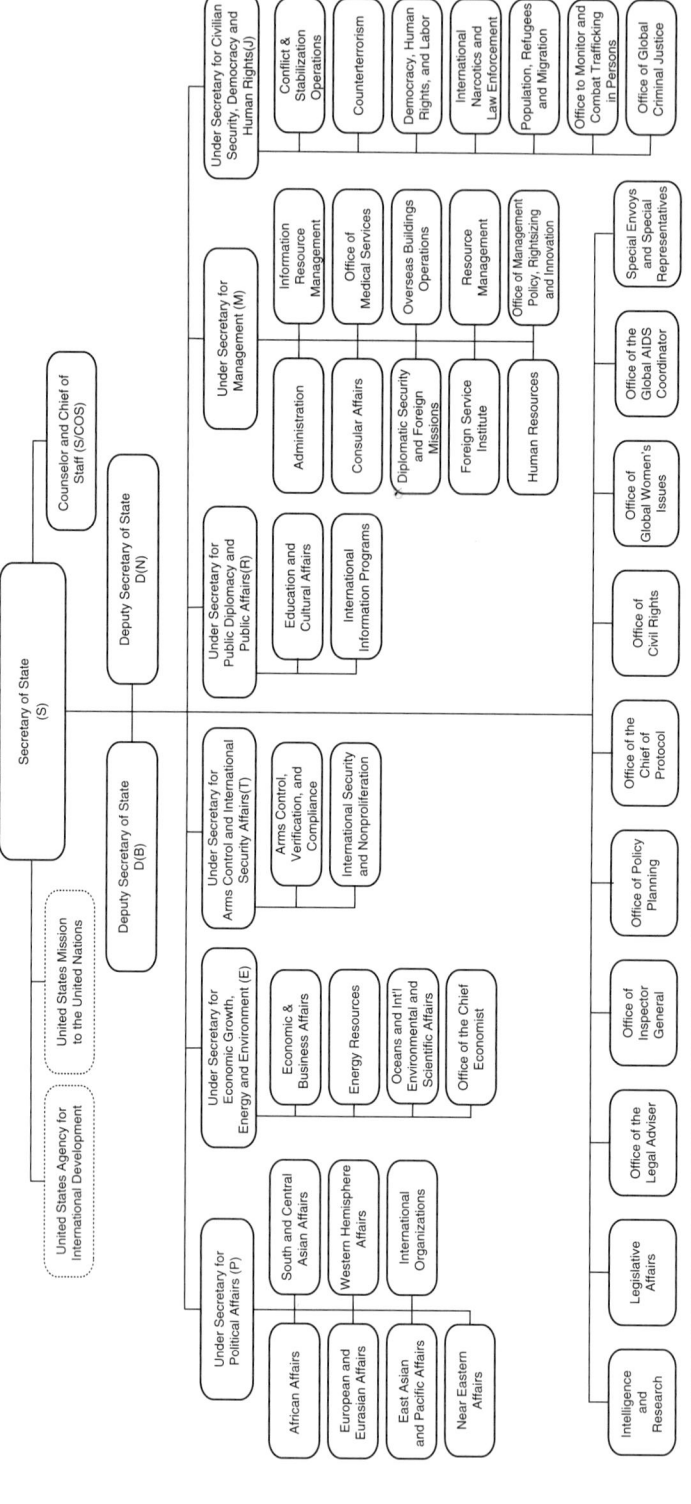

It's important to note in this chart how many special offices report directly to the secretary rather than through other channels. Whether these units are strong or weak depends on the personal preferences of the secretary. The middle and right portions of the chart show the many functional offices in State, but the real power historically has been in the regional bureaus headed by the under secretary for political affairs, usually seen as the number three at State.

Source: U.S. Department of State.

seen to be facing the department and the nation in its international dealings. Each office has a special shorthand designation, rooted in the distant past and often with no obvious connection to the title or subject matter, such as "T" for arms control, "R" for public affairs, and "H" for legislative affairs.

The secretary is at the top of the State Department, as law and tradition require. Next are two deputy secretaries, one as the alter ego of the secretary and the other as the chief manager of the department, especially of its budget and personnel processes. Nestled near the top and reporting directly to the secretary is the executive secretariat (S/ES), which functions as the secretary's right arm—coordinating the work of the department, dealing with the White House and other agencies, and running the 24-hour operations center. The S/ES also polices the flow of paperwork to the secretary, particularly to ensure that all the proper clearances have been obtained from stakeholding offices.

Curiously off to the side are the administrator for foreign aid programs, the U.S. permanent representative to the UN, and the counselor. It's easy to explain the counselor's role as an adviser on various topics who frequently gets special assignments from the secretary, thus removing the position from the regular bureaucratic hierarchy. Similarly, the ambassador to the UN is often a person with independent political standing, sometimes with cabinet rank, perhaps even a rival to the secretary, and thus not necessarily a true subordinate. The head of the Agency for International Development (AID), while dual-hatted as a State Department official, has separate legislated responsibilities, and the AID budget is only coordinated with State rather than determined by the senior department.

At the bottom of the chart are the many offices allowed to report directly to the secretary rather than through the regular bureaus. The important offices include the department's intelligence unit, Intelligence and Research (INR); the Office of Legislative Affairs (H), which handles congressional relations; the legal adviser; and small, specialized offices given special status often for symbolic reasons.

The Office of Policy Planning (S/P) has a celebrated history (George Kennan and Paul Nitze were its first two directors), a talented staff of both career and political appointees, and a mandate to think big thoughts, look ahead, and avoid trivia. S/P houses the secretary's speechwriters, who can shape policy by the simple words they choose. It also wields enormous bureaucratic power because its clearance is required on all policy papers going to the secretary from other offices.

There are five functional units and one regional one, each headed by an under secretary, but they vary widely in power. The under secretary for management (M) runs day-to-day operations as well as personnel management and training. It is also responsible for developing the department's budget but from a much less powerful position than, for example, the Pentagon, where budgets are a major tool of policy making as well as management. The under secretary for public diplomacy and public affairs (R) is the residual presence of what used to be the U.S. Information Agency until it consolidated with and subordinated to the State Department in 1999. In addition to normal public and media relations, R runs the educational and cultural programs that sends U.S. musical groups abroad and brings future leaders on visits to America.

The remaining three functional groups—Economic Growth, Energy, and the Environment (E), Arms Control and International Security Affairs (T), and Civilian Security, Democracy, and Human Rights (G)—all struggle to bring their concerns to bear on the policies largely formulated and implemented by the regional bureaus and the under secretary for political affairs (P), historically the third or fourth highest post in the department, just below the deputies. The regional bureaus house the *country desks,* which are the focal points for messages going to and from overseas posts.

Foreign policy tends to be made on a regional or country basis because that is the way diplomats think and work. Issues that cut across regional compartments are often harder to visualize and even harder to coordinate. Who has the lead in responding to Chinese arms sales to Africa, the China desk or the affected African desk officer? Who at State should be responsible for following Iranian-Venezuelan cooperation on oil and arms? The functional bureaus may weigh in with their concerns and recommendations, but the channels for policy development and action tend to be in and through the regional bureaus. Thus, even within State, there is a need for coordination and compromise in the carrying out of U.S. diplomatic activity.

The Country Team

Overseas, each embassy staff constitutes a country team for conducting American foreign policy. Achieving genuine teamwork, however, is a difficult process. As many as 30 different U.S. agencies may have people assigned to a given embassy. At the larger posts, State Department people may account for only one third of U.S. personnel.[5] Among the other agencies sending large numbers of people abroad are: DOD, with its military attachés; the United States Agency for International Development (USAID), to run assistance programs; Agriculture (USDA), with its Foreign Agricultural Service; Commerce, with its Foreign Commercial Service; Justice, with its legal liaison, drug enforcement, and Federal Bureau of Investigation (FBI) representatives; Treasury, with its attachés; the Peace Corps, with its volunteers; the Department of Homeland Security (DHS), with its immigration, customs, and transportation security offices; and the intelligence community (IC), with its spies.

These agency representatives perform important services for the United States as well as for their home departments. The defense attachés often develop close relationships with host country military leaders that can be helpful in crises. The agricultural representatives provide export services to U.S. producers and administer food aid and technical assistance to locals. The commercial attachés help U.S. businesses establish local markets and contacts. FBI and Drug Enforcement Administration (DEA) agents work with their foreign counterparts to combat crime. Treasury representatives provide on-scene expertise that helps the U.S. government and permits close collaboration with local financial authorities. As these examples illustrate, U.S. foreign policy activities have a wide reach and cover areas that many in the public, who associate American diplomacy more with the secretary of state and U.S. ambassadors, may not expect.

The chief of mission (usually the ambassador) has formal authority over all the people assigned to the embassy, though not over military personnel under the command of the regional combatant commanders. Each chief of mission receives a formal letter from the president designating him or her "the personal representative" of the president and assigning "full responsibility for the direction, coordination, and supervision of all United States government executive-branch employees." The chief of mission also has the right to see all communications to and from embassy officials. While the chiefs of mission can veto the assignment of particular people from the various agencies and insist on the recall of objectionable ones, they do not write the performance reports on those from outside State—and in practice they cannot really oversee the communications that go directly to and from agency home offices, bypassing State's channels.[6]

The presidential letter clearly provides *de jure* authority to the ambassador, but the chief of mission may lack *de facto* authority because the separate agencies often feel free to pursue their own agendas. The non-State people often view the ambassador as representing his or her department rather than the president, a point of view reinforced by the fact that most communications go *through* the secretary of state and most official guidance is developed under State's leadership even if there is interagency coordination.[7]

Each of the agencies sending people abroad has its own programs, goals, and priorities, and these may clash with the overarching goals established by the ambassador and coordinated with policy makers in Washington. The highest priority for the commercial attaché, for example, might be to secure some U.S. export, but that could conflict with embassy efforts to avoid questionable business practices or enriching certain host country officials. The ambassador's efforts to maintain cooperative relations with the national leader may conflict with military or intelligence programs that help political rivals. Former Ambassador Robert Oakley describes the many simultaneous challenges facing an embassy staff: "In Moscow, the Country Team must promote democratic reform efforts while enhancing opportunities for U.S. businesses in a dynamic emerging market, as well as improve nuclear security initiatives and monitor avian flu. It must do this while working on global and regional energy problems as well as traditional diplomacy."[8]

Ideally, potential conflicts should be worked out in Washington or in the local embassy. But, that requires timely communication and sometimes compromise, all of which can be hard to achieve in chaotic circumstances. That Moscow embassy has about 400 Americans plus another 665 local employees. The embassy in Afghanistan has over 800 U.S. personnel spread throughout the country. With the withdrawal of U.S. military forces from

Iraq in 2011, the U.S. embassy in Baghdad was scheduled to take over 310 of the 1,000+ tasks the Pentagon had been performing. Along with about 650 diplomats, the embassy was slated to oversee 17,000 people—about 1,000 from other government agencies, with the rest being mostly third-country nationals working as life support and security contractors. Security and budget concerns led the State Department in 2012 to review those plans, seeking significant cuts.[9]

Various studies have urged changes in the ways embassies operate. Most call for increased personnel and resources. Many envision the use of new technologies even to the point of virtual presence posts. Some call for better management training for senior officials so that they can better oversee and coordinate the multitude of activities underway by the various U.S. agencies. Both Secretary Condoleezza Rice's Transformational Diplomacy and Secretary Hillary Clinton's Quadrennial Diplomacy and Development Review (QDDR) contained new initiatives to strengthen civilian activities abroad.

Leadership

The secretary of state has the preeminent position in the president's cabinet and in the public eye on matters of foreign policy. (See Box 6.1.) Throughout history, some of America's most distinguished political figures have held that post. Recent decades have witnessed the first female secretaries of state—Madeleine Albright, Condoleezza Rice, and Hillary Clinton—and the first African-American Secretary, Colin Powell.

There are two contrasting operating styles among State's leaders. Most tend to run the department with a small circle of advisers, often long-time friends or associates. This was the model, for example, followed by James Baker, Madeleine Albright, Condoleezza Rice, and Hillary Clinton. The other approach, followed by George Shultz and Colin Powell, utilized the full professional hierarchy of the department, empowering subordinates by regularly including them in decision processes. There are pros and cons to each model. The small circle is good for loyalty, speed, political sensitivity, and consistency. The empowered bureaucracy is good for departmental

---

Box 6.1

Secretary of State . . . and President?

Thomas Jefferson was the first of six presidents who had previously served as secretary of state, the most prestigious cabinet post for most of U.S. history. Jefferson, Madison, Monroe, John Quincy Adams, Van Buren, and Buchanan all got significant government and foreign policy experience in that job. Another eight political leaders served as secretary but were defeated in their quests for the White House: Henry Clay, Daniel Webster, John C. Calhoun, William H. Seward, James G. Blaine, William Jennings Bryan, Charles Evans Hughes, and Edmund Muskie.

> **Box 6.2**
>
> **Who Makes Foreign Policy: The Busy Secretary of State**
>
> The secretary of state hardly ever has a day off. White House meetings have been held once or twice a week in the Bush and Obama administrations. In addition, the secretary has to travel abroad for face-to-face meetings with foreign leaders and for international conferences. Secretaries Condoleezza Rica and Hillary Rodham Clinton each averaged about 250,000 miles per year in foreign travel. In 2010, for example, Secretary Clinton visited 54 countries and spent 81 days away from Washington.
>
> *Source:* U.S. Department of State.

morale, professionalism, subordinate buy-in, and fuller consideration of alternative views.[10]

Whether secretaries of state are powerful within the government as a whole, however, depends on their relationships with the president. When presidents rely on others for key foreign policy advice—as Richard Nixon did on Henry Kissinger and George W. Bush did on Vice President Cheney and Defense Secretary Rumsfeld—the State Department suffers a loss of power, influence, and morale. As former Secretary Dean Rusk, who served two quite different presidents, acknowledged, "The real organization of government at higher echelons [is] how confidence flows down from the President."

Any secretary of state is enormously busy, as Box 6.2 indicates. They all have to travel widely and frequently. They appear on Capitol Hill regularly to explain and defend U.S. policy. And as members of the National Security Council (NSC), they are summoned to numerous White House meetings. In fact, the entire State Department is very busy. (See Box 6.3.)

The State Department itself is a large bureaucracy. There are 44 positions important enough to require Senate confirmation in addition to the more than 100 ambassadorial appointments. While most of these officials work in hierarchical channels, some 45 different people are formally authorized to report directly to the secretary—far more than any good manager could handle.[11] Many of these posts are traditionally given to career foreign and civil service personnel, thus enhancing the institutional memory and professionalization of the department. In contrast to DOD, where no career civilian has ever been appointed to a post requiring Senate confirmation, the State Department typically appoints career foreign service officers (FSOs) to half of the assistant secretary posts and to 85% of the deputy assistant secretary positions.[12]

Ambassadorships are awarded to both political appointees and career officials. Some presidents—and host countries—prefer envoys who are personally close to the White House despite their diplomatic inexperience. Some presidential friends and major contributors welcome the prestige of an

| Box 6.3 |

Who Makes Foreign Policy: A Day in the Life of the State Department

Every day, U.S. diplomats are busy around the globe, gathering information, consulting with foreign officials, attending international conferences, urging actions in support of American policies and interests. Some days are busier than others, of course, but here is a sample of the publicly announced activities of senior State Department officials based in Washington on a fairly typical day. While many more meetings are not announced publicly, and those may be even more significant for foreign policy, the breadth of diplomatic engagement shows that the United States must deal simultaneously with dozens of countries and hundreds of issues. When the president chooses to use the diplomatic instrument for a particular foreign policy goal, that action must be integrated with the many ongoing diplomatic interactions.

On May 18, 2011

- The Secretary of State met with a Chinese general; met with the U.S. ambassador to India; met the Icelandic foreign minister; met with the Secretary of Defense and the National Security Adviser.
- The senior Deputy Secretary of State was in Bahrain, heading a U.S. delegation that met with local government officials.
- The junior Deputy Secretary met with the Tunisian finance minister and attended a meeting at the White House.
- The USAID Administrator met with the Israeli ambassador; met with three U.S. ambassadors; attended a meeting in the Senator's Dining Room in the Capitol.
- The Under Secretary for Political Affairs spoke at the opening of a historical exhibit at the State Department and met with a U.S. Senator.
- The Under Secretary for Economic, Energy, and Agricultural Affairs gave speeches to a presidential science advisory group and a study group on the U.S. and Chinese economies.
- The Under Secretary for Arms Control and International Security Affairs traveled to Moscow for meetings with Russian officials.
- The Assistant Secretary for International Narcotics and Law Enforcement Affairs was in Accra, Ghana, discussing the West Africa Citizen Security Initiative.
- The Assistant Secretary for East Asian and Pacific Affairs was in Singapore during a trip to Southeast Asia and Japan.
- The Assistant Secretary for Economic, Energy, and Business Affairs met with the Paraguayan Ambassador and the Paraguayan Vice Minister of Economic Relations.
- The Assistant Secretary for European and Eurasian Affairs testified before the Senate Foreign Relations Committee.
- The Assistant Secretary for Population, Refugees and Migration participated in an intergovernmental consultation on migration, asylum, and refugees held in Miami.

(Continued)

> (Continued)
> - The Assistant Secretary for Educational and Cultural Affairs met with the Panamanian Ambassador.
> - The Ambassador-at-large and Coordinator for Counterterrorism met with an official from the British ministry of foreign affairs.
> - The Special Representative for North Korea Policy held meetings in South Korea.
> - The Ambassador-at-large to monitor and combat trafficking in persons spoke to a conference in Rome on modern day slavery.
> - The Ambassador-at-large for global women's issues met with a delegation of Pakistani female entrepreneurs.
> - The Special Representative for Global Intergovernmental Affairs was in Nigeria meeting with Nigerian governors.
> - The Special Envoy for climate change was in Mexico City for a meeting of the U.S.-Mexico Bilateral Framework on Clean Energy and Climate Change.
>
> Source: U.S. Department of State, www.state.gov/r/pa/prs/appt/2011/05/163617.htm.

ambassadorial title, especially if they can serve in a less stressful post with good weather. In recent decades, with minor variations, careerists have held about 70% of the ambassadorial slots, with about 30% political. Virtually all Caribbean posts go to political appointees, while most African and Middle Eastern positions go to careerists.[13]

The Changing Foreign Service

Until the creation of the permanent career foreign service in 1924 and the establishment of professional pay, housing allowances and other benefits, and retirement pensions, most U.S. officials abroad had to be independently wealthy. Until World War II, most American diplomats were white males, mostly Anglo-Saxon Protestants, and often with Ivy League degrees. Much of the time, the work wasn't very hard and the parties were fun. A career officer who was then ambassador to Poland, Hugh Gibson, told Congress in 1924, "You hear very frequently about the boys with the white spats, the tea drinkers, the cookie pushers, and while they are a very small minority, they make a noise entirely disproportionate to their numbers." He urged professionalization of the foreign service in order to "crowd out those incompetents and defectives."[14] In some circles, diplomats are maligned with such stereotypes.

The road to diversity was uphill and slow. By 1970, the foreign service was still 95% male and 99% white. Women could serve, but they had to resign if they married. Lawsuits forced changes in these practices and opened more opportunities during the 1970s, and the Foreign Service Act of 1980 specifically declared that "the members of the Foreign Service should be representative of the American people."[15]

The foreign service today is much more diverse, both in the backgrounds of people recruited and in the range of assignments they perform. As of 2011, two thirds of the total (including FSO generalists and specialists) were male and one third female. African-Americans constituted 7.0%, Hispanics 5.0%, and Asian-Americans 6.8%; the overwhelming majority of 80.6% were white. Of the total foreign service, over half (about 6,800) are generalists, the people who perform the key diplomatic tasks, and the remainder (about 5,000) are the specialists who handle daily operations of office management, security, technical equipment, health, and other support services. Overseas posts also employ about 38,000 foreign service nationals, local citizens who are support staff to U.S. personnel.[16]

The core of America's diplomatic instrument, foreign service generalists, is outnumbered by many measures in the Pentagon. There are more Pentagon lawyers than FSOs, more colonels (and navy captains) than in all ranks of the foreign service, and more members of military bands than FSOs.

The generalist FSOs enter one of five career tracks. Political officers deal directly with host governments and report on policy developments. Economic officers work on economic, trade, energy, and related issues. Consular officers provide citizen services to Americans abroad, such as facilitating adoptions as well as screening visa applicants. Public diplomacy officers—successors to the once-separate U.S. Information Agency—run educational and cultural exchange programs as well as efforts to explain America and its policies to others. Management officers specialize in budgets and embassy management. While any of these tracks could lead to senior posts and satisfying careers, the political officers are generally seen as the diplomatic elite.

In addition to FSOs, who typically spend two thirds of their careers overseas, the department employs 9,300 civil service careerists, mostly in Washington. These people have professional or scientific backgrounds and perform legal, research, administrative, or management duties. One key disparity is that few FSOs want to serve in the functional bureaus because such assignments are viewed as less career enhancing than in the regional bureaus, so they are largely staffed by civil service personnel.[17]

Although some presidents have had low regard for the State Department and the foreign service, former secretaries have much more positive views. As Henry Kissinger wrote: "Several Secretaries have begun their tours of office with that expressed determination [to 'clean out' the department]. I know of none that left office without having come to admire the dedicated men and women who supply the continuity and expertise of our foreign policy. I entered the State Department a skeptic, I left a convert."[18]

On the other hand, former Secretary Alexander Haig called the service "an asteroid, spinning in an eccentric orbit, captured by the gravity of its procedures and its self-interest, deeply suspicious of politicians who threaten its stability by changing its work habits." And James Baker, while praising

FSOs for talent and loyalty, also noted their tendency "to avoid risk taking or creative thinking."[19]

State Department Culture

There is a dominant culture in the State Department, quite distinctive from those in the other major institutions of American foreign policy. A colonel at the Army War College contrasted the military culture with that of diplomats in his 1998 paper, "Defense Is From Mars, State Is From Venus." While sometimes snarky and condescending—"Venutians frequently find that explaining what they do for a living is met with blank stares"—the colonel also has valuable insights based on scientific evidence.[20]

It so happens that both State and DOD make extensive use of the Myers-Briggs Type Indicator (MBTI) personality evaluation tests, and that the characteristics of people in each department are sharply different. Myers Briggs analyzes people on four contrasting pairs: extroversion (E) versus introversion (I); intuition (N) versus sensation (S); thinking (T) versus feeling (F); and judging (J) versus perceiving (P). There are thus 16 possible combinations.

Both military personnel and FSOs are overwhelmingly introverted, thinking, and judgmental, but uniformed officers tend to rely on sensation, while the diplomats rely on intuition.

Nearly half (47%) of FSOs have the INTJ personality type, compared to only 1% of the general population.[21] Such people, according to the analysts, "convey confidence, stability, competence, intellectual insight, and self-assurance." They are also "intensely individualistic. Stimulated by difficulties, and most ingenious in solving them. Motivated by inspiration." They tend to see the world as a chessboard and like to act independently. Teamwork is hard for them. They embrace theory but avoid long-range planning as they see each problem as unique. They have a much higher tolerance for ambiguity and uncertainty than their military colleagues.

In practice, these differing personality styles help explain why interagency coordination is difficult. But, they also point out State's strengths at seeing the forest as well as the trees and at finding ways to bridge what to others appear to be irreconcilable points of view. Diplomats negotiate. Successful negotiation means reconciling differences, often by compromises that have to be face-saving in order to be durable.

The downside to this way of thinking, however, is that it presumes that blacks and whites can always be combined into a comfortable gray, that artful ambiguity can paper over wide differences, that searching for an agreement is almost always better than giving up, especially if the likely alternative is war. To have to suspend talks, to halt contacts, especially to have to close an embassy because of fundamental disagreements, is a diplomat's worst failure.

Similarly, a diplomat's special skills—the ability to understand foreign governments and cultures, to empathize with them in order to craft agreements—can lead to *clientitis*, that bureaucratic disease that makes foreign concerns seem more important than American ones. Senator Jesse Helms (R-NC), a longtime critic of the State Department, used to complain, "There's no American Desk at the State Department." And, former Secretary George Shultz used to meet with newly named ambassadors and ask them to point on a globe to their country. Almost invariably, they indicated their new postings. The secretary corrected them by pointing instead to the United States. He wanted to inoculate them against that clientitis.

President John F. Kennedy distrusted the State Department because he believed it was too conservative. Richard Nixon distrusted it because he considered it too liberal. Former Speaker of the House Newt Gingrich criticized the department for being insufficiently loyal to President George W. Bush and said that Secretary Colin Powell had "gone native" by adopting departmental views. The common thread in these comments is that State, like all bureaucracies, is fundamentally a force for continuity, and its perspective is necessarily different from that of the White House, where domestic political pressures are most acute.

Representation and Engagement

The State Department's people and organizations form the primary instrument of diplomacy. They are actually used in a wide variety of activities, with specialized skills and responsibilities. Foremost, of course, is representation of the United States, both symbolically and as a point of contact for foreigners. Representation also entails communicating and advocating American policies.

Presidents often deal directly with foreign leaders and frequently use other officials and even private citizens as emissaries to foreign governments. (See Box 6.4.) National Security Advisers (NSAs) Henry Kissinger, Zbigniew Brzezinski, and Brent Scowcroft were each sent on sensitive missions to Beijing to resolve issues in U.S.–China policy. President Bill Clinton used former President Jimmy Carter, Senator Sam Nunn, and then retired General Colin Powell to persuade the Haitian military government to surrender power in order to avoid a U.S. military invasion. Former New Mexico Governor Bill Richardson—who also has been a member of Congress, a cabinet officer, and UN ambassador—has frequently traveled to North Korea to convey messages and resolve particular problems.

These people were not part of the State Department hierarchy, but they often were advised and supported by foreign service personnel in Washington and abroad. Their activities demonstrate the flexibility of America's diplomatic instrument, while the State Department remains the principal agent for international diplomacy.

The Obama administration made even greater use than its predecessors of special representatives or envoys for various foreign policy issues,

> **Box 6.4**
>
> ## Inside View: The State Department Outnumbered
>
> In the George W. Bush administration, the national security policy process was dominated by Defense Secretary Rumsfeld in collaboration with Vice President Cheney. The State Department was frequently bypassed by those senior officials, who went directly to the president, or outnumbered in meetings that were held including the diplomats. The State Department's director of the policy planning staff explained how things worked.
>
> *In this administration, the process didn't work nearly as well [as when Bush's father was president] for several reasons. . . . One is that [the Joint Chiefs of Staff] had a lot less voice in this administration. The Pentagon in previous administration really had two voices. Not in this administration. It was just Rumsfeld. Second of all, the vice president's office has become the equivalent of a separate institution or bureaucracy. When I was in the White House in [Bush] 41, the vice president had one or at most two people doing foreign policy. . . . In this administration, the vice president has his own mini-NSC staff. And at every meeting they had a voice and a vote. The vice president ended up getting, from what I could tell, three bites at the apple. He had his staff at every meeting. He would then come to the principals meetings. And then he'd have his one-on-ones with the president. And given the views that came out of the vice president's office, it introduced a certain bias to the system. As a result, I felt that at just about every meeting, the State Department began behind two and a half to one.*
>
> Source: Policy Planning Staff Director Richard Haass, quoted in David J. Rothkopf, *Running the World* (New York: Public Affairs, 2004), 407–408.

some two dozen by 2010. Former Ambassador Richard Holbrooke was the Obama administration's special representative to Pakistan and Afghanistan. Former Senator George Mitchell was special envoy for Middle East Peace. Retired General Scott Gration was special envoy to Sudan. And there were also special advisors for nonproliferation, North Korea policy, Guantanamo, climate change, and various energy issues. Such arrangements have their own strengths and weaknesses. It helps to have a single point of focus and responsibility for issues that cut across usual bureaucratic borders, provided that person can build a competent team and receive the necessary support from his or her superiors and colleagues. But, such a post can easily be orphaned by higher-ranking officials or policy priorities as few have the legal standing to control their own budgets or give orders beyond their own offices.

Regular diplomatic personnel spend most of their time in the representation function, meeting with foreign officials and reaching out to others on behalf of the United States. They explain and advocate U.S. policies and seek agreement and support from the host governments. Sometimes they cajole; sometimes they threaten; sometimes they deliver dollars or deals; sometimes they deny what the host government most desperately wants.

Negotiations

The most dramatic aspect of international engagement is summit diplomacy. Presidents regularly travel to multinational meetings of organizations like NATO, Asia-Pacific Economic Cooperation (APEC), the G-8 and G-20 economic summits, and the annual session of the UN General Assembly. They also travel abroad for bilateral meetings with foreign leaders and high-profile public events. This is not surprising because the president is the chief diplomat. But behind the scenes, U.S. officials from the White House and State Department frequently lay the groundwork and negotiate the communiqués and agreements announced during these meetings.

Ambassadors and special envoys also negotiate but only subject to guidance and approval from Washington. That guidance can be very specific and constraining, such as on nuclear weapons matters, or it can be more general and flexible. Negotiating teams are also dispatched to major international conferences, some of which last for weeks, months, and even years. For example, negotiations for a follow-on arms control agreement with Russia—called New Strategic Arms Reduction Treaty (START)—began in 2006 and continued for four years under two different presidents.

Negotiations can take numerous forms—informal, highly secret, indirect through third parties, formal meetings and conferences, bilateral and multilateral, and so forth. While the sides may make formal proposals, diplomats often use the device of a *nonpaper,* a proposal not officially attributable to a particular government on blank paper rather than letterhead. In 2006, for example, the Iranian government sent a nonpaper to the United States via a European diplomat suggesting ways for the United States and Iran to engage in diplomatic talks.[22]

Analyzing and Reporting

What Washington wants most from the field, and what FSOs spend most of their office time doing, is crafting brilliant analyses of host country policies, politics, and personalities. Many a young diplomat dreams of writing a new *long telegram,* George Kennan's broad and deep analysis of the sources of Soviet conduct that led to a Washington consensus on the policy of containment and a prestigious job as first head of the new policy planning staff. Short of that, embassy officials hope that they can put daily events into a broader context and that their inside sources can provide more significant information than journalists can obtain.

FSOs get chosen in part on the basis of their analytical and writing skills. They get promoted in part on how well they report on developments in their overseas posts. There are frustrations, of course. Much reporting is to answer the mail to Congress with required reports on human rights and drug enforcement and so forth or to check the box on a required annual survey of key economic sectors or social trends. Only rarely can their reports justify high levels of classification, yet they know that people in Washington tend to read only top secret messages, saving the unclassified ones for the free time that never comes. (See Box 6.5.)

Overseas messages are called cables, echoing the time when they traveled undersea at high cost and were often written in truncated form, combining words and omitting articles in order to minimize per-word pricing. Now, they arrive on secure computer terminals but are still formatted so that anyone will know who cleared it and who gets to see it. By convention, all outgoing cables are signed with the secretary's name, even if he or she never sees it, and incoming ones carry the ambassador's name, regardless of who authored it.

As a result of the flood of diplomatic messages leaked to the news media, the rest of us can see examples of routine analysis and reporting from U.S. embassies. Many are dull; some are clever; few even begin to approach the Kennan model.

Public Diplomacy

Although what we now call public diplomacy was an essential part of the State Department at least since World War II, it had a separate bureaucratic existence until 1999, when it was merged with the department. Many insiders claim that the merger downgraded their programs and weakened America's ability to maintain prestige and influence abroad. Recent studies and statements by Secretaries Rice and Clinton have urged greater emphasis on public diplomacy as a tool of foreign policy.

Some public diplomacy is short-term public relations—seeking publicity of U.S. policy statements and favorable coverage of events in the United States. But, some of the most effective work pays out only in the long term. Cultural exchanges nurture public understanding and appreciation between Americans and foreigners. Sending musicians and other performers abroad adds to American *soft power*. Bringing future leaders to extended visits around the United States, and not just to Washington, makes them more realistic and perhaps more sympathetic about America than if they were dependent on their local media. As these benefits are slow to accrue and hard to quantify, it's easy to cut back when cuts are required.

Citizen Services

Consular officers probably do more to help or hurt America's image abroad, or public approval of the State Department at home, than U.S. ambassadors. They are in the receiving line of those seeking U.S. visas. They help Americans in trouble while traveling as well as facilitate adoptions and business contacts. Their work puts them in danger but also gives them unique insights into the thinking of local people. Their job of assessing visa applicants also puts them in the front line of defense against terrorists. Despite these invaluable functions, consular officers are peripheral to what we usually think of as *doing diplomacy*.

Surprising as it may seem, the United States has embassy-like operations in countries with which it has no formal diplomatic relations. They are used to perform citizen services rather than regular diplomacy. Since 1977, there has been a U.S. interests section in the Swiss Embassy in Havana and a similar Cuban presence in Washington. Switzerland also houses a U.S. interests section in Iran, while Pakistan has one for Iran in Washington. Sweden represents several western countries in North Korea. There is a different arrangement in Taiwan, where the U.S. has a *de facto* embassy, which is technically a private organization staffed by career diplomats who are formally on leave.

Other Operations

Increasingly, State Department personnel are being used to run programs in the field very operationally. While USAID personnel and others in the embassy have long been operational, this is a change for many in the political and economic sections, who were used to working close to the capital wearing business dress. This activity has been most evident in Iraq and Afghanistan, where civilians from State worked alongside U.S. military personnel in the provincial reconstruction teams (PRTs) in their efforts to advise and assist local communities and officials. The teams arranged community meetings, advised local officials on procedures for activities like elections and budgeting, helped facilitate funding for local projects, and myriad other tasks. As forward-deployed Americans, they were also well positioned to report on political and security developments. When the teams were less successful, it was usually because the security situation was too perilous for them to move about easily.

Secretary Rice began a process of shifting several hundred positions out of Washington and Europe in order to put more people in more difficult strategic posts in the Near East, Asia, Africa, and Latin America. Many were sent to Iraq and Afghanistan but also to India, China, Indonesia, and Venezuela.

Policy Making

Diplomats don't just execute foreign policy; they also work to develop it through a sometimes somewhat cumbersome process. Ambassadors routinely conclude their reports on foreign developments with recommendations for actions. Policy planners write options papers and circulate them to other offices for clearance to send the documents to more senior officials. Every day, desk officers draft *talking points* for official spokespeople to use in responding to media inquiries. Speechwriters use public appearances and congressional testimony by senior officials to announce policies in the most persuasive language. Reports to Congress and self-initiated policy reviews may conclude with major policy announcements.

Policy is more than statements of goals and intentions; it's also what governments do. And when what the government says is different from what it does, that suggests that policy is not very well coordinated.

Policy papers may recommend actions in the form of statements—"Let's criticize this example of Chinese abuse of human rights"—or in the form of tangible measures—"Let's halt aid to that corrupt government." State

The Diplomatic Instrument

mandates a careful review of such proposals from the country desk to the regional bureau and then to senior leaders. All potentially interested offices should be asked to comment and ultimately to *clear*—that is to approve sending the paper forward. This process is policed by the S/ES, which has a formal handbook outlining the procedures to be followed. One of the special powers of the policy planning staff is that its clearance is required on all policy papers submitted to the secretary, ostensibly to ensure consistency with other established policies.

Multiple veto points can slow the process down or lead to more ambiguous language or less radical departures from current policy. Bureaucracies, after all, are a predictable force for continuity. On major issues, the paper—with its recommendations or options or key talking points—may go to the secretary for decision.

Box 6.5

Inside View: The Clearance Process

Almost every document going to the secretary of state and other senior officials has to be seen and approved by several subordinate officials. The same is true for official "cables" sent to U.S. embassies abroad, all of which are nominally issued in the secretary's name. This clearance process can be very time-consuming, and dissenting officials can insist on changes to satisfy some of their concerns. The process often involves intense negotiations over what words to use and what positions to take. The bureaucratic hoops are spelled out in this excerpt from the handbook from the office that polices the clearance process.

Write concisely; if you don't, your Principal may not have time to read the memo. Present the facts clearly and in an organized manner; make sure the analysis holds. Give sufficient detail to offer a sound basis for a decision, but don't overwhelm the Principal with minutiae. . . . If there is a difference of opinion within the Department, don't obfuscate—make that difference clear.

It is the drafting officer's responsibility to clear memos involving the interests of other bureaus or agencies with those bureaus or agencies. **Neither the Secretary nor USG policy interests can be well-served by uncleared talking points, recommendations, or briefing materials.** *It is important that the Secretary or other Principal be confident that the memo has been vetted, that its contents is accurate, that the downsides of a policy decision or discussion are clear, and that any recommended course of action is legal.*

Don't let disagreement on substantive recommendations hold up a memorandum's progress; where differences exist, craft the memo to highlight clearly the bureaus' differing views and the full range of reasonable options available. Although memoranda must be cleared fully, drafters should avoid unnecessary clearances. One clearance per bureau is generally sufficient, provided the person clearing has sufficient knowledge of the bureau's interest and the authority to represent it.

Source: *The Executive Secretariat Handbook*, 2000, U.S. Department of State.

As the most important foreign policy matters need to be vetted through an interagency process usually run by the NSC staff, State personnel have an incentive to draft the first paper on an issue because that can frame the matter in a way that points to its favored outcome. And when that first paper arrives from another agency, State may have to raise objections or delays to obtain changes.

Bureaucratic Rivalries Among State, Defense, and the National Security Council

In the interagency process, State is often literally outgunned. What Defense Secretary Robert Gates has called "the defense 800 pound gorilla" tends to dominate foreign policy discussions that have any kind of security component, as most do. If State wants to back diplomacy with the threat of force, the Pentagon insists that that force be ready and credible and usable without interfering with other DOD activities. DOD also represents capabilities for immediate action—aircraft, people, tents, and radios—that no other department has, especially not State.

Whatever deference may be given to State as the lead agency on foreign policy may be insignificant when someone asks, "Who's going to pay for this?" There was a time, the golden year of 1950, when State's budget equaled half the Pentagon's budget. In recent years, the ratio has been more like 1 to 20.

Nevertheless, State brings analytic and diplomatic skills to interagency discussions, so its views can get a fair hearing. The NSC staff, however, has even greater advantages: proximity to the president, access to all of the most sensitive intelligence, and the right to call—or cancel—interagency meetings and set the agenda.

While the formal processes tend to be dominated by the NSC and the Pentagon, there are also informal processes that give State more equal standing. In most administrations, there are regular face-to-face meetings over breakfast or lunch for the secretaries of state and defense and the NSA. These are in addition to the numerous formal NSC-level meetings and permit out-of-channel exchanges: "We're thinking of doing this." "Can you help us resolve this problem our subordinates are having?" In addition to these cabinet-level sessions, departmental deputies also meet frequently both formally and informally and can use those venues to settle disputes. Some analysts believe that the widespread use of informal channels is the result of officials trying to work around a weak and ineffective formal system.[23]

Within State, there are other rivalries that can impede effective action. The regional bureaus have more prestige and people than the functional bureaus, and State's processes channel most activities on a bilateral or regional track. The foreign service similarly tends to dominate civil service personnel on policy questions. And USAID remains in an uncertain status, not fully subordinate to State but not really independent either.

Congress and the State Department

Congress manages and oversees the State Department with a great tangle of frayed ropes. Most basic foreign policy law is contained in the Foreign Assistance Act of 1961, a 400-page measure that has not been substantially amended since 1985. As a result of patchwork changes over the years, the law contains a bewildering array of 33 goals, 75 priority areas, and 247 directives.[24] No State Department authorization bill has been enacted since 2002. Even when the foreign policy committees produce legislation widely viewed as necessary for enactment, individuals and groups may seek to add controversial measures that prolong debates and may undermine support for the basic legislation. The net result of this failure to pass basic legislation is a weakening of the authorizing committees compared to the appropriations committees and thus a weakening of the policy perspectives and basic guidance that those committees are supposed to provide.

Nor has Congress provided funds for international activities in a timely manner. Neither of the appropriations bills for the State Department and foreign operations has been passed before the end of the fiscal year since 1996. Only four times in the past 20 years has the Foreign Operations Bill been passed on time. The figure for State Department funding is only three times. Even worse, four times in the past 10 years, neither bill passed until January or February.

There is no strong domestic constituency for foreign policy funding. Surveys find that a large number of Americans think that foreign aid takes up close to one fifth of the federal budget, when in fact, all international affairs programs, including the State budget, amount to only 1%. Defense programs produce jobs at home; foreign policy programs don't, except to a very minor degree.

As a consequence, Congress feels freer to cut international programs (budget function 150) than defense (budget function 050). Lawmakers routinely cut presidential requests for international affairs programs, often by percentages 5 to 10 times greater than legislative cuts in defense spending. For example, in the Reagan administration, Congress reduced defense requests by an average of 2.73% while cutting international affairs by 7.07%. In the G. H. W. Bush administration, function 050 was cut an average 2.08% each year, while function 150 was slashed by 12.62%. In the Clinton administration, Congress added an average 1.55% to 050 while cutting 150 by 14.49%. In the George W. Bush years, Congress added 0.4% to basic (nonemergency) defense requests on an average annual basis while cutting international affairs by 2.0%.[25] (See Figure 6.2.)

The State Department has many critics and few defenders on Capitol Hill. The two foreign policy committees—Senate Foreign Relations and House Foreign Affairs—offer few political benefits to members. They may gain attention during international crises but get criticized back home for foreign travel. They gain firsthand knowledge of foreign leaders, but can't

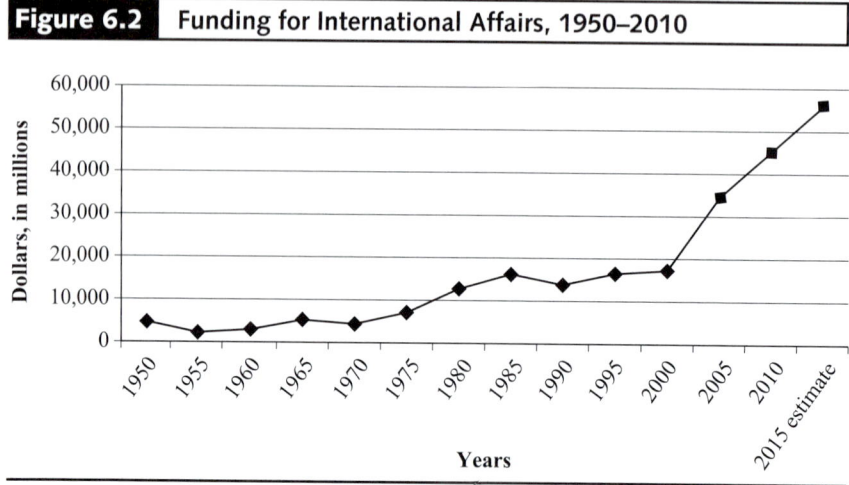

Figure 6.2 Funding for International Affairs, 1950–2010

The major factors for changing funding levels were increased aid to nations in the Middle East after the 1978 Camp David agreements, cutbacks as the Cold War ended, and then the surge of spending after 2001 relating to counterterrorism and the war in Iraq. Costs also climbed as the U.S. added posts in newly independent countries and built more secure embassies. Despite these increases, total spending on international affairs-related programs has remained as only about 1% of the total federal budget.

Source: Office of Management and Budget, Historical Statistics, Table 3.1 Outlays by Function and Superfunction: 1940–2016, www.whitehouse.gov/sites/default/files/omb/budget/fy2012/assets/hist03z1.xls.

accept campaign contributions from foreigners. On the other hand, some members have been effective issue entrepreneurs, becoming key players on particular issues, like Senator Richard Lugar (R-IN) on Soviet nuclear dismantling, or Senator James Webb (D-VA) on Burma, or Congressman Tom Lantos (D-CA) on human rights issues.

Congress treats foreign aid programs the way it handles much domestic legislation, earmarking funds for favored countries and imposing sanctions on miscreants. Programs with strong political support—such as aid to Israel or measures to combat HIV/AIDS—get robust funding, while less favored activities get squeezed for funds. Under Secretary Colin Powell and his successors, the State Department won added funds to increase personnel after years of restraint and even hiring freezes. More recent political pressures for budget cuts may curtail such growth.

Congress tends to prefer procedural legislation to substantive policy laws. For example, it has written laws imposing sanctions on nations supporting terrorism or abusing human rights but gives the president discretion to make such findings—and usually even to waive the sanctions for a higher national security interest. (One reason sanctions on dealings with Castro's Cuba are so hard to change is that they were written into permanent law without the waiver provisions now commonly included.) Similarly, the law requires reports on foreign arms sales and the right to pass legislation vetoing particular sales. Even the War Powers Act, arguably a delegation of Congress's power to declare war, merely requires reports from the president and timely procedures to pass restraining legislation. Observers can debate whether this approach is in recognition of the need for executive discretion or a way of permitting criticism while avoiding congressional accountability.

While it is difficult to pass binding, substantive legislation, Congress often resorts to symbolic gestures, such as a sense of Congress resolutions praising or condemning foreign leaders or their actions. Legislation condemning Ottoman Turkey for "genocide" of Armenians has come close to passage several times, pushed by Armenian-Americans and their friends in Congress, despite warnings that this would cause serious problems for U.S. relations with modern Turkey.

The Senate, with its constitutional powers to advise and consent to nominations to ambassadorships and other senior positions and to approve treaties by a two-thirds vote, plays a special role in foreign policy, sometimes abusing its privileges by delaying or denying votes on noncontroversial nominees in order to gain leverage on some other matters or by complicating treaty consideration with unrelated political issues. In recent decades, the executive branch has tried to get around the treaty hurdles by concluding agreements with other nations that are not labeled treaties and thus do not have to be submitted for the two-thirds vote of approval.

While Congress is usually willing to defer to the executive branch in crisis situations, it has jealously guarded its power of the purse when asked for contingency funds. For example, a small ($25 million) contingency fund for unanticipated opportunities was reduced and then eliminated from the Foreign Operations Appropriations Bill in the 1970s after it was used to pay for a helicopter for a visiting foreign leader. On the other hand, Congress has also been willing to fund over $1.3 billion in annual funds for certain specific contingency situations, including disaster and famine aid, refugee assistance, and peacekeeping operations.[26] It's worth noting, however, that in an era of greater legislative-executive cooperation on foreign affairs, and less virulent partisanship (1960–1961 in particular), Congress was willing to give the president a yearly overseas contingency fund equal to $1 billion to 1.5 billion in current dollars.

As will be clear in Chapter 7, many committees have jurisdiction over matters that affect U.S. foreign policy. The foreign policy committees have primary jurisdiction on, say, policy toward China, but the defense committees can hold hearings and write legislation that relates to Chinese military capabilities and strategy. The trade committees (House Ways and Means and Senate Finance) can set tariffs or authorize trade agreements, but the banking committees can write laws on China's currency. The judiciary committees can write laws on intellectual property rights after looking into China's software piracy activities. Other committees could write consumer laws forbidding importation of Chinese products containing lead or other dangerous products. And, the appropriations committees can condition money for any federal agency on some aspect of relations with China.

There is no requirement—or easy mechanism—for Congress to fashion a comprehensive and consistent grand strategy for China or any other major nation or issue. Political incentives push members toward *ad hoc* responses and prevent much collaboration across party or committee lines. On occasion, Congress has been a strong supporter of the State Department and its people and programs, but more often, it is a fair-weather friend.

***

The diplomatic instrument with its many channels and venues is always available to the president. The State Department manages the infrastructure for international engagement, though other officials may be tasked for particular issues. The real choice for senior policy makers is rarely whether to talk to foreign officials but rather which issues to raise, and when and how, in the context of all issues that may be relevant and outstanding.

Case Study: Building the Gulf War Coalition, 1990

Routine diplomacy involves meetings, conferences, exchanges of views, and occasionally negotiations of international agreements. This is a story of extraordinary diplomacy, when the secretary of state traveled widely and engaged numerous foreign leaders in an urgent effort to build a coalition to challenge Saddam Hussein's invasion of Kuwait. It shows that personal diplomacy can make a difference.

Secretary of State James Baker was in Siberia, talking and fishing with Soviet Foreign Minister Eduard Shevardnadze, when he learned of Saddam Hussein's imminent invasion of Kuwait on August 1, 1990. He told his Soviet counterpart, who checked with Moscow and told Baker not to worry. When confirmation of the invasion came a few hours later, Shevardnadze was angry and embarrassed. Baker seized the opportunity to press for a joint statement condemning the attack and demanding an immediate withdrawal as well as halting arms shipments. Because the USSR was a major weapons supplier and diplomatic supporter of Iraq, Baker saw cooperation with Moscow as the linchpin for building an international coalition against Saddam Hussein. The two sides decided to discuss the matter further.

Baker left for a preplanned visit to Mongolia. Shevardnadze called from Moscow and said it might be difficult to reach agreement on a joint statement. A State Department team in Moscow found Soviet officials opposed to tough language and recommended against a Baker visit. But, the secretary decided he could succeed if he put American prestige—and prospects for further U.S.-Soviet cooperation on other issues—on the line in a face-to-face meeting. The two foreign ministers met and issued a strong statement calling upon the rest of the international community to join in an international cutoff of all arms supplies to Iraq.

The Diplomatic Instrument

President George H. W. Bush had been conducting his own personal diplomacy, calling the leaders of Egypt, Jordan, and Saudi Arabia, and meeting with British Prime Minister Margaret Thatcher. After an NSC meeting, he sent Defense Secretary Dick Cheney to seek Saudi permission to send U.S. troops to help defend that nation.

While the UNSC approved Resolution 661 imposing severe economic sanctions on Iraq, Bush and Baker believed they needed to continue pressing other nations for tough enforcement and for possible additional steps to pressure Iraq. On August 9, Baker headed to Turkey, the first of 20 nations he would visit during the crisis. Turkish President Ozal agreed to halt shipments of Iraqi oil through a Turkish pipeline but sought and received from Baker a pledge for World Bank loans of $1.5 billion to offset lost revenues.

In September, despite five more UN resolutions, Baker began what he called his "tin cup trip" to get financial support for what had become Operation Desert Shield defending Saudi Arabia and preparing for a possible move back into Kuwait. Baker got pledges of $15 billion from the Saudi king and from the emir of Kuwait. He got Egypt to commit some of its troops in return for forgiveness of $7.1 billion in U.S. loans. He secured a troop pledge from Syria and a squadron of fighter planes from Italy. Germany pledged another $2 billion. Ultimately, the U.S. cost of Operations Desert Shield and Desert Storm totaled $61 billion, of which $54 billion was supplied by other nations.

When President Bush decided at the end of October to double the U.S. troop commitment and prepare for war, he also decided to try to get another UNSC resolution authorizing the use of force. Baker undertook a new mission. "I was determined to meet personally with the head of state or foreign minister of every Council member in the weeks before the vote." He also wanted the foreign ministers present for the vote—the first UN authorization of force since Korea in 1950.

During November 1990, Baker visited 12 countries in what he called "an intricate process of cajoling, extracting, threatening, and occasionally buying votes." The Chinese indicated they wouldn't veto a resolution but wanted to arrange a high-level visit. Turkey pledged support. French President Francois Mitterand agreed that war was necessary. Ethiopia was supportive. Zaire (previously and now again called Congo) complained about a congressional cutoff of military aid, which Baker promised to try to reverse. The secretary also promised to try to get additional debt forgiveness for Ivory Coast. Romania, recipient of $80 million in humanitarian assistance only a few months earlier, offered no objections. Yemen's leader said no, but Colombia's president gave his support. Malaysia's foreign minister was noncommittal. After a final flurry of talks just before the UNSC vote on November 29, Baker presided as the members voted 12 to 2 (Cuba and Yemen), with the Chinese abstaining, for Resolution 678 authorizing "all necessary means" to get Iraq to withdraw from Kuwait. The deadline was January 15, 1991.

Despite the international support for possible military action, public opinion in the United States was less enthusiastic. Baker joined in the administration effort to build public support but in a way that backfired. Critics had been saying, "No war for oil," and Baker only reinforced that connection when he told reporters that the global economy would be threatened by allowing Saddam Hussein to control substantial oil reserves. "If you want to sum it up in one word, it's jobs," he declared. That led many in Congress to demand a vote on whether or not to go to war.

Congress ultimately approved a resolution authorizing force but only after Baker went the last mile in a search for peace by meeting with the Iraqi Foreign Minister Tariq Aziz in Geneva on January 9, 1991. The diplomats spent nearly seven hours exchanging points of disagreement then parted. Coalition forces began their war on January 16, and Iraq was driven from Kuwait and ready to conclude a cease-fire on February 28. The coalition that James Baker, President Bush, and other diplomats had built held firmly together through the conflict.

This case shows the value of personal diplomacy by the secretary of state but also the enormous time required on this single issue. It also shows that, although the United States was already engaged with the members of the UNSC, building a coalition required special negotiations with foreign leaders to gain their support for U.S. proposals.

By contrast, in 2002 and 2003, the George W. Bush administration secured UNSC approval, by a unanimous vote, of Resolution 1141. That measure was admittedly ambiguous. It declared Iraq in "material breach" of its obligations under earlier UNSC resolutions, called for renewed international inspections, and warned that Iraq "will face serious consequences as a result of its continued violations of its obligations." After dramatic testimony by Secretary of State Colin Powell, the Bush administration determined that it could not win a second UNSC resolution formally authorizing the use of force and thus never pushed it to a vote.

Sources: James A. Baker, III, *The Politics of Diplomacy: Revolution, War, and Peace, 1989–1992* (New York: G.P. Putnam's Sons, 1995); Condoleezza Rice, *No Higher Ground* (New York: Crown Publishers, 2011).

Selected Resources

The main Department of State website is at www.state.gov/.

Sites that follow State Department activities, policies, and budgets include: www.usglc.org/, http://thewillandthewallet.squarespace.com/, http://thecable.foreignpolicy.com/, http://news.yahoo.com/blogs/envoy/.

What it's like in an embassy abroad is detailed in Robert Hopkins Miller, *Inside an Embassy: The Political Role of Diplomats Abroad* (Washington, DC: Institute for the Study of Diplomacy, 1992). A more recent publication on the same topic is Dorman, Shawn, ed., *Inside a U.S. Embassy: How the*

Foreign Service Works for America (Washington, DC: American Foreign Service Association, 2005).

The Institute for the Study of Diplomacy has reports and case studies at http://isd.georgetown.edu/.

The Association for Diplomatic Studies and Training also has background information on diplomacy and diplomats at www.usdiplomacy.org/index.php.

7 The Economic Instruments

> *Foreign economic policy in the United States is shaped not systematically, but almost by accident. It is a least common denominator, worked out, as some have so aptly put it, by a kind of guerrilla warfare among the Departments of State, Treasury, Agriculture, the Federal Reserve Board, and a whole host of other Executive Branch agencies.*
>
> —former Senator and Treasury Secretary Lloyd Bentsen[1]

Most of the instruments of national power are controlled by the U.S. government. The armed forces are controlled by the president all the time, and he can federalize the national guard as needed. Diplomacy is a federal function, except for those local communities that try to have their own foreign policies on boycotts, human rights, or immigration. Nongovernmental organizations gather information abroad, including news and satellite imagery, but only the intelligence agencies have the resources and the mandate to break foreign laws if necessary to get the desired information.

The economic instruments of national power, however, are nested in a much larger market economy, which itself is subject to international legal and market forces beyond the day-to-day control of the national government. They can be used for national security purposes but only with collateral consequences and with less precision compared with the other instruments.

The president has a broad array of economic tools to support U.S. foreign policy. (See Table 7.1.) The toolkit is not well organized, however, because different institutions control different instruments and there is only a weak coordinating mechanism in the White House. Those institutions have their own cultures and core missions, which can easily come into conflict. The Department of Commerce, for example, may want to promote exports of high-tech devices that the Defense Department (DOD) fears might lead to a loss of U.S. technology. The State Department may want to give aid to a country for political reasons that the Agency for International Development (USAID) views as wasteful or inefficient. Moreover, there is often a domestic component of economic policy that the foreign policy experts are ill-equipped to assess.

Table 7.1 The Economic Instruments Brief

ACTION	EXECUTIVE AGENT	ADVANTAGES	DISADVANTAGES	CONGRESSIONAL ROLE
Sanctions	President, Department of the Treasury, Office of Foreign Assets Control (OFAC)	Highly punitive when supported by others	Unintended consequences, often ineffective if unilateral	Set by general or country-specific law
Capital flows; currency support	Department of the Treasury; Federal Reserve (the Fed)	Few restraints on action	Limited impacts in global economy	International Emergency Economic Powers Act, money laundering laws, International Monetary Fund contributions
Foreign direct investment	Committee on Foreign Investment in the United States reviews; OFAC enforces sanctions	Assures control	Political pressures frequent	Broadened Committee on Foreign Investment in the United States (CFIUS)
Exports	19 agencies promote; Dept. of State runs munitions list; Dept. of Commerce runs commerce control List; OFAC issues licenses	Popular support for export promotion with minor controls	Little coordination, complaints on arms limits	Review of major arms exports, basic law expired, no consensus on renewal
Imports	Department of Commerce; Customs; International Trade Commission (ITC) review	ITC review can reduce political pressures	Reduced presidential discretion	Tariffs; quotas; other restrictions
Trade agreements	U.S. Trade Representative (USTR) negotiates: tariffs, quotas, non-tariff barriers; ITC review of alleged violations	Important outcomes when achieved	Authority limited; lengthy negotiations	Grants negotiating authority; single vote on trade agreements
Military aid	Department of State; Department of Defense	Valued support to allies	Unintended political consequences	Appropriations; many earmarks

(Continued)

Table 7.1 (Continued)

ACTION	EXECUTIVE AGENT	ADVANTAGES	DISADVANTAGES	CONGRESSIONAL ROLE
Economic aid	Department of State; U.S. Agency for International Development; Department of Defense; + 22 others	Appreciated economic support	May not be effectively used	Appropriations; many earmarks
Development aid	Department of State; U.S. Agency for International Development; Millennium Challenge Corp. + 22 others	Noncontroversial aid	Slow to achieve results	**Appropriations; many earmarks**
Humanitarian	Department of State; U.S. Agency for International Development; Department of Defense	Noncontroversial aid	Some unintended consequences	Appropriations; many earmarks
Multilateral	Department of the Treasury votes at International financial institutions (IFIs)	Professional	Little U.S. political benefit	Approves contributions
Culture	Each agency distinctive	Good at core competencies	Hard to coordinate	Tends to view economic instruments through domestic lens

There are many quite different economic instruments in the foreign policy toolkit. Congress plays an active role in some, but many are within the discretion of the president. In the executive branch, there are often overlapping authorities, making it hard to achieve a coordinated foreign policy. Some of the economic tools are quick acting, while others are very slow; some are direct, while others are indirect. A further complication is that these tools operate in a globalized economy, where private sector forces can overwhelm or offset whatever a government may try to do.

Carrots and Sticks

Economic statecraft is conducted with various carrots and sticks—some provide incentives and rewards for other nations; others impose punishment or pressure on those who are not cooperating. Among those carrots are favorable tariff and tax treatment, direct monetary aid and guarantees, subsidies and licenses for imports and exports, and helpful capital flows and foreign investment. Some of these measures are conducted directly by the U.S. government, while others benefit and are used by the private sector for its own profit-making purposes.

The sticks can be heavy and painful. Sanctions can be used to cut off aid and other favorable treatments as well as private sector sales and investments. Exports can be restricted and imports banned. Assets of countries, companies, and even individuals can be seized or denied access to U.S. financial institutions. These penalties can be imposed quickly by presidential order.[2]

What complicates things is how these instruments affect other economic activities and other foreign policy goals. Forbidding sales of U.S. oil drilling equipment, as has been done at different times to punish Libya, Iran, and Iraq, hurt American companies even as it demonstrated a foreign policy principle. Limiting food aid to North Korea for important security goals may hurt the Korean people more than its leaders. Or as one analyst has said, "America continues to place far greater emphasis on bribing nondemocratic states than on promoting their democratization."[3] The challenge for the president is to balance these domestic and foreign policy concerns.

A Disorganized Toolkit

In the U.S. government itself, the economic tools are dispersed and disorganized. Except for the agencies handling foreign assistance, the agencies with responsibilities for international economic policy have a primarily domestic focus. Treasury worries about the strength of the dollar and the U.S. economy as a whole. Commerce wants to help U.S. businesses and domestic markets. Even the U.S. trade representative (USTR) negotiates trade agreements in order to help domestic companies and industries, as the Korea Free Trade Agreement case study makes clear. Several of the important institutions are not under direct presidential control, including the Fed, the International Trade Commission, the Export-Import Bank (Ex-Im), and the Overseas Private Investment Corporation (OPIC).

If the White House wanted to convene an interagency meeting to harmonize export strategy, they would have to invite at least 19 different agency heads, who have mandates to promote U.S. exports along with other responsibilities. A meeting of those involved in providing development assistance would have to include 26 different institutions. Each of those bureaucratic entities has its own laws, often written by different congressional committees to serve different purposes. Unlike most countries with large economies, the United States does not have a department of trade or even a truly central bank.⁴ This multiplicity of agencies with similar activities prompted President Obama in 2012 to seek reorganization authority—subject to a congressional veto—to consolidate several organizations that help U.S. businesses at home and abroad.

Foreign assistance is also dispersed among several agencies. About 20% of development aid is administered by the Pentagon. USAID has its own bureaucratic competition from the Millennium Challenge Corporation (MCC) and the U.S. Trade and Development Agency.

Exports of military or potentially military *(dual-use)* equipment and technologies often have to pass muster with DOD, State, and Commerce. Imports of different kinds may be subject to review and limitations by Treasury, Commerce, DOD, Transportation, and even the Fish and Wildlife Service (which administers the endangered species list).

Americans wishing to invest abroad may be limited by rules from Treasury, which administers financial and trade sanctions and maybe the Securities and Exchange Commission (SEC). Foreigners wishing to invest in U.S. companies might also need permission from Treasury and perhaps other departments as well.

The laws are complex. The bureaucracies are numerous. It is very hard for the United States to pursue a consistent and well-coordinated strategy using international economic policy instruments. As Stephen D. Cohen has written, "International economic policies serve as important means to the end of achieving domestic and external political and economic goals that the official sector has determined would enhance the country's national interests. . . . All too often, however, it is an either/or case, and considerations of global efficiency are unceremoniously brushed aside by perceptions of domestic or international political necessity."⁵

The Globalized Economy

Even if agencies and actions were fully integrated, they would still be subject to larger forces both domestically and internationally. The federal government accounts for only 20% of the gross domestic product (GDP), and its revenues are crucially dependent on the health of the other 80%. Foreign trade accounted for nearly 33% of the economy in 2011, and daily currency transactions totaled $2 trillion. Currency controls are still at least theoretically possible, but electronic transfers in nanoseconds could sink a troubled economy before most could kick in.⁶

International organizations like the International Monetary Fund (IMF), World Bank, and the G-20 have become crisis managers, weighing in with advice and assistance on matters far beyond the control of any small handful of countries. Apart from the governments, multinational corporations dominate the global economy, and they often have great flexibility in choosing the tax and legal regimes to which they subject themselves.⁷

Table 7.2   U.S. Net Economic Engagement With Developing Countries, 2009

SOURCES OF ECONOMIC ENGAGEMENT	BILLIONS OF DOLLARS	PERCENT OF ENGAGEMENT
U.S. official development assistance	$28.8	13% of overall engagement
U.S. private philanthropy	37.5	17% of overall
Foundations	4.6	12% of private sources
Corporations	8.9	24% of private
Private and voluntary organizations	12.0	32% of private
Volunteerism	3.0	8% of private
Universities and colleges	1.8	5% of private
Religious organizations	7.2	19% of private
U.S. remittances	90.7	40% of overall
U.S. private capital flows	69.2	31% of overall
Total U.S. economic engagement	$226.2	100%

Within the developing world, the amount of U.S. government support is dwarfed by the private sector. Remittances sent to home countries by foreign workers in the United States alone amount to triple official government assistance.

Source: The Index of Global Philanthropy and Remittances, 2011, Hudson Institute.

In addition to the numerous financial transactions for profit-making purposes, there are sizable private transactions. (See Table 7.2.) Foundations, corporations, religious organizations, universities, and private and voluntary organizations gave nearly 40% more than official U.S. development assistance. Individual remittances totaled three times the official government total.[8] Thus, whatever government may be doing, the private sector is doing much more and for its own purposes, which may or may not be in sync with U.S. government policy. Government rules can limit or shape many of these private actions through tax treatment and prohibitions to enforce sanctions, but it is harder to direct these resources as a conscious instrument of U.S. policies. Only the institutions of government can reliably be used for that.

Key Institutions

While the president usually orders the use of the economic instruments, the implementation of those orders is done through and by different organizations within the U.S. government. Table 7.3 lists the major institutions and their key responsibilities relating to foreign economic policy along with the organizational culture that dominates them.

Table 7.3 Key Institutions in U.S. Economic Foreign Policy

INSTITUTION	ECONOMIC ACTIVITIES	CULTURE
National Economic Council (NEC)	Coordinates administration of domestic and international policies; provides collective advice to the president	White Houser-centric, supports the president
Federal Reserve	Independent status; crafts U.S. monetary policy; works with foreign central banks	Conservative bankers
Department of Treasury	Administers economic sanctions; monitors foreign investments in the United States; safeguards the financial system from foreign threats; advisers and attachés overseas work with communities and local governments	Conservative bankers plus law enforcement
U.S. Trade Representative (USTR)	Advises on trade policy and negotiates trade agreements when the president has the requisite authority from Congress; reports directly to the president, yet often mediates between both branches	Trade deals are us
Department of Commerce	Enforces import regulations and some export laws; runs the U.S. Commercial Service to help American businesses sell in global markets	Supports U.S. business
Department of State	Develops foreign aid programs for recipient countries, especially security-related assistance; oversees rules and processes for the export of military goods and services	Promotes U.S. foreign policy
U.S. Agency for International Development (USAID)	Manages American foreign aid programs concerned with economic development and improved living conditions	Helps the needy abroad
Department of Defense (DOD)	Manages foreign military grant and loan programs and foreign military sales programs; oversees counterterrorism training and postconflict stabilization programs as well as some humanitarian assistance	Strengthens military ties and improves capabilities of friends
Department of Agriculture (USDA)	Promotes exports of U.S. agricultural products with subsidies, export credit guarantees, and food aid	Keeps U.S. agriculture strong and prosperous

(Continued)

The Economic Instruments   177

Table 7.3	(Continued)	
INSTITUTION	ECONOMIC ACTIVITIES	CULTURE
Other Organizations	Partner with foreign governments to help shift former weapons scientists into nonmilitary research (Department of Energy); work with other nations on container security and law enforcement training (Department of Homeland Security, DHS); liaise abroad on legal issues and counterterrorism and counternarcotics programs (Department of Justice)	Promotes core mission by overseas activities

While Table 7.1 shows the types of economic instruments and the roles of the president and Congress over them, here we highlight the major institutions that have responsibilities over those instruments. You can see from this summary of activities how responsibilities, goals, and actions may overlap across the different institutions.

National Economic Council

The NEC was established by executive order under President Bill Clinton and has been retained by his successors. In theory, the NEC is supposed to coordinate administration domestic and international economic policies and provide collective advice to the president. Its success as a coordinating body has depended on the personal skills and relations of the chairman, for it has no substantive authority. Its membership includes most of the members of the cabinet as well as the senior people in the Executive Office of the President (EOP). Day-to-day operations are handled by National Security Council (NSC)-like committees of lower-ranking officials.

The NEC staff of about 20 people typically run dozens of meetings and conference calls each week to discuss policy matters. A decision paper might require 200 to 300 hours of preparation for a 45-minute meeting with the president.[9]

International economic issues may be handled by the NEC, but its staff also tend to be dual-hatted as NSC staff, so the venue can change. The NEC has been used for some trade issues like North American Free Trade Agreement (NAFTA) under Clinton and for some international economic crises in later years.

Because the NEC is based on an executive order rather than a statute and its leadership is not confirmed by the Senate, it has only informal dealings with Congress. Unlike the NSC, which has a 65-year track record and an established process that departments can rely on, the NEC is an organization-in-waiting, dependent on support and taskings from the president.[10]

Federal Reserve

Also called the Fed, the Federal Reserve is a key player in the U.S. economy at home and abroad, but it has an independent status that allows it to act on its own. It does not participate in NEC deliberations. The members of the board of governors have long-term presidential appointments, while the heads of the 12 regional banks are chosen locally. The Fed system was created by Congress in 1913 in order to have an "elastic currency" and better supervision of U.S. banking. In 1978, Congress gave the Fed a broad and difficult mandate to promote "the goals of maximum employment, stable prices, and moderate long-term interest rates."[11]

While its most visible role is in monetary policy—setting interest rates and trying to limit inflation—it is in regular contact with foreign central banks and regulates the U.S. activities of foreign banks. It also carries out foreign currency operations that affect exchange rates. In the 2007–2008 global financial crisis, and again in 2010–2011, the Fed established swap arrangements with foreign central banks to help provide liquidity.

When finance ministers gather to discuss crisis responses or general international economic policies, the Fed chair and Treasury secretary usually attend for the United States. While legally independent, their institutions are expected to harmonize their activities.

The Fed culture is a banker's culture—conservative, concerned with stability, worried about inflation, viewing international and domestic policies through an economic lens. These are not the hedge fund high fliers but the sober, risk-averse bank managers, skeptical of optimistic forecasts and concerned about collateral for loans. The international economy is seen as a dark forest of wild beasts that can sometimes only be tamed by heavy doses of austerity medicine. The banker's culture is willing to protect the system as a whole but hard-nosed toward any individual country or institution.

As a result, the Fed can be quick to join efforts to provide liquidity to U.S. banks and companies, as it did in 2008–2009, and to help the international system cope with the sovereign debt crisis more recently. But, it is much more cautious of using monetary tools for foreign policy objectives. Fed Chairman Ben Bernanke did call the Chinese currency undervalued, but he avoided endorsing punitive actions favored by many in Congress.

Congress is the only overseer of the Fed as it writes the laws giving its authorities and responsibilities, and the Senate can block appointments to the board. But in general, lawmakers have stood in awe of the Fed chairmen, even as they tried to elicit comments helpful to their own agendas.

Department of the Treasury

The Treasury Department, second oldest in the government, was created to handle federal finances—collecting revenues, paying bills, and managing the public debt. It now has broad responsibilities to promote economic prosperity and ensure the nation's financial security. In international affairs, it administers economic sanctions of foreigners, monitors foreign investments in the U.S., and works to safeguard the financial system from foreign threats.

Although the State Department was historically the primary institution to craft U.S. foreign economic policy, Treasury has gained a preeminent role since the 1960s, reinforced by the increase in political and economic importance of international economic issues and the need to balance domestic and foreign policy concerns.[12] It also represents the United States in the international financial institutions like the IMF and the World Bank. As a consequence, Treasury votes for the U.S. on which assistance programs run by the multilateral development banks go to which countries. Treasury also runs the debt relief program for poor countries with a budget of about $100 million per year.[13]

Treasury has two offices headed by under secretaries that deal with international policies—the Office of International Affairs (OIA) and the Office of Terrorism and Financial Intelligence (OTFI). OIA handles the traditional portfolios of economic issues with regional and functional bureaus for matters like debt, trade, and energy. It also heads CFIUS, the interagency panel that reviews possibly troublesome investments in American companies. OTFI, which was established only in 2004, houses OFAC, which enforces economic and trade sanctions. Another office works with law enforcement agencies domestically and abroad to combat financial crimes. An office of intelligence and analysis is Treasury's subsection of the intelligence community (IC).

Overseas, Treasury has attachés in 16 major posts who relate primarily to foreign finance ministries and central banks. It also has technical advisories in about 40 countries, helping them develop human and institutional capacities for their governments. The State Department also has economic specialists in its embassies, but the Treasury people are often the best connected with the local financial community.

The senior officials at Treasury have the banker's culture—concerned with the health of the dollar and the domestic economy and conservative in approach with a focus on macroeconomic and systemic issues. The people at OIA, OFTI, and OFAC are more often economists and lawyers, trying to use their professional tools to advise on policies and enforce the laws.

Congressional oversight of Treasury is mainly by the tax committees, House Ways and Means and Senate Finance, and their focus is more on domestic than foreign issues. Those committees also handle trade policy, however, but their focus there is on the USTR.

United States Trade Representative

Congress created the post of USTR in 1962 because it didn't trust any other part of the American government to handle what became the Kennedy round of multilateral trade negotiations. Lawmakers wanted someone reporting directly to the president. The system worked well enough that, in 1974, Congress made the post permanent and gave it cabinet rank.

As a creature of the Congress, despite its bureaucratic placement in the EOP, USTR feels a dual responsibility to both branches and often ends up negotiating with one on behalf of the other. The trade representative chairs

19-member interagency committees on trade policy and is on the board of directors of the MCC, OPIC, and Ex-Im.

The primary USTR missions are to advise on trade policy and to negotiate trade agreements when the president has the requisite authority from Congress—something Bill Clinton was denied and George W. Bush was granted for only five years.

The culture of USTR is that of deal makers balancing multiple clients and feeling constant cross-pressures from within and outside the government while they advocate for U.S. interests with foreigners. In their interagency roles, USTR people are the voice for trade as an instrument for various domestic and foreign policy goals.

Department of Commerce

The Department of Commerce is a collection of disparate bureaus with what it calls "cross-cutting responsibilities in the areas of trade, technology, entrepreneurship, economic development, environmental stewardship and statistical research and analysis."[14] It includes the Census Bureau, a Bureau of Economic Analysis, the patent and trademark office, the National Oceanic and Atmospheric Administration, and the National Institute of Standards and Technology. Its key international activities are enforcing import regulations, issuing export licenses and enforcing export laws, and running the U.S. commercial service, which has offices in more than 100 U.S. cities and 80 countries to help American businesses sell in global markets.

Commerce has a probusiness culture overall, though its export and import offices have a law enforcement focus. Its International Trade Administration is primarily concerned with advocating for U.S. businesses that want to export than with other aspects of trade. Congress, over the years, has shifted functions into Commerce when lawmakers felt that another department was ineffective in fulfilling its assigned missions. Commerce reclaimed the commercial service from State in 1978 when lawmakers concluded that diplomats weren't especially interested in promoting U.S. businesses. Commerce gained enforcement of the dumping and countervailing duty laws in 1980 when Treasury was viewed as more interested in macroeconomic issues than in responding to the grievances of individual companies and industries.[15]

Commerce's role may change if the Obama administration's National Export Initiative results in a consolidation of exporting activities in a single organization. In 2012, the president sought reorganization authority to combine the business-related components of Commerce with the USTR, the Small Business Administration, the Ex-Im, and OPIC. Any such changes require congressional approval.

Department of State

The State Department has a bureau for Economic Growth, Energy, and the Environment and numerous economic officers posted abroad, but its primary role in international economic policy involves developing and implementing foreign aid programs for recipient countries, especially security-related assistance. State also oversees the rules and processes for the export of military goods and services.

As discussed in Chapter 6, State is better at diplomacy than program management. It rewards individual accomplishments more than teamwork. Its culture relies on engaging foreigners more than punishing them. In contrast to the more domestically oriented departments of the U.S. government, State tends to "give top priority to foreign policy considerations because they view international economic policy as being mainly the economic aspect of the pursuit of a stable, friendly, and prosperous global environment. Hence, economic considerations should be subordinate to the primary objective of good relations with other nations."[16]

For Congress, State is the perennial whipping boy on the whole range of foreign policy issues, including softness toward bad guys and mismanagement of the limited funds provided. Lawmakers reflect the public mood that historically has wanted to cut foreign aid more than any other activity by the government.

United States Agency for International Development

USAID, as the agency likes to be called, is the primary manager of American foreign aid programs that are concerned with economic development and improved living conditions. It coordinates with State on those programs but has the lead for policy implementation.

Foreign aid programs are governed by the lengthy, complex, and somewhat inconsistent provisions of the Foreign Assistance Act of 1961, which has not been substantially amended since 1985. USAID currently has a checklist of 65 statutory provisions that must be considered when determining country eligibility and budget amounts as well as funding allocations.[17]

Congress complicates USAID programs by earmarking the bulk of foreign assistance for a handful of countries, forcing restraint on more modest and long-term development programs.

Department of Defense

The Pentagon currently manages more than one fifth of the funds that count as overseas development assistance, mainly because of huge programs in Iraq and Afghanistan. But, there has also been a major increase in other DOD-run programs since the 9/11 attacks. The Pentagon launched programs in counterterrorism training and postconflict stabilization and became a major player in humanitarian assistance. In Iraq and Afghanistan, it provided substantial economic assistance through the Commander's Emergency Response Program (CERP) and led most of the interagency provincial reconstruction teams (PRTs).[18]

For several decades, the Pentagon has managed the foreign military grant and loan programs as well as the foreign military sales programs, albeit with inputs from the State Department, which sets guidelines for these programs and must approve all sales and transfers. DOD personnel, however, are usually the ones working with local militaries and developing program requests. DOD has a Defense Security Cooperation Agency (DSCA) for these activities. That agency also manages the International Military Education and Training (IMET) program that brings foreign military personnel into U.S. programs. In 2009, for example, approximately 69,500 students from 159 countries participated in such training.

The defense committees of Congress have supported these DOD activities, but the foreign policy committees have sometimes criticized them, complaining that the Pentagon puts too much of a military face on U.S. foreign policy.

Department of Agriculture

Besides running domestic government farm programs, the USDA has long been active in promoting exports of U.S. agricultural products with subsidies, export credit guarantees, and food aid.[19] Although USAID now administers much of *Public Law 480,* the 1954 measure that created the Food for Peace program, the impetus behind it has always been agricultural interests and their congressional allies. They succeeded magnificently, for agriculture now accounts for 6% of U.S. exports of goods and supports nearly one million jobs in the United States. Market access for U.S. agricultural products is often a key sticking point in negotiating trade agreements.

Other Organizations

Several other parts of the U.S. government run programs that provide security assistance abroad. The Department of Energy has a Nonproliferation and International Security Program costing over $1 billion annually that partners with foreign governments and helps shift former weapons scientists in Russia and elsewhere into nonmilitary research. State and DOD also run related programs with nonproliferation goals. DHS has international programs working with other nations on container security and law enforcement training. The Department of Justice and the Federal Bureau of Investigation (FBI) both send people abroad for liaison on legal issues and counterterrorism and counternarcotics programs.[20]

Other agencies also run their own economic assistance programs. The Department of Health and Human Services (HHS) has numerous programs in the Centers for Disease Control and Prevention (CDC). The Food and Drug Administration (FDA) and National Institutes of Health (NIH) have technical assistance and training programs abroad, as does the Environmental Protection Agency (EPA). The Department of Education has foreign study grants and runs language study centers.[21]

Key Processes

As Table 7.1 shows, many of the economic tools have shared or overlapping control in the bureaucracy. The processes for sanctions and trade agreements, for example, are narrowly held. But, imports and exports and foreign direct investments are overseen by many different agencies, often for differing purposes. Foreign assistance also comes in many varieties, each managed by separate organizations with differing core missions. Even a determined president and an unusually effective White House will have difficulty integrating these disparate organizations into a coherent policy.

Sanctions

One of the most powerful tools of foreign economic policy is the threat or use of economic sanctions. These are from the bag of sticks, seeking to punish objectionable behaviors or to coerce a change in behavior. The president has several legal authorities to use against other nations, and even against individuals and private entities.

The broadest law is the International Emergency Economic Powers Act (IEEPA) of 1977 (PL 95–223, 50 USC 1701 et seq.), which allows the president "to deal with any unusual and extraordinary threat, which has its source in whole or substantial part outside the United States, to the national security, foreign policy, or economy of the United States." If he declares a national emergency, the president can then "investigate, regulate, or prohibit" foreign exchange transactions, banking credits or payments, and importing or exporting of currency or securities. Any such emergency, however, must be renewed annually in order to remain in effect.

IEEPA was enacted to regularize the use and impact of national emergency declarations, some of which dated to the depression and World War II. It also narrowed the 1917 Trading With the Enemy Act to apply only in wartime.

The president also has more specific authorities to control imports and exports of certain goods to or from specific countries, discussed below. But, the limits on financial transactions can be sufficient to block trade in goods.

In addition to trade and financial sanctions, the president can cut off U.S. government assistance to targeted countries and institutions—both direct funding programs and access to programs like loan guarantees. The executive branch can also use its regular discretionary authority to impose very specific sanctions against foreign officials and their families, such as denying them travel visas. These are viewed as *smart sanctions* that try not to punish ordinary citizens for their governments' actions.

Congress has also legislated a large array of sanctions[22] that are supposed to be applied when the president determines that certain conditions exist. In most cases, the law allows the president to waive enforcement for national security interests.

Long-standing law prohibits U.S. assistance to "communist" countries. A related measure, the Jackson–Vanik amendment of 1974, bars most-favored nation trade status and U.S. trade credits to nonmarket economy countries that try to prevent emigration—a provision credited with forcing the Soviet government to permit emigration of Soviet Jews.

Another law requires a cutoff of economic aid to any country whose democratically elected leader is deposed by a military coup. Various laws prohibit U.S. aid to countries that seize ownership or control of American-owned property without paying adequate compensation.

Human rights violators are subject to another set of laws, including bans on security and other assistance and mandates to vote against multilateral aid to such countries. Nations that fail to cooperate with U.S. counternarcotics efforts are supposed to lose their economic aid.

Several laws require sanctions for nations that provide nuclear technology outside of international controls or that test nuclear weapons. A 1998 law imposes sanctions against countries engaged in a pattern of religious persecution.

Long before the 9/11 attacks, Congress passed laws prohibiting aid to governments that support international terrorism. A 1976 law requires the secretary of state to maintain a list of terrorist-supporting countries to which various sanctions should be applied. A 1985 law permitted the president to restrict or ban imports from countries on that list. A 1996 law banned financial transactions with nations on the list. The USA PATRIOT Act in 2001 added provisions prohibiting money laundering that helps terrorists and requiring more extensive reporting and record keeping.

In addition to these more generic statutes, Congress, over the years, has enacted country-specific laws with sanctions against Cuba, South Africa, Iran, Libya, Syria, and Burma. These were typically designed to limit presidential discretion in order to ensure tough policies against the pariah regimes. Congress usually preferred to impose drastic sanctions and get public credit for them, even while allowing the president to set most of the provisions aside if he submitted the required finding. One provision that Congress likes but executive branch officials regularly oppose because of the foreign policy problems it would cause is one with *extraterritoriality*—trying to prevent foreign companies from ignoring U.S. sanctions by allowing actions against them in U.S. courts.

Most of these various laws remain on the books as powerful sticks to use against violators. It would take a new law, not just presidential waivers, for example, to reduce the sanctions currently applied to Cuba, Iran, and North Korea.

Most studies of sanctions conclude that their effects are greatest when they are broadly applied by the international community, especially pursuant to a United Nations Security Council (UNSC) order, rather than by single countries, even ones as powerful economically as the United States. Unless there is broad support, nonsanctioning nations can easily supply what the United States denies.[23]

The key issue for a president to decide is whether the sanctions can be effective or at least whether they punish the target more than they hurt Americans. Once imposed, and especially if they do not seem to be effective, the White House faces the agonizing choice of persisting in futile and perhaps counterproductive gestures or admitting defeat. Sanctions against Iranian nuclear programs, while not effective in stopping them, have set an otherwise encouraging example of increased tightening with UN support in part because U.S. officials identified shell companies and other arrangements that could be targeted, and even international companies decided it was in their own interests to cease operations in Iran.

Trade

As an instrument of policy—in order to persuade other nations to act in particular ways—trade is most powerful when used negatively through restrictions or suspensions. But, trade relationships are also positive forces for political cooperation and economic growth. The United States seeks trade agreements both for economic benefits and for the political goodwill that can accompany good trading arrangements. On the other hand, trade disputes can exacerbate tensions in other areas, especially because trade is, for many nations, a leading foreign policy concern.

Congress is a necessary player for trade to be a policy instrument. The legislative branch sets tariffs and special trade preferences as well as authorizing negotiations for multilateral agreements. Protrade lawmakers endorse the idea that freer trade has economic benefits for all nations, but they are often held in check by legislators concerned about job losses and industrial decline in their home areas. These parochial concerns, understandably, have weakened some of the political benefits of trade deals as Americans resisted threats to domestic textile and steel companies, for example, and Koreans resisted threats to their automobile and cattle producers.

Trade preference laws are a major way of promoting economic growth in less-developed countries by allowing certain specified imports into the United States. The 1974 Generalized System of Preferences (GSP) provides benefits to more than 130 less-developed countries. Under GSP, the president can grant duty-free status to selected imports from qualifying nations. Certain conditions apply, such as reasonable market access, worker rights, support for U.S. antiterrorism programs, and not engaging in practices that would harm U.S. economic interests. Many agricultural, textile, apparel, and import-sensitive products are excluded. In addition to GSP, several regional trade preference programs have been adopted in recent decades, including ones for the Caribbean Basin, Central America, Andean nations, and Africa. Each law has to be extended periodically.[24]

Free trade agreements (FTAs), regional and bilateral, have been used frequently in recent years both for their economic benefits and for the associated political benefits. The negotiations generally seek to eliminate tariffs and nontariff barriers on trade in goods and services. Collateral agreements on investment, intellectual property rights, labor practices, and environmental protection are often demanded by Congress and become part of the negotiating agenda. FTAs have been negotiated by the USTR under time-limited power given by Congress to the president, originally called *fast track* and now renamed Trade Promotion Authority (TPA). From Congress's perspective, TPA is a self-denying process where legislators surrender their tariff-setting power in order to avoid dismemberment of multilateral agreements by parochial amendments. Under TPA, Congress allows only an up-or-down vote on the package. But, the trade committees insist on, and have been granted by USTR, close consultations during the negotiations process, so they can raise concerns and try to forestall objectionable outcomes.

When major international talks on trade liberalization have stalled, U.S. administrations rushed to sign bilateral or regional free trade agreements. America currently has such pacts in force with Israel, Canada, Mexico, Jordan, Australia, Singapore, Morocco, Oman, Bahrain, Chile, Peru, Dominican Republic–Central America, and—in 2011—Colombia, Panama, and South Korea. The most recent three agreements were stalled for more than four years until the Obama administration agreed to revisions demanded by congressional Democrats. More details on the diplomatic and political processes are in the case study on the Korean FTA at the end of this chapter.[25]

To reduce domestic opposition to liberalized trade relations, Congress has established various trade remedy devices. Trade adjustment assistance has been made available since 1974 to workers, firms, farmers, and communities hurt by shifts in trade. For example, workers can get job training, search, and relocation benefits as well as up to 130 weeks of income assistance equal to what they would get as unemployment compensation. Firms can get technical assistance on how to be more competitive. Farmers can get technical assistance and training as well as some financial grants. And, communities can get redevelopment assistance.[26]

Congress has also created a quasi-judicial International Trade Commission (ITC) to investigate and make recommendations in cases where foreign products are subsidized at home and cause economic injury in the United States. Countervailing duties can be imposed if the ITC finds in favor of the complainant. ITC also hears cases under the antidumping laws and can recommend punitive duties. The Commerce Department is also involved in these investigations and determinations. ITC has a culture of professionalism in conducting its investigations despite the enormous political pressures to make judgments in favor of American industries.

Presidents thus have numerous trade tools to pursue their foreign policy goals, but they also face domestic pressures to use trade measures for local benefits. Executive action is also severely limited by the actual authorities granted by Congress.

While trade negotiations are handled by the USTR, and USTR chairs interagency panels on trade policy, the Obama administration has dropped hints that it might propose a consolidated trade department, combining the trade activities now in Commerce with the USTR duties, plus perhaps some of the separate export promotion entities. This might be opposed by congressional trade supporters who want to keep the function in the EOP and by defenders of Commerce who don't want to see its other activities subordinated to trade missions.

Exports

Export promotion is as American as apple pie. In fact, there are at least 19 federal agencies that have that goal as one of their mandates. President

Obama in 2010 announced a National Export Initiative (NEI) to double U.S. exports by 2015. The NEI hopes to increase access to export financing mechanisms already run by the government, such as the Ex-Im and OPIC, and to increase trade missions and commercial advocacy by government agencies. There is little opposition to such activities in principle, but agencies and their congressional overseers may resist particular changes in their established ways of doing business.

Parallel to the NEI is an administration effort to rewrite the laws and reorganize the processes for commercial export controls. An administration review in 2010 concluded that the existing system was overly complicated, had too many redundancies, and tried to protect too much. Defense Secretary Gates spearheaded the reform effort, calling for "a higher fence around a smaller yard." Currently, there are two different control lists, one managed by the State Department covering military items (the munitions list) and one by the Commerce Department (the commerce control list) for commercial items with possible dual use as military items. There are three agency licensing systems that don't tell each other of their decisions and have incompatible information technology systems. In addition to licenses by State and Commerce for items on their respective lists, Treasury licenses items subject to trade sanctions and embargoes. This stovepiped system somehow issues about 130,000 licenses each year.

Each agency tends to apply its own culture and perspective to its licensing system. State, in consultation with DOD, wants to limit exports that might benefit adversaries, except in those cases where it wants to reward cooperative regimes. Commerce wants to say yes to exports wherever possible. And, Treasury wants to apply the rules strictly but professionally.

The Obama administration wants to develop a single control list managed by a single licensing agency using a single IT system and relying on a single primary enforcement coordination agency. This would require legislation passed by Congress.

Congress's record on export controls is not very encouraging. The basic Export Administration Act, first passed in 1949 and then thoroughly revised in 1979, expired in 1989. It has been resuscitated for short periods in later years and remains operative only because of annual presidential declarations under the International Emergency Economic Powers Act. Efforts to extend or amend the basic law have foundered on political and policy disagreements among lawmakers over whether the new law should be more restrictive or more permissive. It doesn't help the process that two quite different committees have jurisdiction over the legislation—the House Foreign Affairs Committee and the Senate Banking Committee.

Export restrictions are allowed for various specified purposes. For national security reasons, restrictions are allowed on items that would significantly improve the military capability of countries that pose a threat to the United States. For economic reasons, restrictions are allowed where items are in short supply or might have harmful impact on U.S. industry or economic performance. Numerous foreign policy concerns can also be used to justify restrictions: regional stability, human rights, antiterrorism, missile technology, nuclear nonproliferation, and chemical and biological warfare.

An additional process is required for exports of major defense equipment valued at $14 million or more and for sales of defense articles or services totaling $50 million. Under the 1976 Arms Export Control Act (PL 90–629), the president must notify Congress of such proposed sales, and Congress then has 45 days to consider passing a resolution of disapproval. Supreme Court rulings on legislative vetoes suggest that such a measure would be subject to a presidential veto and thus would require two-thirds votes for enactment. But, the threat of congressional debate and criticism of the recipient country still can be factors in the diplomacy surrounding arms sales.

Exports are thus an instrument with two sharp edges. They can cut policy makers when they are used and when they are withheld. While export promotion serves mainly domestic American economic goals, it can come in conflict with various foreign policy objectives. The president may thus face conflicting advice from his cabinet on whether to allow certain kinds of exports either in general or to particular countries. Foreign leaders may seek specific items from the United States both to help their nations economically and as evidence of American diplomatic support. The president has to balance the various pressures and considerations. Selling Pakistan military helicopters to allow the army to conduct flood relief operations has humanitarian and political benefits, but such sales may also lead the Pakistani military to discount U.S. pressures related to terrorist networks or better relations with India.

Imports

American laws restrict imports in various direct and indirect ways—thus potentially causing foreign policy problems with the countries wishing to sell restricted items. Basic tariffs limit imports. Eliminating tariffs is the standard practice of free trade agreements. Those measures may also deal with nontariff barriers such as copyright protections for intellectual property or environmental restrictions.

Imports may also be barred by buy-American provisions in law since the Great Depression, which have regularly added to federal spending programs for highways and other infrastructure. The president also has long-standing authority under a 1962 law to restrict imports that "may threaten to impair national security" (19 USC 1862).

As discussed in the trade section, import relief in the form of countervailing duties or other penalties may be imposed by the president after findings by the ITC.

Import quotas apply to certain categories of goods. Sugar and dairy products are subject to quotas that allow a lower tariff for importers with licenses limited to the quota and higher tariffs for any other importers. There are also some absolute limit quotas on some clothing and textiles. Sometimes, nations get others to impose voluntary export restraint as Japan did on its auto exports to the U.S. for several years in the 1980s.

U.S. laws and regulations impose import restrictions on a broad array of goods. For example, imported cars must meet U.S. fuel emission and safety standards; biological specimens require permits from USDA or CDC; items derived from endangered species, as set by the Fish and Wildlife Service, are banned; most merchandise from embargoed countries (Cuba, Iran, Burma, and most of Sudan) cannot be imported.

Import issues can be foreign policy bones of contention that influence the handling of other foreign policy issues. Presidential decisions thus have to balance diplomatic concerns against the domestic economic and other factors that led to the import limitations.

Foreign Assistance

One of the most visible economic tools in foreign policy is government-provided assistance to other nations. (See Table 7.4.) These are actions the president can turn off quickly, if he chooses, or turn on, though at a much slower pace because of the need for congressional approval and contracting procedures. Accumulated controversies over the years have tangled foreign aid programs in a web of restrictions and conditions. The basic 1961 law, now more than 500 pages in length and not significantly amended since 1985, has 33 goals, 75 priority areas, and 247 directives.[27]

Overall, some 26 agencies and offices have foreign assistance programs. In addition to the major organizations—State, USAID, DOD, USDA, Commerce, Justice, and Health & Human Services/CDC—there are foreign programs in the EPA, the Forest Service, the Patent and Trademark Office, National Science Foundation, and National Oceanic and Atmospheric Administration.[28] One study concluded, "At any given time, in any particular developing countries, any or all of over fifty separate government units could be operating separate aid activities with distinct objectives, implementing authorities, and local points of contact."[29]

Some of these smaller programs are technical assistance—sharing best practices of a U.S. agency with a foreign counterpart. But, several large programs have been created in recent decades deliberately outside the State–USAID core. The collapse of the Soviet empire prompted creation of the Support for Eastern European Democracies (SEED) program and the Freedom Support Act and the Nunn–Lugar program for cooperative threat reduction. Under the G. W. Bush administration, Congress created the MCC and the President's Emergency Plan for AIDS Relief (PEPFAR).

Creating new stand-alone programs serves many bureaucratic purposes: It allows greater visibility and budget protection for the effort; it attracts fresh, high-energy personnel in contrast to the established bureaucracies; and it allows officials and lawmakers chances to brag about their farsightedness and accomplishments. On the other hand, the proliferation of special programs leads to coordination problems, conflicts over priorities, and dilution of the assistance effort.

Secretary Hillary Clinton tried to reduce these problems by her 2010 Quadrennial Diplomacy and Development Review (QDDR). On paper, the

Table 7.4	Top Recipients of U.S. Foreign Assistance, 1980–2010, in millions			
	1980	1990	2000	2010
1	Israel $1,868	Egypt $4,977	Israel $4,069	Afghanistan $2,624
2	Egypt 1,470	Israel 4,454	Egypt 2,028	Israel 2,220
3	Turkey 538	Poland 919	Colombia 899	Pakistan 1,457
4	Taiwan 388	Philippines 566	West Bank and Gaza 485	Egypt 1,295
5	Mexico 180	Pakistan 524	Jordan 428	Jordan 542
6	United Kingdom 178	Turkey 367	Russia 195	Colombia 512
7	Bangladesh 175	El Salvador 303	Bolivia 194	West Bank and Gaza 502
8	Spain 159	Greece 282	Ukraine 182	Iraq 466
9	Zaire 148	Philippines 260	Peru 120	Haiti 363
10	Indonesia 137	Zaire 241	Kazakhstan 112	Lebanon 238

The changing priorities of U.S. aid policy in recent decades are evident in the amounts of foreign assistance provided. While the Middle East, and especially Israel and Egypt, have been major recipients, Latin American countries have risen or fallen in priority in response to changing local threats.

Source: Statistical Abstracts of the United States, U.S. Department of State.

QDDR claimed to resolve long-standing disagreements over the roles of State and USAID by saying they would be integrated and coordinated but that USAID would remain bureaucratically separate and would be given increased personnel and resources. It left precise delineation of activities to a midlevel panel, however, and many of the QDDR recommendations also required new legislation from a Congress not especially warm to foreign aid.[30]

While the Bush and Obama administrations gave rhetorical support to the idea of making development equal to diplomacy, their proposed budgets fell far short of that goal. And, there remains a profound disagreement among practitioners—in the government and in the nongovernmental organization (NGO) community that runs assistance programs—over whether and how to separate diplomatic goals from purely developmental ones. Even politically motivated aid can achieve developmental goals; even humanitarian relief can serve diplomatic-political objectives. The overlaps just lead to more disagreements over priorities.[31]

There are three broad types of foreign assistance programs in terms of what they provide: military, economic, and development aid. The State Department is the primary agency for all three, at least in terms of selecting recipient countries and persuading Congress to go along. The Pentagon, however, actually manages the military assistance programs, and USAID runs most of the development programs. The MCC is legally independent.

Opinion polls ever since the 1950s have shown that foreign aid is the least popular program in the U.S. government, the one people are most eager to cut and cut deeply. While every president has supported significant aid programs, they have usually depicted the assistance as an alternative security measure to the use of U.S. military forces or as a humanitarian effort to relieve widespread poverty and disease. Aid advocates are also sharply divided between those who favor programs based on economic and humanitarian needs and those who want aid to serve U.S. foreign policy goals and interests.

Current U.S. assistance is 17.5% military, 27.1% economic for political reasons, 35.5% for bilateral development aid, 14.4% for humanitarian aid, and 5.5% through multilateral organizations, to use the figures for 2009. These figures do not include, however, Pentagon-run programs in Iraq and Afghanistan. Within the regular State–USAID programs, the share of military aid has declined since the 1990s, and the portion for development has increased because of anti-AIDS and other health programs and the new MCC. Total U.S. spending for foreign aid dropped steadily during the 1990s but surged after the 9/11 attacks mainly because of programs in Afghanistan, Pakistan, and Iraq.[32]

In order to use the aid tools, the president needs to be sure he has the authority and the resources. What used to be broad discretionary authority has been whittled down by Congress, which doesn't like contingency funds because they allow spending without congressional guidance or necessary approval. Under Presidents Eisenhower and Kennedy, there was a foreign policy contingency fund equal to $1.5 billion in current dollars. After some questionable expenditures in the 1970s, Congress cut the fund to its current $25 million. In 2009, Congress approved a massive, five-year aid authorization for Pakistan (PL 111–73), but it still requires annual appropriations, which can get caught up in current controversies and budget freezes. In 2011, lawmakers considered a special fund to help Egypt after the resignation of longtime President Mubarak in the wake of proreform demonstrations. Meanwhile, the State Department announced a "reprogramming of $150 million" for Egypt. This turned out not to be new money, however, but funds previously appropriated for Egypt, some in earlier years, but not yet spent. In 2012, however, Congress created a $200 million Global Security Contingency Fund to be jointly managed by State and DOD and subject to advance notifications to Congress.[33]

Most aid programs require advance notification to congressional committees and, in some cases, committee approval before the funds can be spent. The system is confused by the many pots of money created by different sections of the law and the lack, in contrast to the Pentagon, of a clear, consolidated system for Hill consultations on fund transfers.

Military aid programs are often based on collaboration between U.S. defense attachés and the host government military leaders. There are many potential benefits from such collaboration, including deeper knowledge of the military leaders and the capabilities of their forces, adoption of U.S.

equipment and doctrine that can make future cooperation easier, and sometimes reduced costs for U.S. forces because of foreign sales. Grant military aid, called Foreign Military Funding (FMF), helps to finance purchases of American equipment and services. Most FMF goes to Israel and Egypt. Cash sales go through the Foreign Military Sales (FMS) program, where major sales are subject to a potential congressional veto.

The major economic aid program with a clear political purpose is the Economic Support Fund (ESF) that runs about $6.5 billion per year, 77% of which currently goes to friendly countries in the Middle East: Israel, Egypt, Jordan, Afghanistan, Pakistan, Lebanon, and Iraq. While this money may be *projectized,* its real purpose is budgetary support for favored nations. Other politically driven aid goes for counternarcotics programs, nonproliferation programs, and democracy promotion efforts in Eastern Europe, the former Soviet Union, and parts of the Middle East.[34]

Development aid takes many forms and is delivered by many different providers. In addition to the programs for economic growth, the United States has specially targeted programs for countries in transition to democracy and for high-priority health programs, such as the PEPFAR. The programs run by MCC are specifically linked to host government performance in terms of noncorrupt rule-of-law governance, adequate social services, and economic freedom. It spends a bit over $1 billion yearly in countries that work to be eligible for the program funds.[35]

Since the 9/11 attacks, DOD has undertaken several major foreign assistance programs. It has *train-and-equip* programs in Afghanistan and Iraq as well as in other countries helping the United States combat terrorism. It also has *coalition support funds* to reimburse or reward nations like Pakistan and Jordan for logistical and military support for the wars in Iraq and Afghanistan. Especially valued by the U.S. military is CERP, which lets military units provide local assistance without the paperwork and other requirements of a regular aid program.[36] The $11.3 billion for these programs in 2010 equaled 25% of total U.S. foreign assistance that year.

Financial Flows

As long as the United States has a large economy and is heavily involved in foreign trade and investment, the government has to worry about the value of the dollar and the smooth functioning of the international financial markets. America dominated the Bretton Woods system from 1945 until 1971, pumping out dollars to rebuild war-torn economies and then working with others to expand international trade and finance. As the global reserve currency, the United States was largely able to avoid having to make domestic economic policy changes to protect its international role. By August 1971, however, the dollar was under severe pressure because of domestic inflationary pressures and the first U.S. trade deficit in the 20th century. President Nixon abandoned the Bretton Woods system of fixed exchange rates, de-linked the dollar from gold, and imposed immediate 10% surcharges on Japanese and German imports to force them to revalue their currencies.[37]

> **Box 7.1**
>
> ## Inside View: Treasury Versus State During the Asian Financial Crisis
>
> Former Treasury Secretary Robert Rubin describes how policy to handle the 1997 Asian financial crisis was made by an interagency conference call on Thanksgiving Day. Local currencies and then stock markets began collapsing throughout Asia in the summer of 1997, with Thailand, Indonesia, and South Korea most adversely affected. By mid-1998, months after the rescue engineered by Rubin and the IMF, GDP had dropped over 34% in much of the region. Rubin notes that the concerns of Treasury were quite different from the concerns of the State Department and Pentagon, highlighting one of the key challenges faced by the White House when crafting a consistent foreign economic policy.
>
> *On Thanksgiving Day . . . I spent much of the day and evening on a series of urgent conference calls with Treasury and Fed officials, the President, the national security advisor, and the Secretary of State. . . . For understandable reasons, we at Treasury and the foreign policy people in the administration looked at the issue from somewhat different perspectives. Madeleine [Albright] and the other foreign policy advisers on the phone were mainly worried about our relationship with a crucially important military ally, as well as national security issues. They thought any instability in South Korea might encourage a reaction from the North, where some troops had reportedly gone to some heightened state of alert. Their view was that we economic types were insufficiently focused on geopolitical concerns and that the United States needed to move quickly to show support for South Korea through the IMF and a backup loan from the ESF, as we had just done for Indonesia—what we were now calling a "second line of defense." I felt strongly that if economic stability wasn't reestablished, our geopolitical goals wouldn't be accomplished either. . . . Committing the IMF and ourselves to a show of financial support for South Korea without an adequate commitment to reform might even make it less likely that South Korea would get back on track, because providing money without strong conditions would reduce our leverage in getting the country to adopt a program that would work.*
>
> Treasury worked with the IMF, which a few days later, announced its largest-ever assistance package—$55 billion—and which also had obtained the reluctant endorsement of reform measures by all three leading candidates for president of South Korea. Treasury and the Fed also worked out arrangements with major banks for a voluntary rollover of their loans. The final deal was announced on Christmas Day. As this chapter shows, the different agencies involved in crafting U.S. economic policy on an international scale often have overlapping areas of interest and differing perspectives on situations. Consequently, they may clash regarding their goals and approaches. In this case, Treasury wanted an economic solution, while State emphasized foreign policy concerns. The United States also enlisted the IMF to leverage its own economic support.
>
> Source: Robert Rubin, *In an Uncertain World* (New York: Random House, 2003), 232–233.

Oil shocks in 1974 and 1979 forced the leaders of the major economic powers to recognize their interdependence and work together to solve problems. Annual financial summits began in 1975 and have continued to today. In the early years, the participants were usually the Group of Seven (G-7) economic powers, but in the 21st century it has been expanded to G-8 with the addition of Russia and the G-20, which was the principal forum for handling the global financial crisis starting in 2007.

Major nations liberalized their banking systems in the 1980s and 1990s, and the Europeans created a widely shared common currency. The IMF got increased resources and became actively involved in coordinating responses to the inevitable currency crises—in Mexico, Asia (see Box 7.1), and Russia, and more recently among Western European countries. Globalization has removed many of the long-standing tools government had to manage to protect domestic economies. Nations may still try to impose currency controls and restrictions on capital flows, for example, but with foreign exchange markets having an average daily turnover of around $4 trillion, some restrictions may be too little and too late, at least in the short run.

What this means for the U.S. foreign policy process is that the president is regularly engaging with foreign leaders on economic issues. The strength of the economy and of the dollar are important foreign policy concerns. The situation is complicated, however, because the president can give orders only to the secretary of the treasury. The Fed chair has enormous financial powers and tries to cooperate with Treasury, but their perspectives may diverge.

Both Treasury and the Fed have ways to help in currency crises. Treasury can draw on an Exchange Stabilization Fund with over $100 billion in 2009 and vote for action as the U.S. representative on the IMF. The Fed can work out swaps and other arrangements with other central banks. The president, under IEEPA, has broad powers to impose restrictions on economic transfers.

There are large capital flows in portfolio investments above and beyond trade in goods and services.[38] There are also large amounts of nongovernmental foreign assistance by private voluntary organizations, foundations, and religious groups, as Table 7.2 shows. Remittances to families back home total more than $90 billion per year, triple actual U.S. foreign development aid. In 2011, foreigners held 48% of U.S. debt, with China holding almost 12% and Japan nearly 10%.

One of the most important areas for policy action in recent years has been attempts to prevent money laundering by terrorist groups or illegal drug cartels. In 1998, IMF estimated that $800 million to $2 trillion was laundered each year. The laws then required banks to report any transaction of $10,000 or more and suspicious transactions of lower amounts. After the 9/11 attacks, the USA PATRIOT Act extended reporting requirements to securities dealers, casinos, and car dealers, among others. The attorney general also got powers to demand additional information on foreign accounts. These legal measures have been supplemented by efforts to cooperate and coordinate with foreign law enforcement and intelligence agencies abroad.[39]

The Securities and Exchange Commission (SEC) has even expanded its efforts, under congressional pressure, to make judgments about the impact on stocks of various foreign policy problems. It created an Office of Global Security Risk, which among other things, requires companies to disclose whether they are doing business with nations on the supporting terrorism list.[40]

Foreign Direct Investment

Acquisition of foreign companies and real estate is called foreign direct investment (FDI) and is distinguished from the ebb and flow of portfolio investments discussed above. Most countries practice some forms of economic nationalism, although the trend in recent years has been more favorable to foreign investors. Formal restrictions are usually limited to complying with antitrust and competition rules, but governments can use informal pressures to encourage or discourage particular investments.[41]

Because FDI is done by the private sector, the government role is only negative—blocking investments that conflict with other policies. Even so, those blockages raise foreign policy issues that have to be weighed with other economic goals.

U.S. companies had invested more than $3.5 trillion abroad as of 2009, with new investments that year of $269 billion. About 70% of U.S. investments were concentrated in highly developed countries. There has been a shift since the 1990s from extractive and basic manufacturing activities in the less-developed world and toward high technology, finance, and service industries in economically advanced nations. American FDI abroad has averaged about double foreign FDI in the U.S. at least since 2001.[42]

FDI in the United States totaled about $2.3 trillion in 2009, mostly (95%) from developed economies. About one third of this investment is in manufacturing and one sixth in banking and finance. Already on the books are laws restricting foreign investment in the maritime industry and the aircraft industry. Only U.S. citizens or people in the process of acquiring citizenship can buy mining rights on U.S. lands. Only citizens or U.S. corporations can obtain licenses for power plants and transmission. There are also restrictions on foreign ownership of mass communications media. And, buy-American provisions are a standard feature of federal contracts, though they often have to be waived for practical reasons.[43]

Concerns over foreign acquisition of technologies or companies affecting national security led President Ford to create CFIUS by executive order. After a decade of limited activity by this Treasury-led panel, Congress passed the Exon–Florio amendment to codify the CFIUS process and strengthen the president's hand in blocking foreign acquisitions that might impair U.S. national security. While Treasury chairs CFIUS, its other members include representatives from State, DOD, Commerce, DHS, Justice, USTR, and presidential advisers for science, economics, and national security.

Congress amended the law further in 2007 by adding impacts on economic security and critical infrastructure to the established defense criterion.

The new law also requires more regular reporting to Congress on implementation of its provisions. President G. W. Bush took issue with some of the reporting requirements in a signing statement that said some information might be withheld for reasons of foreign policy or executive privilege.

The CFIUS process has been most influential in its preliminary informal phase, when companies report planned acquisitions and the staff raises questions and concerns. Between 1988 and 2005, CFIUS received more than 1,500 notifications of acquisitions and conducted full investigations in only 25 cases. Of those, 13 transactions were withdrawn when the formal review was launched and the remaining 12 were sent to the president. Only one of those was prohibited. Since the law was changed in 2007 through 2010, CFIUS received 451 notices, of which 57 were withdrawn during subsequent review, and no cases went to the president.[44]

Despite the CFIUS process in the executive branch, Congress has weighed in with statements, hearings, and amendments on some controversial cases. In 2005, the Chinese National Offshore Oil Corporation (CNOOC), a government-owned firm, announced a bid to buy Unocal, an American oil and gas company. A firestorm of criticism on Capitol Hill, culminating with passage of an amendment that would have delayed any acquisition pending additional cabinet-level studies, led CNOOC to withdraw its bid. In 2006, an effort by Dubai Ports World to acquire a British company that operated several U.S. ports led to renewed controversy and passage of amendments to block the deal. Faced with that, the company pledged to divest the U.S. operations to an American company within six months.[45]

China poses a special set of problems for use of the economic instruments of U.S. policy. With the world's second-largest economy and huge bilateral trade with America, China is regularly caught up in trade disputes, some of which have gone to the World Trade Organization (WTO) for adjudication. With large, state-owned companies and sovereign wealth funds, China is seeking foreign investments that are bound to raise concerns. It doesn't help that China is the one major U.S. trading partner that is viewed more as an adversary and potential threat than as a steady ally.[46] In recent years, China has complained about the denial of several investments it sought in the United States on security grounds. Whatever the merits of these cases, similar disputes are likely to continue as part of the complex U.S.–China relationship and must be sorted out through the various economic instruments and processes.

***

Each of the economic instruments in foreign policy can be used only in particular circumstances and only for specific purposes. Some can be used actively in support of foreign policy, while others must be used reactively and defensively. Some of the instruments can be used unilaterally by the president, while others require congressional approval, and still others necessarily involve the private sector. Many of the departments and agencies that are part of the toolkit have domestic economic responsibilities and constituencies that may conflict with their foreign policy roles. There is no simple coordination mechanism available to the president. But, the array of tools is ample and diverse. This chapter provides a scorecard of players and their regular positions.

Case Study: The Korean-U.S. Free Trade Agreement

While sanctions are the most powerful negative economic tool for U.S. foreign policy, free trade agreements are one of the most powerful, positive instruments for economic and political linkage. The United States has entered into 20 such agreements with various countries since 1985, mostly with nations with far smaller economies. This is the story of the lengthy struggle to negotiate and approve a free trade agreement with the Republic of Korea, whose strong and emerging economy was the seventh-largest export market for the United States as well as the seventh-largest supplier of imports. The Korean–U.S. free trade agreement, called KORUS FTA in shorthand, was the most economically significant since the 1992 NAFTA linking Mexico, Canada, and the United States.

President George W. Bush gained approval from Congress in 2002 for TPA, the fast-track procedure forcing Congress to act by up-or-down votes within 60 days of submission of completed agreements. The votes were close, however. The House approved fast-track bills by one- and three-vote margins because of overwhelming opposition by Democrats. The Senate was more supportive—66–30—but Democrats were evenly divided. Supporters envisioned expanded export opportunities. Opponents feared the loss of U.S. jobs from foreign competition and outsourcing of production.

The Bush administration, after completing several smaller agreements, began negotiations with South Korea in February 2006. Seoul initiated the talks, feeling competitive pressures from Japan and China and wanting free trade deals with both the United States and the European Union (EU). Korea most wanted changes in U.S. antidumping rules and preferential treatment of products made at the Kaesong Industrial Complex, a joint South–North Korean facility inside North Korea and employing North Korean workers.

American negotiators were keen on improving access for exports of U.S. agricultural products, especially beef, rice, pork, and dairy items; of cars and trucks; and of U.S. financial and professional services and foreign investment. Other U.S. interests chimed in with proposals that would benefit their sectors or companies.

Negotiations proceeded steadily during 2006, with 17 negotiating groups and two *working groups* handling specific issues. They broke down in December 2006 over antidumping rules and rice.

Facing a deadline of July 1, 2007, when the TPA fast-track law would expire, the two sides made significant compromises in order to sign an agreement on June 30. The United States dropped its demands for rice exports and agreed to simpler procedures for dealing with antidumping cases. The two sides agreed to set up a panel to consider particular products made in Kaesong. There were complex agreements on a wide range of other trade issues, including several *snapback* provisions allowing temporary tariffs to offset unexpectedly large imports of some Korean products.

Two issues, however, remained inadequately resolved from the U.S. perspective. Korea kept restrictions on U.S. beef imports because of concerns over mad cow disease. And, U.S. automakers opposed the deal as insufficient. These matters caused enough opposition among Democrats, newly in control of both houses of Congress, that President Bush decided not to send the KORUS FTA to the Hill.

A major agreement between President Bush and congressional leaders on May 10, 2007, paved the way for more favorable consideration of all remaining trade agreements. The president agreed to include labor standards provisions, to enforce multilateral environmental agreements with trade partners, and to add provisions on generic pharmaceuticals, port security, and foreign investor rights. In the case of Korea, the Bush administration also reached an agreement in 2008 for a gradual expansion of U.S. beef exports.

The Obama administration sought changes in the KORUS FTA to make it more palatable to congressional Democrats, especially with regard to the auto provisions, pork, and dairy products. On December 3, 2010, the two sides announced an agreement on modifications. The changes in tariff phaseouts and other provisions relating to cars and trucks were sufficient to win the support of the Ford Motor Company and the United Auto Workers union. Agricultural interests were pleased by more favorable provisions for pork, oranges, and domestic cheeses. Financial services investors were also pleased with the revised deal. The steel and textile industries voiced their opposition.

Under congressional pressure, the Obama administration demanded that approval of three major FTAs, with Korea, Colombia, and Panama, be linked to an expansion of Trade Adjustment Assistance (TAA), the program to help U.S. workers displaced by foreign trade. The House and Senate trade committees held *mock mark-up* sessions in July 2011, when they considered advisory proposals to the administration before final submission of the FTA. The Republican-controlled House panel approved the FTA but not TAA, while the Senate panel approved both items on a party-line vote.

President Obama waited until October 3, 2011, when he received assurances that the House would pass TAA as well as the FTA. He then sent the three major agreements to Congress and started the clock running on the fast-track vote. The real deadline for congressional action, however, was the pending state visit and speech to Congress of South Korean president Lee Myung-bak on October 13. The day before, both chambers approved the KORUS FTA. The House voted 278–151 (with 21 Republicans and 139 Democrats in opposition) and the Senate 83–15 (with 14 Democrats and 1 Republican in opposition).

The long delay in final approval demonstrated the contentiousness of trade issues and the need for a broad coalition of supporters. While there were strong geostrategic arguments for close relations with South Korea—not least the U.S. defense commitment and deployment of 28,500 troops as well as the importance of cooperation on dealing with North Korea—the trade agreement depended on domestic economic support for its approval. The economic instrument of trade may serve foreign policy goals, but it also has to satisfy domestic interests. This case shows how domestic political and economic considerations intersected with and influenced the development and approval of an important foreign economic policy goal.

Sources: Congressional Research Service, *Reports to Congress* and *CQ Weekly Reports.*

Selected Resources

Each of the following government agencies has a website with more information about its activities.

Committee on Foreign Investment in the United States, www.treasury.gov/resource-center/international/Pages/Committee-on-Foreign-Investment-in-US.aspx

Export-Import Bank, www.exim.gov/

International Trade Commission, http://usitc.gov/

Office of Foreign Assets Control, http://www.treasury.gov/resource-center/sanctions/Pages/default.aspx

Overseas Private Investment Corporation, www.opic.gov/

U.S. Agency for International Development, www.usaid.gov/

U.S. Department of Commerce, International Trade Administration, http://trade.gov/

U.S. Department of Defense, www.defense.gov/; Defense Security Cooperation Agency, www.dsca.osd.mil/

U.S. Department of State, www.state.gov/

U.S. Department of the Treasury, www.treasury.gov/

U.S. Trade Representative, www.ustr.gov/

The most thorough discussion of sanctions can be found in Gary Clyde Hufbauer et al., *Economic Sanctions Reconsidered, Third Edition* (Washington, DC: Peterson Institute for International Economics, 2009).

An excellent overview of this topic is in Benn Steil and Robert E. Litan, *Financial Statecraft* (New Haven, CT: Yale University Press, 2006).

8 The Military Instrument

> "Long before September 11, the U.S. government had grown increasingly dependent on its military to carry out its foreign affairs.... The military simply filled a vacuum left by an indecisive White House, an atrophied State Department, and a distracted Congress."
>
> —*Washington Post* reporter Dana Priest[1]

> "The Department is run by intimidation, not by control, when you get right down to it. You have to intimidate people to get anything done."
>
> —Deputy Secretary of Defense John Hamre (1997–1999)[2]

The largest, most capable, best-funded instrument in the foreign policy toolkit is the U.S. military. The Department of Defense (DOD), headquartered in the Pentagon, organizes, trains, and equips the armed forces and, through the military chain of command from the president, controls their conduct in peace and war. Paradoxically, the military is both the sharpest and the bluntest instrument, with stiletto-like capabilities for some missions, yet cumbersome to move about and difficult to use without causing broad and unintended consequences.

Military forces are a tool of foreign policy in many ways: They can back diplomatic and economic policies with the threat of violence and punishment; they can deter hostile actions against America and its interests; they can destroy units and weapons that threaten the United States or its allies; they can train and equip foreign militaries for combined operations. (See Table 8.1.) The United States has large, expensive, and ever-changing military capabilities, populated by an all-volunteer force equipped with technologically advanced weaponry. Pentagon leaders are key players in the interagency process advising the president and implementing presidential orders. This chapter highlights the strength and diversity of the military instrument and the organizational and political challenges it faces.

Nature of the Military Instrument

The instrumental purpose for using military force for broader strategic goals is clear in current U.S. military doctrine: "The chief principle for employment of US forces is to achieve national strategic objectives established by the

Table 8.1 The Military Instrument Brief

PEOPLE	ADVANTAGES	DISADVANTAGES
Secretary of Defense	Authoritative, powerful	Limits on time, multiple demands
Joint Chiefs of Staff (JCS)	Symbolic, best for dealing with other officers	Only advisory power in U.S.
Combatant Commanders (COCOMs)	Seen as pro-consuls, large staffs	Overshadow nonmilitary instruments
Special Operations Forces (SOF)	Secretive, highly capable	May produce blowback
ACTIONS		
Presence	Symbol of commitment and support	Costly over time
Engagement and training	Symbolic, builds relations for future	U.S. may be blamed for repressive governments
Contingency planning	Allows prompt action in crises	Planning may create false expectations regarding war
Warfighting	Can achieve decisive results	Costly, many uncertainties, often unpopular over time
ROLE OF CONGRESS	Supporter and enabler, alternative source of civilian control	Micromanager
CULTURE	Can-do spirit, wants clear guidance and timely decisions	Tends to dominate, resists coordination with civilians; sees issues in black-and-white terms

There are three separate groups of people who are most influential in shaping and using the military instrument, plus the increasingly important SOF, which have become a major foreign policy tool. Each of the components of the military performs four major activities under the direction of the president and subject to various actions by the Congress, thus assuring civilian control. The military's can-do culture makes it a reliable and effective instrument for foreign policy, provided that policy makers can deal with the political and diplomatic consequences of using deadly force.

President through decisive action and conclude operations on terms favorable to the United States."[3] That same doctrine recognizes a wide range of actions that armed forces may be called upon to perform:

The United States employs its military capabilities at home and abroad in support of its national security goals in a variety of operations. These operations vary in size, purpose, and combat intensity within a range of military operations that extends from military engagement, security cooperation, and deterrence activities to crisis response and limited contingency operations, and if necessary, major operations and campaigns.[4]

These statements mark a shift from what had been traditional American military thinking that proclaimed a narrower goal: "The purpose of the Armed Forces is to fight and win the Nation's wars."[5] While many officers still repeat that slogan without qualifications, U.S. military leaders now acknowledge that they will be called upon for more tasks than simply fighting and often with objectives less concrete than "winning" what are called "wars."

After a long tradition of following military theorists who concentrated on the operational level of war, U.S. military leaders now acknowledge the wisdom of the Napoleonic era writer, Carl von Clausewitz, who stressed that war should be judged in terms of its strategic role. Perhaps his most famous statement in *On War* is this: "We see, therefore, that war is not merely an act of policy but a true political instrument, a continuation of political intercourse, carried on with other means."[6]

The U.S. experience in World War II, which had a clear and simple objective—"unconditional surrender" by Germany and Japan—and which was followed by a forceful occupation of enemy lands, along with rewriting their basic laws and reshaping their political institutions, made it hard for many Americans to accept limited wars, where the means used and the goals sought fell short of total war or an unambiguous victory. The wars in Korea and Vietnam, and more recently in Afghanistan and Iraq, lost popular support in part because they were pursued for less ambitious and less satisfying goals and with far more restraints on the use of force than public opinion preferred.

From Vietnam into the 1990s, U.S. military leaders repeatedly argued that force should be used only for vital interests, and then only in an overwhelming way. They used a disparaging term for lesser conflicts: Military Operations Other Than War—MOOTW or *moot-wah*. By the 21st century, however, military leaders and civilians agreed on the need to conduct *stability operations,* and in 2005, this capability was made equal in importance to major wars.[7]

The U.S. military is not always comfortable with the limits that limited war entails, but official doctrine currently lists 20 different types of military operations for which it must prepare. (See Box 8.1.)

Note that only a handful of these operations necessarily involve the use of lethal force. The problem for the military, however, is that any of them could. And, that fact raises the risks for political leaders considering use of the military instrument.

Civilian leaders are also sometimes uncomfortable with the proliferation of missions the U.S. military now undertakes. They see a vicious circle in which civilian capacities are inadequate for urgent tasks, the military comes to the rescue, and the civilians are pushed aside and denied resources to regain their normal roles. Many officials also believe in the just war tradition of exhausting all other means before resorting to the use of force, a

The Military Instrument

> **Box 8.1**
>
> ## How Foreign Policy Is Made: Types of Military Operations
>
> Here is the Pentagon's list of the types of operations the U.S. military trains to conduct. As you can see, many of them are directly part of U.S. foreign policy and only indirectly related to national defense. Assistance and training of foreign forces (including tasks like combating terrorism, counterinsurgency, and nation assistance) are a major use of U.S. forces for foreign policy purposes. The U.S. military also works with U.S. civilians in humanitarian assistance, peace operations, and recovery operations. The list also makes clear that the military can help insurgents and counterinsurgents, depending where U.S. interests dictate. The ability to conduct raids, strikes, and shows of force allows the United States to back its diplomacy with the threat of force. The very diversity of capabilities makes use of the military a valuable instrument for more than killing and destroying enemy forces.
>
> | | |
> |---|---|
> | Major operations, such as war | Nation assistance |
> | Arms control and disarmament | Noncombatant evacuation operations |
> | Homeland defense | Peace operations |
> | Civil support | Protection of shipping |
> | Combating terrorism | Raids |
> | Consequence management | Recovery operations |
> | Counterinsurgency operations | Routine, recurring military activities |
> | Enforcement of sanctions | Show of force |
> | Foreign humanitarian assistance | Strikes |
> | Freedom of navigation | Support to insurgency |
>
> *Source:* Joint Operations, August 11, 2011. Figure I-2. Types of Military Operations from JP 3–0, I-3 at www.dtic.mil/doctrine/new_pubs/jp3_0.pdf.

notion that treats war as a binary choice where the diplomats turn out the lights and leave subsequent decisions solely to the military.

Whether one believes in the moral traditions of just war doctrine or in international law, which has been more aspirational than truly binding on nations, it is hard to justify the killing of others or the deaths of one's soldiers for lesser purposes than national survival. These moral qualms work to make any use of military force a painful and difficult choice for national leaders. (See Table 8.2.)

There are risks of combat and deaths even when military units are used to deter actions by others by making clear that a hostile move could be countered by significant force, as the effectiveness of such threats depends on the credibility of their actual use. Commanders abhor empty, symbolic gestures. And, U.S. presidents have learned that troops sent on peacekeeping missions and even disaster relief operations can come under fire and suffer casualties.

Table 8.2 Major U.S. Military Operations and U.S. Battle Deaths, 1775–2011

CONFLICT/OPERATION	NUMBER SERVING	BATTLE DEATHS
Revolutionary War (1775–1783)	Estimated 184,000–250,000	4,345
War of 1812 (1812–1814)	286,730	2,260
U.S.–Mexican War (1846–1848)	78,718	1,733
Civil War (Union only)** (1861–1865)	2,213,363	140,414
Spanish–American War (1898)	306,760	385
Philippine insurgency (1898–1902)	126,468	1,108
World War I (1914–1918)	4,734,991	53,402
World War II (1941–1945)	16,112,566	291,557
Korean War (1950–1953)	5,720,000	33,741
Vietnam (1964–1975)	8,744,000	47,424
Lebanon UN Peacekeeping (1983)	1,800	256
Urgent Fury, Grenada (1983)	1,900	18
Just Cause, Panama (1989)	27,000	23
Desert Shield/Storm (1990–1991)	2,225,000	147
Restore Hope, Somalia (1992–1994)	30,000	29
Enduring Freedom, Afghanistan* (2001–present)	1,353,627 (combined)	1,850
Iraqi Freedom, Iraq* (2003–2011)	1,353,627 (combined)	4,408

*As of January 3, 2012

**Confederate figures are estimated to be about 850,000 to 900,000 serving, and about 75,000 battle deaths.

Modern weapons and modern medicine have reduced U.S. battle deaths in recent wars. The reliance on volunteers since 1973 has also seen a reduction in the number of Americans who have served in combat operations.

Source: Department of Defense; Congressional Research Service at http://fpc.state.gov/documents/organization/139347.pdf.

They have also learned to distrust advisers who claimed that "surgical" strikes could achieve quick and lasting success.

These experiences have made U.S. political leaders cautious about the use of force but not unwilling to order operations. The growing use of unmanned aerial drones, especially under President Obama, shows the attractiveness of military actions that reduce the risks of American casualties.

Growth and Professionalization of the Military

While the United States has always had an active diplomatic instrument for foreign policy, the development of the military instrument has been much more episodic. For the first 150 years of the republic, except for the Civil War and four short-duration declared wars, the armed forces were small in size and cost, a cheap insurance policy in case of hostile attacks or threats to commercial freedom of the seas. See Table 2.2 for the details. The framers of the Constitution, mindful of English history, opposed the idea of a large standing army and planned to rely on local militias for defense.

The U.S. Army in 1789 was a small force of 718 men, headed by Secretary of War Henry Knox and a single clerk. The navy and marine corps were not reconstituted after the Revolutionary War until 1794. The army was expanded in the 1790s, first to deal with frontier threats from Indians and then to prepare for a possible war with France. The navy got its first new warships, and marines to sail with them, in response to threats from the Barbary pirates and later also to prepare for a possible war with France.

Thomas Jefferson saw the army less as a tool for military action than as a force for civic improvement. In 1802, he worked to create the U.S. Military Academy at West Point, which was to train officers primarily as engineers. The navy did not get its own service academy until 1845 at Annapolis. These measures helped to professionalize military service by creating a corps of well-trained officers schooled in military tactics and in the operation of military equipment.

Limits on the size of the forces, however, kept promotions slow, and the lack of retirement benefits kept many senior officers on active duty long beyond their best days. In 1860, for example, 19 of 33 army officers at the rank of colonel or higher were veterans of the war of 1812, nearly a half century earlier.

U.S. leaders followed the practice of expanding the military only when combat seemed imminent. Shortly before declaring war in 1812, Congress voted a 25,000-man increase in the army for a 5-year enlistment, including a bounty of $16 and a promise, upon honorable discharge, of 3 months' pay and 160 acres of land. A few months later, lawmakers sought another 15,000 men for 18 months.[8] Congress approved fewer ships than Madison proposed, and none was completed in time to join the fight. After the war ended, the forces shrank below their prewar numbers.

In 1846, Congress voted to raise 50,000 volunteers to supplement the regular forces already fighting Mexico. When that proved insufficient, lawmakers added bonuses in 1847. The navy was not expanded, and the army was cut to prewar levels after the war.

The Civil War saw almost 3 million men under arms during its four bloody years, about 2 million for the Union and another 900,000 for the Confederacy. For the first time, men were drafted into service, though with exceptions for those who could hire a substitute or pay a commutation fee of $300. Despite the need for personnel for reconstruction duties in the South, the size of the U.S. Army dropped steadily in the decade after 1865. The late 19th century army was garrisoned on the frontier and used against Indians until the war with Spain in 1898.

The navy in 1865 was one of the largest in the world, with 471 warships, but its force was designed mainly for coastal and riverine operations. Few ironclads were kept in service after the war. Instead, the navy remained tangled in tradition, still preferring sails and wooden hulls until the 1880s. By 1890, the navy's 44 ships ranked America 12th in naval power, below Turkey and Austria–Hungary. By 1898, however, the navy ranked 6th and had its first battleships.[9]

In 1898, Congress approved an additional force of 200,000 men for the army, a fivefold increase, and nearly doubled the size of the navy and marine corps to about 26,000 total. The army remained about 100,000 thereafter, and the navy grew steadily in quantity and quality of its ships in the years leading up to World War I.

To raise the army to join the fight in World War I, which in 1918 had more than 2.3 million Americans in uniform, Congress again enacted a draft. The navy and marine corps were also greatly expanded, but all the forces fell to prewar levels during the isolationist 1920s.

While constrained in size, the U.S. military used the interwar years to pioneer many innovative approaches to future conflict. Both the army and navy developed air forces, the former to conduct strategic bombing and the latter to sink enemy ships at great distances from their own. Some in the army, but far too few at the time, saw that tanks could be used as primary attack weapons and not just mobile artillery for infantry troops. And in a forerunner to the challenges he would face mobilizing 12 million men and women after Pearl Harbor, General George C. Marshall was deeply involved in the recruitment, training, and use of 2.5 million jobless men who joined the Civilian Conservation Corps.

As war began in Europe, President Franklin Roosevelt (FDR) overcame isolationist resistance and persuaded Congress to increase weapons production for U.S. forces, to aid allies fighting Hitler, and even to institute the first peacetime draft in 1940. While programs for atomic weapons, jet airplanes, and other advanced weaponry did not reach the front lines until later in the war, the foundation was laid for the scientific–industrial–military complex, which flourished after 1945.

Consolidation, Nuclear Weapons, and Jointness

In an effort to improve the process for developing and carrying out national security policy—seen as a combination of foreign, military, and economic policy—Congress enacted the National Security Act of 1947. This law created the job of secretary of defense (but didn't create the actual Department of Defense, DOD, until 1949), codified the Joint Chiefs of Staff (JCS), created an independent air force, created the Central Intelligence Agency (CIA), and created the National Security Council (NSC). In fact, the NSC was proposed by the navy as an alternative to a unified military establishment, but its value was recognized by people on all sides of the question.

A separate law created the Atomic Energy Commission, devised so that the development of nuclear weapons would remain in civilian control. (President Truman was unwilling to turn actual custody of the bombs over to the military until war broke out in Korea in 1950. For their part, military leaders like General Curtis LeMay devised nuclear war plans out of sync with civilian guidance.) The American nuclear monopoly ended in 1949 with the first test of a Soviet A-bomb, and the Cold War race to build bigger and better bombs and delivery systems continued into the 1970s, when the first limits were imposed by U.S.–Soviet agreements. Modernization and worst-case fears about what the other side might do in a crisis persisted until the fall of the Soviet Union in 1991. Changes in the size of the armed forces since 1950 are shown in Table 8.3.

Interservice rivalry between the U.S. armed forces led each component to try to develop capabilities to fight the USSR on its own. Each service thought deterrence of Soviet attack depended on matching Soviet offensive capabilities more than building actual defenses against its missiles and bombers. Each nation based threat assessments on what the other might be able to do in the future and rushed to exceed that capability. In practice, however, both sides showed enormous restraint in readying the weapons

Table 8.3 U.S. Armed Forces, 1950–2010

Numbers by Service, End Strength in Thousands

Fiscal year	Army	Navy	Marine Corps	Air Force	Total*
1950	593	381	74	411	1,459
1955	1,109	661	205	960	2,935
1960	873	617	171	815	2,476
1965	969	672	190	825	2,656
1970	1,322	692	260	791	3,066
1975	784	535	196	613	2,129
1980	777	527	188	558	2,063
1985	781	571	198	602	2,207
1990	751	583	197	539	2,144
1995	509	435	174	400	1,583
2000	482	373	173	356	1,449
2005	492	362	180	352	1,455
2010	468	271	181	263	1,183

*Includes full-time national guard and reserve personnel where applicable.

Military force levels have experienced ups and downs throughout American history. Since 1950, the greatest changes have occurred in the ground combat services during and after major combat operations and steady reductions after the end of the Cold War in 1991. Conscription from 1948 to 1973 allowed rapid expansion of the force for the Korean and Vietnam wars, but it has been all-volunteer since the draft law expired. The services also worked to reduce human resource needs with technological improvements in weaponry.

Source: DOD.

for use. Starting in the 1960s, U.S. and Soviet leaders welcomed a *hotline* between Moscow and Washington and negotiated an incidents-at-sea agreement to reduce the dangers of accidental war.

U.S. military doctrine changed under different leaders. President Eisenhower reduced conventional forces and tried to reduce some of the interservice duplication of efforts. President Kennedy and Defense Secretary Robert McNamara limited the U.S. nuclear arsenal, imposed tighter civilian controls, and changed deterrence doctrine by developing precise damage expectancy criteria. President Nixon agreed to forego national ballistic missile defenses. President Reagan resurrected the idea of missile defenses, which President George W. Bush favored to the point of abrogating the Nixon Antiballistic Missile (ABM) treaty.

Military commanders fought the Vietnam War the way they fought World War II and Korea—with large force movements aimed at reducing and defeating enemy forces. At the same time, American advisors tried to build South Vietnamese units into an effective fighting force. There were some programs like what we now call counterinsurgency, aimed at winning civilian loyalty and providing local security, but most of these were not significant until the final period of U.S. military involvement in the early 1970s. When the war ended, the U.S. military tried to forget Vietnam and especially counterinsurgency operations.

Military misadventures—such as the ill-fated attempt to rescue American diplomatic personnel held hostage by Iranians in 1980 and the nearly bungled invasion of Grenada in 1982—led Congress to impose requirements for better military coordination of the armed forces, labeled *jointness* by the Goldwater–Nichols Defense Reorganization Act of 1986. The following year, Congress passed another law creating the Special Operations Command for counterterrorist missions, a capability deemed inadequately developed in the services. Jointness improved over the following decades not only operationally but also in terms of doctrine and management. A provision requiring, as a precondition for promotion to one-star general or admiral, that the officer serve in a multiservice job, such as in a combatant command or the joint staff, led to higher-quality people in those jobs. For that assignment at least, they were *purple suiters*. As a result, senior officers had some familiarity and experience with the capabilities and operations of other services.

The first Gulf War of 1991 demonstrated the apparent success of traditional U.S. military doctrine as well as improved jointness. Main battle units won a quick and decisive victory by destroying and defeating similar enemy units. No effort was made, however, to conquer and occupy Iraq. When that was done in 2003, it rapidly became apparent that the United States had no ready plans or capability to occupy and rebuild the war-torn country.

The minor conflicts of the Clinton years—the botched intervention in Somalia, the collapsed opposition to intervention in Haiti, and the military operations followed by successful negotiations in the Balkans—left U.S. military planners confident that they had learned all the right lessons from the past. They also believed that, by exploiting new information technologies and the realm of space with what they called the *revolution in military affairs*, they could sustain American military superiority for the foreseeable future.

Then came the 9/11 attacks and the search for ways to defeat an elusive but determined enemy comfortable in caves in rugged mountains. This was followed by the invasion of Iraq and the long struggle to build a viable successor government. The ground forces were called into action, and the air and sea forces shifted into supporting roles. The 21st century was starting to look a lot like the start of the 20th. With the withdrawal of U.S. forces from combat activities in Iraq and Afghanistan, the U.S. military faced a readjustment of strategic focus as well as strong pressures to cut spending to help reduce budget deficits.

Box 8.2

Secretary of Defense: A Hard Job to Keep

The secretary of defense has to confront daunting challenges almost daily: managing the sprawling Pentagon, obtaining military hardware at reasonable cost, planning and executing military operations, advising the president and NSC, and winning support from Congress for military programs.

The job is almost impossible to do well. In fact, more than one man in three who has held the post was fired or forced to resign. Ironically, most lost their jobs not because they failed to manage DOD but rather because they lost the confidence of the president or Congress or caused major political problems for the administration.

- James Forrestal (1947–1949) lost the confidence of President Truman, began behaving strangely, and later committed suicide.
- Louis Johnson (1949–1950) lost the confidence of President Truman and was sacrificed in recognition of U.S. military unpreparedness at the start of the Korean War.
- Charles Wilson (1953–1957) became a political embarrassment to President Eisenhower.
- Neil McElroy (1957–1959) lost the confidence of President Eisenhower.
- Robert McNamara (1961–1968) lost faith in his own Vietnam War and lost the confidence of President Johnson.
- James Schlesinger (1973–1975) irritated and caused political problems for President Ford.
- Caspar Weinberger (1981–1987) lost the confidence of Congress and caused political problems for President Reagan.
- Les Aspin (1993–1994) lost the confidence of President Clinton and was sacrificed after military problems in Somalia.
- Donald Rumsfeld (2001–2006) lost the confidence of Congress and caused political problems for President Bush.

Source: Charles A. Stevenson, *SecDef: The Nearly Impossible Job of Secretary of Defense* (Washington, DC: Potomac Books, 2006).

Leadership

The person in charge of the Pentagon is the secretary of defense, known in bureaucratic shorthand as the SecDef. The top official has ample authority to meet his responsibilities. As with the secretary of state, the SecDef is an instrument of the president. (See Box 8.3.) As the basic law says, "The Secretary is the principal assistant to the President in all matters relating to the Department of Defense. Subject to the direction of the President and to [other laws], he has authority, direction, and control over the Department of Defense" (10 USC 113b). He is also supposed to be "appointed from civilian life" rather than directly from the senior officer ranks, as in many other countries. In fact, this law had to be specifically waived by Congress when President Truman wanted to name retired General George C. Marshall as SecDef at the start of the Korean War.

Originally, the job was much less powerful than it is now. The very first Secretary, James Forrestal, was increasingly frustrated in the post. He called it "probably the greatest cemetery for dead cats in history." He also concluded that "the peacetime mission of the Armed Services is to destroy the Secretary of Defense."[10] They succeeded. Forrestal was fired, showed signs of mental illness, and jumped to his death from the 16th floor of the Bethesda naval hospital.

The law was changed in later years to give the secretary more power over the armed services. The first man to exploit it to the full was Robert McNamara, who served under Presidents Kennedy and Johnson. McNamara dominated the Pentagon through a series of processes, all of which went directly through his office. The most powerful was the budget process, which McNamara—and all of his successors—used to set the size of the forces, their military missions, their capabilities, and their research and development (R&D) efforts for the future. Any change in previously approved programs had to be approved by his office, and only on the basis of elaborate justifications, including future year costs.

McNamara ultimately failed, however, when he tried to impose his accounting metrics—and his intrusive personality—on the men fighting the war in Vietnam. The boss wanted numbers, so he was given numbers in accordance with the military maxim, "if you want it bad, you'll get it bad."

Many Pentagon chiefs practiced leadership by intimidation, as former Deputy Secretary John Hamre recommended in the quotation at the start of this chapter. Others, the ones generally judged more favorably by history, listened as well as talked and sometimes even accepted the advice of their subordinates. The quiet successes included men like Melvin Laird under Richard Nixon and William Perry under Bill Clinton.

It's hard to succeed as boss of the Pentagon. (See Box 8.2.) Of the 21 men who have served as SecDef, at least 8 were fired or forced to resign. Most lost the confidence of the president or caused him major political problems. Several also lost the confidence of the defense overseers in the Congress, endangering Pentagon programs and causing additional political problems.

> **Box 8.3**
>
> ## Who Makes Foreign Policy: The Very Busy Secretary of Defense and Chairman of the Joint Chiefs of Staff
>
> Besides the demanding requirements of running the Pentagon and attending White House meetings to advise the president, the secretary of defense has to travel widely to oversee military operations, deal with foreign officials on security issues, and attend conferences with allies. In 2010, for example, Defense Secretary Robert Gates spent 67 days away from Washington on foreign travel, visiting 25 different countries, several more than once. During his four and a half years in office, Gates was away from the Pentagon 282 days, visited an average of 33 countries each year and traveled over 664,000 miles.
>
> The chairman of the JCS also has to travel widely, visiting U.S. forces and conferring with foreign military leaders. In 2010, Admiral Mike Mullen traveled abroad 72 days, visiting 26 countries, several more than once. During his four years in office, he averaged visits to 39 countries each year, traveling 78 days. His four-year total was 157 country visits and 313 days of travel.
>
> Both officials used their travel for diplomatic activities and military consultations as well as overseeing U.S. forces, thus demonstrating how important they are as part of a foreign policy team.
>
> *Source:* DOD.

Success requires the trust and support of the president, collaborative relations with the military leadership in the JCS, and at least a tolerable working relationship with the rest of the administration's national security team. Failure in any of those roles puts the secretary on the exit ramp.

The senior military leader is the Chairman of the JCS (CJCS). The JCS used to be a consensus-based advisory committee whose advice was often slow to come and opaque in form. The 1986 Goldwater–Nichols law gave the chairman special status and allowed him to offer independent advice without logrolling and compromise among the chiefs. This is one of the CJCS's few powers. He is not in the chain of command to warfighting forces and cannot give orders to subordinate commanders. But, his public and private advice is frequently sought and carries great weight throughout government. The JCS still perform important roles as representatives of their service in Pentagon policy making. And while they hold formal sessions in their *tank*, the chairman may also consult them informally, as Admiral David Jeremiah reports. (See Box 8.4.)

The COCOMs in charge of U.S. forces in various regions and for particular missions like the use of strategic nuclear weapons and SOF are independently powerful because of their warfighting responsibilities. They are directly under the secretary in the chain of command and share their war plans with the JCS only as a matter of courtesy rather than law. In planning for the Iraq war, for example, Secretary Rumsfeld and Central Command

> **Box 8.4**
>
> ## Inside View: Joint Chiefs of Staff Meet in the Kitchen
>
> Admiral David Jeremiah, vice chairman of the JCS, 1990–1994, describes how the JCS Chairman, Gen. Colin Powell, scheduled formal meetings but did most work in informal ones. The use of informal meetings and processes is common in government, but it makes it harder for outsiders to know what is happening. Formal sessions require paperwork before and afterward and stimulate interest among subordinates. Informal sessions allow franker exchanges and fewer leaks. That makes it easier for the president to feel comfortable with the advice on the use of the military instrument that the chiefs are established to provide.
>
> *We scheduled—historically, the Chiefs would go in on, say, Tuesdays, Thursdays, maybe Wednesday, and they'd have tank sessions. Tank sessions were wonderful theater. Coffee or tea or seltzer water or whatever the drink of choice was, a candy jar with whatever the candy of choice was, in the old days an ashtray with cigar or whatever. Beautiful. Everybody sat down, everybody had their staff position, and they would settle up defending their staff position that had been worked up through their individual service staffs . . .*
>
> *The product was not of any particular consequence. . . . We met in the tank a lot but we met in [Gen.] Colin [Powell]'s kitchen a lot, sometimes in my kitchen, sometimes in other places, often in the office. Get the Chiefs down, everybody popping in, and we'd talk. He would tell the Chiefs what was going on, what the issue was. What do you think about it? He pretty well knew what he wanted to do. Let's talk about it. Sometimes it got vectored a little bit differently, but when it came out it didn't take up a lot of staff time trying to fool around with the issue. If the issue required a lot of staff time, the staff ought to take care of it. If you really wanted to know something about it and do something about it, then we should be able to deal with it at the service chiefs' level without having to mess around with the whole process.*
>
> *[Powell's approach was:] I think we need a meeting on that, do you? Yes. Makes sense. Get some comments, get the Chiefs together. Or, you just came from the White House and this is what the deputy said to say? Let's get the Chiefs down and you tell them what's going on, where it's headed, something like that.*
>
> Source: Oral history for the G. H. W. Bush Administration, Admiral David Jeremiah at http://millercenter.org/president/bush/oralhistory/david-jeremiah.

(CENTCOM) Commander General Tommy Franks collaborated together and allowed little input from the JCS.

The U.S. military fully embrace the notion of civilian control, but they sometimes chafe at its practice. They prefer to design and execute military operations based on clear, strategic guidance, yet presidents and SecDefs over the years have tended to give only vague guidance and then to insist on close tactical oversight. Military officers tend to resent any civilian intrusion into what they see as their domain, yet with few historical exceptions, they will loyally carry out even orders they think unwise.

Scholar–practitioner Peter Feaver has said that, in the American system of civil–military relations, "The civilians have the right to be wrong." And another professor–policy maker, Eliot Cohen, has recommended regular civil–military consultations, even though it is necessarily an unequal dialogue. Professor Richard Betts has noted that, except for the 1983 intervention in Lebanon, no major military operation in the latter half of the 20th century was conducted when more than one of the JCS was strongly opposed. One might now add another possible exception—the "surge" of additional troops to Iraq in 2007. But I think the evidence there, and elsewhere in the historical record, points to a different conclusion. The U.S. military, because of the enormous deference given them by the public and political leaders, have an implicit veto over the use of force in major operations. They never use the veto as such; they never refuse to follow orders, but they do insist on and obtain terms and conditions that limit the way force is used.[11]

Civil–military relations in the United States have been tense for several decades despite the best efforts of many leaders to build bridges of understanding. Many military officers believe that civilian officials "lost" a war in Vietnam that might otherwise have been "won" because of poor strategy and intrusions into the military domain. Many officers in the 1980s and 1990s objected to being sent on *nation-building* missions because they believed the military should be held in reserve for major, nation-threatening conflicts. Many officers resented Bill Clinton as commander-in-chief because he had avoided the draft during Vietnam. Some senior officers spoke out against Secretary Rumsfeld's intrusive management of the Pentagon.

Rumsfeld managed by *snowflakes,* personal memos raising questions and offering ideas sent at the rate of hundreds per week. "I want to run this department from my outbox, not my inbox," he explained.[12] He also bullied his subordinates but yielded to unshaken and persuasive responses, as described in Box 8.5. He was often quite willing to impose his ideas contrary to military advice, even going as far as demanding changes in the complicated and long-planned timetables for shipping equipment and personnel for the Iraq war. (See Box 8.5.)

Rumsfeld's successor, Robert Gates, had a quite different style and was unusually successful as secretary of defense. He won the confidence of Congress and two different presidents while managing two difficult wars. Gates challenged the status quo in the Pentagon in numerous ways. He enforced accountability on senior officials who made mistakes or were too slow to accept changed approaches to major policy issues. For example, he replaced the secretary of the army, the secretary of the air force, the chairman of the JCS, the air force chief of staff, the commander of CENTCOM, and two U.S. commanders in Afghanistan.

Gates also forced the Pentagon to give priority to ongoing wars and overrode bureaucratic emphasis on future weapons development. For example, he ordered accelerated production and delivery of the mine-resistant, ambush-protected (MRAP) armored trucks that were saving lives in the war

> **Box 8.5**
>
> ## Inside View: Rumsfeld's Assertive Style
>
> Defense Secretary Donald Rumsfeld intimidated his subordinates, even those he admired, according to one of his senior staff, the Defense Department Comptroller Dov Zackheim. He challenged them but appreciated those who had cogent arguments and stood their ground.
>
> *Rumsfeld's style also confused many senior people inside the Pentagon. He would not hesitate to vent his annoyance when he felt a briefer was unprepared or when he perceived that someone had not done his or her homework. Many of us were on the receiving end of comments like 'a trained ape could do better than that,' and not everyone grasped that Rumsfeld was not being personal.*
>
> *[One day Rear Admiral Stan Szemborski] had been called into the secretary's office to outline how efficiencies could reduce the defense budget by 15 percent. . . . Stan told the boss flatly that it couldn't be done. Rumsfeld was outraged. It was not what he had expected to hear; it confirmed his worst suspicions about the pedestrian nature of the military and its adherence to 'old think.' But Stan stood his ground in the face of Don's displeasure. Rumsfeld finally stormed out of the conference room back to his office. The rest of us stared at one another in silence as embarrassment blossomed among us. Finally, I remarked to Stan, 'He really likes you.'*
>
> Source: From Dov S. Zackheim, *A Vulcan's Tale* (Washington, DC: Brookings Institution, 2011), 59, 60.

zones. Within two years, the number of such vehicles with U.S. forces in Iraq and Afghanistan surged from 64 to more than 13,000. Similarly, he compelled the air force to greatly expand its number and use of unmanned aerial vehicles (drones) in combat areas.

He patiently used Pentagon processes to obtain military concurrence in budget cuts and program changes and even to support repeal of the law banning service by gays and lesbians. He arranged for a thorough study of the Don't Ask, Don't Tell law that answered many criticisms and secured the support of most senior military commanders for repeal, which passed Congress in 2010. Gates probably ranks as the most effective and highly regarded secretary of defense in history.

People in Many Uniforms

There are almost 3 million men and women who are the human factor behind the military instrument of national power. Some 736,000 are civilians, and the remaining 2.252 million (1.4 million on active duty, 846,000 in the reserves) are in one of many different uniforms. All share, however, a military ethos of order, sacrifice, loyalty, and other important virtues. All of the people in uniform are volunteers, either for active duty or for reserve assignments that in recent years have included many months in Iraq and

Afghanistan. The draft ended in 1973 and, with it, the incentive to volunteer for safer assignments than combat infantry.

The all-volunteer force is diverse in composition but not a demographic mirror of American society. Whites represent 79.4% of the general population and 70.7% of the armed forces, according to a survey in 2008. Blacks are 12.8% of the population but account for 16.5% of the military. Hispanics are 15.8% of the population and 10.6% of those in uniform. Women are 50.4% of the population but only 14.3% of the active-duty personnel.[13]

Southern states have accounted for a disproportionate share of military recruits throughout the all-volunteer force, from about one third during the 1970s and 1980s to 42% since the early 1990s. The number of enlistees from New England and the Middle Atlantic states is significantly below the national average. While about 30% of the new accessions come from urban areas, nearly half come from relatively small towns and rural areas.[14]

The quality of the armed forces is generally quite high because virtually all enlisted personnel are high school graduates or the equivalent and most officers eventually obtain master's degrees.

The risks of military service are obviously high, but benefits have steadily increased in order to sustain a volunteer force and avoid a draft. For example, men and women serving in Afghanistan or Iraq or some nearby countries could also qualify for hostile fire pay, hardship duty pay, a family separation allowance, and a per diem—with most or all of these payments excluded from federal taxes. Military personnel and their dependents also receive generous health care benefits while on active duty, and they qualify for veterans' benefits and a special retiree health care program more generous than Medicare.

In addition to the active forces, there are over 1 million men and women in the reserve component forces. The army, navy, marine corps, and air force reserve units are designed as replacements or supplements for regular forces if needed. The national guard is different, the modern equivalent of the militia that the framers preferred to a standing army. Unless called to federal duty by the president, the guard belongs to the governor of the state where it was recruited and trained. Even if given advanced weapons and training for ground combat, the guard is used locally mainly for disaster relief and riot control. In recent years, about 6,000 guard personnel have been federalized for border security missions along parts of the U.S.–Mexican border. This is an example of the use of military forces for a domestic homeland security mission that also has significant foreign policy consequences for U.S. relations with Mexico. The president has to weigh both domestic and foreign policy factors before using such an instrument.

The reserve forces used to be a convenient way for people to continue military service, get a little money and eventual retirement benefits, and provide backup skills in case of a major war. As reservists were embedded in civilian life and often community leaders, presidents were very reluctant to call upon the reserves during the Cold War. As the Vietnam War was ending, General Creighton Abrams restructured the army so that large deployments could not occur without calling up reservists. Many police, medical, and transportation units—so-called combat service and combat service support units—were put in the reserves. It was Abrams's way of making sure that future presidents would think twice about major military operations and that civilian society would share in the costs and disruption.[15]

In fact, the numbers of reservists recalled to active duty were low and the domestic political impact small until the post-2001 wars in Iraq and Afghanistan, which became unpopular for many reasons, including the disruptions caused by the use of large numbers of guard and reserve personnel. Reservists were called to active duty frequently during the 1990s and since the 9/11 attacks. Nearly a quarter of a million were activated during the Persian Gulf War of 1990–1991; more than 6,000 were recalled for duty in Haiti during 1994–1996; more than 31,000 were used to support peacekeeping missions in Bosnia after 1995; another 11,500 were used in Kosovo after 1999. About 700,000 reservists have been activated for the wars in Afghanistan and Iraq. Air national guard units have provided about 30% of the aircraft used by U.S. forces in Iraq and Afghanistan. More than one fourth (28%) of the forces deployed to Iraq and Afghanistan during 2001–2007 were from the guard and reserves.[16] In 2011, Congress voted to make the chief of the National Guard Bureau a formal member of the JCS.

Organization

The 2.1 million people regularly in the DOD (civilians and active duty military) pose a major management challenge. As the organization chart shows, DOD is divided into three military departments, 18 defense agencies, 10 combatant commands, 10 field activities, and several other organizations, including the important and powerful Office of the Secretary of Defense (OSD) and the Joint Staff. (See Figure 8.1.) There are about 2,000 people working in OSD and another 1,600 on the Joint Staff.

The military departments organize, train, and equip the armed forces, but most are assigned to the combatant commands for military operations. The defense agencies have special, department-wide tasks, like accounting and payroll, auditing, logistics, and various intelligence activities. The JCS, aided by the Joint Staff, provide advice to the secretary and the NSC, but they do not command any operating forces. OSD is the secretary's management device, with five under secretaries and numerous other officials reporting to him.

The deputy secretary has traditionally been the chief operating officer of DOD, the one managing the major processes of budgeting and weapons acquisition, facing inward, while the secretary is the public face and spokesperson on defense issues. For foreign policy matters, as well as for civilian control of military strategy, the under secretary for policy is the key official. Each secretary chooses which processes and issues deserve personal attention and which can be delegated to the experienced bureaucracy of the Pentagon. Secretary Rumsfeld reached far down the chain of command with

Figure 8.1 U.S. Department of Defense Organizational Chart

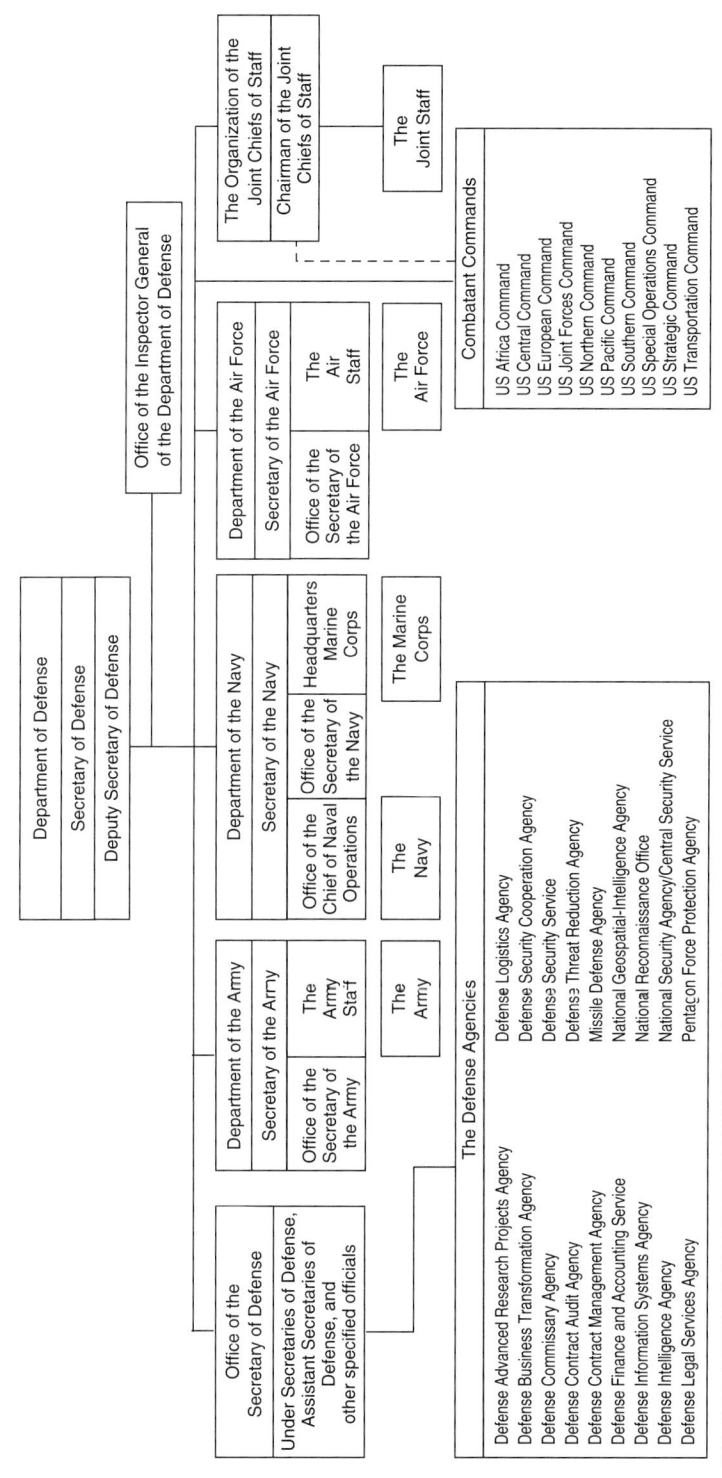

Note the complexity of DOD organizations, the services separate from the combatant commands, and the many defense agencies separate from both. Yet, all funnel into the OSD for management and decisions. On the other hand, the diversity and specialization of DOD organizations has made it easier to militarize foreign policy because the Pentagon usually has people and resources ready to use, and the civilian agencies do not.

Source: DOD, 2010.

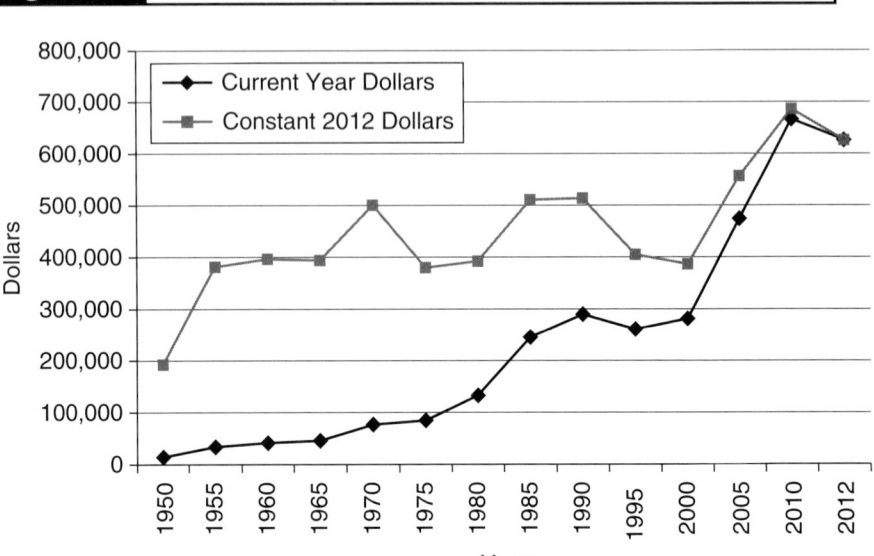

Figure 8.2 U.S. Defense Spending, 1960–2012

There are many different ways to measure military spending. This chart shows the actual budget outlays in current year dollars and in constant dollars, factoring out inflation. As you can see, in constant dollars, recent budgets have been about as high as during the Vietnam War and the mid-1980s military buildup. And even with congressionally mandated cuts during 2012–2017, spending should remain above the Cold War average.

Source: National Defense Budget Estimates for FY 2012, Office of the Under Secretary of Defense, 2011, 141–146 at http://comptroller.defense.gov/defbudget/fy2012/FY12_Green_Book.pdf.

questions and guidance. Secretary Gates relied more on the formal processes that routinely bring matters for high-level decision.

While the budget is the primary process for managing and controlling the Pentagon (see Figure 8.2), the secretary is also at the pinnacle for other processes. The acquisition process supplements the budget process but allows the secretary to reshape the capabilities of the armed forces, sometimes giving them new missions and weaponry, other times denying them the desired but far too costly system they were hoping to acquire. The personnel system gives him, with presidential concurrence, the chance to pick civilian officials and the senior military officers. Some secretaries made a practice of interviewing several candidates for key posts, thus providing them a cadre of loyalists who shared his vision of what should be done and how. The public affairs process allows the secretary to shape the message of the Pentagon to friends and enemies at home and abroad. Rumsfeld's pronouncements about the Global War on Terror, which typically was quickly shortened to GWOT, were an effort to frame how to view the threats from loosely organized but violent groups. The legislative affairs process helps the secretary build a partnership with Capitol Hill, using devices such as classified briefings, locally helpful contracts, and occasional free trips home and abroad on military aircraft. Each of these tools can strengthen a SecDef's power and influence.

The Culture of the Pentagon

There is a distinctive organizational culture in the Pentagon, widely shared by civilians and military alike. In terms of the Myers–Briggs typology, about 90% of military personnel test as thinking and judging, traits related to being logical, firm but fair, goal-oriented, decisive, and organized. Some 30% are introversion–sensation–thinking–judging (ISTJ), compared to only 6% in the population as a whole. ISTJs "have a keen sense of right and wrong," believe in punctuality, are "factual, dedicated, thorough, systematic, steadfast, practical, organized, realistic, duty bound, sensible, painstaking, and reliable."[17] Just listing those words calls to mind warriors.

These personality traits also infuse organizations with an insistence on careful planning, seeking clear goals, and timely decisions. The elaborate DOD processes for budgeting and weapons acquisition are mirrored in war planning by the combatant commands. This culture also focuses on enemy capabilities, which seem measurable, rather than intentions, which can be vague, uncertain, and changeable. It also considers worst-case analysis as reasonable and necessary.

A vivid example of the military can-do spirit is what the author observed in a visit years ago to a live-fire exercise at Fort Benning, Georgia. Seeing M60 tanks crossing a small lake with their turrets open in order to attach flotation gear, he asked a young major, "Can they fire while in the water?" "Yes, sir," the major replied, "once." He explained that the recoil would make the tank take on water, but before sinking, it could contribute one shell to the fight.

All these characteristics make the Pentagon different from the other national security organizations, where multiple objectives (e.g., trade, human rights, support against pariah states) have to be balanced and prioritized and where the planning culture has not taken root. In interagency meetings, it's usually the Pentagon representatives who ask, "What are we really after, not just how do we solve today's problem?"

While the military ethos is widespread, each service has its own individual culture, reflecting its history and the way it views its core competencies. As Carl Builder and others have noted, the army views itself as the servant to society, and it emphasizes cooperation and coordination. Army units have to know who is on each side of them and what each is planning to do in battle. The navy honors its traditions, including the independence of the captain at sea. It also enforces a different standard of accountability, punishing the captain for errors by the crew, while the other services tend to look for the precise locus of error. The marine corps, lean and mean throughout history, has always stressed its willingness and readiness for almost any mission it might be assigned. When army leaders in the 1990s opposed nation-building and stabilization missions, saying "We don't do windows," the marines said they would do them. Despite easy political victories when civilians have tried to disband the corps—as Teddy Roosevelt and Harry Truman learned to their regret—the marines still feel embattled and threatened. The air force, the newest service that achieved independence only after a long struggle, emphasizes technology and the superiority of air power for most military tasks.[18]

There is one curious fact that makes DOD different from the State Department and other national security institutions and which may explain the dominance of the military mind-set: Most of the senior civilian officials in OSD are outsiders, political appointees. Very few careerists have ever been appointed to positions requiring Senate confirmation—in contrast to the State Department, where typically half the assistant secretaries and 85% of the deputy assistant secretaries are career foreign service officers (FSOs). This has numerous pernicious effects. Few talented DOD civilians can be motivated and rewarded by promotion to top posts. There is high turnover of political appointees, weakening institutional memory and learning. And, incoming officials distrust the loyalty of their new subordinates.[19]

Use of the Military Instrument

Current military doctrine sets four strategic goals for the Pentagon, three for security purposes and one for management. They are these: Win our nation's wars; deter conflict and promote security; defend the homeland; and integrate business operations.[20] Plans and budgets are linked to those goals much more specifically than in other departments and agencies. The three security goals are also foreign policy goals that military forces help the United States to achieve.

When it comes to actual use of military capabilities, there is a tight system of civilian control. The secretary of defense may consult with the chairman or the JCS as a body, but only he can give direct orders to the COCOM to engage in military operations. Only he can approve war plans or assign troops to one command rather than another. In fact, the secretary personally must sign any deployment order sending military units abroad, except for small numbers of people sent on temporary duty for nonoperational support tasks.[21]

Within the United States, the limits on the use of the regular armed forces are even more restrictive. As part of the political settlement that ended Reconstruction and led to the withdrawal of federal soldiers from the former Confederacy, Congress passed a *never again law* forbidding the use of troops to enforce domestic law. This is called The *Posse Comitatus* Act (18 U. S. C. 1385), using the common-law phrase for a sheriff's power to call upon local citizens to help maintain law and order. There are some technical exceptions—the law doesn't apply to the navy or marine corps; the coast guard has explicit law enforcement duties; troops may still be used to suppress insurrections and repel invasions. But, the practical result is that the law prevents soldiers from arresting people or conducting searches and seizures to aid civilian law enforcement.

The law also imposes a strong psychological barrier against using troops domestically. For example, only in the 1980s did Congress enact provisions allowing military aircraft to pass along surveillance information that could be used to interdict drug smugglers. Officials reluctant to seek or use military personnel in some domestic matter raise the *posse comitatus* law as a first line of argument. Since 2006, national guard troops have been deployed along the southwest border with Mexico to supplement the activities of the border patrol. About 30,000 men and women have participated in this activity, called Operation Jump Start. They are paid for by the federal government but under the control of the respective state governors. And, they are limited to supporting local authorities, stopping short of actual arrest or search and seizure.[22]

Presidents are sometimes limited by law in their use of force abroad, though some lawyers dispute the validity of such limits. Nevertheless, Congress has passed and presidents have complied with numerous restrictions on troop deployments and warfighting. For example, President McKinley abided by a ban on the annexation of Cuba in the Spanish–American War. FDR agreed, prior to Pearl Harbor, not to send draftees outside the Western hemisphere. President Nixon complied with congressional bans on sending U.S. troops into combat in Laos or Thailand and on conducting bombing raids anywhere in Southeast Asia after August 15, 1973. President Reagan agreed to limit U.S. troops in Lebanon to a self-defense mission. President Clinton complied with troop limitations for Somalia and Rwanda. And, President George W. Bush accepted a ceiling on U.S. military personnel in Colombia.[23] Congress has imposed, and various presidents have grudgingly accepted, other limits on foreign policy activities using armed forces.

Warfighting

The pointy end of America's military instrument is the combat force deployed abroad, armed and trained to fight, kill, and destroy hostile forces, weapons, and supporting elements. Staffs at each of the combatant commands, under presidential directives, prepare contingency war plans and variations to deal with crisis situations in their areas. These can be reviewed by a handful of senior DOD civilians and are periodically updated. See the case study at the end of this chapter showing the planning process followed before the start of the Iraq war in 2003.

In their regions, the COCOMs (formerly called CINCs) are powerful and prestigious. These four-star officers are often treated as American equivalents of ancient Roman proconsuls and are used for diplomatic missions even more than the State Department's ambassadors and assistant secretaries. The COCOMs also have the very practical advantage of dedicated aircraft to expedite their travel.

The regional commanders control all of the air, naval, and ground forces assigned to their regions, regardless of their own particular service backgrounds. They also coordinate with host country civilian and military leaders and are supposed to work collaboratively with the U.S. ambassadors in their areas as well. Sometimes, the civilian and military chiefs work well together, as did General David Petraeus and Ambassador Ryan Crocker in Iraq. Sometimes, the pair are in constant tension, as was the case between General Stanley McChrystal and Ambassador Karl Eikenberry in Afghanistan.

The Special Operations Command (SOCOM) is in charge of warriors who depend on stealth, surprise, and speed. They aren't designed for sustained combat. The 9/11 attacks prompted a rapid increase in SOF, from 35,000 in the late 1990s to about 66,000 in 2013, along with a tripling of its budget.[24] The SOF have land, sea, and air units used primarily to deter, disrupt, and defeat terrorists and their networks. As of 2010, 86% of deployed SOF personnel were in the CENTCOM region including Afghanistan and Iraq, but about 3,000 people were also routinely deployed in more than 75 countries, where they conduct training, advisory, or unpublicized missions.

Congress created an independent SOCOM in 1986, giving it an independent budget so that its capabilities would no longer be treated as an underfunded stepchild of the established armed services. In operations in CENTCOM, however, its forces often are dependent on the regular forces for mobility and some support functions. There are often tensions between the COCOM's chain of command and the somewhat autonomous line of authority for the SOF.

Separate from the uniformed military are the CIA's paramilitary forces, which since the Korean War era, have conducted clandestine operations both to gather intelligence and to pursue other goals. CIA operatives, for example, commanded the forces used in the failed Bay of Pigs attack on Cuba in 1961 and for secret operations in Laos against the North Vietnamese. CIA units have been active in Afghanistan since even before the 9/11 attacks. The president ultimately controls all of these supersecret military units, but the 9/11 Commission recommended moving the CIA paramilitary forces under the command of the Pentagon. Instead, Congress has endorsed closer coordination between the forces.[25]

Engaging With Foreign Governments and Militaries

In recent years, the bulk of U.S. combat forces have been deployed in or near Iraq and Afghanistan. But, there are also substantial numbers of military personnel afloat on naval ships or deployed to other countries. In 2009, for example, the Pentagon had 20,000 men and women on the high seas and 52,000 in Germany, 36,000 in Japan, 25,000 in South Korea, more than 9,000 in Italy, and a similar number in the United Kingdom. Sizable contingents of more than 1,000 people were also in Bahrain, Belgium, Djibouti, Spain, and Turkey.[26]

Some of these people were in support of long-standing treaty obligations for mutual defense. Others were engaged in particular missions to advise or train local forces. Such deployments have long been an important tool of foreign policy, for they integrate local forces in common defense efforts; help to develop an affinity for American people, practices, and equipment; and provide invaluable contacts with those who are often the most powerful individuals in their respective nations.

Since the 9/11 attacks, DOD has undertaken a large share of U.S. security assistance, funneling more than $60 billion mainly to Iraq, Afghanistan, and nearby countries. DOD gained control of these programs because it was viewed as more agile and flexible than the State Department and its rigid legal authorities. The Pentagon also dominates the planning for foreign military sales and financing programs because its people develop the recommendations for recipient countries, which are then reviewed by the State Department. The regional military commanders often have their own resources—like the Commander's Emergency Response Program (CERP)—that supplement regular foreign assistance programs with flexible funds for small-scale civil and humanitarian projects.[27] As Dana Priest argues in the quotation at the start of this chapter, these many Pentagon activities have led to military dominance over much of U.S. foreign policy.

The 911 Force

The U.S. military is a 911 force—large enough, diverse and redundant enough in capabilities, and trained and ready to be used in almost any way a president might wish. In recent years, U.S. military personnel have been sent to help deal with natural disasters like the Indian Ocean tsunami of 2004 and the 2010 earthquake in Haiti as well as domestic American missions after Hurricane Katrina and for wildfire suppression.

Military aircraft can speed supplies and people to far parts of the globe in a few hours. Military medical personnel can supplement overwhelmed local people. Military bulldozers can clear streets filled with rubble, and engineers can install temporary bridges in flood-ravaged countries. These capabilities bring prestige and soft power to the United States and are often welcomed for providing operational experience for military personnel.

Planning and Policy Making

Crisis needs may be surprising, but they are rarely unanticipated in the Pentagon. Military planners may not know precisely where an incident may occur that may lead to a U.S. military response of some kind, but they know that certain kinds of activities will likely be necessary, so they plan, and budget, and train, and practice for them. Since the 1990s, Congress has required DOD to perform a Quadrennial Defense Review (QDR), a regular assessment of defense strategy and force structure that leads to changed priorities and new requirements to deal with current and expected developments.

The secretary of defense leads the QDR process, and it often is the central focus of Pentagon leadership during the first year after each presidential election. Secretary Rumsfeld tried to use the process to encourage a defense transformation toward more high-technology weaponry and other systems, but he was forced to devote more effort to the conflicts in Iraq and Afghanistan. Secretary Gates used the process to shift emphasis from future war planning to meeting urgent needs of deployed forces, especially those in the war zones. Secretary Panetta used the QDR as the baseline for analyzing reductions required by congressional budget ceilings and for planning the *pivot* or *rebalance* to the Asia–Pacific region.

In addition to these long-range, strategic plans, the Pentagon follows an elaborate process for all important policy decisions. Stakeholders at middle levels are convened to discuss and prepare options papers for high-level officials. Coordination is attempted across service or functional or regional lines as necessary. Senior leaders can reach down to force consideration of matters they deem important, or their subordinates can bring issues to their attention for decision and guidance. This is all routine and bureaucratic but fits well within the military's planning culture.

Recurring Tensions

As in any diverse bureaucracy, there are in the Pentagon numerous rivalries and recurrent tensions that can affect the use of the military instrument. Foremost is that between civilians and the military. While the uniformed officers accept civilian control, they prefer that it be gentle and respectful without intruding on their professional expertise. For their part, the civilians want loyalty and obedience, and they get upset when the career military don't adopt the broader and more political perspective they have.

A revealing example of a legitimate disagreement is on the Rules of Engagement, the orders commanders give prescribing when force can and cannot be used in specified circumstances. From the military perspective, these are operational questions they should resolve, given their knowledge of military training and capabilities. From the civilian perspective, tactical matters can have strategic consequences and thus should be subjected to civilian review. Both sides want to protect the lives of Americans, for example, but they may disagree on which measures have collateral effects that undermine the war effort. When enemy soldiers appear to be firing from in or near a mosque or school, for example, the rules need to balance protection of civilians and friendly forces with steps to eliminate the threat. Similarly, the air force makes elaborate calculations of the potential blast effects of hitting certain targets in order to minimize collateral damage. These are not easy questions.

Another tension, quite evident in the Iraq war, is that between the JCS and the COCOMs. The chiefs are the leaders of their services concerned with its long-term capabilities, both human and material. The commanders, especially when engaged in a shooting war, care primarily about today and tomorrow, not next year, and doing whatever can be done to accomplish their missions. Each side has a legitimate perspective, and the policy process tries to balance the conflicting demands. Secretary Gates, much more than his predecessors, emphasized immediate requirements over future programs.

Interservice rivalry has been strong throughout U.S. history and was only slightly diminished by the recent emphasis on jointness. The air force wants the latest and best aircraft; the navy wants a number of aircraft carriers; the marines want to stay at three divisions; and the army wants next-generation weaponry even as it is stretched thin by current wars. It took civilian pressure to acquire airlift and sealift because those assets were going to be used to transport army people and equipment. It took civilian pressure to create the SOF because the regular forces viewed that as a minor mission, last in line for funding and promotions. It took civilian pressure to build up a force of unmanned aerial vehicles because as the military sees it, "real men should be in cockpits, not at computer terminals."

Still unresolved is the perennial conflict between the active forces and the reserves. Despite the valiant performance of reserve units in Iraq and Afghanistan, some senior officials still doubt their capabilities and insist on preserving full active-duty strength. Budget officials recognize the strong political support for the reserves on Capitol Hill and routinely omit full funding of particular programs in expectation of congressional add-ons. For its part, the national guard has embraced the homeland security mission, hoping to grow in size and capability as a consequence.

The Pentagon in the Interagency Process

As Secretary Gates acknowledged, DOD is an "800-pound gorilla" when dealing with others. As a result, the military instrument is the default option even for many nonmilitary tasks, including a large share of U.S. foreign aid. Another consequence is that Pentagon views get special deference from presidents and other cabinet officials. Especially since the Goldwater–Nichols Act, the uniformed military have had their own seat in interagency planning meetings, thus giving military concerns a strong double voice in debates. Pentagon officials are used to careful planning and rapid responses. They can do the *first paper on the block* to frame issues for interagency discussion.

Conversely, when the Pentagon holds back, the whole interagency process comes to an abrupt halt. Two long-serving DOD officials, Frederick C. Smith and Franklin C. Miller, document this effect during Secretary Rumsfeld's tenure. Rumsfeld, they note, had "an abiding animosity" toward the interagency process. Especially in planning for the Iraq war, DOD officials failed to attend meetings or sat in but failed to share information.[28] Other participants have said that Rumsfeld insisted that his subordinates not deal with others on issues until DOD had a position, and then they were not supposed to agree to any alternatives. Such sabotage of the policy process probably contributed to shortcomings immediately after the invasion of Iraq in 2003.[29] Secretary Gates and Secretary Panetta were much more willing team players in the interagency process.

Congress and the Pentagon

Congress shares control of the military through its constitutional powers to raise and support an army, provide and maintain a navy, organize the militia, and "make Rules for the Government and Regulation of the land and naval Forces" (Art. I, sect. 8). It also has functioned historically as an escape valve during civil–military tensions as people in uniform could freely complain to lawmakers, who often were happy to help them for personal or political reasons. Members of defense committees often challenge executive branch policies because of such back-channel reports from dissenting officials.

Key oversight is performed by the House and Senate Armed Services Committees. Most members represent states or districts with major military installations or defense contractors, and they necessarily view their jobs as protecting and enhancing those sources of local jobs. Many members also have personal backgrounds, such as prior military service, that give them expertise and affinities that influence their actions. Former marines are particularly supportive of their service, which is generally regarded to be the most effective on the Hill. Senior lawmakers often have far more experience with specific military issues than their three- and four-star witnesses, who rotate through jobs every two or three years. They can recognize the newly reinvented wheel that was tried but failed a decade or two earlier.

Congress has long insisted on its prerogatives in asserting civilian control over the military. Lawmakers want to hear from military officers and not just from their civilian superiors in the executive branch. For their part, senior officers use formal and informal access to Congress to provide back-channel information and complaints about presidential policies. In 1949, Congress passed a law giving the JCS the right to "make such recommendations to Congress" as they consider appropriate, after first informing the secretary of defense. Starting in the 1950s, the Senate insisted that all senior officers pledge, as a condition of confirmation, that they will provide Congress with their personal and professional judgments when asked. President Eisenhower called this whole system *legalized insubordination,* but it remains a key guarantor of civilian control.

The nature of congressional representation makes committee members more attuned to parochial concerns, like jobs and contracts, than grand strategy or innovative management. They are also steady advocates of military personnel benefits. For a half century, the armed services committees have produced an annual defense authorization bill, one of the *must-pass items* in the opinion of most members of Congress. This measure, now more than 900 pages long, sets personnel ceilings for each of the armed forces and adjusts military pay and benefits. It also authorizes weapons procurement, research and development programs, and military construction projects. Each year, the committees also request numerous reports on defense activities as part of their oversight process.

Actual funding for the Pentagon comes in the Defense Appropriations Bill from the appropriations committees, but the outlines are set in the authorization bills, and only those measures can contain the basic laws on the organization and operation of DOD.

While the committees responsible for the Pentagon tend to be parochial, they have on occasion had major impacts on national security strategy. It was the armed services committees that wrote the landmark National Security Act of 1947 and its later amendments strengthening the secretary of defense and his civilian control. Those committees also enacted the Goldwater–Nichols reforms in the face of vigorous Pentagon opposition. They have also tried to force the executive branch to frame its own grand strategy. A 1986 provision requires the president to develop and submit a national security strategy review that is used as the capstone document for all subordinate national security planning throughout the government. The committees also mandated the QDR—and usually added a requirement for a second opinion by a distinguished panel of outside experts.

In short, Congress, drawing on its own perspectives and prejudices, helps to build and shape the military instrument that is available to the president.

* * *

The military instrument is well trained and equipped for use as the president may direct. The armed forces are especially good at planning complex actions and then carrying them out. But, the use of force raises moral, legal, and political concerns and often entails enormous and unanticipated consequences for those involved and the policy objectives being sought. The United States in recent decades has been more successful in the operational aspects of the use of force than in translating those actions into strategic victories.

Case Study: Planning for the 2003 Iraq Invasion

Modern armed forces plan carefully for combat. Planning is their everyday business until the battle starts, so they are quite skilled at it. But since war is conducted for political purposes, as Clausewitz argued, political leaders have to be deeply engaged in the process. This case illustrates the lengthy and complex process followed to plan for the 2003 war against Iraq. It shows that two individuals—a determined secretary of defense and a stubborn combatant commander—can shape a war plan to fit their personal views.

Even after the Gulf War ended in 1991, the United States conducted regular military operations against Iraq and kept revising plans for major war. No-fly zones were established over northern and southern Iraq, and by 2002, more than 300,000 sorties had been flown. In 2002 alone, Iraq attacked coalition aircraft 500 times, leading to 90 retaliatory air strikes.

When Iraqi leader Saddam Hussein expelled United Nations (UN) monitors in December 1998, the United States responded with three days of bombing and cruise missile strikes in what was called Operation Desert Fox. CENTCOM Commander General Tony Zinni also revised the contingency war plan for a possible invasion of Iraq. His OPLAN 1003–98 envisioned using 380,000 troops.

Many officials joining the George W. Bush administration in 2001 regretted not finishing the job by removing Saddam Hussein in 1991. At the very first NSC meeting, the new president ordered his Pentagon leaders to "examine our military options" in Iraq. In July, Defense Secretary Donald Rumsfeld urged "a more robust policy" against Saddam Hussein.

Immediately after the 9/11 attacks, despite the lack of any evidence linking al-Qaeda to Iraq, Rumsfeld and his Deputy Paul Wolfowitz urged attacks on Iraq. Although Bush deferred that topic, on September 29, Rumsfeld told the incoming Chairman of the Joint Chiefs of Staff, General Richard Myers, to begin preparing military options for Iraq to achieve "regime change" and the location and destruction of Iraqi weapons of mass destruction (WMD).

By the end of November, with the Taliban government in Afghanistan overthrown, Bush ordered a new look at the Iraq war plan. Over the next 16 months, Rumsfeld worked closely and directly with the CENTCOM Commander, General Tommy Franks, supplementing frequent briefings and meetings with his snowflakes and memos. The previous practice had been for defense secretaries to work through the JCS chairman to the combatant commander, but Rumsfeld largely sidelined the chiefs and the Joint Staff. They were not formally briefed on the war plan until September 2002.

During the planning process, the defense secretary was "like a dentist's drill that never ceased," according to Franks. His staff faced a "daily barrage of tasks and questions [that] was beginning to border on harassment." Franks himself objected to JCS oversight of his planning or even participation in his video teleconferences with Rumsfeld. Two days before the start of the war, Franks sent a formal *letter of concern* to the Pentagon leadership. Though politely phrased, the point of his message was this: "Leave me the hell alone to run the war."

What Rumsfeld wanted was a lightning-fast attack followed by a rapid handover of power to Iraqis. He kept pressing Franks to reduce the number of troops needed. On at least six occasions during the course of the planning, Rumsfeld insisted on further cuts in ground troops. The final version called for 140,000 troops, compared to Zinni's 380,000. The secretary also wanted *off ramps* to divert unneeded troops if the battle went better than expected. From the start, the objectives remained unchanged: regime change and location and destruction of the WMDs. Franks never presented options short of major war, such as creating enclaves, supporting a guerrilla war, or limiting combat to airpower and SOF.

According to U.S. military doctrine, the plan had four phases: I, preparation; II, shape the battlespace; III, decisive operations; IV, posthostility operations. CENTCOM had responsibility for all phases but gave scant attention to Phase IV. Franks estimated he might need 250,000 troops for occupation and security duties but did not know how long they might be needed. While most of the military planners expected a quick victory, they shared other assumptions that proved to be incorrect. For example, most military officials believed that U.S. forces would be welcomed as liberators, that the Iraqi people yearned for democracy, that Iraqi could finance its own reconstruction, and that the professionalism of the Iraqi police, army, and government ministries would lead them to help coalition forces establish control and competent governance.

Just as Rumsfeld largely excluded the JCS and Joint Staff from detailed war planning, he also tried to limit the involvement of other departments. Civilian planners were not briefed on war plans until the summer of 2002. Rumsfeld then got Bush to sign a presidential directive in October 2002 giving DOD authority over postwar planning, but the office to do the job was not established until January 20, 2003, just two months before the start of the war. Staff from that office were then delayed in getting into Baghdad until mid-April, when they found that 17 of the 23 ministries they had hoped to restore under new leadership were gone, with the buildings looted and the workers fled. The widespread looting after the fall of Baghdad—which Rumsfeld dismissed as a sign of liberation: "Freedom's untidy," he said—was allowed because U.S. troops had not been given orders to prevent or stop it, and there were probably too few troops to have much success had they tried.

The JCS did influence some aspects of U.S. policy during the development of the final war plan. When civilians pressed for an earlier start to the U.S. attacks, the chiefs sided with Franks in urging more time and better weather. They also reportedly urged that congressional approval be sought for the attack—a position consistent with the U.S. military's post-Vietnam conditions for the use of major force.

Rumsfeld insisted on delaying mobilization deployment orders for some military forces because they were likely to become public. He also tinkered with the complex deployment plans that were designed to bring men and equipment together at the few available ports and airfields with the greatest efficiency. These actions caused enormous disruptions in the field.

In the final weeks before the start of the war, the president met with the JCS and heard their general support for the war plan despite some service-specific concerns. Retaliatory bombing raids were being directed against targets that would have been hit early in the ground combat phase. The battlespace had been prepared. Sufficient troops were in place, and follow-on units were en route. The president decided that diplomacy had failed and it was necessary to employ the military instrument of national power. Major combat began on March 19, 2003.

While tactical military success was achieved quickly and the Iraqi government overthrown, the failure to make adequate plans for the next phase of the operation led to numerous problems and additional years of combat. The war met its immediate military objectives but fell short of accomplishing its broader objectives, which included the creation of a stable, friendly, and democratic government in Baghdad. The military instrument, by itself, was insufficient to attain America's strategic goals.

Sources: Joseph J. Collins, "Opting for War: An Analysis of the Decision to Invade Iraq," *Project on National Security Reform, Case Studies, Vol. 1,* 9–58, accessible via www.pnsr.org.

Douglas J. Feith, *War and Decision* (New York: Harper, 2008).

General Tommy Franks, *American Soldier* (New York: Regan Books, 2004).

Richard Myers, *Eyes on the Horizon* (New York: Threshold Editions, 2009).

Michael R. Gordon and General Bernard E. Trainor, *Cobra II* (New York: Pantheon, 2006).

Bradley Graham, *By His Own Rules* (New York: Public Affairs, 2009).

Ron Suskind, *The Price of Loyalty* (New York: Simon & Schuster, 2004).

Bob Woodward, *Bush at War* (New York: Simon & Schuster, 2002).

Bob Woodward, *Plan of Attack* (New York: Simon & Schuster, 2004).

Selected Resources

The main DOD website opens the door to a broad range of additional sites at www.defense.gov/.

Military doctrine is especially well outlined by these JCS publications:

Jt Pubs: interagency capabilities, www.dtic.mil/doctrine/new_pubs/jp3_08v2.pdf

Jt Ops 3–0, www.dtic.mil/doctrine/new_pubs/jp3_0.pdf

Jt Pub 1, www.dtic.mil/doctrine/new_pubs/jp1.pdf

Think tanks with excellent coverage of defense issues include: The Center for Strategic and Budgetary Assessments, www.csbaonline.org/; The Center for a New American Security, www.cnas.org/; the Center for Strategic and International Studies, http://csis.org/; the Rand Corporation, www.rand.org/; the Federation of American Scientists, www.fas.org/; and the International Institute for Strategic Studies, www.iiss.org/.

There are numerous scholarly and historical works on U.S. civil–military relations, including: Richard H. Kohn and Peter Feaver, *Soldiers and Civilians: The Civil–Military Gap and American National Security* (MIT Press, 2001); Peter Feaver, *Armed Servants: Agency, Oversight, and Civil-Military Relations* (Harvard University Press, March 2003); Charles A. Stevenson, *Warriors and Politicians: U.S. Civil–Military Relations Under Stress* (London: Routledge, 2006); Richard K. Betts, *Soldiers, Statesmen, and Cold War Crises* (Columbia University Press, Morningside edition, 1991).

9 The Secret Intelligence Instruments

> *Policymakers crave certainty and abhor surprise. They come to office with more or less defined policy objectives that they hope to attain. They want to work on their priority agenda, not be sidetracked or deflected by unanticipated events. They look to the permanent civil service bureaucracy of government, including the intelligence community, to help them achieve those goals and feel let down that they do not get more help.*
>
> —Deputy Secretary of State James Steinberg[1]

> *Perhaps the most important thing to understand about covert action is that it is not a routine mission of the CIA, such as foreign intelligence collection or counterintelligence operations. Rather, covert action is very much an element of American presidential statecraft, joining the more familiar components of American foreign policy . . .*
>
> —former CIA operative William J. Daugherty[2]

There are 16 members of the *intelligence community (IC)*, responsive to presidential directions but largely hidden from public view. While much about their activities is broadly known, even more is suspected. The picture that emerges from declassified materials is of a set of large, well-funded organizations that do many things well and some things poorly. They are regularly blamed for alleged failures but cannot disclose many of their successes.

As reporters Dana Priest and William Arkin argue, "The CIA is the president's personal sword of power in foreign lands if all else fails, one he can use without asking Congress first."[3] Their comment applies to the entire IC, for presidents use the intelligence instruments to gather information not otherwise attainable, to analyze all available information, and to conduct activities that need to be kept secret. (See Table 9.1.) Intelligence organizations are thus key tools for U.S. foreign policy, gaining and providing analysis to aid decision making and then conducting operations when ordered. Each one has its own special capabilities and associated culture, though all share a preoccupation with secrecy.

Table 9.1 The Secret Intelligence Instrument Brief

ACTIONS	ADVANTAGES	DISADVANTAGES
Collection	Multiple, highly specialized organizations	Competition for resources
Analysis	Professionalism	Resistance to information sharing
Operations	Highly secret	Subject to congressional oversight and blowback
ROLE OF CONGRESS	Overseer, policy legitimator	Leaks and criticism
CULTURE	Very secretive	Resists sharing information

The nature of the IC's work leads to high competition, secrecy, and a reluctance to share, making each agency in the IC very protective of its independent roles.

Secret Tools

Intelligence activities are cloaked in secrecy for many reasons. Collecting information abroad often requires breaking laws, stealing secrets, and bribing officials to betray their own nation's secrets. Governments do not like to acknowledge those truths. And, they certainly don't want their own spies to be jailed or executed for what they do.

Intelligence operatives want secrecy also in order to protect their sources and methods. Disclosure of information that could only have come from a clandestine listening device could lead to its destruction. Reporting information known only to a handful of people could jeopardize the life of the secret source.

Sometimes, governments want to do things without admitting any involvement, such as supporting a rebel group or financing a friendly foreign political party, where publicity could damage foreign relations or undermine the success of the enterprise.

Of course, secrecy can also be used to hide mistakes and misbehavior or simply to avoid political embarrassment. At least in the United States, there are laws and processes in place to reduce the abuse of secrecy, particularly through congressional oversight.

Secrecy is at the core of the IC's culture, separating members from the rest of the government and binding them together but still separated by *the need to know*. Intelligence personnel are adamant about secrecy when other officials are more relaxed. Confirming what is already reported in newspapers seems reasonable to political appointees used to living in the public sphere but still treasonable to those whose careers require secrecy. As former Director of Central Intelligence (and later Secretary of Defense) Robert Gates has written, "[T]he work of spies makes risk routine and danger the companion of every day's work. For them secrecy is not a convenience or a bureaucratic matter, but the essential tool of their craft."[4]

Most governments concentrate control over secret instruments in very few hands. In the United States, only the president can activate and use the most sensitive tools, and only the president can override the secrecy classifications imposed by subordinates.

The Long History of Secret Programs

The men who won the revolution and created a national government for the United States knew the value of spies and secret dealings. The very First Congress passed a law allowing the president to spend $40,000 per year "for the support of such persons as he shall commission to serve the United States in foreign parts." And despite the Constitution's clear requirement for disclosure of a "statement and account" of expenditures of public money, lawmakers allowed secrecy in this case.[5]

The United States paid spies and gathered intelligence throughout the 19th century, but the effort was small and sporadic, except for wartime increases. The army and navy created military intelligence units in the 1880s. The U.S. government also played a not-very-covert role in the 1903 rebellion of Panama from Colombia, thereby allowing a canal to be built and enabling Theodore Roosevelt to boast, "I took Panama."

Despite U.S. code-breaking successes during World War I and the naval conferences in the 1920s, incoming Secretary of State Henry Stimson cut off his department's funding of the State–Army cryptanalysis office in 1929, famously saying, "Gentlemen do not read each other's mail." He had a different view when he was secretary of war during World War II.[6]

Secret operations peaked in World War II with the building of atomic bombs, very successful code breaking, and the intelligence operations of the Office of Strategic Services (OSS), the direct predecessor of the Central Intelligence Agency (CIA). Although Harry Truman disbanded the OSS at the end of the war, he agreed to the creation of the CIA as part of the National Security Act of 1947.

The new CIA was limited to overseas activities because lawmakers feared creating an American "Gestapo." But, Congress also wanted to prevent another Pearl Harbor, where intelligence was not shared or well coordinated, leading to the devastating surprise attacks of December 7, 1941. From the start, the new agency combined the talents of well-schooled analysts and gung-ho spies.

Throughout the 1950s and 1960s, the CIA and other components of the IC expanded their capabilities of technical collection—such as the high-flying U-2 spy plane and space satellites—and put their human agents to work overthrowing governments in Iran and Guatemala, tried to do so in Cuba and Indonesia, and also worked to prop up friendly governments in Western Europe and South Vietnam.

In the early 1970s, however, disclosures of some of these activities and other questionable ones, like assassination attempts on Fidel Castro, led to a public outcry and major congressional investigations. As a result, Congress created special committees to conduct regular oversight of intelligence activities, and later presidents issued executive orders limiting what intelligence operatives were allowed to do. Special committees were established in the executive branch to review and monitor covert operations.

The 9/11 attacks prompted a reexamination of the IC's structure and processes. As in the case of Pearl Harbor, there was a surprise attack that might have been prevented if those with bits and pieces of information had shared them with others and if senior leaders had responded more forcefully to the warnings they were given. The 9/11 Commission documented the failure and recommended the creation of a stronger central manager, a director of national intelligence (DNI), separate from the head of the CIA. The 2004 law creating the DNI fell short of giving him full directive and budget authority over the members of the IC, however, because of Pentagon resistance. Nor did Congress go along with the commission's recommendation of a single joint intelligence panel on Capitol Hill with both authorization and appropriations power.

Major Institutions

While the components of the IC share a concern for secrecy and are supposed to work together, they have separate and distinct capabilities that they contribute to intelligence products and activities. (See Figure 9.1.) The president has to understand what each can do and what each does well in order to allocate budget resources and to assign special tasks.

Office of the Director of National Intelligence

The IC today is headed by the DNI and a large staff, estimated to be 1,700 federal workers and 1,200 private contractors. Critics of the Direct of Central Intelligence (DCI) system argued that the DCI spent too much time overseeing the CIA and had too little power to direct the rest of the IC. The DNI was made the principal intelligence adviser to the president and the NSC. The official oversees and directs the NIP, which in 2011, was $54.6 billion, but the MIP of $24 billion remains under the control of the Pentagon. The NIP includes activities responding to the needs and priorities of national policy officials, while the MIP is focused on the needs and priorities of DOD and the armed services. These figures are said to be two and a half times the size of the IC budget at the time of the 9/11 attacks.[7]

The law creating the DNI position was a compromise. The DNI was given some added authorities over budget development and for transfers of people and resources but not full hire-and-fire or budgeting power. In fact, lawmakers included a provision demanded by the Pentagon that cautioned the DNI to use his authorities "in a manner that respects and does not

Figure 9.1 Intelligence Community Organizational Chart

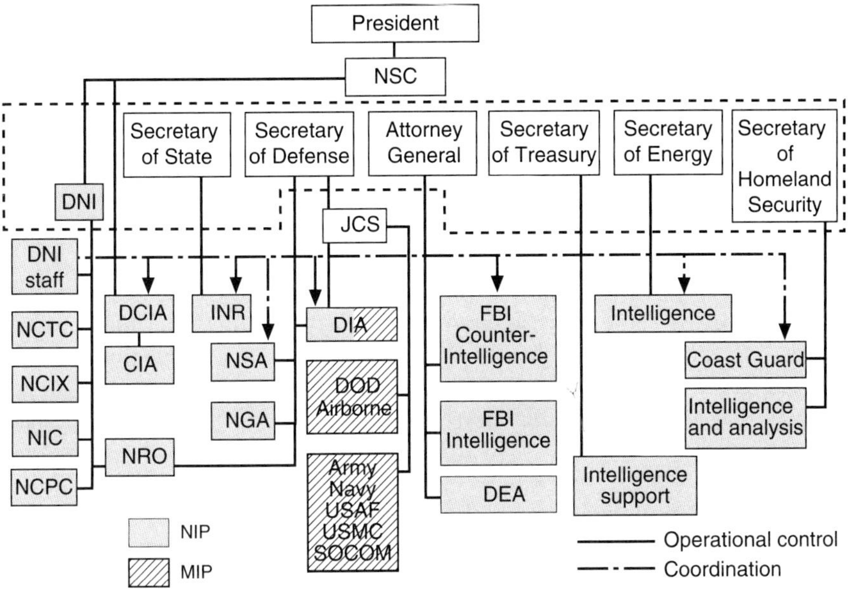

The DNI has direct operational control over only a few components of the IC and relies on coordination with the rest. The congressional intelligence committees oversee the National Intelligence Program (NIP), while the armed services committees oversee the Military Intelligence Program (MIP).

Source: Mark M. Lowenthal, *Intelligence: From Secrets to Policy,* Fourth Edition (Washington, DC: CQ Press, 2009). Used with permission of Mark M. Lowenthal.

abrogate the statutory responsibilities of the heads of the departments of the U.S. government."[8]

As a result, the assessments of the effectiveness of the Office of the Director of National Intelligence (ODNI) are mixed. A congressional research service summary in 2010 found lawmakers unwilling to undo creation of ODNI but also unwilling to create a fully empowered Department of Intelligence. An official who served in one of the top ODNI positions, Thomas Fingar, concluded that the impact of the office on the IC had been "limited by ambiguity, ambivalence, and animosity." He also says, "Key elements of the IC continue to resist that vision [of a single integrating enterprise], view colleagues as competitors, and disparage the work of fellow professionals."[9]

Former CIA Director Robert Gates, who turned down the DNI job before later becoming secretary of defense, said, "My view is that the compromises that were made in passing the Intelligence Reform Act really inhibited the ability of the DNI to carry out what most people thought the DNI should do. He has authorities and he has power, but at the end of the day, he's got to sort of lead and persuade people to follow in all these disparate organizations."[10]

Further evidence of the uncertain standing of the DNI comes from the fact that the first director quit after two years to take a lesser-ranking post at the State Department. His successor complained that he was only the coordinator and not really director of national intelligence. And, President Obama's first nominee for the post was fired after repeated conflicts with the CIA director and other missteps.[11]

ODNI runs several important units, including the National Counterterrorism Center (NCTC), the National Intelligence Council (NIC), and centers for counterproliferation and intelligence coordination. One of its major outputs is the President's Daily Brief (PDB), the highly classified intelligence summary circulated each day to a handful of senior officials.

Observers say the ODNI has not developed its own integrating culture. It "has no hoary traditions, limited staff loyalty, and few routinized procedures."[12] Only half its workforce are permanent staff. The remainder rotate in and out from IC components and thus are expected to show primary loyalty to their home organizations.

Central Intelligence Agency

The CIA is no longer central, but it is still large, skilled, and important. The agency has three core missions: all-source analysis; managing human intelligence (HUMINT) operations, that is, recruiting and running spies; and conducting covert operations.[13]

The CIA has gained a host of critics and defenders over the years. Most of them clash over what the agency has done, especially in the realm of covert actions against foreign governments and whether the acts were effective and morally defensible. Some critics argue that agency analysts made wrong judgments, particularly on Soviet military spending and capabilities. Even former DCI Robert Gates acknowledged that CIA underestimated the pace of Soviet military programs in the 1960s and overestimated them in the 1980s and that it overestimated the size of the Soviet economy and underestimated the burden of military spending on that economy and its people. But, he says actual estimates of current Soviet military strength were quite good.[14]

Some critics say that the agency has become too cautious, perhaps because of disclosures of secret activities or because of past criticism from Congress and the media. Richard Clarke, who was the NSC staffer for counterterrorism under Presidents Clinton and Bush, complained about CIA reluctance to do more in Afghanistan, labeling the agency *risk averse*. He also quotes former Secretary of State Madeleine Albright's observation that CIA acted in a passive-aggressive way, as if "it has battered child syndrome." A retired CIA analyst counters, "What critics call risk aversion, professionals call common sense or good political judgment."[15]

CIA has about 20,000 people and four directorates, each drawing on quite different people and skill sets. The Directorate of Intelligence (DI) does the analysis and prepares the reports. The Directorate of Science and Technology (DS&T) exploits science to improve collection of information and protection of assets. The Directorate of Support (DS) manages the facilities, communications, payroll, and logistics for the agency.[16]

Most notable, or notorious, is the Directorate of Operations (DO), now renamed the National Clandestine Service (NCS). These are the spies abroad and the covert operators whose exploits, real or imagined, are the stuff of thrillers. While the analysts and scientists would not be out of place in a university, the NCS operatives are a separate guild, often recruited from the military and business worlds and trained separately from other agency personnel. They have a can-do culture and an obsession with secrecy.[17]

Agency observers say that the NCS culture dominates the CIA, reinforcing the need for secrecy and the protection of people, sources, and methods. The analysts have their own subset culture, adding commitments to professionalism and objectivity. They like to quote Sherman Kent, an OSS veteran who headed the DI in the early years. He said intelligence officers are supposed "to stand behind [policy makers] with the book open at the right page, to call their attention to the stubborn fact they may be neglecting, and—at their request—to analyze alternative courses without indicating choice."[18]

CIA personnel do feel that they are *the president's own,* on call to the chief executive for analysis and action and responsive to his orders. Often, CIA people are detailed to the NSC staff, and that staff regularly consults with agency people and asks for briefing memos that can be part of NSC submissions to the president. Vice President Dick Cheney developed his own agency contacts and pressed them for information related to his policy interests.[19]

The creation of ODNI posed various challenges to the CIA, once its director was no longer the overall IC director and no longer the daily briefer of the president. President Obama's appointees to the CIA and DNI slots reportedly clashed over who got to assign the top U.S. intelligence official in overseas embassies and other bureaucratic issues. In that case, the CIA won, but turf issues remain unresolved in the IC.

Pentagon Management

Historically, those intelligence activities not assigned to the CIA fell under the control and management of DOD. The armed services had their own intelligence units for tactical and operational needs, and military planners had their own requirements for information about potential enemies and their capabilities.

The Pentagon also had the processes left over from World War II for secret budgets and programs as well as operational units that gathered electronic and signals intelligence. Consequently, the funds for much of the IC's activities are concealed within the DOD budget and ultimately controlled by the secretary of defense. Four major components of the NIP are DOD run: Defense Intelligence Agency (DIA), National Security Agency (NSA), National Reconnaissance Office (NRO), and National Geospatial-Intelligence Agency.

Defense Intelligence Agency. The DIA was created in 1961 in order to corral service intelligence activities and provide coordinated, all-source analyses of matters of interest to the Pentagon and the armed forces. The mission of its 16,500 people is to "provide timely and objective military intelligence to warfighters, policymakers, and force planners." The army, navy, air force, and marine corps retain units for tactical and operational intelligence for their service. But, DIA runs the defense attachés posted to U.S. embassies.[20]

The wars in Iraq and Afghanistan have placed extraordinary demands on military intelligence that sometimes conflict with priorities outside the war zone. One reason Congress limited the DNI's ability to direct DOD-run organizations was precisely the concerns about wartime requirements.

National Security Agency. The NSA was secretly established in 1952 as the principal agency for collection of signals intelligence (SIGINT) and codebreaking. SIGINT includes both communications intelligence (messages between individuals) and electronic intelligence (from electronic signals like radar). NSA is also responsible for information assurance, meaning creating the codes and communications procedures for government agencies with national security responsibilities. Long known as No Such Agency, its 20,000 personnel can now admit they work there.[21]

National Reconnaissance Office. The NRO's existence was not officially declassified until 1992, although it had been in existence since 1961, when it was created as an Air Force–CIA umbrella organization in charge of the U-2 spy planes and intelligence-gathering satellites. NRO has about 3,000 people and spends a lot of money developing, launching, and operating reconnaissance satellites for what is called *imagery intelligence* (IMINT).[22]

National Geospatial-Intelligence Agency. The National Geospatial-Intelligence Agency began in 1996 as the National Imagery and Mapping Agency. It has 8,500 people whose basic job is to turn imagery intelligence into maps and other depictions of geographical spaces that can be used for analysis and operations.[23] They can develop products that overlay terrain features with intelligence reports and weather data. Such information has been used for military operations, humanitarian relief, and support for diplomatic negotiations where terrain issues arise.

State Department's Bureau of Intelligence and Research. The Bureau of Intelligence and Research is the State Department's CIA, its own 300-person office providing all-source analyses on matters of special interest to the secretary, the department, and embassies overseas. Its staff produce regional and functional reports and participate for State in the NIC.[24]

Other Intelligence Community Components

Several other cabinet departments have intelligence units that are part of the IC but are focused on the special responsibilities of their respective departments. The Justice Department has two components—the Federal

Bureau of Investigation's National Security Branch, which has responsibilities for counterintelligence and counterterrorism, and the Drug Enforcement Administration (DEA), which follows drug-trafficking organizations and provides other drug-related intelligence to IC members. The Department of Homeland Security (DHS) has a special Office of Intelligence and Analysis (OIA) to provide intelligence to state and local governments and private-sector partners on homeland security issues. The coast guard, now part of DHS, has long had its own intelligence units, which are now focused on counternarcotics, port security, and immigrations interdictions. The Department of Energy has intelligence units focused mainly on other nation's nuclear capabilities. And the Department of the Treasury has an office of intelligence and analysis under the office of terrorism and financial intelligence.[25]

One emerging issue is the increased use of contractor personnel in intelligence jobs. In 2008, an official said that the roughly 100,000 government employees in the IC were assisted by 36,000 people on contract. About 22% of those contracted people did computer or information technology work, but 19% were involved in analysis. Some 27% were said to be involved in intelligence collection and operations.[26]

While many of these people were added to handle the informational and operational demands of the Iraq and Afghanistan wars and counterterrorism, the large numbers raised questions of government accountability and a brain drain of experienced people seeking higher salaries.

Major Processes

The intelligence process is often described as a predictable sequence from requirements to collection to processing and exploitation to analysis to dissemination to consumption. In practice, there is regular feedback and often backtracking in order to make adjustments before proceeding forward.[27] For our purposes, it is useful to look at the three major processes where the president plays a role: collection, analysis, and operations.

Collection

Several parts of the IC are specialized for collection of particular kinds of intelligence. The CIA has the lead for HUMINT, or old-fashioned spying. NSA is the principal organization for SIGINT, which includes intercepting communications and electronic emissions like weapons telemetry. NRO builds and operates satellites that gather various types of intelligence. NGA acquires geospatial intelligence (GEOINT), including photographic and other imagery intelligence linked to terrain—and processes it with SIGINT from NSA. NGA and DIA are the agencies principally responsible for measurement and signatures intelligence (MASINT), involving identifying and analyzing environmental byproducts of activities like weapons tests and the uses of industrial facilities.[28]

Intelligence collectors are professionals and are proud of their work. But, they may also develop stovepiped thinking that makes it hard for them to acknowledge the value of other collectors, especially if the issue is where to assign the marginal budget dollar when resources are tight.

In order to capture this intelligence, the government needs the collection capabilities and associated people—and then it needs to decide to target particular places and subjects. That means deciding in advance what images or emissions or other intelligence will be important tomorrow and next week and next year, for collection assets have to be assigned, and more focus on one area means less on another. As an example, journalists Dana Priest and Bill Arkin report that collection systems at the NSA intercept and store 1.7 billion e-mails, phone calls, and other types of communications every day and then sort a fraction of those into 70 separate databases.[29]

Starting in the Clinton administration, the president issued a formal order, called a Presidential Policy Directive (PPD) that established a tier system for intelligence collection. As described by the Federation of American Scientists:

> Tier 0 is warning and crisis management. Tier 4 is countries that are virtually of no interest to the United States. The PDD specifically identifies targets that the US intelligence community will not collect against. Under PDD 35 the highest priority is assigned to intelligence Support to Military Operations (SMO). The second priority is providing political, economic, and military intelligence on countries hostile to the United States to help to stop crises and conflicts before they start. Third priority is assigned to protecting American citizens from new trans-national threats such as drug traffickers, terrorists, organized criminals, and weapons of mass destruction. High priority is also assigned to Intelligence support to activities addressing counter-proliferation, as well as international terrorism, crime and drugs. The Directive increased the priority assigned by the intelligence collection and analysis capabilities to the proliferation threat.[30]

The G. W. Bush administration developed an elaborate priority system that is now a matrix of functional issues plotted against nations and other groups. It gets reviewed every six months, and the decision makers have to make hard choices whether to reduce priority for some once-important issues in order to increase attention to something else.[31]

Analysis

Instead of a case study on how intelligence products are developed, we have included in this chapter several declassified documents showing what senior officials were told by the IC. There are, however, numerous public accounts of how the Special National Intelligence Estimate (NIE) on Iraq was fashioned in 2002.[32]

Collected intelligence needs to be processed and evaluated then sent on for further analysis and incorporation into the reports and estimates that are the chief products of the IC. As former DCI Richard Helms wrote, "Casting aside the perceived—and I must admit the occasionally real—excitement of secret operations, the absolute essence of the intelligence profession rests in the production of current intelligence reports, memoranda, and National Estimates on which sound policy decisions can be made."[33]

The culture of analysts is that of skepticism. As former CIA official Mark Lowenthal notes, "Their training teaches them to question and to doubt. Although they may see an optimistic outcome to a given situation, they also see the pessimistic outcomes and likely feel compelled to analyze them as potential outcomes."[34]

Analysts are also human and therefore subject to human frailties. Lowenthal says analysts sometimes are guilty of adopting various mind-sets that shape their analyses. One is mirror-imaging, presuming that other leaders or nations share motivations similar to their own. Another flaw is clientism, when they have become so immersed in a subject that they lose perspective and "go native." Analysts may also commit layering, when they draw upon earlier work and fail to include the assumptions and uncertainties that may have influenced those judgments. Lowenthal also notes that the all-source analysts at CIA, DIA, and the State Department's INR can fall into analytical stovepipes where they disparage the work done elsewhere.[35]

Another flaw, noted by former DCI Robert Gates, is that "the CIA knew how foreign policy was made in every country of the world but one—our own." Analysts didn't realize how the president's schedule of meetings with foreign leaders, overseas trips, or current issue discussions would affect his need for information from the IC.[36]

Still another flaw is the politicization of analysis, where analysts tailor their reports to be consistent with the views and policy preferences of the president and other senior officials. A former senior CIA analyst describes the process as a *joust*. Paul Pillar writes, "Policymakers . . . would press intelligence officers—always in one substantive direction, never in the other—and keep pressing as long as sought-after conclusions were not yet forthcoming. They would stop short of blatant arm twisting to maintain the appearance that the analysts were only being healthily challenged, not pressured. Intelligence officers would cope with the pressure while trying to remain consistent with common standards of analytic tradecraft and objectivity. The joust typically would conclude with inventive wordsmithing that met each side's minimum requirements in the competition."[37] Analysts also know that their careers would be helped by praise from above and could be derailed if superiors concluded they were not team players.

Analysts prepare numerous reports and give briefings on demand, but its premier product is the PDB, the highly classified summary of information deemed most urgent and important for the president to know. (See Box 9.1.) Only a handful of copies of the PDB are circulated to senior officials; other less-sensitive but still highly classified reports get wider circulation in the Worldwide Intelligence Review (WIRe). Since 2004, preparation of the PDB has been done by the newly created DNI's office. At times, depending on the preferences of the president, the DCI or DNI personally briefed the chief executive. At other times, a designated briefer, often accompanied by

> **Box 9.1**
>
> ## How Foreign Policy Is Made: Examining the President's Daily Brief, April 1, 1968
>
> Very few PBDs have ever been declassified, but the example here from the Lyndon Johnson (LBJ) administration during the Vietnam War gives you a flavor of what gets included. Note how short the items are. The in-person briefers can supply longer background materials if requested, but presidents have very limited time.
>
> The PDB leads with the most important information from the war zone but also includes entries on other countries. This PDB addresses North and South Vietnam, Panama, Brazil, Cyprus, and Egypt. Aside from the Vietnam coverage, these are not really breaking-news items but teasers on other developments the analysts want to flag for the president's attention.
>
> On Vietnam, the PDB warns the president that Hanoi is planning a summer offensive and that 17,000 North Vietnamese troops have been discovered moving south. The document also tells the latest in the power struggle among generals in South Vietnam. Neither report could have given the president much confidence about progress in the war.
>
> The PDB alerts the president to unrest in Latin America. It suggests that a political dispute in Panama will lead to a military takeover. And in Brazil, it says that the military dictatorship there is unhappy with the government's handling of student demonstrations, which have "widespread sympathy" among the public but are now being led by "extremists."
>
> The PDB also mentions a couple of developments in order to say that they are not significant—talks in Cyprus aren't likely to lead to anything, and Egyptian President Nasser's political reform promises won't amount to much.
>
> If you received this PBD, what follow-up questions would you ask? What taskings, if any, would you send to your advisers and cabinet members?
>
> * * *
>
> SANITIZED
>
> The President's Daily Brief
>
> 1 April 1968
>
> 1. North Vietnam [■■■■] Hanoi reports the Vietnamese Communists are organizing a broad offensive to take place in South Vietnam this summer. [■■] Hanoi expects the offensive to set the stage for a settlement on Communist terms and that the US will accept an "armistice" by early next year. [■■] report that a special mobilization of manpower is under way in North Vietnam to provide large numbers of new forces for the South.
>
> * * *
>
> What appear to be eight more infiltration groups were discovered [■■■■] over the weekend, raising the number of units en route through central North Vietnam in March [■■■] More than 17,000 troops could be involved.
>
> 2. South Vietnam   Vice President Ky, chief of the Joint General Staff Vien, and at least three of the four corps commanders plan to submit their resignations en masse unless Thieu resolves certain doubts and agrees to consult them closely on

> (Continued)
> policy, according to [█████] These doubts include rumors that Thieu is embarking on wholesale personnel changes which would revive the influence of the Dai Viet party at the expense of the military hierarchy.
>
> The commanders are already disturbed by Thieu's recent provincial appointments which they see as a substitution of Thieu's followers for their own protégés or as creating unrest among province chiefs and military officers in general.
>
> 3. Panama   The Supreme Court will reconvene today to decide on the constitutionality of the Assembly's impeachment of Robles. No matter how the court rules, the situation is likely to deteriorate further.
>
> The people around Arnulfo Arias are now working on more legal moves against the government, and are also keeping pressure on Robles and the National Guard through demonstrations and disorders. If the court invalidates the impeachment, Arias and company are prepared to impeach the court.
>
> Pro-Arias demonstrators plan to be in the streets "to create an atmosphere of tension" while the court is deliberating. Influential families on both sides are becoming more and more convinced that a takeover by the guard is the only solution . . .
>
> *Source:* The PDB, CIA, April 1, 1968.

an issue expert on the day's major topic, would perform that task.[38] To see the sorts of things included in a PDB, look at the copy of one of the few ever declassified.

The PBD document and knowledgeable briefers go to the president every day. (See Box 9.2.) In the Obama administration, the regular briefing usually included the vice president, the White House chief of staff, the NSA, and the deputy for homeland security. The sessions ranged from getting presidential directions for work on particular issues to what was called *blue sky* thinking on policy development. Presidents often raise questions or make comments that lead to additional activities by the IC. Those questions, of course, indicate areas of presidential interest or inquiry, creating valuable feedback to analysts preparing the next day's PDB and future activities. Throughout the process, analysts and senior officials recognize that the president is *the first customer,* and that intelligence materials have to be suited to his needs. This process of daily production creates a sense of urgency and time pressure. One analyst comments that he had not joined a university so much as a government-run newspaper business.[39]

Longer-term and broader focus intelligence studies include the all-source, all-community NIEs that may take months to prepare under the direction of specialists on the NIC. (See Box 9.3.)

From the standpoint of senior policy makers, there are two key problems with current intelligence analysis. There are too many reports: The sheer size of the IC probably involves a proliferation of reports that may overwhelm the intended recipients. Priest and Arkin estimate that more than 50,000 intelligence reports are published each year under 1,500 titles. The number

> **Box 9.2**
>
> ## Inside View: The President's Daily Intelligence Briefing
>
> Former DCI George Tenet describes his regular morning sessions in the Oval Office with an oral version of the PDB. He shows how much personal chemistry and management style mattered. These briefings remain the most important way a president can give the IC guidance and taskings.
>
> *Around 8:00 A.M., the briefer and I would go across the street to the West Wing of the White House and troop up the back stairs to the Oval Office. The actual briefing would generally take between thirty and forty-five minutes—an hour when things were really busy. The vice president, Dick Cheney; Condoleezza Rice, then national security adviser; and Andy Card, the president's chief of staff, always sat in unless they were out of town. The briefer would usually 'tee up the piece,' explaining each PDB article's background or context, and then hand each item to the president to read. Often there would be additional material to flesh out the story—the nitty-gritty on how we had stolen the secrets contained in the item, and the like. Everyone loves a good spy story. More important, it was an opportunity to pull back the curtain, to talk to the president about a sensitive source or a collection method. The written items were generally short, and the president would read them carefully. Sometimes he would start tossing out questions before getting to the bottom line ...*
>
> Source: George Tenet, *At the Center of the Storm* (New York: HarperCollins, 2007), 32.

is so large that, in 2010, a new online newspaper, *Intelligence Today*, was created to summarize the greatest hits appearing elsewhere.[40]

The second problem is that the products often fail to give officials the certainty and clarity they most want, as indicated by Jim Steinberg's quote at the start of this chapter. Analysts respond that they live in a world of uncertainty and can only try to manage it. They also argue that prediction is not the best way to judge intelligence products because it performs so many other functions—identifying trends, documenting threats, listing possibilities and even likelihoods—that are helpful to policy makers even if they do not predict the timing of particular events.[41]

Operations

Various activities are conducted to collect intelligence, some of them illegal in the places they are carried out. That's what espionage historically involves. It takes people with certain mind-sets and skill sets to run agents and steal secrets successfully. Collection in denied areas like the Soviet-era Kremlin or behind enemy lines in war zones also requires skill and bravery. Observers have noted that this operational culture pervaded the upper ranks of the CIA for many years, not only in the clandestine service.[42]

Since the 1970s, Congress and the president have made an important legal distinction between operations to gather intelligence and operations

> **Box 9.3**
>
> ## How Foreign Policy Is Made: Key Judgments From a National Intelligence Estimate, Saddam Hussein, June 18, 1992
>
> A year after the end of the first Gulf War, the IC produced this National NIE on Saddam Hussein's hold on power in Iraq. Policy makers wanted to know how viable the regime was and what might lead to its overthrow. While many senior officials had expected Saddam Hussein to be ousted after losing the war, the NIE judgment was that he had grown stronger in the past year and that the greatest threat to him was a military coup, not a popular revolt.
>
> Policy makers also wondered whether international sanctions were being effective. The NIE's judgment pointed to two effects: increased public disaffection with his leadership but also increased popular resentment toward the West. Analysts said Saddam Hussein probably concluded that international support for continuing the sanctions was lessening, so he had weathered the storm.
>
> One immediate policy question facing the George H. W. Bush administration was whether to continue Operation Provide Comfort, the U.S. flights enforcing a no-fly zone over northern Iraq. The NIE does seem to support the operation as it warns that, otherwise, the Iraqi leader would likely act to suppress the Kurds if Operation Provide Comfort were halted.
>
> If you were a senior official receiving this report, how would it influence your policy choices for Iraq? Would you favor continued sanctions or other courses of action?
>
> * * *
>
> Key Judgments
>
> Saddam Husayn [sic]: Likely to Hang On[■]
>
> Saddam Husayn is likely to survive the political and economic challenges of the next year. Although he is significantly weaker than he was before the Gulf war, he appears stronger than he was a year ago. The only real threat to Saddam remaining in power over the next year is from a sudden, violent effort to remove him by one or more people with access to him.
>
>
>
> If we are wrong in our judgment about Saddam's survival, it is most likely in underestimating the current degree of unhappiness in the military and in the Sunni core that have provided Saddam's base of power. Important individuals in the inner circle and in the Republican Guard might be ready to mount a coup against Saddam. A popular revolt is much less likely. [■]
>
> Saddam will continue to use the Army, the Republican Guard, and intelligence and security forces to stifle dissent, reassert his control over Iraq, and prevent the emergence of any potential rival. The resumption of Air Force fixed-wing flight activity in April probably added to public perceptions that the regime is growing stronger and that citizens are powerful to bring about change [■]
>
> Economic sanctions alone are not likely to bring about Saddam's removal, but they will contribute to public disaffection with his leadership. Sanctions may also
>
> *(Continued)*

> (Continued)
> be increasing popular resentment toward the West. Despite sanctions, Saddam has managed his core support group by providing goods and services not available to the masses. Saddam probably believes that Iraq has withstood the brunt of the sanctions and that international support for sanctions is flagging. [▪]
>
> Saddam will continue to test coalition resolve by using economic pressure and increasingly intimidating military positioning against the Kurds in northern Iraq. Should Provide Comfort not be extended, he would be freer to expand his operations in the north—and may hope for Turkish collusion in suppressing the Kurds. He will also be more likely to act against the Kurds if he thinks they are acquiring attributes of statehood. In addition, his success in restricting international attention to the plight of the Shias in the marshlands of southern Iraq permits him to carry out a ruthless, but probably only partially effective, military campaign against them. [▪]
>
> *Source:* DCI, NIE: Saddam Husayn: Likely to Hang On, NIE 92–7, June 18, 1992.

for certain other purposes. These latter are called *covert actions* or *special activities* and are subject to careful presidential review and approval. President Reagan issued Executive Order 12333, still in effect, that defined covert actions as "special activities conducted in support of national foreign policy objectives abroad which are planned and executed so that the role of the United States Government is not apparent or acknowledged publicly" but are not intended to influence domestic U.S. policies or public opinion.[43]

Congress enacted a similar definition in 1991 in setting forth a process for conducting such operations. It says: "Covert Action is an activity or activities of the United States Government to influence political, economic, or military conditions abroad, where it is intended that the role of the United States Government will not be apparent or acknowledged publicly." This law also excluded intelligence acquisition or counterintelligence activities, "traditional diplomatic or military activities," and law enforcement activities.[44]

Simply put, these definitions make clear that covert actions are to influence foreigners secretly in support of American foreign policy goals. The techniques involved are usually labeled propaganda, political action, paramilitary activities, and information warfare.[45]

Propaganda is said to be the most extensive type of covert action, spreading messages to support U.S. policy through various overt and covert channels. In the early years of the Cold War, the CIA secretly funded Radio Free Europe and Radio Liberty to broadcast programs behind the Iron Curtain.

Political actions are used to influence the political situation in a foreign country. Starting with efforts to build up anticommunist parties in Italy and France after World War II, money, advice, and equipment to support political movements and candidates are the typical tools for political action. In the 1990s, the CIA gave support to Iraqi dissident groups. CIA personnel were reportedly sent to Libya in 2011 to give certain kinds of assistance to anti-Qaddafi rebels.[46]

Paramilitary operations can secretly train foreign military and security forces. This was done on a large scale in Laos in the 1960s and more modestly in Persian Gulf states in the 1980s. CIA support to U.S. military operations was a major activity in Somalia and Bosnia in the 1990s. CIA-run paramilitary operations were significant in Afghanistan after the 9/11 attacks and have continued in recent years in Iraq, Afghanistan, and Pakistan.

Information warfare now includes hacking and full-scale cyberwar where the purpose is to hinder a target's capabilities and not merely obtain intelligence. The IC is only one part of the diverse U.S. government array of agencies involved in cybersecurity, both offensive and defensive, as discussed further in Chapter 10.

Close cooperation between CIA paramilitary forces and regular American special operations forces (SOF) is highly valued but hard to achieve. Many of their missions overlap. Both can conduct and train others in unconventional warfare, foreign internal defense, information warfare, and psychological operations. Yet, both value their independence, especially their freedom from a heavy, bureaucratic chain of command. Some analysts contend that Defense Secretary Rumsfeld's promotion of DOD-run SOF and his resistance to the use of CIA paramilitary forces in Afghanistan was driven both by a determination to win credit for the Pentagon and avoid the process of notifying Congress that is required for covert action missions.[47]

Notifying Congress was a special requirement added by the Hughes–Ryan Amendment in 1974 and revised to be more specific in the 1991 legislation. In response to news articles disclosing CIA covert operations in earlier years, Congress adopted the Hughes–Ryan Amendment to (1) require the president personally to approve all such operations and (2) require notification of the appropriate committees of Congress of all covert actions not merely to collect intelligence. In 1991, Congress revised the law to cover ambiguities exposed in the Iran-Contra scandal. The still-current law requires a presidential finding in writing in advance of the operation with a specification that the action is "necessary to support identifiable foreign policy objectives," with a list of all participating U.S. government entities, followed by notification to Congress within 48 hours. The law allows the president, in "extraordinary circumstances," to limit notification to the House and Senate leadership and the four senior intelligence committee members—sometimes called "the gang of eight."[48]

To comply with the law, subsequent administrations established a careful process, starting with a presidential request to the CIA to begin planning a covert action. The CIA has review groups to process the paperwork, including the required finding that the president must sign. Those materials go to the NSC staff, which moves it from the lowest interagency committee on intelligence matters to the deputies committee and then to the president and full NSC.[49] One of the few declassified presidential findings is the one by President Reagan on Nicaragua. (See Box 9.4.)

> **Box 9.4**
>
> ## How Foreign Policy Is Made: Presidential Finding for Covert Action: Nicaragua, September 19, 1983
>
> Congress passed a law in December 1982 forbidding support for the antigovernment contras in Nicaragua "for the purpose of overthrowing the government of Nicaragua or provoking a military exchange between Nicaragua and Honduras." The Reagan administration claimed that it was abiding by the law, but some intelligence committee members believed it wasn't. To help calm fears and win support for its covert action, the president signed a new finding governing the operation on September 19, 1983, and informed the intelligence committees, as required by law.
>
> As you can see from the provided excerpt, the finding says that the "goal" is persuading the Sandinista government to have "meaningful negotiations" with its neighbors and to end their support for regional insurgencies. It says that U.S. agents will train paramilitary units to attack various targets in order to "raise the price" for Cuban and Sandinista forces. It also reports that "financial and material" support will be given to opposition leaders in Nicaragua, including support for propaganda efforts. The cost is estimated to be $33 million. On the basis of this finding and assurances from the CIA director, the intelligence committees voted to allow the program but capped its cost at $24 million.
>
> If you were on the intelligence committee receiving this finding, would you be reassured that the law was being followed? What questions would you raise in a classified hearing?
>
> ### SCOPE OF CIA ACTIVITIES UNDER THE NICARAGUA FINDING
>
> The Finding replaces the 1 December 1981 Finding which authorized certain covert action programs in Nicaragua and Central America. This program remains a critical element of U.S. policy in the region which recognizes that Nicaragua's Sandinista regime, with Soviet and Cuban active support, is implementing a strategy of full support for insurgent elements whose aim is the overthrow of democratic governments in the region. The political and paramilitary pressures created by this program are linked and are essential (1) to enable friendly Central American nations to strengthen democratic political institutions and achieve economic and social development, free from Soviet, Cuban, and Sandinista interference and (2) to induce a negotiated political resolution of international tensions in Central America.
>
> This Finding authorizes the provision of material support and guidance to Nicaraguan resistance groups; its goal is to induce the Sandinista government in Nicaragua to enter into meaningful negotiations with its neighboring nations; and to induce the Sandinistas and the Cubans and their allies to cease their provision of arms, training, command and control facilities and sanctuary to regional insurgencies. This support is to be provided [■] in cooperation with others, as appropriate. The provision of political support and funding to opposition leaders and organization [■] in order to maintain their visibility is also authorized.
>
> **POLITICAL ACTION**: Financial and material support will be provided to Nicaraguan opposition leaders and organizations to enable them to deal with the Sandinistas
>
> *(Continued)*

> (Continued)
>
> from a position of political strength and to continue to exert political pressure on the Sandanistas to return to the original premises of the revolution—free elections political pluralism, basic human rights and a free press.
>
> **PARAMILITARY ACTION**: Arms and other support will be provided to Nicaraguan paramilitary forces operating inside Nicaragua for the purpose of pressuring the Sandanista government and its Cuban supports to cease their support for regional insurgencies. [■] instructors will train these forces to attack targets in Nicaragua in order to deny facilities, interrupt support networks and to raise the price the Cubans and Nicaraguans and their allies must pay for continued support of insurgent groups elsewhere in Central America. [■]. . . .
>
> **FUNDING REQUIRED**: $19,000,000 is included in the Fiscal Year 1984 CIA budget for this program. Additional funding requirements, to be determined by developments in the area, could be as much as $14,000,000. Any such additional funding will have to come from the Agency's Reserve for Contingencies or other authorized sources . . .
>
> *Source:* Presidential Finding for Covert Action, Scope of CIA Activities under the Nicaragua Finding, September 19, 1983.

Covert actions are deliberate tools of presidential statecraft, as former CIA operative William Daugherty argues at the start of this chapter. Congress insisted on undeniable presidential approval, and presidents realized that it was in their own best interests to keep a close eye over operations that could inflict political and diplomatic damage on their presidencies. Despite the high risks and heavy secrecy, however, covert actions are reportedly only a small fraction of CIA activities and budgets. One estimate is that, while as much as half the CIA budget went for covert actions in the 1950s and 1960s, since the Kennedy years, the figure has been 5% or below. In the 1990s, the figure was said to be more like 1%.[50] Perhaps it's just harder to be covert or less important to preserve the secrecy in many cases.

What Presidents Want

If the president is first customer of intelligence products and the necessary decision maker on covert actions, what is it that presidents want from the IC? George Tenet says that presidents like to hear the spy stories and they like to ask follow-up questions. Robert Gates says that presidents and their senior advisers "usually are ill-informed about intelligence capabilities." As a result, "they have unrealistic expectations about what intelligence can do for them." When they do learn the limitations, Gates says, "they are inevitably disappointed. Presidents usually learn the hard way that, although intelligence can tell them a great deal, it only rarely—and usually in crises involving military forces—provides the kind of unambiguous and timely information that can make day-to-day decisions simpler and less risky." Nevertheless, Gates says, presidents keep the CIA around and budget large sums for intelligence because they want "the politician's mother's milk of factual, accurate information" and they like to retain the option of using covert action in dealing with some problems abroad.[51]

James Steinberg, deputy national security adviser under Clinton and deputy secretary of state in the Obama administration, says "policymakers crave certainty and abhor surprise." He admits that policy makers "harbor unrealistic expectations" of the IC, hoping for omniscience. Policy makers also tend to view the analytic community as "cautioners" or naysayers rather than supporters of administration policy. Senior officials can rarely say "too hard." They have to make choices despite the uncertainties. Many policy makers, Steinberg says, feel that analysts are too insulated from the "on the ground reality" that they have experienced in their professional lives, such as direct interactions with foreign leaders.[52]

Former intelligence officials see the same cultural divide. Former Deputy Director of CIA John McLaughlin says that policy makers tend to have a "culture of optimism." They "live in a world heavily influenced by political considerations, and intelligence is only one factor weighing in their decision calculus." Of course, some officials cannot tolerate analysis or reporting that disagrees with their own views.[53]

Mark Lowenthal also says policy makers are optimists. "They believe they can make things happen for the better." Intelligence officers have different motivations. "What [they] want more than anything else is access. They want to know what policies are being developed so they can focus their analysis on these areas and thus contribute to the policy process. They want policymakers to read their analysis. They want to brief senior policymakers, which is the ultimate form of access."[54]

To bridge this cultural divide, analysts say participants on both sides need to understand the perspectives and expectations of each other. For policy makers, what they want most from intelligence professionals is accuracy, clarity, timeliness, and a willingness to revise their judgments. For intelligence professionals, the big red line is any answer to "what should we do?" They can assess the consequences of different actions but are culturally barred from making recommendations. They also want to avoid being blamed for judgments made under acknowledged uncertainty that turn out to be wrong. Former officials like John McLaughlin also point to *warning fatigue,* when policy makers stop listening because they want something harder and more actionable than just a warning of a likelihood.[55] In other words, cries of "wolf" are most valuable and most likely to be heeded when the animal has been spotted and is within range.

Over time, presidents learn the strengths and weaknesses of the intelligence tool, ideally without making any catastrophic decisions as they go through that learning process. The IC is big, costly, responsive, effective at many things, and pretty good at much else, but still far from perfect in its estimates or its operations.

President Obama fired his first DNI after only 15 months, reportedly because he wanted the DNI to be more a coordinator and manager rather than a kind of czar imposing his will on the entire IC. The president was said to be unhappy with the bureaucratic conflicts between the DNI and the CIA director. Obama subsequently expressed some dissatisfaction with perceived intelligence failures at the time of the December 2009 underwear bomber and in advance of later turmoil in Egypt and elsewhere in the Middle East. Such reactions are not unusual. Presidents want the IC to help and forewarn, not cause problems for the administration.[56]

Policy makers want intelligence instruments to make a difference for them, to make their jobs easier, yet there are numerous examples where intelligence assessments have been ignored. Sometimes, senior officials have fixed ideas about other nations or strategic principles, or they may think their policies can change the situations reported to them. As Paul Pillar sadly concluded, "Notwithstanding some instances (such as with terrorism) of intelligence enlightening policy, the overall influence—for good or ill—of intelligence on major decisions and departures in U.S. foreign policy has been negligible. Most notorious intelligence failures have similarly had almost no effect on U.S. policy or U.S. interests."[57]

Congressional Oversight

Congress created the IC, regularly funds it in the multibillions of dollars, and frequently criticizes its performance. Some insiders claim that congressional investigations in the 1970s and since have weakened the intelligence instruments and made them less effective. What every president needs to know is that Congress claims coequal jurisdiction over intelligence activities, regardless of how skilled lawmakers are at their jobs.

Until 1974, only a handful of senior lawmakers on defense appropriations knew details of the intelligence budget, and many of them didn't really want to know. The 1976 Church Committee concluded that prior congressional oversight had been "more perfunctory than rigorous." And, some members declined to be briefed, fearing inadvertent disclosure. Senator John Stennis (D-MS) once brushed off a CIA briefer ready to tell him about a covert action by saying, "No, no, my boy, don't tell me. Just go ahead and do it—but I don't want to know."[58]

On the other hand, a fuller historical investigation found much more evidence of congressional knowledge, oversight, and advice to the executive. David M. Barrett concluded that, while oversight was not comprehensive, it was not simply passive or static prior to 1961. There were numerous hearings and briefings, though few records were preserved. Members were often quite hawkish on covert actions when they learned of them. Barrett also notes that Congress in 1951 approved an amendment authorizing $100 million to arm and train residents or escapees from communist countries into military units for North Atlantic Treaty Organization (NATO) defense. Although never put into practice as envisioned, the endorsement of

U.S.-funded forces to overthrow of Soviet and Eastern European governments was a green light for other operational planning.[59]

By the 1970s, however, Congress had grown more skeptical about CIA covert actions and other seeming dirty tricks abroad as more and more information was becoming available. A series of news articles in 1974 revealing U.S. involvement in the overthrow of the Salvador Allende government in Chile prompted Congress to act. One of the first measures was an amendment by Senator Harold Hughes (D-IA) requiring that covert operations could be conducted only if and after the president made a finding that the action was "vital to the defense of the United States" and transmitted a report to Congress. This provision was later merged with a similar one authored by Congressman Leo Ryan (D-CA) and passed by the House. The Hughes–Ryan Amendment was then followed in 1975 by full-scale investigative committees in both chambers and by creation of intelligence committees in each body.

The Senate Select Committee on Intelligence (SSCI, commonly called the *sissy*) and the House Permanent Select Committee on Intelligence (HPSCI, called the *hip-see*) are the oversight panels with regular access to finished intelligence and classified reports circulated widely in the executive branch. To protect sources and methods, they are denied routine access to *raw*, unevaluated reports. Each has a staff of about 40 professionals who arrange briefings and hearings and help prepare authorization bills. Various controversies prevented Congress from enacting an authorization bill between 2004 and 2010, but the 2010 measure broadened congressional access to intelligence information by requiring eventual (after 180 days) notification of all committee members of covert actions, creating an inspector general in the ODNI, and requiring some access by Government Accountability Office (GAO) auditors.

The intelligence panels, like many legislative committees, tend to pay closest attention to scandals and controversies rather than routine reviews of programs—what the political scientists call *fire alarm* hearings rather than *police patrol* oversight.[60] For example, they investigated the Aldrich Ames spy case and intelligence failures connected to the 9/11 attacks and the absence of weapons of mass destruction (WMD) in Iraq.

Congress has also sought out information that the executive branch seemed reluctant to provide, even for itself. Despite administration resistance, Congress created the independent 9/11 Commission in order to get a fuller investigation than was made available to a joint congressional panel. In 2002, lawmakers demanded an NIE on Iraq's WMD before voting on the use of force resolution, something the Bush administration had never prepared. One of the later defenses of that flawed estimate was that it had been done in only four weeks instead of the usual several months. In 2006, Congress required a new NIE on Iranian nuclear programs.

The 9/11 Commission called congressional oversight of intelligence *dysfunctional* and tried to shame lawmakers into creating a single joint committee to do both authorizations and appropriations. The appropriations committees, who routinely review intelligence budgets and approve funds in the Defense Appropriations Bill—along with a detailed classified annex—refused to go along, although the House, for the 110th and 111th Congresses, had a special panel consisting of intelligence and appropriations members. Nevertheless, the authorizing committees have enormous influence over the IC through their hearings and, when enacted, their bills.

Covert actions are probably the intelligence operations of greatest concern to Congress. Regular collection has costs and risks, and analyses can be reviewed and critiqued, but covert actions can lead to diplomatic crises and wars if they go badly. That's why Congress demanded to be informed about such operations. The 1991 law allowed the president to restrict notification in extraordinary cases to only the gang of eight—the Senate and House leadership, plus the two senior intelligence members in each chamber. One reason for the 2010 change in the law to require eventual notification of all intelligence committee members was the Bush administration's routine practice of limiting notifications to the gang of eight. Very sensitive collection activities that do not fall under the definition of covert actions are briefed only to the four senior committee members.

From a congressional perspective, the notifications on covert actions have served their intended purpose. They are consulted, and they usually have an opportunity to give their own advice. That process forces the executive branch to respond to congressional concerns, either with changes or cancellation of the proposed action. On some occasions, the covert action briefings have been so unpersuasive to lawmakers that presidents have decided to cancel the plans. In 1989, for example, the Senate oversight committee specifically voted against a program to assist overthrow Panamanian strongman Manuel Noriega in Panama by aiding opposition military officers. The committee favored nonlethal aid but did not want U.S. complicity in an assassination attempt.[61]

The expanded use since 2001 of SOF and military drones for actions that previously were conducted only by the IC has led some members of Congress to call for an extension of the law to cover Pentagon activities that fall into the covert action category so that Congress will be given timely notification.

Do lawmakers abuse their access to secret information? Journalists say that leaks come from both the executive and legislative branches, usually from people who disagree with the proposed action. But, some members caught divulging classified information have been admonished or punished, so the risks are known. Secrecy is one of the levers each branch has over the other.

* * *

The intelligence instruments are a very important part of a president's foreign policy toolkit. They can reduce uncertainty but not eliminate it. They gather information but still require a process of evaluation that can be influenced by personal and political factors. Some of the instruments can be used to great effectiveness but also at great risk. Their secrecy enhances their value to policy makers even as it leaves outsiders uncertain as to the benefits of the large sums expended.

Selected Resources

Gateway websites for the DNI and CIA are available at www.dni.gov/ and www.cia.gov/index.html.

Much is available at the CIA's Center for the Study of Intelligence at www.cia.gov/library/center-for-the-study-of-intelligence/index.html.

Each of the components of the IC has its own site with links from ODNI at www.dni.gov/members_IC.htm.

The congressional intelligence committees also have sites with current and historical information at www.intelligence.senate.gov/; http://intelligence.house.gov/.

Several excellent books on the intelligence instruments have been published in recent years: Mark Lowenthal, *Intelligence: From Secrets to Policy, Fifth Edition* (Washington, DC: CQ Press, 2012); Paul R. Pillar, *Intelligence and U.S. Foreign Policy* (New York: Columbia University Press, 2011), and Dana Priest and William M. Arkin, *Top Secret America* (New York: Little, Brown, 2011).

10 The Homeland Security Instruments

> *Americans will likely die on American soil, possibly in large numbers.*
> —Hart-Rudman Commission warning of need for homeland security agency, September 15, 1999[1]

> *Terrorism is a tragic fact, an unwelcome but immutable reality of life in the twenty-first century.*
> —First Secretary of Homeland Security Tom Ridge[2]

The tools to preserve homeland security have been around since 1789. For the first 212 years, they were called national defense and relied primarily on the armed forces and a federalized militia. The framers empowered the federal government to oppose invasions and insurrections and guaranteed all states a Republican form of government without saying how that should be accomplished. The 9/11 attacks, however, prompted lawmakers to create a cabinet department and other institution specifically focused on homeland security.

Domestic defense is a supreme obligation for any president, but in today's world of globalized transportation and trade, electronic communications, and transnational threats, homeland security requires international cooperation and coordination. Whatever other goals the United States has in dealing with other countries, securing help in fighting terrorists has to rank high. Similarly, American intelligence and security best practices are tools to be shared with others for mutual protection. In short, homeland security instruments are used both at home and abroad for domestic and foreign policy goals. (See Table 10.1.)

A Brief History of United States Homeland Security

Other than the War of 1812 and some later attacks on places that were U.S. protectorates but not states in the union—such as Pearl Harbor in Hawaii in 1941—all of America's wars with foreign enemies were fought on foreign soil. Many Americans felt protected by large oceans and the absence of

Table 10.1 Homeland Security Instrument Brief

AREAS OF RESPONSIBILITY	ADVANTAGES	DISADVANTAGES
Critical infrastructure	Coordinator for government	Requires cooperation from private sector
Cybersecurity	Responsible for domestic agencies	Conflicts with Department of Defense (DOD)
Biological protection	Narrow responsibilities	Center for Disease Control and Prevention (CDC) has greater role
Border security	Coordination for government	Many political and budgetary pressures
Transportation security	Broad authority, overseas presence	Costly, often unpopular
Emergency preparedness and response	Federal Emergency Management Agency (FEMA) experienced, well resourced	Domestic and budgetary pressures
ROLE OF CONGRESS	Enabler and overseer, program defender	Multiple overseers
CULTURE	High priority on homeland security	Components retain prior focus and distinctiveness

Most of the major activities performed for homeland security are domestically focused, even though many of them involve other nations, either participating in the efforts or reacting to U.S. actions in their diplomatic dealings.

technology that could penetrate naval, coastal, and air defenses to reach the homeland. And, political leaders recognized the imperative of preventing attacks.

The advent of nuclear weapons brought a recognition of U.S. vulnerability to attack. At first, defense planners sought protection through military superiority then through deterrence based on secure retaliatory forces. The United States also developed bits and pieces of a civil defense program but never embraced the concept enthusiastically.

By the 1970s, most U.S. civilian and military leaders concluded that ballistic missiles with nuclear warheads could not be stopped, or at least not at a reasonable cost. That realization led Richard Nixon to conclude a treaty with the Soviet Union banning national missile defenses on both sides. Some Americans still believed in the feasibility and desirability of such defenses. Ronald Reagan proposed a strategic defense initiative that critics labeled *Star Wars*, and George W. Bush abrogated the missile defense treaty in order to continue U.S. programs that still have not produced a deployed nationwide system.

Internal threats have always been dealt with by local law enforcement officials, supplemented by the Federal Bureau of Investigation (FBI) and ultimately backed by the threat of U.S. military force. Congress has always insisted on limiting the intelligence agencies to overseas activities and trusting the FBI to investigate and prosecute domestic lawbreakers, whether they use ordinary criminal or terrorist tactics. The FBI had long (and sometimes highly criticized) experience investigating alleged communists, antiwar activists during Vietnam, violent groups like the Weather Underground, and civil rights organizations considered prone to violence. In the 1980s and 1990s, the FBI set up joint terrorism task forces in New York and other cities, numbering 35 by the time of the 9/11 attacks.[3]

In the late 1990s, several national security analysts began warning of potential terrorist attacks on mainland America and urged actions to protect the homeland. They were divided on whether that threat would be nuclear or conventional, delivered by aircraft or suitcases, but they believed some sort of threat was real, and the United States was woefully unprepared. The Defense Science Board in the mid-1990s forecasted that the United States would face enemies whose command and control system was the Internet with logistics by Federal Express. The Hart–Rudman Commission first warned in 1999 about direct attacks on American soil and then told the incoming Bush administration in March 2001 that it should create a national homeland security agency linking FEMA, the coast guard, customs, and border patrol. The warning was placed on the back burner, not ignored but not considered urgent.

Creation of the Homeland Security System

The attacks on September 11, 2001, in which a foreign group attacked the United States on its own soil, killing nearly 3,000 people, forced the U.S. government to examine and refashion all of its instruments for homeland security. Previous studies like Hart–Rudman were dusted off and their ideas turned into actions. The most significant idea was the creation of a federal agency with the specific mandate of protecting the homeland from terrorist attacks, such as that proposed by Hart–Rudman. But, there were other ideas as well: changes in the law to allow intelligence agencies to talk to crime-fighting agencies; new measures to protect nationwide networks for power, finance, transportation, and communications from disruption; and better border security to prevent dangerous people or materials from reaching the homeland.

The USA PATRIOT Act (formally the Uniting and Strengthening America by Providing the Appropriate Tools Required to Intercept and Obstruct Terrorism Act, Public Law 107–56) was signed into law six weeks after the 9/11 attacks. One of its most important sections reduced the "wall" separating law enforcement from intelligence officials so that they could share information on potential terrorists. The law also gave expanded authorities for domestic surveillance and investigating money laundering. Several terrorist-related acts were specifically made federal crimes. Several provisions were *sunset* with expiration dates, thus forcing Congress to revisit them and decide on renewal, as was done most recently in 2011.[4]

The goal of initial efforts was simple: to link the disparate agencies and operations, coordinate them with a homeland security focus, and provide them with additional legal and investigative tools. One of President Bush's first actions—on September 20—was to create a Homeland Security Council (HSC) modeled on the National Security Council (NSC)—a White House-based group headed by a presidential aide tasked to coordinate federal actions aimed at protecting against terrorist attacks. As any bureaucrat could tell you, however, coordination is easier said than done. Established agencies had their existing laws, programs, procedures, priorities, clients, and overseers in Congress. They had to be cajoled or coerced into cooperating with others on additional goals while still trying to meet their existing ones.

Members of Congress objected that the presidential assistant for homeland security was not subject to Senate confirmation or congressional testimony or any law setting the rules for the HSC. They pushed for, and after nine months of pressure got the president to support, creation of a Department of Homeland Security (DHS). The law was a compromise, moving 22 government organizations now with more than 180,000 people into the new department. (See Figure 10.1.) The resulting system posed enormous challenges to its initial leaders.

Several long-standing organizations were transferred from their home departments to the new DHS: the U.S. Coast Guard (USCG) from Transportation; the Secret Service from Treasury; and FEMA from the Executive Office of the President (EOP). Several other organizations were split, with only parts going to DHS: the Customs Service, Immigration and Naturalization Service (INS), and Animal and Plant Health Inspection Service (APHIS). Visa issuance stayed in the State Department; the FBI remained in Justice; the Federal Aviation Administration (FAA) remained in Transportation, but the newly created Transportation Security Administration (TSA) was moved to DHS; Health and Human Services (HHS) kept the CDC and the National Institutes of Health (NIH); and the Bureau of Alcohol, Tobacco, Firearms, and Explosives was moved from Treasury to Justice.[5]

The antiterrorist purpose in creating DHS was unmistakably clear in the law:

The primary mission of the Department is to—(A) prevent terrorist attacks within the United States;

(B) reduce the vulnerability of the United States to terrorism;

(C) minimize the damage, and assist in the recovery, from terrorist attacks that do occur within the United States;

(D) carry out all functions of entities transferred to the Department, including by acting as a focal point regarding natural and manmade crises and emergency planning[6]

The mandate from the law was simple: Do everything you've been doing, but worry first about terrorism, both domestic and foreign in origin, that threatens the security of the United States. Congress recognized that this

Figure 10.1 U.S. Department of Homeland Security Organizational Chart

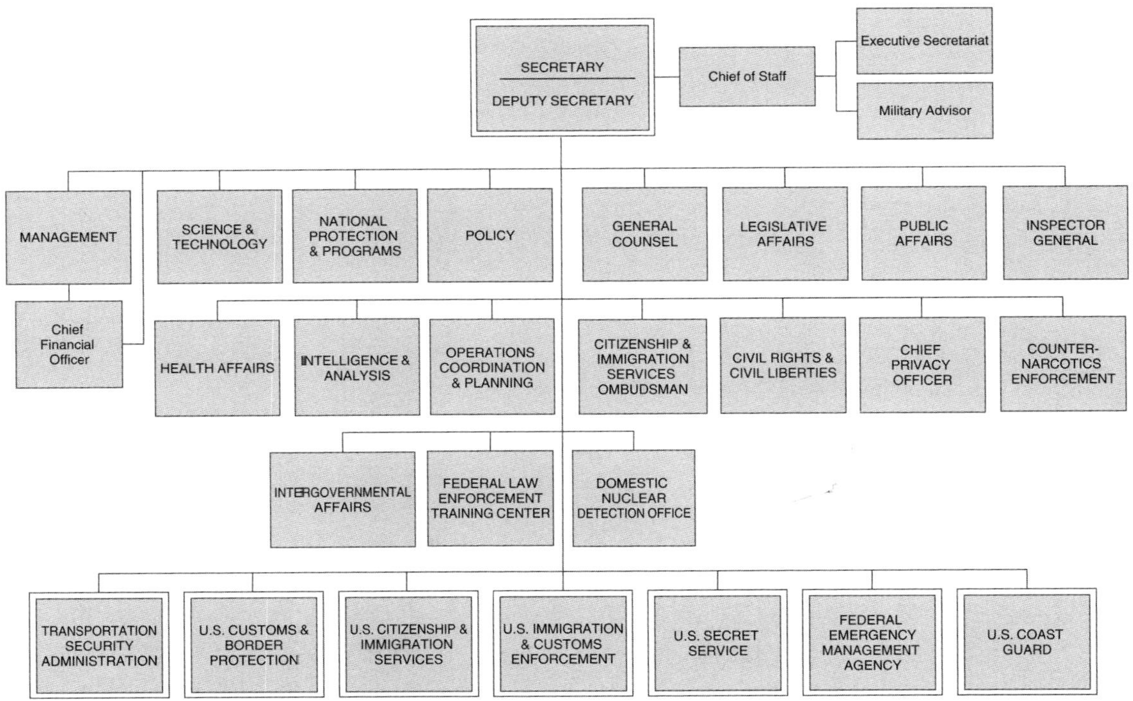

DHS has many special offices reporting directly to the secretary, but they do not supervise the several large organizations that form the bulk of DHS and that have their own distinctive missions and cultures.

Source: U.S. DHS, 2010.

mission might conflict with existing agency missions but insisted that activities not directly related to homeland security be "not diminished or neglected." That has been hard to achieve in practice, not least because the congressional committees that previously had jurisdiction over DHS components for those other missions retained jurisdiction and oversight even after creation of the new department. Within DHS, there is ongoing competition for resources and influence among the many newly combined organizations and, within them, between legacy and new missions.

The budget process for homeland security is enormously complicated. Only about half the total federal spending for that purpose goes through DHS. DOD and HHS also have major programs, with the rest of the spending scattered among 28 other federal agencies. Only about two thirds of the DHS budget goes specifically for homeland security activities, with the remainder going for traditional programs like maritime safety and mitigation of oil spills. While listing all the spending information across the government, the Office of Management and Budget (OMB) still has not created a separate homeland security budget function.[7] That means that budgeteers trade off homeland security programs against other activities in each agency rather than against homeland security programs across the government. A similar situation prevails in national security, where defense and international affairs activities are in separate functions, making it hard to trade off military and civilian activities that are similar in objectives but separate in execution.

The Defense Mission

Fears of an attack from abroad arose now and then throughout U.S. history, at first from Canada and later from the sea. Long before the United States had a blue-water navy, it was building coastal forts with artillery and shallow draft gunboats. In World War II, German submarines threatened ships near U.S. ports, and some coastal cities imposed blackout restrictions to thwart attacks. On the Pacific coast, Japanese submarines attacked ships and some shore facilities and later launched fire balloons that did minor damage. These real but minor attacks and numerous false alarms caused major public concern.

Military operations within the United States were strictly limited by the *Posse Comitatus* Act of 1878, which prohibited the use of federal troops for domestic law enforcement. The law halted federal prosecutions of violations of civil rights and other laws in the southern states and marked an end to Reconstruction after the Civil War. Only in recent years were exceptions written into law allowing counterdrug assistance (military personnel can identify drug-trafficking activities but cannot conduct arrests) and emergency assistance in case of the theft of nuclear materials or situations involving chemical or biological weapons of mass destruction (WMD).[8]

One early response to the Soviet nuclear threat was the creation of the North American Air Defense Command (NORAD) in 1958. With Canadian support, the United States built radar systems to detect enemy bombers flying over the North Pole and later upgraded the system to warn of enemy missiles. After the end of the Cold War in the 1990s, some defense officials worked to create military units to deal with threats from smaller nuclear devices—*suitcase bombs*—that might be carried by ships or aircraft.

The 9/11 attacks demonstrated that serious damage could be done using civilian airliners rather than explosive weapons. While DOD remained focused on foreign military threats and defense of American airspace, civilian agencies undertook to defend against threats that traveled on common carriers or were already resident in the United States. The creation of DHS brought most of those agencies under a single umbrella and gave them a new highest priority—preventing terrorist attacks.

DOD spends about 26% of the money counted government-wide as being for homeland security, with the bulk of that going for DOD programs to protect military facilities, personnel, and infrastructure like computer and communications systems. In 2002, DOD created the Northern Command (NORTHCOM) and gave it area responsibilities for the continental United States, Canada, and Mexico and important functional roles including aerial monitoring and defense as well as *military support to civil authorities,* the Pentagon's phrase for everything from disaster relief to riot control. NORTHCOM took over the joint task force that worked on drug interdiction along the Mexican border and expanded its mandate to surveillance and detection for homeland defense. It also controls the joint task force established in 1999 to prepare to deal with any chemical, biological, radiological, or nuclear incident on U.S. soil. NORTHCOM today has about 1,200 personnel regularly assigned and an annual budget of about $70 million. These activities suggest that the Pentagon still treats its domestic security role as secondary to its external security missions and is primarily concerned with dealing with the consequences of threats to the homeland.

The USCG, now part of DHS, has long been an instrument for foreign policy activities as well as for domestic purposes. It has its own military operations at home and overseas. Besides interdiction of drug traffickers and illegal migrants, the USCG has been involved in Haitian earthquake relief and training missions to 51 nations. It has deployed six patrol boats to U.S. Central Command (CENTCOM) for Middle East activities and has sent port security units to Kuwait and Iraq.[9] USCG has 42,000 military personnel and 8,000 civilians, with an annual budget of about $10 billion.

Intelligence Collection and Integration Mission

Prevention of terrorist attacks relies heavily on what the intelligence community (IC) can learn from its many techniques and sources. But, the intelligence agencies are limited to overseas activities. (For more detailed discussion, see Chapter 9.) One of the government's most important tools to bring together domestic and foreign threat information is the National Counterterrorism Center (NCTC), a 500-person organization drawing on all 16 members of the IC. Its task, basically, is to connect the dots pointing to terrorist threats. Formally, its responsibility is to analyze the threat, share that information, and integrate all instruments of national power to obtain unity of effort.[10] NCTC manages a terrorist identity database and provides regular reports to other parts of the government, including threat reports, incident tracking, and daily teleconferences. It reports directly to the president and the Director of National Intelligence (DNI).

In practice, NCTC has been judged as providing added value to the rest of the government but facing "numerous obstacles," including "systemic impediments" and culture clashes among agencies. A congressionally commissioned study found that planning and operations have been hindered by overlapping authorities, especially among NCTC and State and the CIA. Relations with the NSC staff were also judged "not well institutionalized."[11]

DHS is part of the IC. It has a 1,000-person component for analysis and operations with a budget around $350 million that does both operational planning and intelligence analysis. DHS does not do the foreign intelligence collection that is the responsibility of other parts of the IC, but it does gather unique information as part of its regular activities at airports, seaports, and the border. It also gains information from local law enforcement officials as well as the private sector.

Given these multiple sources of information, the DHS intelligence and analysis unit prepares intelligence warnings and security assessments as well as monthly *security monitors* and an annual threat assessment. The unit's analytic thrusts are narcotics trafficking, alien and human smuggling, money laundering, radicalizations and extremism, groups that could be exploited by terrorists or criminals, critical infrastructure and key resources, WMD; and health threats. The intelligence office is responsible for providing actionable intelligence to departmental officials and for sharing threat information and assessments with state, local, and private-sector partners. As part of this process, DHS has provided people and secure communications equipment to 72 state and local fusion centers across the country.[12] The coast guard has a separate intelligence unit that works with maritime fusion centers and conducts signals intelligence (SIGINT) operations for the National Security Agency (NSA).

In 2010, the Government Accountability Office (GAO) reported to Congress that DHS was making progress on sharing and managing information related to terrorism but still lacked a comprehensive approach. On this activity, as well as on several other DHS functions, GAO for several years has rated DHS problems as "high risk."[13]

Critical Infrastructure Mission

As terrorist threats became a major concern of the federal government in the 1990s, analysts pointed to several infrastructure systems that seemed potentially vulnerable, such as the electric power grid, oil and gas pipelines, financial networks, key transportation nodes, and various communications networks. Those systems that, if disrupted or destroyed, would have a debilitating effect on the national economy, or homeland security, or public health and safety were deemed critical infrastructures, and DHS was given overall responsibility for prioritizing and executing infrastructure protection programs. It spends about $5 billion per year on such activities.

Presidential directives identified 17 key sectors, each of which is supposed to develop protection plans.[14] These include agriculture and food; banking and finance; chemical; commercial facilities; communications; critical manufacturing; dams; defense industrial base; emergency services; energy; government facilities; healthcare and public health; information technology; national monuments and icons; nuclear reactors, materials, and waste; postal and shipping; transportation systems; and water. While DHS has overall responsibility for developing strategies for protection, other departments have lead agency roles for the sectors they know best—such as the Environmental Protection Agency (EPA) for water and chemical, Justice for emergency services, and Treasury for banking and finance. As sector plans have evolved in recent years, DHS has put added emphasis on resiliency and not just protection. Planners recognize the need to prepare to deal with possible attacks in case preventive measures fail. For example, DHS has now developed web portals for specific incidents for real-time exchange of sensitive information.

The challenge for DHS and the rest of the federal government, of course, is that 85% of the critical infrastructure is privately owned and operated, and businesses resent and resist government interference, especially costly government regulations.[15] There are often major barriers to cooperation, such as from the antitrust laws or competition-sensitive information. Government officials also worry about providing information that is based on classified data. A 2011 study noted the inherent conflict between the electric industry's efforts to build Internet-based, smart grids for more efficient pricing and delivery of power and the heightened vulnerability to disruption such a system would be at risk for without major security features. But, security is a low priority for these efforts, and it is unclear who would have to pay for the enhancements.[16]

Cybersecurity Mission

The Internet developed from a military program to allow communications even in the event of nuclear war through the use of packet switching. The Pentagon has always had programs for secure command, control, and communications linkages and has recently expanded both its defensive and offensive capabilities against potential threats. Increasing civilian reliance on cyber networks has made their protection against disruption similarly important in recent years. Analysts fear that attackers could hack into computer systems to destroy nuclear reactors, crash trains or planes, or disable banking and financial transactions. A think tank report in 2011 noted that U.S. government networks faced 1.8 billion cyber attacks of varying sophistication each month. It concluded that "cyber attacks are more than a nuisance and more than criminal activity. They constitute a serious challenge to U.S. national security."[17]

Cybersecurity became a special priority of the Obama administration, with nearly $1 billion budgeted for this purpose in the first two years. In 2009 and 2011, the administration announced programs involving DHS in liaison with the private sector and DOD for protecting governmental and allied networks. The White House named a cybersecurity coordinator to manage the interagency process. The Pentagon in 2010 established the U.S. Cyber Command as a component of the strategic command with missions to defend U.S. networks and if necessary conduct "full spectrum military cyberspace operations." The administration also announced plans for working with other nations on a joint cyberspace strategy.[18]

Coordination just within the U.S. government will pose major challenges, however, because several agencies and military commands already have large cyberdivisions. In fact, 21 federal organizations dealing with cybersecurity have been created since 2001.[19]

For its part, DHS is preparing to deploy the EINSTEIN 3 system to prevent and detect intrusions on government computer systems. The department also has been working to identify U.S. companies deemed most important for cyber infrastructure and get them to develop security plans. Additional legislation is needed from Congress to codify and implement the strategic plans and deal with related issues of privacy and intellectual property. There has been some push back from the private sector, however. The U.S. Chamber of Commerce complained that the plans developed so far amount to "regulatory overreach" by imposing heavy burdens on U.S. businesses.[20]

Biological Protection Mission

There are no easy answers as to how to handle threats to public health. Several civilian agencies have long-standing programs, enormous scientific expertise, and well-established connections to national and local medical communities. On the other hand, DHS has special expertise on biological threats and unique capabilities for integrating whole of government responses to disruptive threats and emergencies. So far, the tendency has been to tilt in favor of the doctors.

Public health and safety programs are divided between DHS and the HHS, which manages the NIH and the CDC. While both departments are supposed to work closely in responding to disasters, HHS was given lead agency status for medical emergencies by Congress in 2006.[21] DHS is mainly responsible for biological defense and surveillance programs. The department also has a $1 billion annual science and technology program that, among other things, funds research and development of biometric detectors and surveillance systems. The federal government is also developing an Early Warning Infectious Disease Program (EWIDS) that seeks early detection, identification, and reporting of infectious diseases associated with bioterrorism agents and other major threats to public health, which may originate at home or abroad.

Border Security and Immigration Missions

The largest single component of DHS is called U.S. Customs and Border Protection (CBP), with 61,000 people and an annual budget of over $11.5 billion. It combined the customs bureau from Treasury and the border patrol from Justice, along with inspectors from the INS and the Department of Agriculture. CPB's job is to prevent the illegal entry of people and forbidden items at the U.S. borders. CPB officials also work at airports and seaports, both domestic and overseas.

Investigations and law enforcement of immigration and customs matters are handled by a separate part of DHS, the Immigration and Customs Enforcement (ICE), with 20,000 employees and an annual budget over $5.5 billion. ICE goes after transnational criminal organizations and runs deportation programs.

A third agency, Citizenship and Immigration Services (CIS), processes immigration and naturalization requests as well as asylum petitions. It has 11,000 employees and a nearly $3 billion budget.

Managing the CPB, ICE, and CIS has been a major challenge because of the differing cultures and practices developed in their legacy institutions and the need to impose greater commonality for homeland security purposes.[22] The task has been made even more difficult by the political disputes over immigration and naturalization issues. Some political leaders demand tougher entry barriers and more aggressive enforcement of sanctions against undocumented persons and their employers as a precondition; others seek immigration reform and paths to citizenship for some people already resident. This political dispute complicates DHS management as it weighs spending more money on border fencing versus, say, port security or whether to target employers or undocumented workers in their enforcement efforts.

Transportation Security Mission

The third largest component of DHS is the TSA, with 14% of the budget and 58,000 employees. (CBP is first, with 21% of the budget and 61,000 people. The coast guard is next, with 18% of the budget and 50,000 people.) TSA was created shortly after the 9/11 attacks, combining the existing air marshal program with newly federalized airport screeners. There are more than 500 commercial airports in the United States with airline service, but about 70% of passenger boardings occur at just 31 sites. In 2010, TSA reached its mandated goals of 100% screening of all passengers on designated flights to, from, and within the United States against government watch lists as well as 100% screening of cargo on passenger aircraft. In addition to the airport screeners and their advanced imaging machines, DHS has 3,336 behavior detection officers and 900 canine teams for added security.[23]

TSA is also responsible for developing programs for security of surface transportation in cooperation with state, local, and private operators. There, too, the challenge is huge. There are 45,000 miles of interstate freeways and 600,000 bridges. Freight rail networks extend for 300,000 miles.[24]

TSA faces a no-win problem. Passengers resent the intrusive inspections, even of small children and the disabled, as *security theater*, but inspectors want to avoid blame if they overlook what becomes a threat. Rules have been changed to guard against new techniques, such as liquid chemicals or underwear bombs.

Emergency Preparedness and Response Missions

Federal help in cases of natural disasters was ad hoc until the 1930s, when federal funds were authorized for repair of public facilities and roads that suffered damage. Broader federal programs were enacted in the 1960s and 1970s, and in 1980, several programs were merged into FEMA.[25] At first, FEMA was under the direct control of the president, but it was moved into DHS when that department was created in 2003. Some observers feared that would lead to a subordination and diminution of an effective government agency. Others argued that it was only logical to link homeland security protection and prevention programs to response planning if those measures fail. FEMA has about 10,000 permanent employees and an annual budget about $10 billion. About half the people are assigned to disaster relief operations, the remainder to other FEMA activities.

While the terrorism focus of DHS adds another set of concerns for FEMA, its actual toolkit would be the same for natural disasters and for terrorist attacks. In either case, it would need to plan for evacuations; search and rescue; medical support; temporary housing; food, water, and fuel supplies; communications; and evacuee registration. There are important differences, however, in how to train and interact with first responders and local communities depending whether the emergencies are terrorism, natural disasters, infectious diseases, or industrial accidents—the broader spectrum of incidents FEMA is now mandated to handle.[26]

When FEMA does well, there are no limits to the praise and budgets it receives. When it does poorly, as after Hurricane Katrina, Congress reacts with predictable anger. Some critics say that FEMA does too much, pushed by Congress and pulled by presidents who want to show their concern and support to local communities. The number of presidential disaster declarations has soared in recent decades, from an average of 43 per year in the 1980s to 130 per year under President Bush the younger and 108 per year in President Obama's first two years. Local officials want such declarations, of course, because then the federal government pays 75% to 100% of the disaster response bills. Congress then helps out by passing supplemental emergency funds.

While FEMA's role remains essentially unchanged, its relation to the rest of DHS is conflicted. Departmental officials don't like to think of failure to prevent and protect against terrorist attacks. They also have a bias in favor of additional protective measures over funding for relief and recovery.

FEMA officials lament their loss of White House status and the need to compete for funds with the rest of DHS.

The Anomaly of the Secret Service

Also in DHS is the Secret Service with its 7,000 people and nearly $2 billion annual budget. Most people think of the Secret Service primarily as the protectors of the president and other current and former officials. But, the agency was created in 1865 to catch counterfeiters and received the presidential protection mission only after the McKinley assassination in 1901.

Part of its mission remains safeguarding the financial infrastructure and payment systems and the investigation of electronic crimes. While formally under DHS, the Secret Service has substantial autonomy—plus the special benefit of daily access to the president.

Culture of the Department of Homeland Security

The integration of the 22 agencies moved under the DHS umbrella is still a work in progress. Most of the components had well-honed bureaucratic cultures and practices. Some had a law enforcement mission and viewed the world in black and white. Others performed services for the public and developed strong ties to civilian communities. Still others had technical skills and professionalism, isolating themselves somewhat from outsiders. If there is an emerging DHS culture, it seems to be one emphasizing coordination—coordination of the units and activities within the department and coordination with the many other government agencies who perform related tasks.[27]

A second aspect of DHS organizational culture seems to be a kind of hyper vigilance combined with risk aversion. Officials are right to be worried; that's their primary job. But, that focus on worst-case threats makes it hard for them to perform another important task—reassuring the public. As former counterterrorism official Michael Sheehan has written, "No terrorism expert or government leader wants to appear soft on terrorism. It's always safer to predict the worse; if nothing happens, the exaggerators are rarely held accountable for their nightmare scenarios."[28] The Obama administration discontinued the color-coded threat levels precisely because they were numbingly vague and unhelpful in terms of what ordinary citizens should do.

The risk aversion component of DHS culture can be seen in reviews of its risk assessment methodologies. Critics say there is a preoccupation with "low probability/high consequence" events and that risk assessments exaggerate the probability and likely costs of terrorist incidents. A National Research Council assessment in 2010 placed only "low confidence" in DHS risk analyses and said they were inadequate to support decision making except in the case of natural disasters.[29] Such critiques make it even harder to increase DHS prestige within government or the morale of its employees.

Homeland Security Council

The law creating DHS also created the HSC and staff to advise the president. The membership was to be the president, vice president, secretary of homeland security, secretary of defense, and "such other individuals as may be designated by the President."[30] President Obama took the advice of national security analysts and decided to merge the HSC and NSC staffs as their subject matters had so much overlap. He retained a separate position for an assistant to the president for homeland security and counterterrorism.[31]

HSC is still an immature organization with no track record of effective planning and execution—in contrast to the NSC. Nor does the special assistant have any directive power over the interagency process. There is little evidence that the HSC has achieved significant bureaucratic status in the White House or that it has created distinctive bureaucratic processes for presidential management of homeland security issues. Presidents can call any meetings they want and then decide whether to call the gathering an HSC or NSC meeting.

Strengths and Weaknesses of the Homeland Security System

As long as there is no major terrorist attack on U.S. soil, the homeland security system will receive a passing grade from the American public. But, most experts argue that the government needs to do better overall and that DHS in particular needs major improvements. The GAO has repeatedly documented DHS administrative shortfalls and has listed DHS as a "high risk" agency with numerous programs vulnerable to fraud, waste, abuse, and mismanagement and in need of transformational improvements. Some fixes require better management, but others require different laws or more money, both of which are much harder to come by.[32]

The federal system is fragmented, with DHS managing only half of the federal money spent on "homeland security." DHS is the designated principal federal office (PFO) for management of domestic incidents but is not really empowered to integrate and manage an interagency response. As the Project on National Security Reform (PNSR) concluded in its 2008 report, "The DHS lacks the authority necessary to fulfill its national security mission."[33]

While a good case can be made for letting other departments run the programs where they have experience and expertise, the potential problem remains that, in an emergency, there should be an effective coordination mechanism. DHS is really a *department of coordination,* and thus reasonably suited for such a role with other agencies, but coordination works best when someone has directive authority, not merely persuasive opportunities. Still unproven is how well DHS can mobilize cooperation with state, local, and private-sector officials on many of its tasks. There are committees and conferences, but they have not been tested in crises.

DHS itself is still at the toddler stage. There is much staff turnover and low morale. DHS ranks near the bottom of federal agencies in terms of worker satisfaction.[34] The component organizations are still torn between the new structure and missions and the legacy programs they were most comfortable carrying out. While senior leaders know they will be judged primarily on how well they prevent terrorist incidents and protect the nation, their subordinates know they will also be judged on how well they perform those legacy missions.

The president of Rand Corporation has written that DHS goals and strategy are ill defined. "DHS leaders are thus left to 'manage by inbox,' with the dominant mode for DHS behavior being crisis management." James Thomson also said, "DHS implements most of its programs with little or no evaluation of their performance."[35]

Since that was written in 2007, DHS has followed the good government practices of further internal reviews and reorganizations. In 2009, it conducted, on the Pentagon model, a quadrennial homeland security review and, in 2010, did a bottom-up review. Despite those commendable efforts, the GAO and others say much more needs to be done.

Another critic, Stephen Flynn of the Center for National Policy, says, "The United States has made a mess of homeland security." He complains that DHS and other agencies "are subsumed in a world of security clearances and classified documents" and fail to reach out to the people they are supposed to serve. Instead of doing their work behind closed doors in windowless offices, Flynn urges DHS to reach out to the private sector and the public and involve them more actively in planning both protection and responses. "Building societal resilience requires a bottom-up, open and participatory process," he says, "that is, the exact inverse of the way U.S. policymakers have approached homeland security to date."[36]

Congress and Homeland Security

There is widespread agreement that congressional oversight of DHS is a burden for the department. An estimated 108 congressional committees and subcommittees have some sort of jurisdiction over DHS—compared with 36 for DOD. In addition to the House and Senate homeland security and appropriations committees and their subcommittees, many other panels have legacy jurisdictions over the nonsecurity activities of DHS components, which account for more than one third of the DHS budget. Lawmakers concerned about the coast guard's maritime safety programs or about immigration issues beyond infiltration of terrorists demand continued oversight rights and want to call witnesses from DHS and write new laws.[37]

As a result of the multiple panels with jurisdiction, DHS had to prepare testimony and send witnesses to 376 hearings during the 110th Congress, only half of which involved the two committees with primary homeland security focus. By comparison, the Pentagon, with its much larger budget and range of activities, appeared before only two thirds as many hearings

(261) during the same period.[38] And while the secretary of defense can designate subordinates to testify in most cases, the DHS secretary and the heads of the major agencies find it harder to say "no."

Redrawing jurisdictional lines, as outside observers suggest, is much harder to achieve within Congress. It took four years before the House granted its committee on homeland security legislative authority and then only after protecting the jurisdictional claims of other committees. The Senate counterpart also has primary jurisdiction over laws reorganizing government and was strictly limited in which parts of DHS it could oversee. Members on other committees argued that they have expertise on the legacy operations of the DHS components and that the law required that those programs not be "diminished or neglected." Thus, Congress mirrors the tension within the executive branch between focus on security and prevention, not to mention shared focus on the other activities by the organizations within DHS.

Further evidence of the weakness of the two principal authorizing committees is their failure to pass a homeland security authorization bill since the creation of the department. As with foreign aid, this failure prevents Congress from giving timely guidance and program adjustments except in spending levels through appropriations.

On the other hand, homeland security has had a relatively protected budget in recent years. Both Republicans and Democrats lump DHS spending with defense and veterans affairs and then impose less restraint than for the rest of the civilian portions of the budget. Some lawmakers still criticize some DHS programs; however, preparedness grants have been given to 63 different urban areas, far more than are deemed high risk.

International Aspects of Homeland Security

Just as America's defense strategy and efforts start far from the shoreline, so does homeland security. The case study in this chapter on Mexico illustrates how cooperation on homeland security requires foreign policy deftness and involves many domestic issues for both the United States and Mexico. DHS has agents at 58 overseas ports that handle 86% of container ship traffic. TSA has negotiated aviation security declarations with African, European, and Latin American nations. The United States has numerous agreements with Canada and Mexico regarding border management. DHS has cooperation agreements on homeland security with 10 other nations.[39] And, the United States has sensitive arrangements with several nations for intelligence sharing and other cooperation regarding terrorist threats.

Reaching these various agreements is as important a diplomatic activity as any other pursued by the State Department. They are part of the network of cooperative relations that bolster U.S. national security overall. While Americans may view functional arrangements for passengers and goods as noncontroversial, other nations treat them as political matters that are part of their overall foreign policy. Immigration laws and visa requirements have long been major foreign policy issues in many countries and have to be dealt with diplomatically. For example, the U.S. government can include visa requirements as part of a larger bargain, granting fewer restrictions as a reward for international cooperation or denying privileges as a punishment.

The homeland security instruments are thus part of America's foreign policy toolkit because their use almost always involves foreign nations or individuals and thus becomes part of the context in which international policies are developed. Since the 9/11 attacks, America has developed techniques and processes for terrorist identification and safety procedures, inspections and monitoring that have been widely shared and adopted by friendly nations. Some parts of DHS can also be sent on overseas missions, as has been done by sending coast guard units to Haiti and the Middle East and by sending TSA to work out aviation security agreements.

If the homeland security instruments are weak or faulty, that could have enormous foreign policy consequences. An insecure America could seek to withdraw from international engagements. America's enemies could be emboldened by even a minor successful attack. U.S. leaders could be shaken and distracted by security challenges. And in case of another significant attack, lawmakers and the public might succumb to demands to deny civil liberties to large segments of the population.

Areas of Presidential Choice

Within the U.S. government, the president can try to impose integration and coordination. Presidents Bush and Obama have issued executive orders that point in the right direction, but their subordinates have limited powers, and the integrative mechanisms are weak and untested. Going further requires congressional assent and action as well as close executive supervision.

The president can also try to reorient homeland security activities while reassuring the public that best efforts are being made to protect them, their communities, and the economy. He can try to modify the DHS culture's focus on preventing worst-case events so that it can prepare and deal with more likely threats and associated recovery efforts. In 2011, President Obama issued a policy directive ordering the development of a *national preparedness goal* that would weigh specific threats and vulnerabilities, including regional variations, and recommend "concrete, measurable, and prioritized objectives" to mitigate the risks.[40] The administration has also stressed the goal of "build[ing] a ready and resilient Nation,"[41] terminology that suggests a slight shift away from a preoccupation with prevention of attacks. This may be bureaucratic wheel spinning, or it may produce a more nuanced and balanced homeland security strategy.

***

The U.S. government has a broad array of institutions involved in some way or another with homeland security. To perform their missions, they often have to work with other nations and thus become part and parcel of

U.S. foreign policy instruments. The largest coordinating entity, DHS, still faces enormous bureaucratic challenges as it tries to fashion integrated plans for the protection of the American people and U.S. infrastructure.

Case Study: U.S.–Mexican Collaboration on Security

This case study on Mexico illustrates how homeland security is a major tool for both U.S. domestic and foreign policy. The United States and Mexico share a common border nearly 2,000 miles long as well as numerous problems relating to trade, migration, and criminal activities. The Mexican government under President Felipe Calderón launched a major effort to combat drug-trafficking organizations (DTO) that have threatened the governments, judiciary, and law enforcement activities of several Mexican states and communities. He increased Mexico's security budget from about $2 billion in 2006 to $9.3 billion in 2009 and mobilized thousands of soldiers and federal police to arrest drug traffickers, establish checkpoints, and interdict drug shipments. On its side of the border, the United States increased the number of border patrol agents, installed additional detection systems, and deployed 1,200 national guard troops.

Despite Calderón's efforts, between 2007 and 2010, the Mexican government estimated that 34,500 people died in violence related to organized crime. Murders and kidnappings soared within some border cities and spilled over into the United States. Circumstances were so dire that Mexico set aside 150 years of anti-Yanqui feelings and accepted a broad range of U.S. assistance, including U.S. military personnel to train Mexican antidrug units. The most comprehensive plan was the 2007 Mérida Initiative of counterdrug and anticrime assistance and cooperation.

Presidents George W. Bush and Barack Obama expanded the number and types of collaborative efforts. Today, the two nations work together in a broad range of intergovernmental organizations, from the White House to the border-crossing level. In addition, of course, there are transnational groups in the private sector and between state and local governments. Included among the collaborative efforts of the two countries are meetings among the executive leadership, cabinet-level representatives, and defense and diplomatic contacts. For instance, the U.S. and Mexican presidents meet about once a year, sometimes with the Canadian prime minister, under the umbrella of the North American Free Trade Agreement (NAFTA), and in 2010, Secretary of State Clinton chaired a cabinet-level delegation including the U.S. secretaries of defense and homeland security, the chairman of the Joint Chiefs of Staff (JCS), and the director of national intelligence (DNI) that met with its Mexican counterparts.

The State Department runs numerous contacts and midlevel task forces via the U.S. embassy, while the Pentagon's NORTHCOM regularly meets with its Mexican counterparts. Similar meetings down the ranks address drug trafficking and environmental issues, while more active collaboration includes the creation of 11 border enforcement security task forces containing U.S. and Mexican representatives. Under the 2007 Mérida Initiative to fight drug trafficking and organized crime, the United States provided more than $1.8 billion in assistance through 2011, and between 2008 and 2010, DOD has provided counternarcotics assistance in the form of equipment and training to the total of nearly $100 million. The United States has located offices of 16 agencies in Mexico City to work with partner agencies on these counterdrug programs.

While meetings are not the same thing as progress against the threats, they are a necessary precondition. The breadth of collaboration between the two governments illustrates the importance the two nations place on improving their mutual homeland security. This effort also shows that homeland security instruments have both domestic and foreign policy functions.

Sources: David A. Shirk, *The Drug War in Mexico: Confronting a Shared Threat,* Council on Foreign Relations, March 2011; Clare Ribando Seelke, "Mexico–U.S. Relations: Issues for Congress," *CRS Report for Congress,* February 15, 2011.

Selected Resources

U.S. government sites for homeland security include DHS, which also has links to its component organizations at www.dhs.gov

The two principal congressional committees dealing with homeland security are the Senate Committee on Homeland Security and Governmental Affairs—http://hsgac.senate.gov/public/—and the House Committee on Homeland Security—http://homeland.house.gov/.

Many think tanks have active programs in homeland security. A list is here at www.hlswatch.com/thinktanks/.

Two books with deeper backgrounds are: Donald F. Kettl, *System Under Stress: Homeland Security and American Politics, Second Edition* (Washington, DC: CQ Press, 2007) and Gordon Adams and Cindy Williams, *Buying National Security* (Routledge, 2010).

11 The International Institutions Instrument

The United States should invest time and resources into building international relationships and institutions that can help manage local crises when they emerge.

—President George W. Bush, 2002[1]

Indeed, our ability to advance peace, security, and opportunity will turn on our ability to strengthen both our national and our multilateral capabilities. We need to spur and harness a new diversity of instruments, alliances, and institutions in which a division of labor emerges on the basis of effectiveness, competency, and long-term reliability. This requires enhanced coordination among the United Nations, regional organizations, international financial institutions, specialized agencies, and other actors that are better placed or equipped to manage certain threats and challenges.

—President Barack Obama, 2010[2]

International organizations are part of America's foreign policy toolkit. They can be partners, leveraging U.S. capabilities and power, or substitutes, carrying the burdens the United States would prefer not to bear. Using such organizations, however, creates a separate set of challenges. International organizations can be valuable partners in the pursuit of shared goals, but their participation may impose constraints on U.S. actions. They can be force multipliers for U.S. diplomacy, but they can also be impediments, limiting freedom or speed of action by a need for consensus. Multinational groups may also create expectations, norms, and opportunities that affect American decisions. The United States may be pressured to use or support these organizations when America might prefer to act on its own.

U.S. leaders tend to be pragmatic, embracing international cooperation when it seems to be helpful and avoiding it when it limits U.S. choices. This chapter examines some of the major international institutions and the ways they have been used or could be used as instruments of U.S. foreign policy.

Established institutions are ready forums for consultations and negotiations as well as venues for collective action. They can help in many ways to reduce the risk of conflict by the rules and norms they set, such as the United Nations (UN) Charter's provisions on resort to force and the UN's more recent declaration of a "right to protect" civilians. They can help to prevent crises by actions such as monitoring elections and political transitions (as in several African nations); working to case ethnic tensions (as in Central and Eastern Europe); helping to resolve boundary disputes (as in Africa, Latin America, and Southeast Asia); and by special investigations (as in Lebanon and Sri Lanka). And, they can work to mitigate conflicts that do break out both through diplomacy and by sending military peacekeepers.[3]

When problems arise, the United States can sometimes choose deliberately to use one or more of the major international organizations. The president can turn the issue over to others to avoid the costs and the hassles or to take advantage of the organization's special capabilities. At other times, however, the president will have to act defensively when an organization asserts itself into a foreign policy matter in ways that complicate or influence U.S. decisions. (See Table 11.1.)

It helps to share burdens and responsibilities. But, sharing also entails consultation and coordination, and sometimes, partners have differing perspectives and goals. On more than one occasion—including Lebanon in 1983 and Somalia in 1993—the United States suffered major military disasters because of confused lines of authority and differing approaches among the international partners. On the other hand, the UN has been an indispensable neutral force in many peacekeeping operations, and the North Atlantic Treaty Organization (NATO) has shared major burdens in Kosovo and Afghanistan. As is so often the case, the value of multilateral actions depends on the particular circumstances.

The Role of International Institutions

For major security issues, the UN will be involved whether or not the United States wishes. Only the UN can give an international imprimatur to arms embargoes or comprehensive economic sanctions. Only the UN Security Council (UNSC) can authorize major peacekeeping operations or the use of force against violent dictators and aggressive regimes. Acting with UN support gives legitimacy and moral standing to a nation's own policies.

Regional organizations like NATO, the OAS, and ASEAN can also be useful vehicles for security and other policies. They can mobilize political coalitions and even military forces to police problem areas in their regions. Annual meetings can be important venues for exchanging views, resolving problems, and launching initiatives. Where they have established infrastructures, they can be used to plan and implement agreed policies.

Economic crises and problems requiring economic solutions can often best be handled through the existing multilateral economic institutions—the G-8 and G-20 for high-level economic policy coordination, the IMF for advice and assistance on currency problems and debt, the World Bank and regional banks for development advice and assistance, and the WTO for managing trade disputes.

Table 11.1 — International Institutions as U.S. Instruments Brief

MAJOR INSTITUTIONS	ADVANTAGES	DISADVANTAGES
United Nations (UN)	Broad membership, much experience in relief and peacekeeping	Security Council veto, resistance to some U.S. views
International Atomic Energy Agency (IAEA)	Professional, authoritative	May self-censor reports
North Atlantic Treaty Organization (NATO)	Capable military forces	Requires consensus
Organization for Security and Co-operation in Europe (OSCE)	Broad forum	Little real power
Organization of American States (OAS)	Symbolic power when it acts	Limited by regional rivalries
Association of Southeast Asian Nations (ASEAN); ASEAN Regional Forum (ARF); Asia–Pacific Economic Cooperation (APEC)	Valuable forums	Little beyond meetings, small staffs
Group of Eight (G-8); Group of Twenty (G-20)	Valuable economic forums	Limited follow-through
International Monetary Fund (IMF) and international financial institutions (IFIs)	Experienced, powerful	May provoke local resentment
World Trade Organization (WTO)	Authoritative	Slow, technical
International courts	Symbolic	No enforcement powers
Nonstate actors	United States can help or keep distance	Groups limited; may be competitive with others
ROLE OF CONGRESS Funding and oversight	Necessary supporter	Reflects domestic political pressures

This list of some of the major international organizations includes many that the United States has deliberately chosen to use for its own foreign policy purposes as well as ones where others have challenged U.S. policies and forced American engagement. Each has its particular advantages and disadvantages as an instrument for U.S. policy.

The very fact that most of these organizations have regular meetings and expert staff make them useful for diplomacy. Meetings are action-forcing events for government agencies, prompting them to develop agendas and find measures that can be resolved as signs of success at the meeting. This is true also of bilateral meetings, such as presidential visits, but those lack the regularity of organizational summits. Whether a president or cabinet officer takes the time to attend one of these periodic meetings often depends on whether things will be accomplished—usually after having been worked out in advance by subordinates—that can be portrayed as justifying the trip.

International organizations also function as interest groups trying to influence U.S. policy decisions. (For different types of IOs, see Box 11.1.) They make demands, exert pressure, and offer rewards for support. They become part of the policy calculus as a matter of course.

Ad Hoc Versus Institutional Multilateralism

Too often, policy debates focus on *multilateral* or *unilateral* as if that were an enduring binary strategic choice. Even the most committed multilateralist cannot always rely on IOs. Even the most determined unilateralist will at times find multilateral approaches necessary or at least useful. The multilateral condemnation of Iraq in 1990 and 2002 by the UNSC empowered and strengthened U.S. foreign policy and added to the roster of nations willing to lend support to the subsequent military operations. UN reluctance to authorize combat operations against Serbia over Kosovo in 1999 was partially offset by the willingness of another IO, NATO, to endorse the mission.

Most international problems are either bilateral, between two parties alone, or multilateral and multifaceted. Bilateral disputes can be resolved without the involvement of third parties, but sometimes, those onlookers can be helpful in facilitating exchanges or weighing in on behalf of one of

---

Box 11.1

International Instruments and Entities

Given the widespread use of *international* in the naming of things, it's useful to keep several distinctions in mind. *International organizations* (IOs) as used in this book are organizations with national governments, and sometimes other international organizations, as members. They are usually established by treaties, have permanent staff, and perform regular activities, like the UN and its specialized agencies. They may be used as instruments of U.S. foreign policy as a forum for debate or negotiation or as a means of acting, such as giving aid or conducting military operations.

Nongovernmental organizations (NGOs) are groups separate from governments, usually not for profit, that conduct activities in other nations. They may deliver services, like Doctors Without Borders, or advocate for particular policies, like Amnesty International and numerous environmental groups. For U.S. foreign policy purposes, NGOs function either as advocacy groups or as potential instruments abroad when their goals coincide with the U.S. government's.

Multinational corporations (MNCs) are business organizations operating in more than one country. For U.S. foreign policy purposes, they are usually stakeholders and policy advocates, seeking support and favorable treatment by government. As such, they more often try to use the U.S. government as an instrument for their purposes than the other way around.

the disputants. Issues involving more than one country often benefit from having several participants involved in the discussions and actions. How to proceed thus depends on numerous factors that need to be considered, not simply a *go it alone* or *let's all work this out together* approach. *Coalitions of the willing* can act with fewer constraints than coalitions that form within a particular IO, but coalitions of the willing already trained and practiced can act even better and faster.

Different organizations have different strengths and weaknesses that make them more or less suitable for particular activities. The UN, for example, was designed to resolve disputes among smaller powers on the assumption of great power unanimity. When the Cold War fractured that agreement, the organization lost much of its effectiveness. The UN has become stronger and more effective since great power unity became more common in the 1990s. The G-8 served as a useful forum for economically advanced countries to coordinate policies among themselves but had to be broadened to the G-20 when economic problems became more global in both cause and remedy. APEC has made formal statements on North Korean nuclear programs and has taken preliminary actions on infectious disease control as well as other issues not directly related to its primary focus on economic relations and trade.

Some IOs have large staffs; others make do with small staffs. Some make decisions by formal votes; others require consensus and thus unanimity in order to act. While a few have the capacity to act to implement their decisions, most are limited to making recommendations to member states.[4] All these factors affect how and whether the United States can work with an organization in pursuit of its own foreign policy goals.

Other nations face similar choices and often choose to utilize IOs for their own purposes. They can shop for the forum most likely to be sympathetic to their positions. They can build coalitions within and among international groups. And, they can resort to *ad hoc multilateralism* for particular issues. The United States has joined several of these entities, often called *contact groups,* to deal with issues like Bosnia and Kosovo, Tajikistan, and Haiti. They can be a useful supplement to the established, larger organizations.[5]

International Institutions

For U.S. foreign policy, the most important international institutions are those concerned with international politics and security. These are the ones that can give international legal authorization for sanctions and military operations and that serve as venues for negotiations. Because other member nations can also use these organizations to challenge U.S. policy, America needs to engage with them and understand their capabilities.

United Nations

The UN is an important and at times unavoidable instrument for American foreign policy. Designed in 1945 to protect U.S. interests with a UNSC veto, headquartered in New York City, and funded to a significant extent—currently 22% of its core budget—by U.S. contributions, the UN is *the* global organization, with 192 member nations, and the symbolic guarantor of peace and security in a turbulent world. Its other members often disagree with U.S. policies, but their support, when it comes, can legitimate and leverage American actions.

The UN is a large organization with a $2.6 billion annual budget, not counting the costs of peacekeeping operations (around $8 billion in 2010) and the various specialized agencies (about $3 billion). The professional staff of the Secretariat has about 2,500 people, chosen both for their expertise and for geographical diversity. There are four major action centers at the UN: the General Assembly (UNGA), the UNSC, the Secretary-General (S-G) and the Secretariat, plus the specialized agencies.

General Assembly. The UNGA is the forum for discussion of the UN's 192 member nations. While it can be disparaged as a toothless debating society that ritually passes high-sounding resolutions that are then mostly ignored, the assembly's annual session, starting in September, is a major venue for international discussions. Leaders of many nations come to speak—and to use the occasion for private meetings with other officials. The U.S. president usually spends a day or two in high-level meetings in addition to his annual address, and the secretary of state regularly spends one to two weeks in New York in talks with foreign officials.

UNGA votes are important indicators of international sentiment on some topics, and even the United States can respond to opponents by ignoring them or by working harder to persuade or accommodate them. In 2009, the United States voted against UNGA resolutions more than any other member. Over all, the American position was supported by other members 39% of the time on recorded votes. (The State Department is required to report to Congress each year on UN voting patterns.) The level of support has varied over time and by particular issue, from about 50% support in the mid-1990s to around 23% to 25% in the mid-2000s. The most frequent disagreements have come on Middle East issues, where other members have voted with the United States only about 10% to 11% of the time since 2003. Not surprisingly, the nation voting with the U.S. most often is Israel at 97% of the time.[6]

Despite its many divisions and factions, the UNGA has acted in at least two important ways on peace and security issues. In 1950, it adopted the Uniting for Peace resolution that declared the GA's right to act to restore peace and security when the UNSC was unable to agree. (The United States pushed for the resolution as a way of getting around the usual Soviet veto in the UNSC.) And in 2005, at the world summit commemorating the UN's 50th anniversary, national leaders approved an *outcome document* that included a declaration that both individual states and the international community have a "responsibility to protect" their citizens. This doctrine underpinned the UNSC's decision in 2011 authorizing military intervention in Libya. The GA also acted to promote the Ottawa Convention banning antipersonnel mines when the major powers were reluctant to support it.[7]

Security Council. The UNSC is the most powerful UN body because it can vote binding measures on all UN members on matters of war, peace, and security. Such votes are subject to a veto by any of the five permanent members: the United States, United Kingdom, Russia, China, and France. Avoiding a veto, therefore, often requires crucial negotiations among the Perm 5 (P-5) as they are called. The UNSC has developed a series of informal practices for consultations and negotiations, sometimes among the whole membership, sometimes just among the P-5.[8] There is even a special room for such meetings separate from the regular UNSC chamber.

Corralling votes in the UN is similar to winning votes in Congress: The president and senior officials make arguments, listen to concerns that often relate to side issues, and then respond with arguments, threats, promises, or changes. U.S. officials made major efforts to win support for the UNSC resolutions against Iraq in 1990, and in subsequent years, they bypassed the UNSC when they knew they lacked the votes for action against Kosovo in 1999 and for tougher language against Iraq in 2003.

The UNSC has authorized numerous major policy actions over the decades since 1945. (See Table 11.2 for a listing of major UN military operations.) In 1950 it authorized, while the Soviet delegate was boycotting the organization, an American-led force to counter the North Korean invasion of South Korea. In 1992 it authorized *all necessary means*—the phrase permitting military force—to create safe havens and a no-fly zone in Bosnia. In 2001, it approved the British-led international force helping the United States in Afghanistan. In 2008, it authorized all necessary means against piracy and armed robbery at sea. In 2011, it authorized use of force to protect Libyan civilians and establish a no-fly zone there.[9]

In addition to authorizing hostile force, in what are called *Chapter VII peace-building operations,* the UNSC has approved many Chapter VI peacekeeping operations, where the opposing sides have agreed to stop fighting but need outside forces to keep them compliant or apart. The United States welcomed each one of these either as the best available means to reduce the level of violence or the threat of war or as a way of avoiding direct U.S. military involvement in the conflict. These have included more than 3,000 troops sent to the Suez Canal and Sinai Peninsula in 1956–1957 and another 7,000 in 1973–1979; 6,400 military observers sent to Cyprus in 1964, with 1,000 still there; 1,400 military observers sent to the Golan Heights in 1974 and still there; 6,150 military observers sent to Lebanon in 1978 and more than 12,000 still there; and more than 4,000 troops sent to the Ethiopian–Eritrean border in 2000, with more than 600 still there. Sizable UN operations with both troops and civilians have also been conducted in Namibia, Somalia, Cambodia, East Timor, Bosnia–Croatia, Kosovo, Sudan–Darfur, and the Democratic Republic of Congo. In fact, of the 74 peacekeeping operations voted by the UN since 1948, 12 are still in

Table 11.2 Major United Nations Military Operations, 1948–2011

PLACE	NAME	DATES
Palestine, Israel	UNTSO	1948–present
India/Pakistan border	UNMOGIP	1949–present
Korea	UNC	1950–present
Suez, Sinai	UNEF	1956–1967
Cyprus	UNFICYP	1964–present
Suez, Sinai	UNEF II	1973–1979
Syria, Golan Heights	UNDOF	1974–present
Lebanon	UNIFIL	1978–present
Namibia	UNTAG	1989–1990
Cambodia	UNTAC	1991–1995
Bosnia/Croatia	UNPROFOR	1992–1995
Somalia	UNOSOM II	1993–1995
East Timor	UNTAET	1999–2002
Democratic Republic of Congo	MONUC	1999–present
Kosovo	UNMIK	1999–present
Ethiopia/Eritrea	UNMEE	2000–2008
Liberia	UNMIL	2003–present
Cote d'Ivoire	UNOCI	2004–present
Haiti	MNUSTAH	2004–present
Sudan	UNMIS	2005–present
Central African Republic/Chad	MNURCAT	2007–present
Darfur	UNAMID	2007–present

This list shows how many UN military operations have become semipermanent as well as how many have been started in recent years, especially in Africa. It illustrates as well how the UN gets stuck with a lot of operations that nations prefer to outsource, such as Darfur. Many nations eagerly participate in these operations because it gives their military forces valuable training, free equipment, and UN-paid salaries.

being, 7 of them dating from before 2000. In 2010, more than 100,000 UN personnel were involved.[10] While the United States has paid about 25% of UN peacekeeping costs as part of its regular assessment, it has made major troop contributions only in Korea, the Sinai, Somalia, and the Balkans. The U.S.-led Gulf War coalition against Iraq in 1991 was not a UN operation, though force had been authorized by the UNSC.

Short of the use of force, the UNSC has enacted comprehensive sanctions against pariah regimes, including Southern Rhodesia, Iraq, Yugoslavia, and Haiti. It also has approved at different times arms embargoes against South

Africa, Angola, Libya, Afghanistan, Haiti, Sierre Leone, al Qaeda and the Taliban, Iran, and North Korea.[11] Some of these actions can be considered successful, but others fell short. Achievement of international sanctions has been a major U.S. goal, especially in confronting Libya, North Korea, Iran, and al Qaeda and the Taliban as sanctions tend to be ineffective unless broadly applied.

An important reason for seeking UN sanctions even if the prospects are limited is to build momentum and international support. The UNSC adopted a series of progressively tougher sanctions against Iraq prior to the U.S.-led invasion of 2003. The same process has been followed with regard to Iran's nuclear program, allowing the United States to win support for ever-tighter sanctions as Iran fails to comply with earlier resolutions.

Avoiding a veto often requires delicate diplomacy with the other permanent members, but sometimes, the pressure of the international community can be effective, as appeared to be the case in the Russian and Chinese abstentions from the resolution imposing a no-fly zone in Libya in 2011. While those nations did not really want to endorse UN action on general principles, they were reluctant to ignore the Arab League's call for action to protect civilians. (See the case study for this chapter for more details.)

Secretary-General. The S-G is the chief administrative officer of the UN, and he has the crucial power of initiative to raise issues before the UNSC and otherwise engage UN organizations. Forbidden to seek or receive instructions from member states, he can be the impartial facilitator of the peaceful resolution of disputes and the management of crises. He can be actively involved himself, or he can name special envoys or representatives to mediate particular conflicts or monitor certain issues. More than 60 people have been assigned to such tasks in recent years.[12]

The S-G has to work most closely with members of the UNSC and is beholden to them for his job. While the UNGA votes him into office, the UNSC must first approve the nomination on a vote subject to a P-5 veto. The United States has worked hard to see that friendly, or at least non-hostile, people are chosen for that position. In 1996, after clashing repeatedly with the S-G, Clinton administration officials worked openly to deny Boutros Boutros-Ghali a second term, replacing him with Kofi Annan.[13]

The United States conducts its UN operations through a special mission in New York, headed by an ambassador who, in many administrations, is given cabinet rank by the president. The American delegate has often been a controversial figure who has strongly criticized the organization to which he or she has been posted. Jeane Kirkpatrick, UN ambassador under President Reagan, once said, "What takes place in the Security Council more closely resembles a mugging than either a political debate or an effort at problem-solving." One of George W. Bush's nominees for the post, John Bolton, said, "If the U.N. building in New York lost 10 stories, it wouldn't make a bit of difference." Another indicator of controversy is that Bolton was never confirmed by the Senate and had to leave his post after 15 months.

One of his predecessors, Richard Holbrooke, faced a Senate delay of over a year before winning confirmation. Opposition to both men was partly in an assertion of senatorial power and partly in disagreement with the nominee's policy positions, but in both cases, the message received abroad was that filling the UN post was not that important.

Congress and the United Nations

Congress blows hot and cold toward the UN, usually hot with criticism and cold in terms of support. During the Cold War, members frequently criticized the UN as ineffective because it was often stymied by the U.S.–Soviet rivalry. Individual countries earned praise or blame on Capitol Hill on the basis of their voting percentage in agreement with the United States.

Starting in the 1980s, Congress began voting cuts in U.S. contributions to the UN in response to programs and activities it strongly disfavored, including actions that seemed to benefit the Palestine Liberal Organization (PLO) and the UNGA resolution equating Zionism with racism. A 1985 law required a 20% cut in U.S. contributions unless certain reforms were adopted. This measure seemed to work, and similar efforts were enacted in the 1990s to achieve additional reforms. Further reform-forcing bills and amendments were adopted in the mid-2000s, but they did not become law.

What was achieved was a reduction in the U.S. share of basic UN costs from 25% to 22% and a cut in the share of peacekeeping costs from about 30% to 27%. (By comparison, the top contributors to the regular UN budget in 2010 were: Japan, 16.6%; Germany, 8.6%; UK, 6.6%; France, 6.3%; Italy, 5.1%; Canada, 3.0%; Spain 3.0%; China, 2.7%; and Mexico, 2.3%.) Nevertheless, in dollar terms, the United States now pays more than $6 billion each year for the UN, and pressures are rising in Congress to cut U.S. contributions further. The major current costs include $1.2 billion in regularly assessed contributions, $450 million in voluntary contributions to specialized agencies like the UN Development Program and UNICEF, and $2.1 billion for peacekeeping. As of 2010, the UN calculated that the United States still owed $860 million in arrearages that accrued during the earlier congressionally mandated ceilings.

Less controversial, most of the time, are the activities of the UN's specialized agencies and programs. The World Food Program spends about $3 billion each year feeding the hungry in more than 80 nations. The Food and Agricultural Organization spends more than $900 million in technical assistance to fight hunger. The UN Children's Fund, UNICEF, spends about $2.4 billion in long-term humanitarian and development assistance for children and mothers. The High Commissioner for Refugees spends about $1.2 billion in relief and resettlement of more than 20 million people in 116 countries. The World Health Organization (WHO) has global vaccination campaigns and responses to pandemics and other health emergencies, spending more than $470 million. Many of these activities are partnered with charitable groups and NGOs. The UN also runs many other programs, some of a technical nature like the World Meteorological Organization and the Universal Postal Union, as well as programs on drug control, the environment, and prevention of HIV/AIDS. The World Bank and IMF are also legally part of the UN system.

In 2011, however, the UN's Educational, Scientific and Cultural Organization (UNESCO), which runs programs in literacy and science education and designates World Heritage Sites, admitted the Palestinian Authority to membership, triggering U.S. laws passed in the 1990s that required the United States to stop funding the organization. Prior to that action, UNESCO had an annual budget of $653 million and 1,955 regular personnel.

As these examples indicate, the UN and the S-G are important actors in international affairs that can affect U.S. decisions and actions. UNSC disagreements over Kosovo in 1999 led the United States to get NATO approval instead for the operations against Serbia. Similarly, UNSC divisions over sanctions on Iran have prevented the United States from achieving the breadth and severity of sanctions that America preferred. If the president chooses to work with or through the UN, the United States can gain valuable legitimacy for its policies. Its membership also requires the United States to engage with those who want to use the UN and its components against U.S. policies and interest. International organizations are a two-way street.

International Atomic Energy Agency

The IAEA is part of the UN system, though autonomous, and reports to the UNGA and the UNSC. Created in 1957 and headquartered in Vienna, it now has 151 member states, a staff of 2,300 people, and an annual budget of more than $450 million. Its original mandate was to promote safe, secure, and peaceful nuclear technologies, but it gained significant additional responsibilities under the 1968 Non-Proliferation Treaty (NPT) because that pact requires signatories to conclude comprehensive safeguard agreements with the IAEA. There are now 171 states with safeguard agreements.

Policing those agreements has put the IAEA at the center of international efforts to limit the spread of nuclear weapons. In 1991, with strong U.S. support, the UNSC tasked the IAEA with inspecting and dismantling suspected Iraqi nuclear programs. The UNSC adopted additional resolutions to force Iraqi compliance with IAEA inspections in 1993 and 1997. When Saddam Hussein refused further cooperation in 1998, inspectors were pulled out of the country.

In November 2002, after a UNSC resolution declaring Iraq in "material breach" of its obligations under various prior resolutions, UN and IAEA teams were again allowed back. When the teams reported lack of evidence of Iraqi weapons of mass destruction (WMD) in early March 2003, the United States insisted on the withdrawal of inspectors so that military operations could begin.

IAEA has also been a key player in international efforts to limit North Korea's nuclear capabilities. Pyongyang withdrew from membership in

1994 after a long dispute over IAEA inspections but reached an *agreed framework* with the United States allowing renewed inspections in return for fuel assistance and two light-water nuclear reactors. In 2002, after evidence emerged that North Korea had a secret uranium enrichment program that would have been in violation of its earlier agreements, the government dismantled the inspection devices and expelled the IAEA inspectors. They were allowed to return in July 2007 but left in April 2009 after North Korea decided to cease all cooperation with the IAEA.

When Iran began building its first nuclear reactor in 2002, the IAEA criticized Tehran and was allowed to send inspection teams. This was the start of a series of IAEA findings and UNSC resolutions that has continued for several years. Each time the IAEA found that Iran had failed to meet important obligations, the UNSC voted additional, tougher sanctions.

This history shows that the IAEA is an important tool for the United States and the international community to try to enforce and then verify compliance with nonproliferation promises. Once the agency gets engaged, it seems to act on professional and institutional bases without the need for diplomatic vote gathering.

Regional Institutions

There are many organizations with regional focuses and memberships that are important actors in international affairs. The European Union (EU), for example, is a supranational government with its own, albeit fledgling, institutions for diplomacy and foreign affairs. In this chapter, however, we consider only organizations of which the United States is a member and which, therefore, might be utilized as instruments of U.S. foreign policy.

North Atlantic Treaty Organization

The most robust and operational regional group is NATO. Formed in 1949 as a defensive military alliance against the Soviet bloc, NATO has grown in size to 28 nations and has deployed military forces both in Europe and beyond. It has a civilian secretariat, a military committee and staff, and even a parliamentary assembly that functions as a liaison to national legislatures and the broader public. The large 13,000-person staff is slated to be cut to 9,000 over the next few years. The current budget totals $2.2 billion annually, $1.8 billion for military activities and $390 million for the civil budget, of which the U.S. share is about 22%. These figures do not include the operational costs of deployed units.

The original membership of 12 was expanded in 1952 by the addition of Greece and Turkey, in 1955 by West Germany, and in 1982 by Spain. See the full list in Table 11.3. After the end of the Cold War, the alliance created a process for grooming former Warsaw Pact nations for membership. In 1999, the Czech Republic, Hungary, and Poland joined. Several more countries were added in 2004: Bulgaria, Estonia, Latvia, Lithuania, Romania, Slovakia, and Slovenia. Albania and Croatia joined in 2009, bringing the total to the current 28. Georgia and Ukraine are considered future members, pending resolution of various issues, and active negotiations are under way with Macedonia, Montenegro, and Bosnia–Herzegovina. On many foreign policy issues, the longtime members of NATO have different views from the newer members that were formerly part of the Soviet bloc.

During the Cold War, NATO organized and equipped itself for war with the Soviet Union and its allies. It developed institutions for consultation—the ambassadorial-level North Atlantic Council—and for military planning, with a military committee with representatives of member chiefs of staff, a defense planning committee, and a nuclear planning group. It developed programs for weapons standardization and logistics and created 11 command bases, now slated to be cut to 7.

Although some NATO members contributed troops to the conflicts in Korea and the 1991 Gulf War, the first NATO-authorized military operations were in the Balkans in the 1990s. Allied aircraft conducted operations in August through September 1995, which led to the Dayton peace talks and accords. NATO then contributed peacekeepers to the implementation force (IFOR) that became the stabilization force (SFOR), which lasted until 2005. The most recent major NATO military operation was in Libya in 2011, as described in the case study for this chapter. In each case, the United States joined with its allies and provided key capabilities, but NATO involvement allowed burden sharing of the costs and risks of the operation.

The North Atlantic Council, the senior decision body composed of ambassadors from the member nations, decides matters largely by consensus. No formal votes are taken. Instead of requiring formal unanimity, however, an objecting nation must file a formal notice of opposition. Because the pressure for agreement can be high, as it was when missions were launched in Kosovo in 1999, some countries preferred to abstain rather than become obstructionists.

When the UNSC was unable to agree on measures to halt Serbian repression of ethnic Albanians in Kosovo in 1999, the United States pressed for, and NATO agreed to take action in, what became a 78-day air campaign. U.S. forces delivered more than 80% of the weapons used in the attacks. NATO troops then formed the UNSC-blessed Kosovo Force (KFOR), which remained in place as of 2011. KFOR units also deployed to Albania during 2001–2003, when they were succeeded by the EU force.

On September 12, 2001, the North Atlantic Council, for the first time in NATO's history, formally invoked Article 5 of the 1949 Washington Treaty, which declared that "an armed attack against one" member "shall be considered an attack against them all." Despite that show of solidarity, the U.S. government consciously decided to bypass NATO in forming its coalition to fight in Afghanistan.[14] Nevertheless, several NATO members participated in the U.S.-led Operation Enduring Freedom in Afghanistan and then in the UN-mandated International Security Assistance Force (ISAF) created in December 2001 and likely to remain in Afghanistan at least until 2014.

In 2011, NATO members accounted for about 90% of the non-U.S. military personnel in ISAF.

While NATO members were sharply divided over the 2003 U.S.-led Iraq war, NATO agreed in 2004 to operate a training mission in Iraq. The numbers involved were small—only 170 troops in 2011—but there has been broad symbolic support and participation by 23 member nations.

As further evidence of the alliance's willingness to conduct out-of-area operations, NATO forces gave support to the African Union's mission in Sudan during 2005–2007 and in Somalia in 2007. Since 2008, NATO has also conducted antipiracy operations in the Gulf of Aden. These operations, strongly supported by the United States, allowed others to shoulder the burden while U.S. forces remained committed in large numbers in Iraq and Afghanistan.

In 2011, NATO undertook to conduct military operations in support of the UNSC resolution calling for the protection of civilians in rebellious Libya. NATO aircraft imposed a no-fly zone, and ships enforced an arms embargo. Between March 19 and October 31, NATO aircraft conducted more than 26,500 sorties, of which 9,700 were strike sorties. After taking the lead in the initial weeks, the United States deliberately switched to a supporting role. In the end, only 25% of the air sorties were flown by U.S. aircraft.

In 2003, the alliance formally decided to create a NATO Response Force (NRF) so that it would have some readily deployable units to contribute to international coalitions. The plan is to have an immediate response force of about 13,000 that could grow to as much as 25,000 in a short period. The NRF, composed of units assigned on rotation, took shape over the following years and was used for humanitarian relief after a major earthquake in Pakistan in 2005 and even after Hurricane Katrina in the United States in 2005.

Some Europeans see the NRF as a means of having a military force separate from the United States, while many U.S. analysts see it as a welcome addition to NATO's usable capabilities.

NATO faces several political challenges as well as the practical military one of maintaining ready and modernized forces at a time of severe governmental austerity throughout the alliance. While formally open to membership for all European democracies, Russia is still strongly opposed to NATO expansion. While concerned about nuclear proliferation, terrorism, cyber attacks, and instability outside Europe, alliance members often disagree among themselves or with the United States on how to proceed. Nevertheless, NATO remains a strong institution, a ready forum for consultations and decision with a diverse set of military and diplomatic instruments.

Organization for Security and Co-operation in Europe

Larger in membership than NATO but more limited in institutional capacity is the OSCE. Of its 56 members, the United States is the only non-European nation, but OSCE has partnership arrangements with Japan,

South Korea, and Australia as well as with Israel and some North African nations. It has an annual budget of about $215 million, derived from voluntary contributions by members, and a staff of 2,900, most of whom are assigned to one of 18 field missions in Central Asia and the nations of the former Yugoslavia.

The organization began as the forum for promulgating the Helsinki Final Act in 1975, which codified post-World War II European borders but also endorsed civil rights, leading to the growth of dissident groups in the Soviet Union. The organization continued as the Conference for Security and Cooperation in Europe until renamed and given permanent institutional status in 1995. It served as a useful venue for East–West dialogue during the Cold War, and has since undertaken programs to help many former Soviet bloc nations develop national capacities to manage their borders, regulate the transfer of weapons, and promote media freedom and other aspects of good governance. It is one of the leading organizations in providing international election observers.

These numerous activities make OSCE a good vehicle for outsourcing some nation-building tasks that the host nations request as well as a forum for multinational dialogue of issues that directly involve members. Some nations apparently hoped that OSCE would become the hub of security cooperation in Europe, especially because it was more inclusive in membership, but in recent years, Russia has complained that the organization was too much dominated by the United States and NATO.[15] The United States uses OSCE mechanisms to oversee several arms control agreements involving Europe and to engage in its weekly *security dialogue* on regional issues.

Organization of American States

The OAS is the world's oldest continuous regional organization that serves as a forum for hemispheric dialogue and an institution to resolve conflicts among members and promote democratic practices. Begun in 1889–1890, then reorganized as the Pan American Union in 1914, the OAS charter of 1948 created the modern institution. It has 35 members, a staff of nearly 700, and an annual core budget of about $90 million that does not include voluntary contributions to particular programs and activities. The U.S. share is around 59%. The OAS operates under a secretary-general, has a permanent council and an annual general assembly, and is the vehicle for annual Summits of the Americas since 1995.

The organization suspended Cuba and imposed sanctions in 1962 but, in 2009, lifted the suspension and opened a dialogue with Havana that is aimed at returning Cuba to the group if it meets certain conditions. The United States has regularly tried to use the OAS as a tool for hemisphere-wide pressure on the Castro regime but has also felt counterpressure to be more flexible.

There is an inter-American defense pact—the Rio Treaty of 1947—that contains language similar to NATO, declaring an attack on one to be an attack on all, but the OAS has never developed military institutions to buttress that treaty. Instead, as part of its work, the OAS has been a forum for hemispheric dialogue and for trying to resolve conflicts among members. It regularly sends missions of election observers throughout the hemisphere as part of efforts to promote democratic practices. Under a 1992 amendment to the OAS charter, members can be suspended if their democratically elected governments are overthrown by force. This provision was broadened in 2001 and has led to a series of high-level missions, conflict resolution actions, multilateral diplomacy, and sanctions in several countries. In 2009, for example, the OAS, with strong U.S. support, condemned the ouster of the Honduran president and arranged mediation leading to free elections of a successor.

While the OAS has been involved in various border disputes and the defense of democracy against coups, it has a mixed record and has often been bypassed in favor of subregional ad hoc groups.[16] While other members were divided over U.S. anticommunist policies in the 1980s, with many unwilling to support actions against the leftist government in Nicaragua, they have found more common ground in recent years in counterdrug activities as well as acting against coups.

For military consultation and coordination on counterdrug and humanitarian missions, the United States uses the Southern Command (SOUTHCOM), headquartered in Florida. It is one of the regional military commands and works closely with the military in countries of the Western hemisphere.

Association of Southeast Asian Nations, the Association of Southeast Asian Nations Regional Forum, and Asia–Pacific Economic Cooperation

Asia has several regional organizations, two of which have the United States as a member and which range in size from 10 members to 27. See Table 11.3 for a list of the different organizations. What they share are limitations in size, focus, and institutional capacity. As Margaret Karns and Karen Mingst say, "Asian and Asia-Pacific regional institutions tend to be informal, having few specific rules, no binding commitments, small secretariats, consensus decisionmaking, and a strong emphasis on process over substance and outcomes. Informal processes include extensive meetings, consultations, and dialogues; informal outcomes typically refer to agreements on general principles and nonbinding codes of conduct."[17]

The oldest of these regional Asian organizations is ASEAN, established in 1967 and limited to nations of the region. In 1994, ASEAN created ARF to consider security questions with a much broader membership, including the United States, the EU, Japan, China, Russia, India, and others. ARF seeks to promote dialogue on issues like maritime security, confidence-building measures such as notification of military exercises, illegal migrations, and terrorist financing.[18]

APEC has economies rather than states as members and includes most of the nations on the rim of the Pacific Ocean. Created in 1989, it has gained visibility and utility because of annual summits and regular meetings of member foreign and trade ministers. The United States has used the

Table 11.3 — Membership of Asian Regional Organizations

ASEAN	ARF (ASEAN members +)	APEC (ASEAN members +)
Brunei	Australia	Australia
Cambodia	Bangladesh	Canada
Indonesia	Canada	Chile
Laos	China	China
Malaysia	European Union	Hong Kong
Myanmar	India	Japan
Philippines	Japan	Korea
Singapore	N. Korea	Mexico
Thailand	S. Korea	New Zealand
Vietnam	Mongolia	Papua New Guinea
	New Zealand	Peru
	Pakistan	Russia
	Papua New Guinea	Taiwan
	Russia	United States
	Sri Lanka	
	Timor Leste	
	United States	

There are many overlapping regional organizations in Asia, each providing a forum for collaboration or conflict and thus allowing members some choices for venue shopping when they wish to raise issues. As is shown here, membership is not restricted just to those nations geographically in Asia. For instance, Canada, the EU, and the United States are members of ARF.

summits for dialogue on foreign economic issues, and APEC itself has been a venue for cooperation on contagious diseases and climate change.[19]

The organizations are used, as the members see fit, as forums for regional engagement. The United States has used APEC in particular to push trade and economic cooperation, and it serves as an annual gathering at which to raise current economic and political issues. Insofar as U.S. policy pivots toward Asia and faces rising powers like China, these Asian organizations become important stages where the United States can build support for its policies.

Economic Institutions

The United States worked to establish the postwar global economic system after 1945 and remains a key player in its many institutions. While each has its own mandate, membership, rules, and goals, the United States has used its memberships to pursue its national policies and its vision of a world economic order. Instead of trying on its own to manage the global economy, it relies on the IMF to promote economic stability, on the World Bank and similar regional banks to promote long-term development, and on the WTO to enforce trading rules and agreements.

G-8 and G-20

As the global economy entered a series of crises beginning in 2007–2008 and continuing to the present, the United States and other economic powers have made increasing use of groups originally set up just to provide periodic consultations. Regular meetings of the finance ministers and heads of the central banks of the major economic powers began in the 1970s as the Group of Six—France, Germany, Italy, Japan, the United Kingdom, and the United States. In 1975, France formalized the G-6 and hosted a summit of heads of government, a practice that has continued ever since. In 1976, Canada was added to make the G-7, and in 1997—for political more than economic reasons—Russia was invited to be part of the G-8. Together, the member nations account for about 14% of the world's population and 60% of the gross global product.

Now, in addition to the annual summits, there are regular meetings of foreign ministers, finance ministers, and environment ministers. The agenda each year is set by the host government, whose leader heads the G-8 in rotation. There is no permanent secretariat.

As the 2008 financial crisis hit in the United States and began spreading worldwide, President George W. Bush convened a summit in Washington, D.C., of a larger group, now called the G-20. See Table 11.4 for the membership of each group. In addition to the G-8, the G-20 has ten other members, including Argentina, Australia, Brazil, China, India, Indonesia, Mexico, Saudi Arabia, South Africa, South Korea, Turkey, and the EU. Together, those nations and the EU account for 85% of gross global product. But, the organization still has no permanent staff or structure.

The Washington summit created a venue for international cooperation on major financial matters, and at the London summit in April 2009, the leaders committed to add $1.1 trillion for the IMF, the multilateral development banks, and other organizations. At the third summit, in Pittsburgh in September 2009, the G-20 leaders formally declared their organization the premier international economic forum. Spain and the Netherlands have also been allowed to sit in, though they are not yet formal members.

The G-20 held twice-yearly summit meetings through 2010 and one in 2011. These have been supplemented by meetings of finance ministers. The agendas so far have been largely confined to major financial issues like IMF reform, financial regulation, and trade. Meanwhile, the G-8 meetings continue, and the national leaders have added more noneconomic topics to the agenda, like climate change, aid to Africa, and some security issues like piracy and nonproliferation. If this division of focus continues, the United States has two additional forums in which to raise its own foreign policy issues. The value of regular meetings and institutional organizations is that

Table 11.4	G-8 and G-20 Members with 2010 Gross Domestic Product in Billions
G-8 MEMBERS	**G-20 MEMBERS (G-8 MEMBERS +)**
Canada, $1,577	Argentina, $369
France, 2,560	Australia, 924
Germany, 3,280	Brazil, 2,088
Italy, 2,051	China, 5,927
Japan, 5,459	EU*, 16,220
Russia, 1,480	India, 1,727
United Kingdom, 2,249	Indonesia, 707
United States, 14,587	Mexico, 1,035
	Saudi Arabia, 435
	South Africa, 364
	South Korea, 1,014
	Turkey, 734

* The EU includes G-8 members France, Germany, Italy, and the United Kingdom. The EU gross domestic product (GDP) figure reflects their inclusion. EU GDP minus those states is $6,080 billion.

The original grouping of major economic powers has been expanded in recent years in recognition of the growing economic strength of the additional nations and in order to craft more broadly based economic policies.

Source: GDP figures from the World Bank, Gross Domestic Product 2010, http://databank.worldbank.org/databank/download/GDP.pdf.

they allow for advance planning and consultation so that agreements might be achieved. Ad hoc meetings are usually less effective. A scheduled meeting is also action forcing on governments and their bureaucracies to decide on policies and priorities.

The International Monetary Fund and Other International Financial Institutions

The IMF and the World Bank were established at the end of World War II to provide a stable monetary system and to finance reconstruction and development, first in Europe and later across the globe. Both make use of financial contributions by members and turn a profit from their operations. Members have voting power proportionate to their contributions—the U.S. leads at about 17%—and votes on major issues require supermajority support of 70% or in some cases 85%.

The IMF has a staff of about 2,650 people and an annual operating budget around $740 million. Most nations are members—186 in all. The IMF performs three main tasks: surveillance of the economic and financial policies of nations and dialogue with them; financial assistance such as lines of credit, currency purchases, and loans; and technical assistance to improve their local financial systems. The IMF helps countries with problems on the basis of conditionality, linking the assistance to acceptance and performance of specific policy actions.[20]

The World Bank, including the subsidiary institutions of the International Finance Corporation and the International Development Association, lends money to development projects—and expects payback. It has a staff of about 10,000 people. Both the IMF and the bank employ many professional economists and have strong organizational cultures described as "apolitical, technocratic, and economic rationality."[21]

Both institutions have come under criticism in recent years—the IMF, for perpetuating the *Washington consensus* (so-called because the two organizations were headquartered in the U.S. capital and their economists were of one mind) requiring loan recipients to impose severe domestic austerity with few deviations from the template, and the bank, for approving loans on narrow criteria with insufficient consideration of social and environmental effects.[22] Both are adopting various reforms in response to these and other criticisms.

In addition to the World Bank, in order to represent its interests, the United States belongs to several regional development banks: the Inter-American Development Bank, the Asian Development Bank, the African Development Bank, and the European Bank for Reconstruction and Development. The Treasury Department represents the U.S. government and votes the U.S. shares in each institution.

The United States has used these institutions for its own foreign policy goals in addition to the specific economic objectives of the banks and the IMF. Scholars have found significant correlations between a country's support for U.S. policies and approval of IMF help, whether or not the United States acted consciously to those ends. For example, analysts point to IMF's support for friendly Zaire (now the Democratic Republic of Congo) during the Cold War; generous help to Egypt; and very favorable conditions on help to Pakistan soon after the 9/11 attacks. Other studies show that countries that voted less often with the United States in the UN received IMF loans less often and that the punishment period for nations falling into noncompliance with the IMF was shorter for U.S.-favored ones. Moreover, U.S. allies tended to receive IMF support with fewer conditions attached.[23]

These studies demonstrate that the United States can—and probably does—use these international financial institutions as an important tool of foreign policy. The mechanisms may be less overt, but their outcomes are visible.

During the global economic crisis of 2008–2009, IFIs were surprisingly responsive and flexible. Pushed by decisions at the G-20 leaders meetings, they mobilized an additional $1.1 trillion in resources to help troubled economies and to buttress trade finance. The IMF provided timely advice and lending commitments of more than $170 billion in the early months and then, urged by the United States, agreed to expand its borrowing pool by up to $500 billion. The multilateral development banks launched a fast-track facility to expedite loans to the poorest countries and, at a time when few institutions were lending, provided $222 billion in financing.[24]

World Trade Organization

The WTO was established in 1995 to replace the less-structured system of the General Agreement on Tariffs and Trade (GATT) that had been created after World War II. One of the main features of WTO is its Disputes Settlement Body (DSB) that supervises consultations between disputing members and establishes panels to hear disputes and issue reports. Findings by those panels are automatically accepted unless vetoed by all WTO members. When the DSB makes a ruling in favor of the complainant, the responding nation has a period of time to come into compliance, usually by repealing or modifying the law, rule, or policy that was found to be in violation. Delays can trigger punitive tariffs.

As this process indicates, WTO is less of an executive body than a legislative and judicial one. It makes rules to enforce the principle of non-discrimination under various international agreements, and it adjudicates complaints of violations of those rules. It has a secretariat staff of about 600 people and a budget just over $200 million. The U.S. contribution is about 13%. Voting is by unanimity, including the admission of new members beyond the current 153. With Russia and Iran as the most economically significant countries still awaiting approval for membership, WTO members account for 91% of the world's population, 98% of the global GDP, and 96% of world trade.[25]

As discussed in Chapter 7, the United States has several trade remedies including use of the WTO when U.S. firms or workers are harmed by foreign practices, notably enforcement of antidumping and countervailing duty laws, as well as by providing trade adjustment assistance to affected parties. The United States can also raise disputes in the WTO system, though that is a costly and lengthy procedure. As only member states can bring cases, whether or not to raise a dispute for WTO consideration is a significant political choice for a country like the United States, which has numerous political and economic issues with any major trading partner.

According to a 2009 report by the U.S. trade representative (USTR), the United States has won most of the cases it brought before WTO. On the other hand, it has lost a little over half the cases where others complained about U.S. practices. These figures probably reflect the fact that cases are not brought unless the complainant has a strong case and lots of evidence. Of the 90 or so cases where the United States brought the complaint, the U.S. prevailed on the core issue 35% of the time and did not prevail in 4% of the cases. Another 30% of the cases were resolved to U.S. satisfaction without completing the litigation process, and the remaining 30% were ongoing or inactive. In 128 complaints against the United States, the U.S. prevailed only 12.5% of the time, and lost 29%. Another 15% of the cases were resolved to U.S. satisfaction before formal findings. Almost half (44%) were in progress or inactive at the time of the report.[26]

This record suggests that the United States benefits from this professional legal process even if the results sometimes anger lawmakers whose protectionist measures are ruled illegal. Nevertheless, there remains strong domestic political opposition to a more liberalized trading system and to procedures like fast-track or Trade Promotion Authority (TPA) to negotiate free trade agreements (FTAs). The WTO process is nonpolitical at a time when political forces in many nations want to be able to prevail.

Presidents have the freedom to choose to bring WTO cases, but outside observers have detected a recurring practice going back to the days of GATT. Jeffrey Dunoff says there is a "historic American pattern of initiating new disputes when the country is facing negative trade balances, rising protectionist voices at home, or when an administration is about to seek new trade negotiation authority from the Congress."[27] In other words, raising trade disputes can serve domestic political ends as well as economic goals.

International Courts

There are now about 18 permanent international courts and tribunals, some highly specialized on matters like trade law and human rights, others dealing with general questions of international law. In recent years, in fact, observers have noticed an increasing *judicialization* of international relations.[28] The United States is a member of only some of these bodies and has actively opposed many of the operations of at least one, the International Criminal Court, because of concerns that U.S. military personnel and policy makers might be unfairly subjected to prosecution. Nevertheless, international tribunals are in the toolkit of the United States and other nations to be used when they choose.

Throughout its history, the United States has often created or made use of judicial instruments for the settlement of disputes and claims. The 1794 Jay Treaty with Great Britain, for example, created two commissions that heard claims on ship seizures and colonial era debts. In recent decades, the American government worked actively to create three significant tribunals in order to achieve specific foreign policy goals. One was the Iran–United States Claims Tribunal that paid compensation in numerous cases and functioned despite the continuing break in diplomatic relations between Washington and Tehran. Second was the series of mechanisms created under U.S. pressure to compensate victims of the Holocaust. Third was the UN Compensation Commission set up after the 1991 Gulf War. When it completed its work in 2007, it had paid out about $22 billion in compensation.[29]

As part of the UN system, the United States supported the creation of the International Court of Justice (ICJ) as successor to the League of Nations Permanent Court of International Justice (PCIJ), which the United States had held at arm's length, never ratifying its charter. In joining the ICJ, the U.S. Senate insisted on the Connally Reservation denying jurisdiction to disputes "which are essentially within the domestic jurisdiction of the United States of America as determined by the United States of America."[30]

The United States used the ICJ actively in its early decades then treated it as inconsequential. The United States withdrew from participation after losing a bitterly contested case over Nicaragua in 1986 and wound up on the defensive against cases brought by others in more recent years. Interestingly, the Connally Reservation proved to be a double-edged weapon because the court allowed its applicability to nations the U.S. tried to bring into the dock. Despite some adverse rulings—in cases involving Nicaragua, Libya, Yugoslavia, and Iran—analysts conclude that the ICJ cases have had little or no practical effect on U.S. foreign policy.[31]

America's mixed record in the ICJ does constrain risk-averse political leaders. They recognize that public opinion surveys show majority and sometimes strong majority support for the use of international tribunals, even for U.S. participation in the International Criminal Court (ICC).[32] But, they also recognize the public resonance with notions of American exceptionalism and protection of sovereignty.

The Clinton administration negotiated the ICC treaty and then formally signed on to the pact but declared that it would not seek ratification without further changes. There was sharp division among Clinton's advisers, with opposition in particular from the Joint Chiefs of Staff (JCS) and the Defense Department (DOD). The Bush administration went further and withdrew from signature, thereby freeing it legally from obligations not to undercut its provisions. In 2002, Congress went on to enact the American Servicemembers' Protection Act, which limits U.S. participation in peacekeeping missions unless U.S. personnel are exempt from ICC prosecution and which cuts off certain economic aid to nations that fail to conclude exemption agreements with the United States.[33]

U.S. policy in recent years has become more pragmatic regarding the various criminal courts, including the ICC. Officials say they decide on participation on a case-by-case basis. As Professor John P. Cerone concludes, "The United States has tended to support international criminal courts when the U.S. government has (or is perceived by U.S. officials to have) a significant degree of control over the court or when the possibility of prosecution of U.S. nationals is either expressly precluded or otherwise remote."[34]

Pragmatism has its benefits and its limitations. Avoiding the international courts means the United States cannot help shape their jurisprudence. On the other hand, limiting U.S. involvement helps deal with the problem cited by Professor Cesare Romano: "[N]ot only are international courts just one tool among many, but they are also second best to most. They are unwieldy instruments, difficult to steer and control. If they rule in favor of the United States, their main problem is that they lack their own enforcement powers. If they do have bite, then they are dangerous because they might be used by another state against the United States."[35]

Major Nonstate Actors

There are many international organizations that are privately organized yet very active in influencing the policies of governments. Further consideration of some of them can be found in Chapter 12 on nongovernmental actors and interest groups. For our purposes here, it is sufficient just to note that these include: multinational corporations (MNCs); foundations; NGOs like the International Committee of the Red Cross and various human rights and environmental groups; and transnational networks and coalitions like the ones that deal with land mines. These groups research and publicize issues, participate in global conferences, and mobilize support for their views. They can be allies or adversaries of national governments, and that's how they will be treated in return.[36]

***

To some extent, IOs can be influenced more by the effects of American *soft power* than by direct actions of U.S. officials. When the United States is widely admired and its policies broadly supported, it is easier for IO leaders to work with Washington. When America falls into international disfavor, however, even routine cooperation can be contentious. However much the U.S. president may want to outsource an issue to an IO, his ability to do so depends crucially on the international political context at the time.

It also helps to have a permanent U.S. presence at the institution, as has long been the case with regard to UN and European institutions and the OAS, but only in 2009 did America assign a resident ambassador to the African Union and ASEAN. Having such representation can help the president better choose whether and when to try to use the organization as an instrument for U.S. policies.

Congress is also a necessary partner in any outreach to IOs. Yet, Congress historically has resisted measures that seemed to risk a loss of domestic sovereignty—hence the Connally Reservation and frequent criticism of the UN. Lawmakers hate to see America outvoted or otherwise embarrassed in international assemblies and hate even more to pay for the privilege of losing in public. Even if U.S. officials weigh the use of IOs on a case-by-case basis, Congress is asked to appropriate money for U.S. contributions to keep the groups in operation. That leads to permanent tension and occasional retribution, as in the case of UNESCO in 2011.

To use international institutions as a policy tool, presidents need to persuade Congress as well as foreign governments of the value of such actions.

Case Study: Using North Atlantic Treaty Organization as an Instrument of Foreign Policy in Libya, 2011

In February 2011, President Obama made a conscious decision to try to use NATO as a tool of U.S. foreign policy in order to avoid a more direct American combat role in the uprising in Libya. What some called *leading from behind* was also *burden sharing* of costs and risks.

When protests erupted in Libya in mid-February, the Obama administration faced difficult choices. For the previous decade, U.S. policy had been to engage with the regime of longtime leader Muammar Qaddafi, using more carrots than sticks. In 2003, Qaddafi had agreed to dismantle his nuclear weapons and long-range missile programs in return for the lifting of sanctions and diplomatic recognition, thus allowing Western trade and investment. When Qaddafi ordered his troops to fire on protestors and threatened further bloody retaliation, many U.S. officials doubted that he would be toppled, as had just happened to aging leaders in Tunisia and Egypt.

Just in case, Obama ordered the U.S. military to develop some possible options for action. Meanwhile, the State Department arranged for the evacuation of Americans by sea and air, and the Pentagon began moving some warships closer to Libyan waters. But, the president did not really want to launch a third U.S. war against a Muslim nation, especially not when U.S. forces were still heavily committed in Iraq and Afghanistan and the chances of a quick and easy overthrow of Qaddafi seemed remote.

With French President Nicolas Sarkozy and British Prime Minister David Cameron pressing for military action, Obama agreed only to impose economic sanctions. On February 25, within minutes of the evacuation of the last Americans, the president signed an executive order freezing more than $30 billion in Libyan assets held in U.S. banks and imposing sanctions on top-ranking Libyan officials. American and European leaders, after a flurry of conversations, agreed to a UNSC Resolution 1970, adopted unanimously on February 26. That resolution imposed an arms embargo on Libya but did not authorize the use of force.

The most widely discussed military option being considered by the diplomats was a no-fly zone to prevent Qaddafi from attacking opposition forces and civilians from the air. Defense Secretary Gates warned that it would require a major military effort, including suppression of Libyan air defenses, and would probably not, by itself, lead to Qaddafi's overthrow. Secretary of State Clinton was also initially reluctant to support U.S. military action.

Drawing on the other instruments in his foreign policy toolkit, Obama ordered diplomatic efforts to meet key conditions prior to American use of force: strong support from Arab nations, authorization by the UNSC, NATO management of the military operation, and no involvement of U.S. ground troops. Surprisingly, deft diplomacy by Obama, Clinton, and others led to fulfillment of those conditions by mid-March.

On March 7, the Gulf Cooperation Council called for a no-fly zone and demanded that the UN take *all necessary measures* to protect Libyan civilians. That is the phrase historically used by the UN to authorize member states to use force. On March 12, the Arab League, a regional institution, announced support for UN action imposing a no-fly zone and creating safe havens for civilians. Two days later, Secretary Clinton obtained commitments from Qatar and the United Arab Emirates (UAE) to provide warplanes for operations over Libya.

On March 15, the president held a National Security Council (NSC) meeting to review policy options. Intelligence reports suggested that a loyalist attack on Benghazi would succeed and might be followed by a massacre of civilians. There was a consensus that a no-fly zone would be insufficient to prevent widespread slaughter. Obama ordered more robust military options and directed his UN ambassador to seek a new UNSC resolution allowing all necessary measures.

On March 17, after frantic diplomacy to convince Russia and China not to veto and other members to support tough action, the UNSC approved Resolution 1973 allowing force to protect Libyan civilians, imposing a no-fly zone, and freezing of Libyan assets. The measure specifically prohibited, however, any foreign occupation force in Libyan territory.

On March 19, French aircraft launched the first attacks on Libyan forces moving toward Benghazi, and the United States attacked Libyan air defenses and air force in what was called Operation Odyssey Dawn. U.S. officials said that the attacks would last "a matter of days, not weeks" and that operational control would soon be turned over to NATO.

In fact, NATO was involved in military activities from the very start of the Libyan uprising. NATO ministers had agreed on February 25 to deploy its airborne warning and control system (AWACS) aircraft to monitor Libya. Obama and Clinton, as well as other foreign leaders, consulted back and forth throughout March, gradually developing the concept for a NATO-led operation. The difficulty was that NATO operated by unanimity, and several members, notably Germany, were reluctant to support the use of force against the Qaddafi regime. On March 22, NATO ministers agreed to take over only the maritime arms embargo. After the Turkish parliament approved participation in the no-fly zone and arms embargo on March 24, Germany agreed to approve the mission but not participate. Final NATO agreement to take over the military operation was secured on March 28. On March 29, the much larger Libyan Contact Group was established for diplomatic coordination. It included 21 nations from Europe and the Middle East plus several IOs.

On March 31, Operation Unified Protector began under NATO command. U.S. units retreated to primarily support roles: electronic warfare, aerial refueling, logistical support, search and rescue, and intelligence, surveillance, and reconnaissance. American ground attack aircraft were put on a standby basis in Italy. Gradually, the air attacks degraded Qaddafi's forces and the noose tightened. Tripoli fell to rebel forces on August 20. Qaddafi's final defeat and death came on October 20. At that point, NATO voted to end its operations on October 31.

The U.S. Congress was divided over the Libya operation and failed to take a firm or consistent position. The Senate, on March 1, had approved a resolution supporting the idea of a no-fly zone and call for a transition to a democratic government. A subsequent measure supporting U.S. military action was sidetracked by filibuster threats. In June and July, the House defeated measures cutting off funds for the operation but did approve a resolution demanding answers to questions about U.S. policy and later approved a ban on aiding Libyan rebels. Members preferred complaining about Obama's circumvention of the War Powers Act rather than voting for or against the policy.

Over the seven months of Operation Unified Protector, NATO and affiliated aircraft from Sweden, Jordan, Qatar, and UAE conducted more than 26,500 sorties, including more than 9,700 strike sorties against Qaddafi's forces and in defense of civilians. U.S. aircraft conducted only 25% of the sorties. Costs to the United States totaled $1.1 billion.

President Obama achieved his explicit and implicit goals by letting NATO lead the operation against Qaddafi. He avoided the diplomatic and military costs and risks of a U.S.-dominated operation and built instead an international force that not only protected Libyan civilians but also allowed the opposition forces to oust Qaddafi. He used an IO as an instrument of American foreign policy in an ultimately successful operation.

Sources: The New York Times; Anthony Bell and David Witter, "The Libyan Revolution: Part 2, Escalation & Intervention," Institute for the Study of War, September 2011, accessible at www.understandingwar.org/report/libyan-revolution-part-2-escalation-intervention.

Selected Resources

Each of the major IOs has its own website.

APEC, www.aseansec.org/

ASEAN, www.aseansec.org/

G-8, www.g8.utoronto.ca/

G-20, www.g20.0rg/

IAEA, www.iaea.org/

ICJ, www.icj-cij.org/

ICC, www.icc-cpi.int/Menus/ICC/Home

IMF, www.imf.org

NATO, www.nato.int

OSCE, www.osce.org

OAS, www.oas.org

UN, www.un.org

WTO, www.wto.org

In addition, the American Society of International Law has numerous links and background materials, such as at www.asil.org/erg/?page=io, as do think tanks like the Council on Foreign Relations at https://secure.www.cfr.org/issue/international-organizations/ri37.

12 Elephants in the Workshop

> *Presidents sometimes lead, sometimes follow, and sometimes ignore the American public. In a sense, then, the American people loosely hold the reins of U.S. foreign policy, periodically giving them a tug but all too often just going along for the ride.*
>
> —Professor Thomas Knecht[1]

> *All [presidential assistants interviewed] agree the national media play a very significant role in the White House decision-making process, A few respondents reported that in White House meetings, on the whole, more time is spent discussing the media than any other institution, including Congress, and that all policies are developed and presented with the media reaction in mind."*
>
> —White House Bulletin (a nongovernmental news publication)[2]

> *When we refer to interest groups as "stakeholders," they are legitimate; when we refer to the same people as "lobbyists," they grow horns.*
>
> —former Senate and White House aide Patrick Griffin[3]

The president and other policy makers are never really alone. In the workshop where they craft American foreign policy, they are constantly aware of several *elephants*—looming presences that influence what they think and do and the foreign policy instruments they choose and use. One powerful presence is public opinion, sometimes clear, sometimes confused, often changing, but too large and potentially powerful to be ignored. Another is the gaggle of things called the news media, often shouting and pointing at situations that require presidential responses. A third looming presence is what we call advocacy groups, pleaders for policies that fit their particular interests, whether those interests are financial or emotional.

Each of these external sources of influence on policy makers interacts with the others. (See Table 12.1.) The media affect what the public thinks; advocates try to persuade both the media and public opinion of the value of their views. Policy makers feel they have to find ways of fashioning their policies in ways that are sensitive and responsive to these outside pressures, and they in turn try to persuade the public, the media, and advocates of the wisdom of their choices.

Table 12.1 External Influences on Uses of the Toolkit

EXTERNAL INFLUENCES	MEANS OF INFLUENCE	LIMITATIONS
Public opinion	Strongest with high salience and broad consensus; more constraint than action forcing; warning of anticipated reactions; validation of decisions; significant on use of force	Distinguishes crises and noncrises; distinguishes elite, attentive, and mass publics; much mass ignorance; pretty prudent on basic choices; target for persuasion by others
Media	Participant–observer in process; can draw attention, frame issues, accelerate or impede decisions, affect public opinion; interagency cues; object of manipulation (leaks); tend to support US policies and frames	Cutbacks in coverage; proliferation of sources; competitive framing
Advocacy groups	Target public opinion, media, policy makers; policy makers seek allies	Status quo usually prevails; change faces multiple veto points
Stakeholders	Economic pressure; try to influence public opinion and media	Countervailing competitors; change harder than obstruction
Ethnic and identity/affinity groups	Moral pressure; personal contact	Sometimes outweighed by "national interest"; groups often small in size and narrow in focus
Lobbyists	Direct contact and public relations	Detailed legal requirements and limits
Contributors/fund-raisers	Campaign contributions	Legal limits (in flux)
Think tanks	Develop and publicize ideas; often connected to advocacy groups	Ideas need influential advocates

Many of the external influences on U.S. foreign policy come from determined advocates, deliberately seeking to persuade or pressure the president and Congress to act in certain ways. Public opinion and the media, however, are targets for both government officials and those advocates, all of whom fight to gain attention and support.

Public Opinion

While democratic theory might prefer that foreign policy reflect public opinion, history shows a much more complicated pattern. As Thomas Knecht concluded, as quoted above, presidents sometimes lead, sometimes follow, and sometimes ignore public opinion. Scholars have developed various models for how and when public opinion makes a difference.

Politicians routinely claim that they ignore public opinion surveys when making tough decisions, especially on foreign policy, but all the evidence since Gallup began polling in 1935 is that presidents and their administrations want to know what the people think. Sometimes, the White House would commission its own polls, but now with a proliferation of pollsters and newer, less-expensive technologies to conduct them, we all can get instant readings on policy questions.

Presidents seem to be most sensitive to public opinion when an issue has *high salience*—the public is aware of the matter and thinks it important—and there is a broad consensus on how to respond.[4] Those, of course, are the easy cases: an attack on Americans, fight back; earthquake in Haiti, send relief. Presidents have more latitude in crafting policy responses when the public isn't caught up in the issue—what should America do about the conflict in Yemen or Greek debt—or when the public is sharply divided over policy options—do or do not sign a free trade agreement (FTA) with South Korea.

Presidents also have more freedom of action in crisis situations, where prompt action is required and they then can persuade the public to support it.[5] There are some constraints on presidential choice in crises, however, based on what policy makers think the public might support. In fact, anticipated public reactions seem to be the most potent influence public opinion has.[6] When President Clinton ruled out the use of U.S. ground troops in Kosovo and President Obama did the same regarding Libya, both seemed to view public opposition to ground combat as a major constraint on U.S. actions. The power of anticipated public reactions is strongest, of course, when a president thinks about his reelection prospects, especially in the second half of a first term.[7] Overall, public opinion seems to be stronger in setting limits on presidential choices than in forcing action on reluctant officials.

The Elite, Attentive, and Mass Publics

Policy makers are keenly aware of different segments of the population when factoring considerations of public opinion—the elite 1% of government and business leaders and interest groups, the attentive public of 15%, and the remaining mass public.[8] Policy makers focus most on the top 16%, hoping that they will be opinion leaders for the rest. The elites follow foreign policy matters closely and often have direct interests in particular issues. They also have access to the media and thus the ability to promote or oppose specific policies. The attentive public pays at least some attention to events, can develop a keener interest in certain cases, and may develop policy preferences that can influence policy makers.

The mass public, on the other hand, doesn't know or care much about foreign policy most of the time. Surveys often disclose widespread public ignorance about other countries, their leaders and policies, and key facts about international issues. For example, in 2006, half the respondents said that Iraq had weapons of mass destruction (WMD) when the U.S. invaded in 2003. And, a poll in 2007 found one third believing that Saddam Hussein was personally involved in the 9/11 attacks.⁹ Of course, everybody's opinion, well informed or not, can matter, especially at election time. As the politicians say, you don't have to be well informed to vote, just registered.

Mass opinion is also often inconsistent or volatile on foreign policy questions. The wording of a question can also make a significant difference. For example, 71% of the people say the United States should play the leading role or a major role in solving international problems, but 56% say America should not be a "world policeman." When the question is whether FTAs have been a good thing or a bad thing, they line up 47% good and 34% bad. But when the question is whether "free trade has been mostly good for the U.S. economy and American workers," opinion shifts to only 31% "mostly good" and 41% "mostly bad." In a two-week period in 2003, four national polls asking, with slightly different wording, whether the United States should send troops to participate in an international peacekeeping force in Liberia produced startlingly different majority results—respectively, 57% in favor, 51% opposed, 58% in favor and 57% opposed.¹⁰

It's useful to keep in mind a distinction by Daniel Yankelovich almost three decades ago between opinion and judgment. Opinions are reactions to events and questions, and the responses to pollsters can vary widely over time and depending on variations in the wording of questions. Judgments come after fuller consideration of the issue, and the responses there tend to be quite stable, regardless of particular wording.¹¹

Despite the inconsistencies and volatility in some opinions, most analysts have found a strong set of core attitudes on how to deal with foreign policy. A 2010 report by the Council on Foreign Relations found more steady consistency than might have been expected. "Contrary to conventional wisdom, the digest suggests substantial consistency in the views of Americans and their counterparts abroad regarding the importance of international law, international institutions, and multilateral cooperation to address global challenges. Far from being insular or obsessed with sovereignty, Americans convey support for internationalist principles and a willingness to compromise for effective multilateral cooperation."¹²

Bruce Jentleson has also found that Americans are "pretty prudent" in judging military actions in terms of their primary objectives. The U.S. public generally views use of force as a last resort, only after using other instruments like diplomacy, economic pressure and sanctions, and military aid and arms sales to possible surrogates. He says Americans also prefer limited operations and air strikes to ground combat forces, a preference presidents have taken as a constraint. But, the public is willing to support use of force to stop aggression and provide humanitarian aid, though not to bring about internal political change. Those views explain why nation building is viewed as unwise, even if it is a chosen tool of policy.¹³

Polling Opinions

Instant polls on current questions still have value for policy makers, if only to understand what arguments might resonate with the public.

The first Bush administration consciously tested a series of messages to justify action against Saddam Hussein after the invasion of Kuwait before settling on "another Hitler" who invaded a neighbor. The second Bush administration emphasized WMD because, as then Deputy Defense Secretary Paul Wolfowitz admitted, "The truth is that for reasons that have a lot to do with the U.S. government bureaucracy, we settled on the one issue that everyone could agree on which was weapons of mass destruction as the core reason." That argument also resonated with public opinion, which supported sending ground troops to remove Saddam Hussein from power throughout 2002 as well as during the invasion in 2003. Public opinion soured on the Iraq war, that is, support dropped below 50%, only in the spring of 2004.[14]

Policy makers look to opinion polls for signs of validation or warning. Support for a policy position strengthens an official's belief in it, while growing opposition is taken as a warning that the policy, or at least the explanations of it, may have to change. Presidents have many tools, of course, to try to shape public opinion, but the number of issues on which they can be engaged is necessarily limited.

Presidential Message and Public Support

When the president ponders the use of force abroad, anticipated public reactions are a major consideration. Public support often seems to depend on proximity to the United States, whether other countries support the U.S. action, the objectives of the operation, and whether the war will eventually be successful.[15]

There is a major scholarly dispute over whether the American people will support military operations when Americans suffer significant casualties. Work by John Mueller on surveys during the Korean and Vietnam wars found a steady drop in public support for those conflicts as the casualties climbed. Other scholars echoed the notion of public aversion to U.S. casualties. More recent research by Peter Feaver and Christopher Gelpi, however, concludes that "casualty aversion . . . appears to be a self-imposed restriction." What generates public opposition is not the absolute level of American losses but whether the type of mission seemed justified and the prospects for success were evident.

Feaver had a chance to try to put his theories into practice when he worked on the Bush National Security Council (NSC) and drafted the 2005 paper, "Strategy for Victory in Iraq," which restated in several ways that victory was vital and possible and that the administration strategy was working.[16] President Bush seemed to agree with Feaver's analysis, for he told reporter Bob Woodward, "First of all, a president has got to be the calcium in the backbone. If I weaken, the whole team weakens. If I'm doubtful, I can assure you there will be lots of doubt. If my confidence in our ability declines, it will send ripples throughout the whole organization. I mean, it's essential that we be confident and determined and united."[17]

The lesson here is that policy makers need to assure the public that their actions abroad are important, worth doing, and not destined for failure. There is also evidence that success matters. Many major U.S. military operations in the late 20th century—Grenada (1983), Panama (1988), Persian Gulf War (1991), and Kosovo (1999)—lacked majority support when begun but soared in popularity as they proved relatively successful. The wars in Vietnam and Iraq, on the other hand, began with strong public support, but opinion soured as the conflicts dragged on and success seemed elusive.[18]

The Bully Pulpit and Framing

When feeling the pressures of public opinion, presidents have a powerful tool to try to move and shape that opinion. They have the *bully pulpit* of the White House and news media professionally compelled to report presidential comments. Presidents can use that forum to set their own agendas and elevate foreign policy issues into public discourse—that is, to increase issue salience and public attention. This is especially helpful for noncrisis issues, like arms control or environmental issues, or otherwise neglected matters like human rights in Burma or Darfur. It is less effective on foreign policy issues where there is already vigorous public debate.

Policy makers can *frame* issues in ways that build support for their decisions. Stopping aggression or preventing genocide is a much stronger reason for military intervention in Kuwait or Kosovo than, say, protecting Western oil interests or choosing sides in a messy ethnic conflict. They can selectively divulge secret information that helps to persuade the public, as the Bush administration did regarding supposed Iraqi WMD.[19]

There is much historical evidence that presidents use public opinion less for policy design than for policy marketing. As L.R. Jacobs and R.Y. Shapiro put it, Politicians "track public opinion not to make policy but rather to determine how to craft their public presentations and win support for the policies they and their supporters follow."[20]

Public opinion is thus a target for policy makers as well as an influence on them. It provides notions and concepts that can be responded to and manipulated. And, as will be seen, it is powerfully influenced in turn by the news media.

Media

The media are participant–observers in the policy process.[21] As observers, journalists report what they see and hear about the development and implementation of foreign policy. Foreign correspondents can provide a useful corrective to what diplomats gather in official channels. Washington reporters can learn of developments even before others in the government. But, the media are also active participants in the policy process. They are used by officials to convey and promote their views. Policy makers can manipulate the media into sharing their interpretations of foreign events and supporting U.S. policies. On the other hand, media reports can force the government to pay attention to issues that have been a low priority and to act sooner than officials might want in response to the pressure to do something about a crisis situation.

Most journalists espouse a belief in certain professional standards, such as nonpartisanship and independence of opinion. Yet, certain biases creep into their coverage, not least because of what they define as newsworthy. Scandals are more newsworthy than the orderly functioning of government. Change is more interesting than continuity of policy. What presidents say is automatically more newsworthy than the pronouncements of a junior member of Congress. Perhaps the most significant bias is that something the government wants to keep secret is deemed inherently more significant than what it admits openly.

Shaping the Media

Policy makers care what the media cover and how issues are portrayed, as confirmed in the quotation at the start of this chapter. Presidents and other senior policy makers use the media as a means of governance. They use it to inform others in government regarding policy preferences. They try to shape public opinion by means of media coverage. They use the media to inform and respond to public concerns and interests.[22]

Media traits allow outsiders to manipulate the news media for their own purposes. The media emphasize very recent developments, not old news. They prefer conflict to consensus and setbacks to progress. When there are political disputes, they resort to he-said-she-said coverage to suggest fairness. To take advantage of these traits, officials repackage news to hang on a current news "peg." They try, often in vain, to make "progress" newsworthy. Officials routinely release bad news late on Friday afternoons, when the chance is best to limit press and public attention because of reduced viewership of television news on Friday evenings and weekends and similarly smaller newspaper coverage and readership on Saturdays.

On the other hand, officials maximize publicity for their actions by orchestrating a full *rollout,* often beginning with an advance release exclusive to one news organization in order to set the stage for wider coverage. Individual reporters may be cultivated by senior policy makers, who grant access and offer comments more freely than to other reporters—and who receive more favorable coverage in return.

These techniques seem to work in foreign affairs. As Doris Graber concluded, "the thrust of most foreign news stories supports government policies. The media usually accept official designations of who are friends and enemies of the United States and interpret these friends' and enemies' motives accordingly."[23]

Outsiders and other officials get valuable cues from news coverage about what is being planned, who's up and who's down in the White House or the Pentagon, or what is the administration line on a controversial issue. President Kennedy's National Security Adviser (NSA) McGeorge Bundy, complained that, during the 114-day New York newspaper strike of 1962–1963, "we lost the best interoffice memo we had."

Leaks as a Policy Making Tool

Leaks are a widely used and sometimes abused tool of policy makers—and have been since the early days of the republic. (See Box 12.1.) They can be accomplished by private and off-the-record interviews, or actually handing a document to a reporter, or just giving a vague hint to look into something. Reporters can then leverage their inside information to seek confirmation or an opposing argument. It's hard for even the most vigilant secret protector to resist the reporter's question, "Don't you want me to include your side of this issue?"[24]

Many leaks are fully planned and authorized as part of a media and political strategy. As the *Los Angeles Times* reported in 2006, "Today, leaking has become such a basic part of the way Washington works that officials hold meetings to decide when, where and how to leak. They cultivate reporters who can be counted on to make good use of leaks. They draft memos spelling out official leak policies so that lower-level officials will know how to leak correctly."[25]

These kinds of leaks are tolerated, at least in the executive branch, as part of the government's sales strategy for foreign policy. What governments deplore, however, are unauthorized disclosures of secret or sensitive information. That usually comes from insiders—or congressional sources—who oppose the current or planned policy. They want to shoot down the trial balloon or expose embarrassing facts about current activities. Or, they want

---

Box 12.1

A Long History of Leaking

The terminology of leaking information, as well as the fact of leaks, is more than 210 years old. Here's John Quincy Adams, then posted abroad, writing to a colleague about leaks in 1798. This passage shows that even secret diplomatic dispatches were routinely shared widely in the early years of the republic. Officials had no guarantees that their views and reports would remain confidential. Still today, policy makers warn their colleagues not to put in writing anything they would not want to see on the front page of the *Washington Post* tomorrow.

The circumstance which you mention, proving that your private letters in cipher to the Secy. Of State, cannot escape the inspection of persons [not] entitled to them, is provoking. Our Government (I'm ashamed to say it, but it is a lamentable truth) our Government has in fact no more retention than a sieve. Everything leaks out, either through treachery or ungovernable curiosity or misplaced confidence [emphasis added]. There is not the least safety for a man to tell them any thing that he is not willing to have proclaimed upon the house tops. I have complained again & again upon the subject, but to no purpose. I now give up the point, take it for granted that secrecy is not understood to be a property of good government with us, and mean to act accordingly.

Source: John Quincy Adams to William van Murray in Berlin, July 7, 1798.

to get the attention of the president or foreign governments, so they will weigh in to the policy dispute.[26] In other words, officials go outside bureaucratic channels to influence policy in another way.

Secret sources are as important to journalists as they are to spies. They reveal what others won't and give insights that might otherwise not be apparent. But, their motives may be quite self-serving, such as stabbing a rival or embarrassing another agency. Perhaps the most significant foreign policy leak in recent times was Daniel Ellsberg's release of the Pentagon Papers, a classified study of Kennedy and Johnson administration Vietnam policy that undermined public support for the war in the Nixon administration. Disclosures of long-secret intelligence operations in the 1970s led to new restrictions and tighter oversight of the Central Intelligence Agency (CIA). The George W. Bush administration leaked information to bolster support for the war in Iraq and suffered from counter-leaks by its critics.

The Media as the Shaper

With or without leaks, the media influence foreign policy in numerous ways, as agenda setting, framing, an action-forcing accelerant, a force multiplier, or an impediment. The media contribute to agenda setting by drawing attention to particular countries or foreign problems that otherwise would not be a high priority for officials. In one of the first examples of what was called the *CNN effect,* television drove the United States to intervene in Somalia and later drove U.S. forces out. Pictures of starving people forced the U.S. government into action, and pictures of dead and wounded servicemen convinced the public that the price of intervention was too high. Likewise, coverage of prodemocracy demonstrations in the Middle East in 2011 also forced the U.S. government to develop policies and messages to respond. Policy makers try to counter media agenda setting by their own actions for their own purposes. They can direct media attention to a place, as official travel, especially by the president, routinely does.

While the American media tend to adopt the frames on foreign policy issues set by policy makers,[27] others inside and outside of government can offer competing frames. Are China's and Russia's leaders partners or adversaries? Was Libya's Qaddafi a reformed terrorist or still a bloody dictator? Are Palestinian militants terrorists or freedom fighters? The frame an issue is given can limit the policy options available for dealing with it. That is why the president works so hard to set a frame that fits U.S. policy, as George W. Bush did in stressing Saddam Hussein's potential for using WMD rather than his less-threatening prewar behavior toward his citizenry and his neighbors.

By pushing issues and events into public view, the media can pressure policy makers into quick decisions and actions rather than careful review, what scholar Steven Livingston calls an *accelerant,* shortening the time policy makers have to make decisions.[28] Where President Kennedy had a week to plan a response to Soviet missiles in Cuba, and President Reagan took 10 days to plan retaliatory strikes on Libya after an attack on U.S. servicemen in Berlin, recent presidents have had to act more quickly and often in the glare of action-forcing media inquiries. President Clinton held his first top-level policy review on Somalia and ordered a U.S. troop withdrawal within three days of the Blackhawk Down deaths of 18 army rangers in October 1993. As shown in Chapter 11, President Obama was repeatedly pressured to make announcements on U.S. policy toward various countries in response to the changing developments during the Arab Spring of 2011.

The media reach multiple audiences at home and abroad, making it a megaphone, or force multiplier, for the government. The diversity of media also allows the government to send multiple signals to an adversary. One official can beat the war drums, while another emphasizes diplomatic actions. One can work for a trade agreement with a country, while another complains about human rights. Foreigners may not know what to believe U.S. policy really is.

Actual or possible media coverage can also work to limit or prevent the use of foreign policy tools. Fears of leaks can lead a president to cancel a covert operation by the CIA. That almost happened at the time of the Bay of Pigs invasion of Cuba, but President Kennedy persuaded the publisher of *The New York Times* not to run a story in advance. Fear of U.S. casualties and the accompanying stories and pictures have frequently limited how presidents chose to use military forces. It's also why the Bush administration banned photos of caskets arriving at Dover air force base during the second Iraq war. The news media can also be a threat to operational security if they inadvertently reveal information about military plans or movements.

Shrinking Coverage and Shrinking Audience

It's important to remember that, despite the proliferation of Internet news and opinion sites and social media, the Washington policy community is still largely focused on the old, legacy media—printed newspapers and the broadcast and cable news outlets. Favorable coverage in those venues is a key measure of validation and effectiveness. When prodded by younger associates, they may start their own blogs or use Facebook or Twitter, but being on the front page or op–ed page of *The New York Times* is still considered more important.

In contrast, the legacy media are paying less attention to foreign policy, except when a dramatic crisis breaks somewhere. Fewer newspapers have overseas correspondents any more, and many of those "parachute" in to trouble spots as they try to cover several countries from a single home base. Fewer television outlets have foreign bureaus, so they have to rely on photos and footage instead of insights of international developments. Television news coverage of foreign affairs has also shrunk in response to low viewer interest. In 1980, 45% of the network evening news shows were devoted to international affairs, compared with 8% in 2009. The cable networks devoted only 2% to 5% of their coverage to foreign news that did not involve the United States. Media coverage of Iraq dropped to 1% of the *newshole* (the amount of space or time devoted to news compared to the total pages or broadcast length) in 2010, and that of Afghanistan was only 4%.[29] Foreign news reaches Americans only in limited amounts.

Meanwhile, the Washington policy community is also largely self-absorbed in each day's cable coverage of news and opinion, following CNN or Fox News as if the whole country were watching and caring what was said. Policy makers and pundits vie for attention and explain domestic and foreign policy issues with bumper-sticker brevity. Most of the general public never hears. In fact, the prime-time audience for cable news programs in 2010 was only 3.2 million viewers, compared with 22 million for broadcast network evening news shows. In 1980, however, the networks had 50 million viewers each night. Media audiences are now highly fragmented.[30]

Advocacy Groups

The many types of advocacy groups are the third presence looming over policy makers. We use that umbrella phrase rather than the more common *interest groups* because the latter phrase is often wrapped with emotion (special interests vs. public interest) and because what matters in influencing foreign policy is that groups of various types support and promote particular policies and actions. Focusing on advocacy also allows us to distinguish types of activities as well as the motivations and sources of support that different groups have.

The number and size of such groups have grown in recent decades. They are better financed and better organized, more sophisticated in their communications strategies and more closely connected to both Congress and the executive branch.[31] The proliferation of advocacy groups has increased competition and led to countervailing groups. Various analysts conclude that, in this clash of groups, the end result is usually stalemate. Those seeking a policy change face multiple veto points, whereas those defending current policy need only to safeguard one.[32] A comprehensive study of lobbying and political contributions reached the same conclusion: "Defenders of the status quo usually win in Washington." The status quo reflects the existing power balance, which is hard to overturn. And on controversial issues, sizable forces and their money are usually mobilized on each side of an issue, leading to a standoff.[33]

Another reason policy changes are hard to achieve and the status quo usually prevails is that stakeholders often seize upon tactics that slow down or obstruct the path to a decision—further study in the executive branch and reporting requirements set by Congress. Delay can be better than an unfavorable decision and easier for an official to support because it avoids making choices that could anger some stakeholders.

Members of advocacy groups know what they want. They have questions, suggestions, complaints, warnings, congratulations, requests, and demands. Clutching their Constitutions, they know they have a First Amendment right "to petition the Government for a redress of grievances"—the words that empower citizen activism and lobbying. Even without those guarantees, policy makers in a democracy would have incentives to listen to these outsiders, sometimes to heed them, and always to grant a respectful audience. While opinion polls might be treated as surrogates for public feelings, real people with strongly expressed views are harder to ignore or discount, especially in election years. While foreign policy issues are only rarely major factors in national elections, antiwar activism was significant in the 2006 congressional balloting.

Everyone in America is a member of multiple interest groups, some very well organized and others lacking staff and structure for forceful advocacy. People share affinities of gender, race, ethnic background, religion, geography, occupation, economic status, and hobbies, as well as politics. Though these affinities do not always result in membership in an organized group, they often do form the foundation for formal organizations that foster shared activities and information. Interest groups are not an abnormal cell growth but a very normal result of a democratic polity. That does not mean, however, that their influences are always benign. Groups that enter the realm of public policy and advocate particular measures are then subject to the rules governing lobbying, such as the laws relating to tax exempt status and reporting expenditures in lobbying Congress.

The size and organizational effectiveness of advocacy groups makes them targets of policy makers seeking allies. Outside support can help officials win internal struggles against rivals and then prevail against adversaries in the contest for public opinion. NATO expansion in the 1990s, for example, succeeded in large part because officials inside government allied with diaspora groups of Eastern Europeans and prevailed against those officials more concerned about and sensitive to Russian opposition.

The most visible and influential advocacy groups on foreign policy issues are those that have direct, usually financial, interests in the policy; those that derive from a common heritage abroad; and those that are active under the rules governing lobbyists and campaign contributors. These are also the groups that have been most closely studied by scholars and the media.

Stakeholders

We use an uncommon term for those groups that have direct personal or institutional stake in a policy issue, usually economic.[34] They often are private corporations or associations, but they could also be nonprofit organizations that advocate policies with economic or financial effects on others. The most obvious stakeholders are the contractors or potential contractors, the businesses or nonprofit organizations that will be better off if the government acts as they recommend. Most of these stakeholders, therefore, want jobs, one of the most potent benefits the government can bestow.

When money and jobs are at stake, the competition for the attention and support of policy makers can be intense. The *military–industrial complex* that President Eisenhower warned about has a long history of fighting for its programs and budgets, using every legal and sometimes illegal tool on both branches of government. These companies hire lobbyists and make political contributions, as discussed below. But, they also promote their products to the public at large and try to build alliances with opinion leaders and think tanks that might improve their chances of success with governmental decision makers. They use economic arguments to influence the media and public opinion as well as policy makers.

What the defense industry wants primarily is funding for their programs. But, it also supports a strong defense and global engagement. Just as exporting companies want lower trade barriers abroad, defense companies want solid alliances and extensive military cooperation. Private interests do not hesitate to tell officials where they stand on foreign policy issues. Sometimes, of course, the stakeholders have clashing interests: a trade agreement has corporate winners and losers; friendly relations with India may make it harder to have good relations with Pakistan, and U.S. firms may suffer as a result. As shown in Chapter 7, stakeholders clashed over provisions in the Korean FTA as different groups sought provisions helpful to their sales. In addition, U.S. nuclear power advocates were effective in winning support for the 2008 law granting India an exemption from certain U.S. nonproliferation requirements.

In addition to defense contractors who build weapons, there are a growing number of firms that provide other services, like security and logistics supply, and are important factors in U.S. activities overseas. In Iraq and Afghanistan, the number of U.S.-funded contractors is larger than the number of American military and civilian personnel. The contractor services are vital, but their use has foreign policy and other implications that policy makers have to take into account. Does the U.S. government have the same obligations to protect and assist contract people as it does official personnel? When contractors are accused of crimes, whose laws and courts should judge them?

Nonprofit organizations and humanitarian nongovernment organizations (NGOs) may also have financial stakes in U.S. foreign policies, for many of them deliver goods and services abroad. Over half of U.S. foreign disaster assistance goes through NGOs. CARE gets 40% of its revenues from the U.S. government; Catholic Relief Services gets 37%; Church World Service gets 43%. These groups are strong advocates for nonmilitary foreign aid as well as stakeholders in those programs.

Ethnic Identity or Affinity Groups

Harder to categorize but still quite important in U.S. foreign policy are what are usually called *ethnic identity* or *interest groups*, which are based around common heritage. They organize, have shared concerns, and try to influence public policy. They share a purpose more than tangible benefits, and they tend to seek emotional rather than financial rewards, and that may make their commitments more intense and less subject to argument. In addition to ethnic groups, there are other affinity groups that organize to influence policy makers, such as those that form among people sharing a religion, or a concern for human rights, or limiting nuclear weapons and warfare.

The most obvious examples of groups active on foreign policy issues are the people with ancestral or other ties to other countries—Ireland, Poland, Greece, Cuba, Israel, Armenia, Taiwan, India. Many African-Americans have organized on behalf of particular African nations or issues affecting the continent as a whole. Diaspora populations understand that they can help their homeland where the U.S. government is concerned by organizing and advocating here in America. One study has identified 85 groups or organizations representing 38 ethnicities that conduct lobbying activities.[35]

The term *ethnic interest group* has pejorative connotations because of repeated instances in American history when dominant groups opposed the special pleadings of these smaller organizations. Those in power like to say they represent the national interest in contrast to the narrow special interest of the minority group. They often have a persuasive case: Why should the embargo on Cuba remain unchanged after half a century when it has clearly failed to achieve the overthrow of the communist regime?

On the other hand, the national interest is only what the nation says it is and what the people are willing to defend and promote by various policies. Ethnic identity groups have their own moral, economic, and security arguments to weigh against the so-called realists who have a different calculus of the national interest. They press these arguments as they lobby and make political contributions, as other stakeholders do.

One could argue that, for most of American history until recent decades, foreign policy was shaped by a single particular ethnic group—white, male, Anglo-Saxon Protestants (WASPs) who dominated American politics and culture. This group resisted pleas to pressure Britain over Ireland, or any of the colonial powers over the ways they carved up Africa, or Ottoman Turkey and Russia over their pogroms. These WASPs were also slow to endorse the idea of a Jewish homeland.

As more immigrants came to America and gained political power, they used it to push for a redress of grievances regarding their ancestral homelands—nationhood for the Poles, a homeland for the Jews, security for Taiwan, democracy in Cuba, independence for the Baltic states, and so forth. They used the tools of interest groups to pressure Congress and the executive branch to adopt their recommendations.

Some were successful, others not. Thomas Ambrosio has a good checklist of what it takes for an interest group to succeed.

1. Organizational strength: Size and capacity to act matter.

2. Membership unity, placement, and voter participation: A group that is united, well-positioned socioeconomically and geographically, and willing to vote as a group has important electoral implications for policy makers.

3. Salience and resonance of its message: A group that can sway public opinion can persuade policy makers.

4. "Push on an open door": It really helps when the group is advocating something policy makers already favor.

5. Strength of opposition: Many of the groups most active on foreign policy issues have weak opponents.

6. Permeability of and access to the government: Groups can be more effective when the Congress, responsive to voters, plays a major role in the policy issue.

7. Mutually supportive relationship: It helps when groups can help the policy makers do other tasks, as pro-Israel groups have done by helping maintain congressional support for the entire foreign aid program.[36]

Note in Box 12.2 how well the group American Israel Public Affairs Committee (AIPAC) measures up on these criteria for success.

Box 12.2

How Foreign Policy Is Made: Why the American Israel Public Affairs Committee Is So Effective

AIPAC is generally regarded as one of the most effective special interest groups. Why? Comparing it against Thomas Ambrosio's checklist of what makes a successful interest, we see that AIPAC measures up on all counts.

1. Organizational strength: AIPAC has a large membership, more than 100,000 who can be mobilized to contact Washington in support of Israel.

2. Membership unity, placement, and voter participation: AIPAC has a large staff of about 100 people, with an annual budget of perhaps $15 million. It lobbies actively on Capitol Hill, spending $2,749,992 in 2010.

3. Salience of its message: AIPAC members are often major contributors to political campaigns, thus assuring them access when needed.

4. "Push on an open door": AIPAC's support of Israel is bolstered by strong support of Israel in public opinion polls.

5. Strength of opposition: Pro-Palestinian groups are fragmented, small, and ineffective.

6. Permeability of and access to the government: AIPAC can get large numbers of members of Congress to sign pro-Israel letters on short notice. Many members are reluctant not to be among the signers.

7. Mutually supportive relationship: AIPAC remembers what politicians say and do, and its members tend to reward their friends and punish their enemies.

AIPAC has been a model for other diaspora organizations seeking to influence U.S. foreign policy, but few have been as effective in so many of the factors for success. AIPAC tends to win its battles preemptively by votes and letters before policy makers decide an issue demonstrating the costs and risks of pursuing a course likely to be strongly opposed.

Many of these groups work closely with foreign embassies, and many of those embassies have congressional liaison staff and contract lobbyists to promote their interests. But, foreigners cannot vote or make political contributions, so those influential activities are left to the Americans. The grassroots basis of most of these organizations, of course, contributes to their political effectiveness.

These ethnic and affinity groups tend to use strong moral arguments, especially historical grievances and current threats. Those can be successful unless countered by economic or security arguments, which are precisely the kinds of points made by stakeholders with jobs or officials dealing with larger strategic issues.

Lobbyists

Lobbyists comprise another category of advocacy groups that deserves special analysis. The term *lobbyist* has misleading connotations because it originally referred to someone in the meeting area outside a legislative chamber. If you take the accepted definition as "a person who represents an interest group in order to influence government decisions in that group's favor,"[37] it clearly includes those who seek to influence the executive as well as the legislative branch.

In the United States, lobbyists approaching officials in either branch are required to register by filing forms with Congress if they expect to spend at least $3,000 on lobbying activities in any three-month period. This threshold is intended to exclude ordinary citizens from the paperwork requirements. Charities, religious groups, and other nonprofit organizations that are exempt from federal income taxes are limited in how much lobbying they can do: It can't be a "substantial part" of their activities. Once registered, lobbyists then need to file quarterly reports on their activities on behalf of each client.

There are several types of lobbyists: private individuals; representatives of citizen or volunteer groups; in-house lobbyists for established institutions; contract lobbyists; and government legislative liaison staffs.[38] Many of the full-time lobbyists are lawyers. Most have some government experience that gives them contacts and inside knowledge of issues, procedures, and personalities. Few had childhood dreams of being lobbyists.

By law, government officials are forbidden to lobby Congress, but they can provide "information," and that's good enough as far as the executive branch is concerned. Besides approaching Congress, executive branch officials have strong incentives to work with outside lobbyists and interest groups. Outreach can give legitimization to administration policies and build public consensus and support. It can also bring outside groups together in coalitions they might not otherwise form.[39]

The most prominent lobbyists are those representing associations or businesses, either on contract or as in-house employees. In 2010, there were 12,964 registered lobbyists, and they reported spending $3.47 billion on their activities.[40] The number of people has remained roughly the same for the past dozen years, but the expenditures have more than doubled.

Those expensive activities include billable hours spent in meetings and in drafting letters, testimony, and amendments. Lobbyists also arrange events publicizing their clients' points of view and organizing support outside of government. They try to get favorable media coverage for their clients. They solicit messages and phone calls from grassroots supporters. They produce issue briefs and circulate favorable materials from outside sources. They need to show action and momentum even if they can't achieve their primary goals. After all, they charge $25,000 per month for most clients as a retainer fee and have annual fees between $700,000 and $1 million according to *The Washingtonian Magazine*.[41]

The defense industry as a whole spent $138 million on lobbying activities in 2010 and contributed nearly $24 million to political candidates in the 2008 election cycle. These are large sums for which the industry expected a good return. There are about 1,100 defense lobbyists working for about 400 different clients.[42]

Lockheed Martin, for example, is the top government contractor, earning $36 billion in 2008. While $29 billion of that figure came from Pentagon contracts, the company was also the top contractor for the Departments of Energy and Transportation, and number two for the State Department, number three for the National Aeronautics and Space Administration (NASA), and number four for the Departments of Justice and Housing and Urban Development. That much government business led Lockheed to spend $15 million on lobbying and campaign contributions in 2009.[43]

Other defense firms with large lobbying programs and political contributions include Boeing ($18 million for lobbying, $2.6 million in contributions), Northrop Grumman ($15.7 million and $1.6 million, respectively), and United Technologies ($14.5 million and $1.2 million). It is noteworthy, however, that the defense sector spends less on lobbying and contributes far less to politicians than many other sectors. Contributions have been heaviest from trade associations (realtors, home builders, bankers) and unions. In 2010, the U.S. Chamber of Commerce spent almost as much ($132 million) on lobbying activities as the entire defense industry combined.[44]

To do their work, lobbyists need access to policy makers. Sometimes, they buy access by making campaign contributions or by helping to raise funds above and beyond what they can lawfully contribute. (See Box 12.3.) But, they can also gain access by offering information important to the policy maker. One of the single most important pieces of information for lawmakers is, "this affects people in your district." The impact could be an increase in jobs, or a loss of jobs, or other costs or benefits. Once in the door, the lobbyist can tailor the approach for greatest impact. He or she can also learn more about how the issue is viewed in each office and what other issues are in play. All that information feeds back into the lobbying strategy.

Lobbyists also try to reach policy makers indirectly by gaining publicity for their causes and by mobilizing others to contact the officials. Lawmakers are particularly sensitive to messages from their voters and from people who are close friends and supporters. A well-crafted issue campaign will seek to find the best person to approach a particular policy maker. The pro-Israel organization AIPAC is especially good at finding the best of their members to make the key call to an official.

The value added that lobbyists provide for their hefty fees is information. Good lobbyists spend much of their time just monitoring the issues of importance to their clients and the offices and committees where decisions may be made. They are experts in the policies they lobby for and in the processes that are followed to deal with those issues. The more contacts they have, the more they can learn. They gain information in each meeting they have and can trade on that information in subsequent sessions. What they learn about the status of an issue and the lineup of supporters and opponents can be important in persuading potential supporters. Such information is also valuable to executive branch officials, who want to know the politics affecting an issue as well as how the matter may affect their own careers. Providing information can build contacts and trust, whatever the impact on the immediate issue at hand.[45]

Some of the techniques lobbyists used to use are no longer allowed. Lobbyists used to provide free meals and tickets to major sporting events and golfing vacations under the guise of "seminars." Members of Congress and their staff are now forbidden to accept free meals or gifts from lobbyists, and lobbyists are banned from even offering gifts. Campaign contributions are covered by separate laws.

However sleazy some lobbyists may seem, they dare not lie. They depend on a relationship of trust both with their clients and with the people they approach on behalf of their clients. If they misrepresent the truth and are discovered, they'll be shut out forever by the angry official. They package their truth in the most persuasive ways, to be sure, but they have a powerful incentive to be honest. As former White House aide and longtime lobbyist Bryce Harlow said, "The coin of lobbying is trust . . . truth telling and square dealing are of paramount importance in this profession. If [one] lies, misrepresents, or even lets a misapprehension stand uncorrected—or if someone cuts his corners too slyly—he is . . . dead and gone, never to be resurrected or even mourned."[46]

Foreign policy lobbyists represent a diversity of clients, most often foreign governments, U.S. businesses with financial interests in the outcomes, and citizen groups concerned with particular issues or countries. They use the same tactics as domestic issue lobbyists and fight for the attention of officials and lawmakers.

Contributors

Lobbyists are frequently campaign contributors as well. They give money to gain access to busy lawmakers. They contribute to reward past support and to try to encourage future support. Sometimes, they raise funds as insurance policies, especially for people in gatekeeper positions on an issue, such

> **Box 12.3**
>
> ### Inside View: Fund-Raising by Lobbyists
>
> Former senator Chuck Hagel (R-NE) acknowledges that lobbyists are the key to political fund-raising. They derive strength and influence not only from their direct contributions but also from their willingness—often eagerness—to help bring others into the fold. In addition to fundraising for individual candidates, lobbyists also help by contributing to party war chests, as the special case described here.
>
> *We let the lobbyists run it all because we have these big fund-raising dinners, for example. Democrats and Republicans. And we raise $20 million, $25 million at these things [for the House and Senate campaign committees]. Who do we go to make sure that we get $20 to $25 million? I've run these dinners so I know what I'm talking about. You go to a committee of twenty-five lobbyists, a steering committee. And you say, Okay, you guys each have to come up with a million dollars. . . . So we go to them for that fast money.*
>
> Source: Quoted in Robert Kaiser, *So Damn Much Money* (New York: Knopf, 2009), 291.

as a senior member of the committee with jurisdiction over the lobbyist's issue or issues.[47]

Contributions also come from relatives, friends, home state voters, political action committees (PACs), and the candidate's political party committees. Foreigners may not contribute to U.S. campaigns directly or indirectly (such as a pass-through to a lobbyist), but their American lobbyists can give their own money. PACs are groups of contributors in an organization, usually a business or union, who bundle their political funds and can give candidates $5,000 per election cycle. Many senior congressional figures have *leadership PACs* that raise funds and then give them, under limits, to other federal candidates, often as a way to build support for themselves as party leaders or committee chairs.

Congressional campaigns cost a lot of money, much of it going to television ads. In the 2010 elections, House and Senate candidates raised more than $1.8 billion. Incumbent senators raised an average of $9,153,000 for their campaigns; House incumbents averaged $1,560,000. To reach those targets, representatives would have to have to raise $15,000 every week they are in office, and senators would need to bring in $30,000 per week every week for six years.[48]

With those soaring campaign costs, candidates seek out contributions wherever and as often as they can. One lobbyist for defense clients says that the invitations to fund-raisers will come and may seem like "blatant arm-twisting," but he recommends "it is in the lobbyist's best interest to participate and have his client represented rather than not pay the price of admission." In recent years, PAC contributions have amounted to 43% of the funds raised by congressional incumbents and 20% of money for incumbent senators.[49]

Lobbyists usually have specific goals behind their contributions. Other contributors may be happy being on a winning team and having some level of special access to the lawmaker. Many lawmakers obtain contributions from across the country because they are seen as issue leaders in the House or Senate. An organization's mailing list can be a way for a candidate to reach out beyond his or her state or district for support.

The laws governing campaign contributions are complex and changing. A 2010 Supreme Court decision (*Citizens United v. Federal Election Commission*) invalidated century-old provisions barring corporate contributions to federal campaigns and allowed companies and unions to run unrestricted *issue ads* that favored a particular candidate. Still in place are laws restricting most individual contributions to $2,500 per election cycle and PACs to $5,000. A primary contest is viewed as a separate election, thus allowing a total that is double the listed amounts.

Impact of Lobbyists and Contributors

Despite media coverage—and the conventional public belief—that equates contributions to vote buying, academic studies can't prove the linkage. An extensive survey of the literature concludes that "the research is inconclusive." Clive Thomas says that most scholars do agree on three propositions regarding PAC influence. First, that money can buy access to lawmakers but not necessarily their votes. Second, that PAC money can influence behavior when one or more conditions apply. Those conditions are that the legislators themselves have no strong preferences; that the issue has low visibility; or that the public at large is inattentive or indifferent. Third, while PAC money may not influence voting, it does affect behavior in other less-visible parts of the legislative process, for example, in committee maneuvering.[50]

Contributions buy access because lawmakers and their staffs have limited time, so they tend to give it to longtime associates and people who can help them in various ways. Contributors help with money; lobbyists can help with information and coalition building. Accepting a contribution creates an obligation at least to listen to the contributor's case on an issue.

Many foreign policy and national security issues also meet the conditions cited for money to make a difference. Few lawmakers feel strongly about policy toward Burma or which jet engine is better for a new fighter. The public knows little and cares less about such matters. And, much of the action is at the committee level—the inside game—rather than on the floor of the Senate or House. On the other hand, cause and effect are still hard to prove because members may have staked out their positions long before lobbyists got directly involved, so any contributions need to be seen as rewards rather than bribes.

Votes are easy to measure, but other actions on behalf of contributors may not be. A member can talk to the committee chair, or press for a hearing, or urge the staff to give sympathetic consideration to a proposal. All these actions may be more significant for the contributor than a floor vote, which is rare in any case on all but the most significant foreign policy and national security issues.

On many foreign policy issues, there is only one side that is large and mobilized—and that's why that group prevails over its rivals. The Greek and Armenian communities in the United States are far larger and more politically active than Turkish groups. The number of Jews and Muslims in America is more closely balanced, but pro-Israel groups are skilled and united, while Muslim groups are fragmented organizationally and concerned about a much wider range of issues than Palestine. The diaspora from Poland and the Baltic States is active and organized, in contrast to whatever émigré Russians might feel about, say, Kaliningrad. A large and growing contingent of South Asians have mobilized in support of India, as evident in the votes for waiving restrictions relating to India's nuclear programs, but Pakistanis are not much in evidence.

On many other foreign policy questions, there are few if any votes, so the competition among interest groups and lobbyists is over the framing of issues and their inclusion on the agenda for action.

Think Tanks

Separate from other advocacy groups, though sometimes allied with them, are public policy research institutions, colloquially known as *think tanks*. These idea merchants are important participants in the policy process. A 2011 report identified 1,816 think tanks in the United States, of a worldwide total of more than 6,480. Some of the oldest are the Carnegie Endowment for International Peace (established 1910), the Brookings Institution (1916), the Hoover Institute at Stanford (1919), and the Council on Foreign Relations (1921). There are about 350 think tanks in Washington. Some are nonpartisan and centrist; others are linked to the left or right.[51]

The federal government funds several think tanks of its own, including the U.S. Institute of Peace, the Woodrow Wilson Center for Scholars, and the Congressional Research Service. The Pentagon has a network of federally funded research and development centers (FFRDCs) like the RAND Corporation, Institute for Defense Analyses, and the Center for Naval Analysis.

Think tank analysts have many advantages compared to government officials and organizations. They can often go places and meet people policy makers cannot. They can make controversial proposals without risking political punishment. They have more time and perspective than harried officials. These traits make their products potentially more valuable than something generated within the bureaucratic chain of command. For influence, however, they need to find influential advocates, either in government or among the advocacy groups.

Competition is sometimes fierce among think tanks. They compete for funding from private patrons and large foundations. They compete for attention to their ideas. They compete to have their proposals adopted by policy makers. The closer their ties to political parties and movements, the more they compete with their partisan rivals. The Center for American Progress, for example, regularly issues op-ed pieces and reports defending Obama administration policies, while the Heritage Foundation publishes articles criticizing those policies.

To market their ideas, they shape their products to appeal to their audiences. A four-page paper in memo form may be more effective than a 200-page book with charts and tables. Practical advice with feasible options is more welcome than theoretically pure but politically impossible proposals. Even the best ideas somehow need to break through the attention barrier of senior officials. As Eliot Cohen noted, "To a remarkable degree, government talks only to itself." When serving in the State Department, he says "the buzz on the outside was just that—a background noise of which I was dimly aware."[52] The more effective think tanks find ways to get their ideas on the radar screens of senior officials, either directly or through the news media.

Besides their ideas, think tanks are important as holding pens for former officials when they are out of office. Clinton administration officials flocked to think tanks after 2000, and Bush administration officials did the same after 2008. Such people bring prestige, inside knowledge, contacts, and a practical perspective to the research institutions. They can recharge their batteries, reflect on what they experienced, and still stay networked. By writing articles and holding conferences, they stay in the public eye as they await other opportunities at public office.

From the government's standpoint, think tanks are valuable resources for developing, testing, promoting, and evaluating new policies. As John Hamre, former deputy secretary of defense and now head of a think tank, says, "Bureaucracies do not invent new ideas. They elaborate old ones." One source of those new ideas is think tanks, which he calls "important incubators of policy innovation."[53] That's why officials reach out to think tanks and their analysts and welcome their suggestions.

Lawmakers are bombarded by think tank products, and they, too, often collaborate with institutions or individuals whose ideas they find congenial. They summon think tank researchers as witnesses in policy hearings and often turn their ideas into legislation.

One valuable example of think tank work shaping foreign policy was the early 1990s efforts by analysts at the Brookings Institution, Harvard, and Stanford, who recommended ways to reduce the dangers of nuclear proliferation as the Soviet Union disintegrated. Lawmakers and executive branch officials joined in support of the Nunn-Lugar program for Cooperative Threat Reduction that includes nonweapons work for scientists and tighter controls over nuclear materials.[54] Think tanks in recent years have also developed an array of ideas to improve interagency collaboration on national security policies, modeled on the Goldwater–Nichols law that brought more *jointness* to the armed forces.

* * *

The "elephants" looming over the White House make a difference in how and when the foreign policy tools are used. Public opinion can prod presidents to action, while sometimes constraining his choices, especially the use of military forces. The news media can also force the president to act directly or indirectly by influencing public opinion. In return, policy makers have techniques for manipulating the media, including leaks and obtaining favorable coverage of their policies. It remains to be seen whether changes in the media, especially the proliferation of news and quasi-news sources, will change this pattern.

Advocacy groups try to influence the media and policy makers. They often draw upon ideas nurtured in think tanks, many of which are connected to them. On foreign policy issues, the groups tend to use economic arguments or moralistic ones and sometimes supplement their activities with lobbying and campaign contributions. Most evidence suggests that, with many competing groups at work, the end result tends to be a continuation of the status quo.

Selected Resources

The Program on International Public Attitudes at the University of Maryland has extensive poll data at http://worldpublicopinion.org/.

The Chicago Council on Global Affairs has a regular series of polls on U.S. foreign policy at www.thechicagocouncil.org/files/Studies_and_Publications/Public_Opinion_Studies/files/Studies_Publications/Public_Opinion.aspx?hkey=4deab5a5-dc29-40b2-be42-4aba0046cccd.

Pew Center reports on journalism are available at www.journalism.org.

Lobbying and campaign contribution data are available at www.opensecrets.org.

Other valuable resources include Allan J. Cigler and Burdett A. Loomis, *Interest Group Politics, Eighth Edition* (Washington, DC: CQ Press, 2012) and Doris A. Graber, *Mass Media and American Politics, Eighth Edition* (Washington, DC, CQ Press, 2010).

13 Missing Tools

> *Radical additions to our existing policy machinery are unnecessary and undesirable.*
> —Senator Henry M. "Scoop" Jackson, November 15, 1961[1]

> *"[S]ignificant changes must be made in the structures and processes of the U.S. national security apparatus. . . . Otherwise, the United States risks losing its global influence and critical leadership role."*
> —Hart–Rudman Commission Final Report, March 15, 2001[2]

The old adage, "If all you have is a hammer, every problem starts looking like a nail," applies to the foreign policy toolkit as well. America already has diplomatic, military, and economic versions of hammers, and screwdrivers, and vises, and saws, and so forth. But, many analysts and practitioners would like to see some better-designed versions or some special-purpose instruments to do the tasks more efficiently or effectively. Just as a power drill with a magnet to hold the screw in place is far better than a traditional hand screwdriver, so is a trained interagency team better for advising foreign officials than a random pickup squad of people just back from leave.

The United States has a long tradition of establishing commissions of notables to study big issues and make well-considered recommendations. And every four years, just before presidential elections, think tanks and other organizations produce glossy reports to guide the next president and the new administration. Such groups and reports are regular features of the American policy advocacy system, and their ideas are often adopted and put into practice. This chapter highlights several of these proposals and their prospects for inclusion in the U.S. foreign policy toolkit.

Legacy of Reform Proposals

Previous commissions have had significant impacts in shaping and adding to America's foreign policy toolkit. In 1937, the Brownlow Commission, appointed by Franklin Roosevelt (FDR), concluded that "the President needs help" and recommended the creation of a presidential staff. A 1939 law allowed the president to hire six assistants and also gave him significant powers to reorganize the executive branch. Prior to this time, presidents had only secretarial staff and government reorganizations required new laws by Congress.[3] FDR used this authority not only for better coordination of domestic policy but also for national security. Just as war broke out in Europe, he moved the Joint Board of the Army and Navy into the Executive Office of the President (EOP), where he later created the Joint Chiefs of Staff (JCS) and a war council for World War II planning. Adoption of the Brownlow Commission's proposal marked the start of the growth of the staff advising the president and communicating his decisions, thus reducing the role of cabinet members and centralizing more power in the White House.

In 1947, Congress created a blue ribbon commission to study the organization and management of the government—hoping, of course, for ways to reduce duplication and waste. Former President Herbert Hoover headed the group and soon-to-be Secretary of State Dean Acheson was vice chairman. The Hoover Commission made many recommendations that were soon adopted, including major changes to the Pentagon and State Department. The commission said that the military establishment was "perilously close to the weakest type of department" and urged giving the secretary of defense "singleness of control" over it. It also recommended creating a chairman of the JCS.[4] Both of these ideas were written into the 1949 Defense Act. These changes helped to give the secretary of defense greater control over the military establishment and established a single military officer as the principal military adviser to the civilian leaders.

The commission also recommended increasing the senior management of the State Department by allowing 10 assistant secretaries, a counselor, and a legal adviser and revising existing law to vest all authority in the secretary, which previously had been assigned to lower-ranking officials. This was done without controversy. On the other hand, Hoover also proposed the amalgamation of the higher levels of the permanent civil service with the foreign service within a few years. This was not accomplished at the time in part because of concerns about low morale in the foreign service and the disruptive effects of the McCarthy-era security investigations of the department.[5] The State Department still has both civil service and foreign service people competing for jobs in Foggy Bottom rather than having a full integration of the civilian career services for foreign policy.

Senator Henry M. "Scoop" Jackson (D-WA), used his subcommittee of the Government Operations Committee to investigate and report on policy machinery for national security just before and during the early years of the Kennedy administration. Instead of adding to the toolkit, however, he favored downsizing. Jackson's subcommittee took a dim view of the Eisenhower National Security Council (NSC) system, labeling it a cumbersome bureaucratic machine that protected bureaucratic interests and failed to innovate or make systematic plans. Other reports called for giving the secretary of state more staff resources and a greater role in politico-military matters and for using the Budget Bureau to monitor and coordinate foreign and defense policy using *the pocketbook nerve*. The Kennedy team agreed with Jackson's analysis and dismantled the NSC system in favor of a small group to work directly with the president as his eyes and ears rather than as strong interagency coordinators.[6] While that arrangement suited the Kennedy management style, it limited the White House's ability to oversee and control all aspects of foreign policy. President Nixon recentralized power under his national security adviser (NSA), a system that has continued ever since.

In 1972, Congress created another commission to study and report on the "Organization of the Government for the Conduct of Foreign Policy." This group, headed by former Ambassador Robert Murphy, commissioned additional studies that eventually filled seven volumes and did not report until 1975. Murphy's group was not unanimous in its recommendations, and few of its ideas were adopted. The commission declared that the two major challenges confronting U.S. foreign policy would be global interdependence and the merger of domestic and foreign policy issues within the United States. It then recommended a central coordinating role for the State Department and the creation of a Joint Committee on National Security in the Congress that would combine authorizing and appropriations functions. It seemed to suggest that the Defense Department (DOD) would somehow be subordinate to State for political-military guidance.[7] Few officials outside of the State Department considered the first proposal feasible or desirable, and none of the congressional leaders on defense and foreign policy issues joined to support the consolidation of committees.

Another commission that had a much greater impact was the Tower Commission appointed by President Reagan to review what went wrong in the Iran–Contra affair. That panel consisted of former Senator John Tower (R-TX), former Senator and briefly Secretary of State Edmund Muskie (D-ME), and former and future NSA Brent Scowcroft. Its focus was the NSC system around the president, and it recommended a model organization for the NSC that was adopted and remains essentially the same today, with a hierarchy of committees at the cabinet, deputy, and assistant secretary levels. The panel also urged that the NSC staff not get involved in operational matters.[8] These changes made the NSC and its staff the key tool and a permanent institution for formulating U.S. foreign policy.

A decade later, Congress created the Quadrennial Defense Review (QDR) process for DOD and included a National Defense Panel (NDP) to give a second opinion on future defense needs and plans. In its 1997 report, the NDP forecast threats to "domestic communities and key infrastructures" and urged "a much larger role for homeland defense." It recommended a transformation strategy for military forces, saying the United States was on "the cusp of a military revolution" driven by information technologies and needed to move beyond "legacy systems" that would increasingly be at risk.[9] This approach was heartily endorsed and pursued by Defense

Secretary Rumsfeld until U.S. forces got preoccupied by the war in Iraq in 2003. Until forced to concentrate on urgent military problems, Rumsfeld shortened the military budget process, urged cuts in military personnel, and proposed advanced weaponry under the umbrella of *defense transformation*.

The Hart–Rudman Commission (formally the U.S. Commission on National Security/21st Century) starkly warned in 1999, almost exactly two years to the day before the 9/11 attacks, that terrorists would obtain weapons and "Americans will likely die on American soil, possibly in large numbers." In its final report in March 2001, the commission recommended creation of a National Homeland Security Agency linking the Federal Emergency Management Agency (FEMA), the U.S. Coast Guard, and Customs and Border Patrol. It also offered a wide array of other proposals, from enhanced educational benefits for people who enter public service to merging the Agency for International Development (AID) with the State Department and cutting DOD headquarters staffs. But, it was the homeland security focus that was prescient and not heeded until months after the 9/11 attacks.[10]

Those attacks led to a series of inquiries, most notably the 9/11 Commission, which recommended the creation of the Director of National Intelligence (DNI) and other measures to connect the dots regarding possible terrorist threats. Most of its recommendations were promptly adopted. As a result, Congress created the structure, if not the reality, for better coordination of intelligence activities relating to threats against American territory. It also lowered the legal "firewall" between intelligence operatives and law enforcement agents. Lawmakers failed, however, to give full budget power to the DNI or to consolidate congressional oversight panels as the commission proposed.

The difficulties of interagency policy coordination drew increased attention after 2001, with many groups and officials calling for "a Goldwater–Nichols for the interagency," a vague phrase that somehow meant comprehensive reform of the national security policy process. Details of the law that might be required were lacking, but many suggestions were offered under that rubric. A group at the Center for Strategic and International Studies (CSIS), several of whose members later held high positions in the Obama administration, recommended such steps as: a broad Quadrennial National Security Review backed by presidential policy guidance; a national security professional career path that would lead to service in more than one department; an interagency planning unit for "complex contingency operations;" and creation of rapidly-deployable civilian capabilities."[11]

Another CSIS group, its Commission on Smart Power, recommended increased civilian capacity for foreign policy operations, a training *float* for civilian agencies, higher priority to knowledge and communication activities, and other emphasis on the use of *soft power* as *smart power*.[12]

Many of these ideas were also advanced in 2008 by the Project on National Security Reform (PNSR), several of whose members were later named to senior positions in the Obama administration. Its 700-page final report discussed several of the proposals outlined below.[13] While some of its approaches were adopted administratively, the new administration did not seek new legislation to make more significant changes.

Each of these major reports had the imprimatur of distinguished former officials and tended to reflect an emerging consensus of the policy community at the time on what was wrong and what could be fixed. Few recommendations were truly radical, though many were still fiercely resisted by those who feared a loss of power or status for an entity they valued. Each of these reports also reflected the tendency to find fixes for the last war, the most recent serious problem. The Jackson Subcommittee saw the NSC process as too ponderous. The Murphy Commission was reacting to the reduced power and prestige of the State Department when Henry Kissinger was in the White House. The Tower Commission solved the problem of a rogue NSC staff. The NDP had an answer for how to defend America better while spending less, by embracing the revolution in military affairs technologies. And, Hart–Rudman foresaw that terrorist threats would grow and proposed a cabinet agency to protect the nation. The reports since 9/11 reflected policy makers' dismay over weak interagency coordination and over the militarization of foreign policy because of the lack of civilian capacity to operate overseas.

One frequent phrase in most of these reports was a call to *strengthen* a particular office or program or department. That sounds tough and significant, but in fact, it is a highly ambiguous term. At a minimum, it seems to connote giving greater influence over a policy area, but influence also depends upon many factors, some personal, some legal. What these reports often fail to provide is specific detail on the measures deemed necessary to confer increased influence and strength. Sometimes, it requires additional legal authority, sometimes budget authority, sometimes the power to decide issues, which is quite different from the power merely to recommend. Sometimes, the enhanced status can be obtained simply by having a seat at the table where particular issues are discussed.

What the critics often mean but are reluctant to say is that one agency needs to be strengthened by reducing the strength of another, often one already active in the contested policy realm. In recent years, the Pentagon has often been the implicit or explicit target of what even Defense Secretary Gates called the *militarization* of U.S. foreign policy. There are many different ways to improve the status and influence of an organization in the national security system. Consult the hierarchy of types of bureaucratic power when deciding which particular changes might actually strengthen a currently weak actor in the policy process. (See Box 13.1.)

Recommended New Tools

Because the United States still faces many of these same problems, it is useful to reexamine some new and some old proposals to add to the president's

> **Box 13.1**
>
> ## Bureaucratic Power Ladder
>
> Reformers often call to *strengthen* particular officials or organizations, but this is a very ambiguous term. It depends on where that official or organization is on the bureaucratic power ladder. Moving up a single step can be a significant strengthening but still fall far short of genuine power. Here's the hierarchy:
>
> - Power to act subject only to presidential concurrence
> - Power to act subject to congressional concurrence
> - Power to shift money between activities
> - Power to spend money
> - Power to hire and fire subordinates
> - Presidential appointment confirmed by Senate
> - Authority based in permanent law
> - Authority based in executive order or departmental directive
> - Verbal authority only
> - Veto power over peers from right to clear documents
> - Power to convene meetings and set agendas
> - Permanent seat at the table
> - Attendance by invitation only
>
> Each of these steps can be significant, but the higher levels convey more power than the lower. Simply having a seat at the table draws organizations into the decision loop where they see the papers under consideration and have a chance to voice opinions. That's why efforts have been made over the years, for example, to add the marines to the JCS, and in 2011 to add the chief of the national guard bureau, and to add formal members to the NSC. Presidential appointees confirmed by the Senate have legal authorities unconfirmed personnel lack, as Richard Holbrooke discovered as special envoy for Pakistan and Afghanistan in the Obama administration when he had to cajole and could not give formal orders to state and defense officials.
>
> Having final authority over budgets is an enormous power, which most cabinet officers have but which Congress refused to grant to the otherwise empowered DNI.

toolkit. These range from new organizations and capabilities, such as creating a national security professional service, to new processes like an overall national security budget, and new emphases and priorities, such as a stronger concentration on policy implementation and not just formulation.

New Organizations and Capabilities

Creating new organizations and capabilities has the advantage of circumventing bureaucracies set in their ways but the disadvantages of start-up delays and uncertainties. New entities have to be encouraged and nourished with resources and high-level attention.

Broadened National Security Council. In recognition of the larger scope of issues that are now recognized to affect national security—health, environmental, demographic, and numerous economic issues—the president could increase the staff and conduct issue-specific NSC studies that draw on the relevant departments and agencies. Formal membership could include almost all of the regular cabinet, but attendance at any given session would be by invitation and dependent on the subject matter. The Obama administration took a step in this direction by merging the Homeland Security Council (HSC) staff and operations with the NSC. Some of the National Economic Council (NEC) staff have long been dual-hatted on the NSC staff if they handle trade and foreign economic issues. This change would allow the president to compel interagency attention to issues that might otherwise be neglected or fall in the cracks between departments. This proposal builds on the existing power and processes of the NSC staff but risks dilution of efforts and confusion over priorities.

Statutory Standing for National Security Adviser. Until now, the NSA has had no legal standing or authority. Establishing the post in law—as is already done for many other White House advisers, including the budget director, and economic, environment, and science advisers—could give him legal authority over other executive branch officials and make him better able to issue orders in the president's name. The NSA could be empowered to prepare strategy and resourcing documents and assign personnel to special task forces and otherwise better coordinate and supervise administration policy. On the other hand, statutory standing would subject the NSA to Senate confirmation, which has the risks of opposition or delay and the potential benefit of closer legislative-executive consultation on national security matters. The Tower Commission strongly recommended against this, arguing that confirmation would deny the president the chance to name and consult with his own chosen advisers or would taint their advice. Supporters of the change note that Henry Kissinger testified to Congress 43 times while simultaneously serving as NSA and secretary of state, answering freely all questions except his personal advice to the president. While the change has legal benefits empowering the NSA, it faces strong opposition from former officials, in part because they fear Senate involvement in the selection of advisers.

Strategic Planning Unit at the National Security Council. Many reports and former officials have urged the creation of an organization in the NSC that can do long-range strategic planning. The Bush and Obama administrations made steps in this direction, but those efforts were limited by the number of staff and the number of issues on which they could gain high-level attention.[14] While such limitations may always be present, the value added from strategic visioning and planning can be significant.

National Security Professional Service. Personnel assigned to the NSC staff and to the offices of senior policy makers are still dependent on the vagaries of their home departments and their rules. The armed forces are better because of the Goldwater–Nichols law requiring experience in multiservice posts, but civilians cannot easily move across departmental lines to gain interagency experience. The foreign service remains administratively and culturally separate from the civil service, and even senior executive service (SES) personnel cannot easily move between agencies. A professional service could have its own education and training program and could be subjected to rotational assignments that could make its people more effective interagency officials. One major cost of such a system is the need for a personnel *float* of 10% to 15% to allow for midcareer education and training. The military has had such a system for decades, but civilian agencies do not.[15]

Expeditionary Civilian Forces. For several years, officials have recognized the need for rapidly deployable civilians to serve in the messy and chaotic situations that exist in war-torn countries even after major combat has ended or in natural or humanitarian disaster zones. While some of the field operations can be contracted, government officials are needed to deal with the local government and supervise the programs. Yet, the rules and expectations of the civil service make it hard to find people willing and qualified to serve in hardship posts abroad, especially on short notice. Civilian health and life insurance, for example, doesn't adequately cover such situations. Various proposals have been offered for creating this capability. Some suggest a kind of standby reserve of people who sign up with a willingness to be called later. Others prefer having administrative units that regularly train like military reservists. Another idea is to recruit a corps of retirees or former officials for possible future service. The main obstacle to creating some sort of capability has been the cost.

Increased Foreign Language Proficiency. Numerous studies and Government Accountability Office (GAO) reports confirm that far too few Americans sent abroad have adequate foreign language skills. GAO found persistent gaps in the language proficiency of State Department, DOD, and Department of Homeland Security (DHS) personnel. Numerous programs are being tried to close those gaps—such as DOD's foreign language proficiency pay and targeted recruitment and training efforts—but the shortfalls remain. There is a small nationwide education grant program, the Boren National Security Education Program, started in 1991, providing funds for the study of languages deemed critical to U.S. security. These programs could be expanded or modified to produce more significant results.

Interagency Oversight by Congress. The legislative branch still writes laws, approves money, and conducts oversight via turf-conscious committees. Only rare acts of comity bring members of the defense and foreign policy committees to discuss shared problems like policies for Afghanistan, Pakistan, Russia, or China. Even rarer is coordination between the national security committees and those with an economic focus as foreign economic policy is often treated as only a subset of domestic economic policy. Rarest of all is collaboration between authorizers and appropriators. Congress could do its job better if it created a select committee on national security for these multiagency operations or at least made use of joint committees or subcommittees for shared problems and integrated solutions.

Revisit Recent Creations. Congress created several major new organizations in the aftermath of the 9/11 attacks, notably the DNI, DHS, and the National Counterterrorism Center (NCTC). Each has had problems that might be attributed to start-up challenges or perhaps to flawed design. Congress and the president should revisit the composition and functioning of each of these organizations with an open mind.[16]

New Processes

The existing machinery for foreign policy lacks some features–*apps*, in information technology (IT) terms—that arguably would make it more effective and thus a better tool for the U.S. government. Each of these proposals comes from practitioners with long experience in foreign policy.

Empowered Interagency Teams. One of the most far-reaching proposals by PNSR was to create, directly under the NSA, interagency teams with specific charters to deal with issues. The proposal was to give each team a mission, legal authorities, and some budget resources and allow the team leader the ability to request specific people from elsewhere in the government. Giving such teams their own limited budgets for programs could greatly increase their abilities to act speedily and flexibly in response to changing conditions. Such teams could function at the Washington level to coordinate interagency approaches and at subordinate regional and country levels as well. In order to have sufficient authorities, the positions would probably need legislative action and perhaps even Senate confirmation of the team leader.[17]

Overall National Security Budget. Several groups in recent years have recommend the preparation of a single, integrated national security budget in contrast to the current system, where each agency and department prepares its own budget in consultation with Office of Management and Budget (OMB), but elements are not traded off or in direct competition with each other either in the White House or in Congress. One presumed benefit from such budgeting would be to highlight to lawmakers and the public the contributions to national security of less-popular activities like foreign aid. Another possible benefit is that such a budget arrangement would better allow policy makers to shift resources between agencies in order to take advantage of special capabilities rather than defaulting, as so often at present, to the resource-rich DOD. Given an overall budget, the president could then institute a process, as in DOD today, for giving multiagency planning guidance to accomplish missions while staying within fiscal limits.

Office of Management and Budget and National Security Council Linkage During Policy Formulation. Most foreign policy decisions are made without specific consideration of budgetary factors. OMB gets tasked to find money to carry out policies only toward the end of the process. Many studies have recommended joint NSC staff and OMB participation throughout the policy analysis and formulation process, not least so that the cost implications and possible constraints are well understood. This would require a difficult merging of quite different perspectives, skills, and organizational cultures.

Contingency Funds. One of the greatest deficiencies cited by executive branch officials is the lack of emergency spending authority except for traditional natural disaster and refugee relief. What used to be (in 2011 dollars) a billion-dollar presidential contingency fund for foreign policy activities is now $25 million, slashed because of abuses and because of a congressional reluctance to give the president too much ability to get America involved in foreign problems without legislative consent. Existing transfer and reprogramming authority is well established for DOD but confusing, complex, and quite slow for State and the United States Agency of International Development (USAID). It might be possible to win congressional support for modestly larger contingency funds in return for demonstrated willingness to consult in advance on their use—in effect, a grand bargain trading funding flexibility for closer oversight. A modest step in that direction was made in 2012, when Congress enacted a $200 million Global Security Contingency Fund to be jointly administered by the State Departments and DOD and requiring advance notifications to Congress.[18]

Rationalized and Reorganized Foreign Assistance Programs. As discussed in Chapters 6 and 7, the State Department and USAID have different authorities over foreign assistance and often disagree over its purposes. The Quadrennial Diplomacy and Development Review (QDDR) process under Secretary Clinton, which reviewed the structure, priorities, and goals for the civilian foreign policy agencies, was supposed to resolve those differences administratively, but many issues remained unresolved, and the final resolution requires legislation. Much could be done to improve the foreign assistance tool if a comprehensive new law could be enacted removing the underbrush of outdated provisions and establishing clear guidance for the future.

New Emphases and Priorities

While the previous sections discussed missing organizations and processes, reformers have also pointed to missing mind-sets among policy makers. Senior officials face enormous pressures to concentrate and deal with only the most urgent matters, and that leads to a preoccupation with short-term, often short-sighted, measures that can be quickly accomplished, regardless of long-term costs or consequences. These reform proposals urge policy makers to think differently about their duties and opportunities.

Long-Range Strategic Focus. Many commentators lament that U.S. national security policies tend to be ad hoc and short range without the long view and strategic focus they favor. They recognize the tyranny of the inbox, the inevitable priority given to the urgent issues that sometimes displaces attention to the more important issues. The most telling example was the Bush administration's postponement of attention to the Hart–Rudman Commission's recommendations on homeland security until September 2001. The recommendation above for an NSC strategic planning cell is part of this shift of emphasis, but it also requires deliberate actions by all senior decision makers—to make time for strategic thought and to demand strategic analyses by their subordinates. It may also require *strategic patience* in awaiting desired results. This emphasis was clearly stated in a formal letter by President Obama's first NSA General Jim Jones, but it remains to be seen to what extent it has been followed.[19] The rhetoric is satisfying, but one would need to know whether officials have changed their behaviors in significant ways to be more strategic.

Concern With Implementation, Not Just Formulation. Many former officials complain that policy making seems to end when the president signs off on the options paper or the decision directive. And since the Iran–Contra scandal and the Tower Commission's reforms, the NSC staff has been warned not to get involved in operational matters. As a consequence, policy oversight and midcourse corrections are infrequent rather than regular functions within the executive branch. It would be better for officials to consider in advance the questions that might arise during the implementation of a new policy and to settle anticipated problems before they arise or at least set up a process for review and adjudication. Implementation was also set out as a specific concern for the Obama NSC in the Jones letter mentioned above.[20]

Revitalized Public Diplomacy and Smart Power. The CSIS report on smart power, cited earlier, was one of several to stress the importance of public diplomacy, which was bureaucratically diminished by the abolition of the U.S. Information Agency in the late 1990s and its merger into the State Department. The QDDR also urged renewed emphasis on public diplomacy. Because so many activities like educational and cultural exchanges take years before they have concrete payoffs, it has been hard to justify those efforts at times of budgetary restraint. It will also be a challenge to increase emphases on public diplomacy at times of cutbacks and austerity budgets.

Increased Institutional Capacity of International Organizations. While there is little the United States can do besides giving encouragement and paying its assigned share of international organization (IO) costs, the United States would be better able to pursue its national interests and shared global interests if the major IOs of which it is a member had their own increased institutional capabilities to act. Until they do, the United States will be the default first responder. When they do, burdens can be shared more equitably and American costs more limited. The United Nations (UN) still lacks the military and other contingency planning staff that would allow it to recruit and operate peacekeeping missions better. The North Atlantic Treaty Organization (NATO), as became glaringly clear during the Libya operations in 2011, can do little without major U.S. military and logistical support. Other organizations could also benefit from increased staff and other capabilities.

Impediments to Reform

When there is so much consensus on what needs to be done, when there are so many hardy perennials that keep blooming in expert reports, why does so little happen? It is not cynical to acknowledge this problem, for there are plausible explanations, even if they may be painful to consider. Impediments to change can be found in mistakes, entrenched interests, honest dilemmas or disagreements, lack of resources, and lessons from past reforms.

Mistakes

Some of the reforms are, in fact, misdiagnoses of the problems or misapplications of remedies. Many reformers tend to favor structural solutions for what might really be process problems. Moving boxes on an organizational chart has a clarity far greater than achieving understanding of how the people in that box will act once they are moved. Will they fit in and be loyal or resist and make everything worse? Maybe a process change, some coordination or consultation device, would work nearly as well. Similarly, creating a new organization has many advantages over trying to make an existing one perform new tasks or act in a quite different way. But, that creates its own set of start-up problems, as DHS discovered.

Too many reformers assume that an order to act differently is sufficient to achieve desired results. That overlooks the bureaucratic and cultural adjustments that might be required. Giving 22 once-separate organizations a common homeland security mission was not enough to create a cohesive and effective DHS, in part because each organization had long been performing other missions and would still be doing them in addition to homeland security. They had to be cajoled and coerced into working together. Often, the greatest payoffs can come when employees are given incentives, and not just orders, to do the right thing. Personnel and pay incentives can be powerful motivators.

Another mistake of reformers is to assume away cultural differences and difficulties in changing the way people in organizations think and act. The army and navy think quite differently about coordinating the battlespace and the chain of responsibility. The differences between military and foreign service officers are even greater. The military is ingrained to think strategically about accomplishing a single mission—defeat the enemy. The diplomats worry every day about how to accomplish and adjust many competing, simultaneous goals with particular countries. Policy planners like to think about results, not budgets and spending authority. It's hard to bridge some of these bureaucratic or professional cultural differences.

Another error is failure to anticipate how things might go wrong despite best efforts and intentions. Military planners build branches and sequels into their war plans, but even they have to cope with surprise and uncertainty. As USAID reduced its personnel levels in response to budget pressures, few realized that it would lose its capacity to run operations and be able only to administer contracts. The Obama administration created several foreign policy *czars* without realizing that their lack of statutory authority would hinder their performance.

Many reforms fix a particular problem for a particular agency while creating others across the rest of the government. The Nixon–Kissinger centralization of power over national security solved the coordination problem and minimized the leak problem, but it left the rest of government ill informed, underutilized, and low in morale. The downgrading of the NSC in the Reagan administration solved the problems of maintaining focus on domestic issues and avoiding Kissinger-like egotism, but it allowed the staff to cause the greater problem of the Iran–Contra scandal. Avoiding the problems of confirmation of the NSA and the foreign policy czars solved that problem but left them with inadequate authority and no ready liaison with Congress.

Finally, there is the attribution error. Many foreign policy problems are not matters of organization or process but of substance. The policies just aren't working, or they are unpopular. Bureaucratic fixes won't fix them. Cosmetic changes are, as the advertising people say, like putting lipstick on a pig. U.S. problems in the Arab world were not caused by dismantling the U.S. Information Agency, and they won't be solved simply by reinvigorating public diplomacy. The failure to find weapons of mass destruction (WMD) in Iraq in 2003 was not caused by an intelligence failure but by the fact that they weren't there.

Entrenched Interests

Government bureaucracies have their own selfish interests, their established roles, missions, and budgets, and they want to defend them. If drones are to be flown, the U.S. Air Force wants to fly them. If talks are being held that might affect the strength of the dollar, Treasury wants to be in charge. If budget estimates are to be made, OMB insists on making them. No agency wants to surrender its authorities, and certainly not a chunk of its budget, to another agency. When Congress wanted to create the DNI with broad budget power, the defense secretary trumped that ace by getting legislation preserving his authorities over the parts of the intelligence community (IC) housed in DOD.

Congress is often the protector of the organizations it sets up, funds, and oversees. And, Congress is itself divided by chambers and committees into self-protective units. Although the 9/11 Commission recommended creating a single congressional committee with authorizing and appropriations power over the IC, the appropriators successfully resisted. Opposition to contingency funds will last just as long as lawmakers feel underappreciated and under consulted by the executive branch and as long as they fear the president might do something stupid or dangerous contrary to congressional advice.

Serious reforms have to take these interests into account and either accommodate them in some way or find a way of overcoming resistance without causing even bigger or longer-lasting problems. That happened with Goldwater–Nichols and with the creation of the congressional budget process, but each took time and effort.

Genuine Dilemmas

Some reforms are blocked by honest disagreements, especially when each side has valid arguments. Centralization and decentralization each have costs and benefits, and different people can weigh those differences with opposing final judgments. The call for close, centralized coordination but decentralized execution sounds simple in theory but can become quite difficult in practice.

The same is true of structural versus functional organizations and flat versus hierarchical ones. Each approach has its advocates both in general administrative theory and in application to particular programs. Whatever importance the secretary of state may want to give to a functional problem like arms sales or human rights, the fact remains that the regional bureaus and country desks have the real power in the State Department. An NSC staff that is flat generates a span of control problems and allows too many people to interact with the president. A strict hierarchy limits those problems but also limits the flow of information and alternative perspectives to the president.

How to run a multiagency operation also has no easy answer. A lead agency provides authority and accountability but no assurances that others will follow and do their share. A coordinated approach run out of the NSC might achieve better integration but has little power over shirkers.

The call for increased civilian capacity ran into its own chicken-and-egg problem. Many officials, including lawmakers, wanted the State Department to build up its staffing and planning but feared that it could not handle a large infusion of new funds. It couldn't get extra resources until it proved that it could wisely spend extra resources, so it never got them for the proof.

Still another impediment that is quite rational is the lower priority given to reform because of the demands of current problems. Scheduling time for a discussion of distant, future threats might take time away from a meeting on next week's hearing or next year's budget.

Reorganizations, in particular, are time-consuming and highly disruptive, so they often have to wait. Changing the personnel system is much harder than rearranging the organization chart and longer to show a payoff.

The secretary's priorities may be different from a subordinate official's, and only one of them is likely to win.

Lack of Resources

The biggest obstacle to reform is often a lack of resources to make it happen. Human resources can't be acquired overnight, and colonels and program managers can't be grown in a month or two. Many U.S. government departments are likely to lose large fractions of their senior leadership to normal retirement in the next few years, and with them goes the institutional memory and real-world experience that their replacements will need years to acquire. Substituting contracted personnel solves the staffing problem while creating questions of loyalty and accountability. Similarly, the adoption of digital technologies and advanced information systems promises benefits but risks high costs, short-term obsolescence, and the cultural divide between early adopters and senior people still accustomed to paper documents and analog equipment.

Money has always been a problem for reform efforts, and budgetary austerity will only make that problem worse in the years ahead. Growing civilian capacity takes money. Even the float for training and education is an added cost when every cost has to be minimized. Creating specialized units—whether civilian reconstruction teams or military constabulary forces—is harder to justify than multipurpose organizations. High-tech systems solve some problems, but they also bring added costs.

The risks of delay are harder to quantify than the costs of proceeding with a change. And, the opportunity costs of failing to make reforms are next to impossible to quantify in advance. These factors do not make reform unacceptable, only harder to justify persuasively.

Warning Lessons

In addition to these specific problems facing particular reforms, there are some lessons earlier reformers identified and which today's reformers should learn and heed. Robert McNamara achieved major reforms in the Pentagon, taking on and defeating entrenched military interests year after year. But even he acknowledged, "One can slay only so many dragons each day." Vice President Biden, when a senator, said, "Don't die on a small cross." Their point was that officials need to pick their battles carefully, for their time, energy, and resources are necessarily limited.

Another painful lesson is that today's reform is often tomorrow's problem. The U.S. government now depends on contractors for many important activities—including one fourth of the people in the IC and half the staff staffing the Office of the Secretary of Defense—not to mention the large contractor contingents supporting U.S. personnel in Iraq and Afghanistan. America grew dependent on contractors because it wanted to reduce the number of career government employees. Broadening military health care benefits responded to immediate medical and morale needs, but it also created high long-term costs. The Goldwater–Nichols requirement of joint assignments in order to gain senior rank left some officers concerned that younger officers will not gain sufficient grounding in their core competencies. Strengthening the combatant commanders tilted the Pentagon focus more toward current operations but with the risk that long-term force recruitment and sustainment might be neglected.

Perhaps the most double-edged lesson is George Shultz's famous comment, "Nothing ever gets settled in this town." Officials who feel strongly will continue to fight for their preferred positions. Losers in one debate will seize targets of opportunity during the next one. There are no final victories in bureaucracy. Reforms accomplished may be undone, while reforms stymied may yet be achieved.

❖ ❖ ❖

America's foreign policy toolkit could be strengthened by some new tools, some reshaped tools, some new processes, and some changed priorities and emphases in how they are used. Reforms, however, are difficult to implement because of bureaucratic resistance, limited resources, and unavoidable dilemmas. Change has its winners and losers, so it often faces vigorous opposition. One reason for hope is that America has a more diverse and capable toolkit today thanks to earlier reform efforts that succeeded against the odds. Even the U.S. government can be changed.

The Changing Foreign Policy Toolkit

Reform, like policy making itself, is a journey and not a destination. America's foreign policy toolkit has been undergoing continuous change since 1789, responding to the ideas of its leaders and the challenges and opportunities the nation faced. Individuals have made a difference, as George Washington did by creating cabinet government and a system of civilian control of the military; as Thomas Jefferson did by shrinking the armed forces and trying to keep America out of the Napoleonic wars in Europe by use of a trade embargo; as Lincoln, McKinley, Wilson, and FDR did by running wars from the White House; as Harry Truman did by insisting on a single DOD and by strengthening the civilian foreign policy agencies; as Richard Nixon and Henry Kissinger did by creating a powerful NSC staff.

The organizations and institutions created over time gave America better tools for the conduct of its foreign policy: a professional, widely deployed foreign service, armed forces trained and equipped for traditional combat as well as counterinsurgency, armed forces integrated in planning and truly joint in operations, a multiplicity of organizations designed to handle specific aspects of foreign economic policy, and a large though secret IC. These organizations have also been staffed by lesser-known people who themselves have made differences in the conduct of U.S. foreign policy by their professionalism, their dedication, their bravery, their innovations, and their honest but not always welcome advice.

Similarly, having specialized institutions gives the president options that would not exist in their absence. It would have been much harder to fight terrorists if the Special Operations Command (SOCOM) had not been created, nurtured, and empowered. It would have been much harder to promote overseas economic development—or to bribe foreign governments to support U.S. positions—without a major foreign aid program. It would have been much harder to anticipate and counter potential threats without a large and capable IC—and now DHS. It would have been much harder to harmonize international security and economic policies without the international institutions the United States encouraged and joined.

People matter. Organizations matter. And processes matter, too. It made a difference, early in the 20th century, when the army and navy began joint planning and when the State Department was later included in interagency discussions. It made a difference when key stakeholders sat around the same table, and the NSC gave advice to the president. It made a difference when presidents were forced to prepare annual budgets and create offices for controlling spending and even when Congress launched its own big-picture budget process. It made a difference when presidents were required to take responsibility for Central Intelligence Agency (CIA) covert actions and also to inform Congress.

This book has focused on the institutions and processes for U.S. foreign policy rather than on the substance and details of that policy. Instead of recommending what to do to strengthen national security, this volume is intended to be a ready reference book on how to do what is decided and who is best suited for particular tasks. That knowledge can be used by advocates or opponents of change. But without arguing rigid determinism, one can see that process does have some influence over substance. A resource- and capability-rich Pentagon makes it easier to have a militarized foreign policy. A disintegrated collection of foreign economic policy organizations makes it harder to have a consistent, coherent foreign economic policy. A White House-centered NSC system and staff is more politically attuned and responsive than most cabinet departments. A large vice presidential staff can make the vice president a more engaged and influential official than just a small staff.

Some reformers may want to change the substance of U.S. foreign policy in general or in particular details. If this book has any applicable lesson for them, it is that it is insufficient merely to announce a change in policy. To have real force and effect, that change must be propagated through the institutions and processes that make policy day to day. The toolkit must be made responsive. The budgeteers need to assign resources to carry out the change. The departments and agencies must insist on compliance with the change and develop oversight and feedback loops to make sure. Personnel offices must find the people with the appropriate skills, assign them to the changed tasks, and reward their performance over time. Processes will need to be reshaped to monitor and reinforce the change.

America's foreign policy toolkit doesn't just belong to the president. It also belongs to the Congress that empowers and funds it and to the people who work within it. Ultimately, it belongs to the rest of us, who through our own processes of paying taxes, voting, speaking, and petitioning, influence what the president and Congress do. Thus, whether that toolkit is capable and wisely used depends in part on us.

Notes

Introduction

1. Jack Anderson, *Peace, War & Politics: An Eyewitness Account* (New York: Forge Books, 1999), 134.
2. Bob Woodward, *Bush at War* (New York: Simon & Schuster, 2002), 38; *The 9/11 Commission Report* (New York: W. W. Norton, 2004), 330.
3. Donald Rumsfeld, *Known and Unknown: A Memoir* (New York: Sentinel, 2011), 346; Hugh Shelton, *Without Hesitation* (New York: St. Martin's Press, 2010), 440.
4. *The 9/11 Commission Report,* 333, www.911commission.gov/report/911Report.pdf
5. Public Law 107–40.
6. Public Law 107–56.
7. Charles A. Stevenson, *Congress at War: The Politics of Conflict since 1789* (Washington, DC: Potomac Books, 2007), 18.
8. Public Law 107–296.
9. Graham Allison and Philip Zelikow, *Essence of Decision: Explaining the Cuban Missile Crisis, Second Edition,* (New York: Longman, 1999), 6, 300–301.

Chapter 1

1. George C. Herring, *From Colony to Superpower: U.S. Foreign Relations Since 1776* (New York: Oxford University Press, 2008), 53.
2. Christopher Collier and James Lincoln Collier, *Decision in Philadelphia* (New York: Ballantine Books, 1986), 348.
3. Quoted in Richard B. Morris, *The Forging of the Union, 1781–1789* (New York: Harper & Row, 1987), 266.
4. Morris, 130–132, 154–159; Frederick W. Marks, III, *Independence on Trial: Foreign Affairs and the Making of the Constitution* (Baton Rouge, LA: State University Press, 1973), 59.
5. Marks 111, 113; Morris, 209.
6. Marks, 16; *Journal of Continental Congress,* June 21, 1786; October 30, 1786; and July 18, 1787.
7. Marks, 37–44, 49.
8. *Journal of the Continental Congress,* February 8, 1786.
9. *Journal of the Continental Congress,* October 18, 1786.

10. Quoted in Morris, 266.
11. Address of the Annapolis Convention, September 1786.
12. Marks, xvii–xix, citing Forrest McDonald, Page Smith, James MacGregor Burns, and Merrill Jensen.
13. Herring, 49.
14. Marks, 170, 142–145; Richard H. Kohn, ed., *The United States Military Under the Constitution, 1789–1989* (New York University Press, 1991), 63–71.
15. Collier & Collier, 103–4; Richard Beeman, *Plain, Honest Men: The Making of the American Constitution* (New York: Random House, 2009), 67.
16. Collier & Collier, 114–115.
17. Collier & Collier, 198–200.
18. David O. Stewart, *The Summer of 1787: The Men Who Invented the Constitution* (New York: Simon & Schuster, 2007), 103–104.
19. The original allocation of seats in the House of Representatives gave Southern states 45% of the seats and Northern states 55%. After the first census in 1790, along with the addition of Vermont and Kentucky, Southern states had 46.5% using the three-fifths ratio. The actual house apportionment was 44.8%. If only free inhabitants had been counted, the Southern percentage would have dropped to 41.0%. If slaves had been counted wholly, the figure would have been 49.9%. George William Van Cleve, *A Slaveholders' Union* (University of Chicago Press, 2010), 121.
20. Farrand's *Records of the Federal Convention,* vol. 1, 24–26, http://memory.loc.gov/ammem/amlaw/lwfr.html
21. Collier & Collier, 121, 123.
22. Collier & Collier, 316, 322–323.
23. *Federalist* 51, http://thomas.loc.gov/home/histdox/fed_51.html
24. Quoted in Cecil V. Crabb, Jr., and Pat M. Holt, *Invitation to Struggle* (Washington, DC: CQ Press, 1992), ix.
25. Quoted in Collier & Collier, 340–341.
26. Beeman, 373–376.
27. Pauline Maier, *Ratification: The People Debate the Constitution, 1787–1788* (New York: Simon & Schuster, 2010), 124; Marks, 197.
28. Beeman, 386–90.
29. Beeman, 391–392; Maier, 459.
30. Beeman, 394.
31. Beeman, 395–400.
32. Beeman, 400–403.
33. Maier, 429, 433.
34. Quoted in David P. Currie, *The Constitution in Congress: The Federalist Period, 1789–1801* (University of Chicago Press, 1997), 4n.
35. Maier, 446.
36. Maier, 446.

37. Statutes at Large, I Stat. 119, http://memory.loc.gov/ammem/amlaw/lwsl.html; Richard H. Kohn, *Eagle and Sword* (New York: Free Press, 1975), 108, 126.
38. Currie, 42.

Chapter 2

1. Charles A. Stevenson, *Congress at War: The Politics of Conflict Since 1789* (Washington, DC: Potomac Books, 2007), 1.
2. Fred I. Greenstein, "The Policy-Driven Leadership of James K. Polk: Making the Most of a Weak Presidency," *Presidential Studies Quarterly*, vol. 40, no. 4, December 2010, 725.
3. Charles A. Stevenson, *Warriors and Politicians: U.S. Civil–Military Relations Under Stress* (London: Rutledge, 2006), 31.
4. Leonard D. White, *The Federalists: A Study in Administrative History, 1789–1801* (New York: Free Press, 1948), 103, 106.
5. White, *Federalists*, 210–236.
6. White, *Federalists*, 61–63; George C. Herring, *From Colony to Superpower: U.S. Foreign Relations Since 1776* (New York: Oxford University Press, 2008), 77–79; Gordon S. Wood, *Empire of Liberty* (New York: Oxford University Press, 2009), 196–199.
7. Kenneth J. Hagan, *This People's Navy* (New York: Free Press, 1991), 32–34, 36–37.
8. Stevenson, *Warriors*, 79–92.
9. Stevenson, *Warriors*, 88–92.
10. Leonard D. White, *The Jeffersonians: A Study in Administrative History, 1801–1829* (New York: Free Press, 1951), 4, 213; Wood, 292.
11. White, *Jeffersonians*, 35, 48, 52.
12. Stevenson, *Congress*, 16.
13. White, *Jeffersonians*, 30–31, 36–37; Stevenson, *Congress*, 38.
14. White, *Jeffersonians*, 248.
15. Herring, 134, 144–151.
16. Herring, 138; 74. William Barnes and John Heath Morgan, *The Foreign Service of the United States* (Washington, DC: Department of State Historical Office, 1961), 74.
17. Herring, 139–143, 155–157.
18. White, *Jeffersonians*, 94, 99.
19. Herring, 178–183.
20. Kinley J. Brauer, "1821–1860: Economics and the Diplomacy of American Expansionism," in William H. Becker and Samuel F. Wells, Jr., eds., *Economics and World Power: An Assessment of American Diplomacy since 1789* (New York: Columbia University Press, 1984), 56–60, 82–83.
21. Herring, 182–183.
22. Herring, 164, 169; Russell F. Weigley, *History of the United States Army, Enlarged Edition* (Bloomington: Indiana University Press, 1984), 161–162.

23. Greenstein, 725.
24. Herring, 191–192.
25. Herring, 198–201.
26. Leonard D. White, *The Jacksonians: A Study in Administrative History, 1829–1861* (New York: Free Press, 1954), 53–54, 63–65.
27. Henry Bartholomew Cox, *War, Foreign Affairs, and Constitutional Power, 1829–1901* (Cambridge, MA: Ballinger, 1984), 147–148; Herring, 201–205.
28. White, *Jacksonians*, 69, 92; Greenstein, 731.
29. Herring, 214–221; Brauer, 104–112.
30. Herring, 210–213, 221; Stevenson, *Congress*, 20.
31. Herring, 228–230, 236–237.
32. Herring, 240–245.
33. See Stevenson, *Warriors*, 230–251.
34. W. Stull Holt, *Treaties Defeated by the Senate* (Baltimore, MD: Johns Hopkins University Press, 1933), 122–124, 139.
35. Leonard D. White, *The Republican Era: A Study in Administrative History, 1869–1901* (New York: Free Press, 1958), 49.
36. Holt, 142–145, 148.
37. David M. Pletcher, "1861–1898: Economic Growth and Diplomatic Adjustment," in Becker & Wells, 120–124, 136, 146.
38. White, *Republican Era*, 158–160.
39. Herring, 308.
40. Herring, 310.
41. Herring, 328; Stevenson, *Congress*, 13–14, 36–37.
42. Herring, 317; White, *Republican Era*, 147–148.
43. Herring, 316–320.
44. Holt, 165–177.
45. Herring, 321–325, 332, 364.
46. Stevenson, *Warriors*, 141; Herring, 367–372.
47. Herring, 345–346; Warren Frederick Ilchman, *Professional Diplomacy in the United States, 1779–1939* (University of Chicago Press, 1961), 3; Barnes, 154.
48. Stevenson, *Warriors*, 143–146, 148.
49. Stevenson, *Warriors*, 149–150.
50. Herring, 372–374.
51. Herring, 358.
52. Herring, 351–352, 356.
53. Herring, 382.
54. Herring, 381, 386, 388–389, 395–396.
55. Herring, 399–401; William H. Becker, "1899–1920: America Adjusts to World Power," in Becker & Wells, 209.
56. Herring, 404–405; Weigley, 348; Hagan, 253.
57. Stevenson, *Congress*, 40, 48.

58. Ernest R. May, *The Ultimate Decision: The President as Commander in Chief* (New York: George Braziller, 1960), 117; Herring, 417–431.
59. Herring, 429–434.
60. Herring, 436.
61. Stevenson, *Congress*, 69; Herring, 439, 452.
62. Herring, 453–455, 489.
63. Richard B. Morris, ed., *Encyclopedia of American History* (New York: Harper & Brothers, 1953), 322–324; Herring, 504–505.
64. Herring, 470–474, 487; Melvyn P. Leffler, "1921–1932: Expansionist Impulses and Domestic Constraints," in Becker & Wells, 254.
65. Becker, in Becker & Wells, 213; Herring, 443.
66. Stevenson, *Warriors*, 96.
67. Ernest R. May, "The Development of Political-Military Consultation in the United States," *Political Science Quarterly*, vol. 70, no. 2 (June 1955), 166–173.
68. May, *Political Science Quarterly*, 172–175; Henry L. Stimson and McGeorge Bundy, *On Active Service in Peace and War* (New York: Harper & Brothers, 1947–48), 495.
69. See Stevenson, *Warriors*, 99–108.
70. Stevenson, *Warriors*, 93, 108–112; Herring, 526, 533–534.
71. Herring, 556–559.

Chapter 3

1. Morton Halperin, *Bureaucratic Politics and Foreign Policy, Second Edition* (Washington, DC: Brookings, 2006), 226–227.
2. Foreign Assistance Act of 1961, Public Law 87–195, sect. 620G and sect. 602.
3. Public Law 105–277, sect. 103.
4. 1 Statutes at Large 96, 561.
5. Public Law 104–201, sect. 1411.
6. Richard E. Neustadt, *Presidential Power and the Modern Presidents, Revised Edition* (New York: Free Press, 1991).
7. See John Yoo memo at www.justice.gov/olc/warpowers925.htm
8. Theodore Sorensen, *Decision-Making in the White House* (New York: Columbia University Press, 1964), 44.
9. Alexander L. George, *Presidential Decision-Making in Foreign Policy: The Effective Use of Information and Advice* (New York: Westview, 1980).
10. Thomas Preston, *The President and His Inner Circle* (New York: Columbia University Press, 2001).
11. Gordon M. Goldstein, *Lessons in Disaster: McGeorge Bundy and the Path to War in Vietnam* (New York: Henry Holt, 2008), 207.
12. Henry L. Stimson and McGeorge Bundy, *On Active Service in Peace and War* (New York: Harper & Brothers, 1947–48), 495.

13. Mark A. Stoler, *Allies and Adversaries* (Chapel Hill: University of North Carolina Press, 2000), 103.
14. See Charles A. Stevenson, "Underlying Assumptions of the National Security Act of 1947," *Joint Forces Quarterly*, 48 (1st quarter 2008), 129–133.
15. Public Law 80–253, sect. 101(a).
16. Ivo M. Saalder and I. M. Destler, *In the Shadow of the Oval Office* (New York: Simon & Schuster, 2009), 70; David Auerswald, "The Evolution of the NSC Process," in Roger Z. George and Harvey Rishikof, *The National Security Enterprise: Navigating the Labyrinth* (Washington, DC: Georgetown University Press, 2011), 40; David Rothkopf, *Running the World* (Public Affairs, 2005), 267; John P. Burke, *Honest Broker?* (College Station: Texas A&M University Press, 2009), 347.
17. Saalder & Destler, 68.
18. Auerswald, 35.
19. See Burke, *Honest Broker?*
20. Saalder & Destler, 70.
21. Rothkopf, 407.
22. Memorandum from James L. Jones, "The 21st Century Interagency Process," March 18, 2009, www.fas.org/irp/offdocs/ppd/nsc031909.pdf
23. Auerswald, 33.
24. Rothkopf, 405.
25. This section is based on www.ndu.edu/icaf/outreach/publications/nspp/docs/icaf-nsc-policy-process-report-10-2010.pdf, 35–45.
26. Morton H. Halperin et al., *Bureaucratic Politics and Foreign Policy, Second Edition* (Washington, DC: Brookings, 2006), 131.
27. George Tenet, *At the Center of the Storm* (New York: HarperCollins, 2007), 449–475.
28. Saalder & Destler, 218.
29. See Peter Feaver and William Inboden, "A Strategic Planning Cell on National Security at the White House," in Daniel W. Drezner, ed., *Avoiding Trivia: The Role of Strategic Planning in American Foreign Policy* (Washington, DC: Brookings, 2009), 98–112.

Chapter 4

1. Cecil V. Crabb, Jr., and Pat M. Holt, *Invitation to Struggle* (Washington, DC: CQ Press, 1992), 242, 187.
2. Rebecca K. C. Hersman, *Friends and Foes* (Washington, DC: Brookings, 2000), 67–70.
3. Crabb & Holt, 237–238; Patrick J. Haney, "Why Do We Still Have an Embargo of Cuba?" in Ralph G. Carter, *Contemporary Cases in U.S. Foreign Policy: From Terrorism to Trade, Fourth Edition*, (Washington, DC: CQ Press, 2011), 340.
4. Michael John Garcia and R. Chuck Mason, "Congressional Oversight and Related Issues Concerning International Security

Agreements Concluded by the United States," *CRS Report for Congress,* October 1, 2009, 3.
5. Glen S. Krutz and Jeffrey S. Peake, *Treaty Politics and the Rise of Executive Agreements* (Ann Arbor: University of Michigan Press, 2009), 71–73.
6. U.S. Congress, Senate Committee on Foreign Relations, *Treaty With Russia on Measures for Further Reduction and Limitation of Strategic Offensive Arms (The New START Treaty),* Executive Report, 111th Cong., 2d sess., October 1, 2010, Exec. Rept. 111–6.
7. Lee H. Hamilton with Jordan Tama, *A Creative Tension: The Foreign Policy Roles of the President and Congress* (Washington, DC: Woodrow Wilson Center Press, 2002), 56.
8. See Thomas E. Mann and Norman J. Ornstein, *The Broken Branch: How Congress Is Failing America and How to Get It Back on Track* (New York: Oxford University Press, 2006); David Epstein and Sharyn O'Halloran, *Delegating Powers: A Transaction Cost Politics Approach to Policy Making Under Separate Powers* (New York: Cambridge University Press, 1999).
9. Gerald Felix Warburg, "Congress; Checking Presidential Power," in Roger Z. George and Harvey Rishikof, eds., *The National Security Enterprise: Navigating the Labyrinth* (Washington, DC: Georgetown University Press, 2011), 230–234.
10. Hamilton, 7.
11. Hamilton, 60.
12. Alexis de Tocqueville, *Democracy in America,* vol. 1 (New York: Vintage Books, 1945), 243.
13. David R. Mayhew, "Actions in the Public Sphere," in Paul J. Quirk and Sarah A. Binder, *The Legislative Branch* (New York: Oxford University Press, 2005), 71.
14. James M. Lindsay, *Congress and the Politics of U.S. Foreign Policy* (Baltimore, MD: Johns Hopkins University Press, 1994), 4.
15. Quoted in Stephen R. Weissman, *A Culture of Deference* (New York: Basic Books, 1995), 14.
16. Quoted in Weissman, 12.
17. Weissman, 14.
18. Bruce W. Jentleson and Rebecca L. Britton, "Still Pretty Prudent," *Journal of Conflict Resolution,* vol. 42, no. 4 (August 1998), 395–417.
19. Ralph G. Carter and James M. Scott, *Choosing to Lead: Understanding Congressional Foreign Policy Entrepreneurs* (Durham, NC: Duke University Press, 2009), 27, 224–225.
20. See Charles A. Stevenson, *Congress at War: The Politics of Conflict Since 1789* (Washington, DC: Potomac Books, 2007), 11–33.
21. Hamilton, 64.
22. David P. Auerswald and Peter F. Cowhey, "Ballotbox Diplomacy: The War Powers Resolution and the Use of Force," *International Studies Quarterly,* vol. 41 (1997), 507.

23. Stevenson, *Congress at War*, 54–55.
24. Stevenson, *Congress at War*, 4.
25. Crabb & Holt, ix.

Chapter 5

1. *John Quincy Adams Memoirs*, vol. vii (Philadelphia, PA: Lippincott, 1875), 359.
2. Shelley Lynne Tomkin, *Inside OMB* (Armonk, NY: M.E. Sharpe, 1998), 55, 62.
3. Gordon Adams, "The Office of Management and Budget: The President's Policy Tool," in Roger Z. George and Harvey Rishikof, *The National Security Enterprise: Navigating the Labyrinth* (Washington, DC: Georgetown University Press, 2011), 58. For a comprehensive look at budgeting for defense, international affairs, and homeland security, see Gordon Adams and Cindy Williams, *Buying National Security* (New York: Routledge, 2009).
4. Adams, 56, 63–64; Tomkin, 118–137.
5. Tomkin, 121–125.
6. See "How Government Plays the Budget Game," *National Journal*, September 30, 2002.
7. Adams, 76.
8. Louis Fisher, *Presidential Spending Power* (Princeton University Press, 1975), 238; William C. Banks and Peter Raven-Hansen, *National Security Law and the Power of the Purse* (New York: Oxford University Press, 1994), 71–72.
9. Public Law 112–81, sect. 1207.
10. The HELP Commission Report on Foreign Assistance Reform, Beyond Assistance, December 2007, 30.
11. Fisher, 204–207.
12. See www.wired.com/dangerroom/2009/05/pentagons-black-budget-grows-to-more-than-50-billion/. For more on secret spending, see Banks & Raven-Hansen, 51–52, 100–105.

Chapter 6

1. Arthur M. Schlesinger, Jr., *A Thousand Days: John F. Kennedy in the White House* (Boston: Houghton Mifflin, 1965), 406.
2. *Foreign Relations of the United States, 1969–76*, vol. II (Washington, DC: U.S. Government Printing Office), 768.
3. U.S. Statutes, I, 28–29; 22 U.S. Code 2656.
4. Leonard D. White, *The Federalists* (New York: Free Press, 1948), 136.
5. Center for Strategic and International Studies (CSIS), *The Embassy of the Future* (Washington, DC: Center for Strategic and International Studies, 2007), 47.
6. Edward Peck, "Chief of Mission Authority: A Powerful but Underused Tool," *Foreign Service Journal*, December 2007, 30; Robert B. Oakley

and Michael Casey, Jr., "The Country Team: Restructuring America's First Line of Engagement," *JFQ*, 47 (4th quarter 2007), 150.
7. Oakley & Casey, 150.
8. Oakley & Casey, 146.
9. See U.S. Senate Foreign Relations Committee, "Iraq: The Transition From a Military Mission to a Civilian-Led Effort," Committee Print, S. Prt. 112–3, January 31, 2011, 7; Karen DeYoung, "U.S. Evaluating Size of Baghdad Embassy, Officials Say," *Washington Post*, February 17, 2012.
10. Marc Grossman, "The State Department: Culture as Interagency Destiny?" in Roger Z. George and Harvey Rishikof, eds., *The National Security Enterprise: Navigating the Labyrinth* (Washington, DC: Georgetown University Press, 2011), 80.
11. Advisory Committee on Transformational Diplomacy, *Final Report of the State Department in 2025 Working Group*, U.S. Department of State, 2008, 28.
12. Frederick C. Smith and Franklin C. Miller, "The Office of Secretary of Defense: Civilian Masters?" in George & Rishikof, 109.
13. Data from American Foreign Service Association.
14. William Barnes and John Heath Morgan, *The Foreign Service of the United States* (Washington, DC: Department of State, 1961), 207.
15. Harry W. Kopp and Charles A. Gillespie, *Career Diplomacy: Life and Work in the U.S. Foreign Service* (Washington, DC: Georgetown University Press, 2008), 20.
16. "A More Representative Foreign Service," Association for Diplomatic Studies and Training, www.usdiplomacy.org
17. Grossman, 83.
18. Henry A. Kissinger, *Years of Upheaval* (New York: Little, Brown, 1982), 442–443.
19. Alexander M. Haig, Jr., *Caveat: Realism, Reagan, and Foreign Policy* (New York: Scribner, 1984), 27; James A. Baker, III, *The Politics of Diplomacy: Revolution, War, and Peace, 1989–1992* (New York: G.P. Putnam's Sons, 1995), 31.
20. Col. Rickey L. Rife, "Defense Is From Mars, State Is From Venus," Army War College, 1998.
21. Rife, "Defense Is From Mars, State Is From Venus."
22. Jim Hoagland, "Fighting Iran—With Patience," *Washington Post*, February 25, 2007.
23. Project on National Security Reform, "Ensuring Security in an Unpredictable World, Preliminary Findings," July 2008, 36–37.
24. Center for Strategic and International Studies (CSIS) Report, *A Steep Hill: Congress and U.S. Efforts to Strengthen Fragile States*, March 2008, 23.
25. Figures based on congressional action in annual budget resolutions as reported in *CQ Almanacs*.

26. Charles Flickner, "Removing Impediments to an Effective Partnership With Congress," in Lael Brainard, ed., *Security by Other Means* (Washington, DC: Brookings, 2007), 242; CSIS Report, *A Steep Hill*, app. G, 85.

Chapter 7

1. Stephen D. Cohen, *The Making of United States International Economic Policy, Fifth Edition* (Westport, CT: Praeger, 2000), 263.
2. David A. Baldwin, *Economic Statecraft* (Princeton, NJ: Princeton University Press, 1985), 41–42.
3. Lael Brainard, *Security by Other Means* (Washington, DC: CSIS & Brookings, 2007), 18.
4. The Fed is legally independent of the Treasury Department, though they try to harmonize their operations. Decentralization is built into the system, with 5 of the 12 members of the Fed's key open market committee chosen by regional banks dominated by local banking interests.
5. Cohen, 5.
6. Commerce Department figures; Benn Steil and Robert E. Litan, *Financial Statecraft* (New Haven, CT: Yale University Press, 2006), 3.
7. Joan E. Spero and Jeffrey A. Hart, *The Politics of International Economic Relations, Sixth Edition* (New York: Thomson/Wadsworth, 2003), 387–388.
8. Index of Global Philanthropy and Remittances 2010, www.hudson.org/files/pdf_upload/Index_of_Global_Philanthropy_and_Remittances_2010
9. See KeithHennessey.com, "Roles of the President's White House Economic Advisors," August 8, 2010.
10. Brian Katz, "International Trade and Economic Policy, Planning and Strategy in the USG: The National Economic Council (NEC)," paper for the Project on National Security Reform, 2008.
11. George Thomas Kurian, ed., *A Historical Guide to the U.S. Government* (New York: Oxford University Press, 1998), 235–241.
12. Cohen, 47.
13. Gordon Adams and Cindy Williams, *Buying National Security* (New York: Routledge, 2010), 55.
14. Department of Commerce homepage, www.commerce.gov/about-department-commerce
15. Cohen, 55–57.
16. Cohen, 12.
17. Steven Radelet, "Strengthening U.S. Development Assistance," in Brainard, 94.
18. Adams & Williams, 86–90.
19. Adams & Williams, 64.
20. Adams & Williams, 90–92.

21. Adams & Williams, 62–64.
22. Gary Clyde Hufbauer et al., *Economic Sanctions Reconsidered, Third Edition* (Washington, DC: Peterson Institute for International Economics, 2009), 148–154.
23. Steil & Litan, 27.
24. Vivian C. Jones et al., "Trade Preferences: Economic Issues and Policy Options," *CRS Report for Congress*, September 24, 2010.
25. William H. Cooper, "Free Trade Agreements: Impact on U.S. Trade and Implications for U.S. Trade Policy," *CRS Report for Congress*, February 23, 2010.
26. Vivian C. Jones, "Trade Remedies: A Primer," *CRS Report for Congress*, July 30, 2008.
27. Radelet in Brainard, 94.
28. Gerald F. Hyman, "A Cabinet-Level Development Agency: Right Problem, Wrong Solution," Center for Strategic and International Studies (CSIS), January 2009, 2.
29. Brainard, 33.
30. For QDDR, see www.state.gov/s/dmr/qddr/index.htm
31. Brainard, 5.
32. Curt Tarnoff et al., "Foreign Aid: An Introduction to U.S. Programs and Policy," *CRS Report for Congress*, February 10, 2009.
33. Public Law 112–81, sect. 1207.
34. Adams & Williams, 67–77.
35. Adams & Williams, 46–49.
36. Adams & Williams, 86–90.
37. Spero & Hart, 14–24.
38. Steil & Litan, 3.
39. Steil & Litan, 32–41.
40. Steil & Litan, 64–66.
41. Spero & Hart, 148.
42. James K. Jackson, "U.S. Direct Investment Abroad: Trends and Current Issues," *CRS Report for Congress*, February 1, 2011.
43. James K. Jackson, "Foreign Direct Investment in the United States: An Economic Analysis," *CRS Report for Congress*, February 1, 2011; Michael V. Seitzinger, "Foreign Investment in the United States: Major Federal Statutory Restrictions," *CRS Report for Congress*, January 26, 2009.
44. James K. Jackson, "The Committee on Foreign Investment in the United States (CFIUS)," *CRS Report for Congress*, February 4, 2010; CFIUS Report to Congress, November, 2010.
45. Edward M. Graham and David M. Marchick, *U.S. National Security and Foreign Direct Investment* (Washington, DC: Institute for International Economics, May 2006), 128–141.
46. See Graham & Marchick, 95–121.

Chapter 8

1. Dana Priest, *The Mission* (New York: W. W. Norton, 2003), 14.
2. Oral history interview, Historical Office of the Secretary of Defense, May 18, 2001, 9.
3. Joint publication 3–0, Joint Operations, 22 March 2010, I-2.
4. Joint Publication 1, Doctrine for the Armed Forces of the United States, 20 March 2009, xi.
5. Joint Publication 1, x.
6. Carl von Clausewitz, Michael Howard, and Peter Paret, eds., *On War* (Princeton, NJ: Princeton University Press, 1982), 87.
7. Michael Meese and Isaiah Wilson III, "The Military: Forging a Joint Warrior Culture," in Roger Z. George and Harvey Rishikof, eds., *The National Security Enterprise: Navigating the Labyrinth* (Washington, DC: Georgetown University Press, 2011), 125.
8. Charles A. Stevenson, *Congress at War: The Politics of Conflict Since 1789* (Washington, DC: Potomac Books, 2007), 38.
9. Kenneth J. Hagan, *This People's Navy* (New York: Free Press, 1991), 194–195, 208–209; John Whiteclay Chambers II, ed., *The Oxford Companion to American Military History* (Oxford University Press, 1999), 488–489.
10. Charles A. Stevenson, *SecDef: The Nearly Impossible Job of Secretary of Defense* (Washington, DC: Potomac Books, 2006), 7.
11. See Charles A. Stevenson, *Warriors and Politicians: U.S. Civil–Military Relations Under Stress* (New York: Routledge, 2006), 205–209.
12. Bradley Graham, *By His Own Rules* (New York: Public Affairs, 2009), 216.
13. 2010 U.S. Census; Population Representation in the Military Services, Defense Equal Opportunity Management Institute (DEOMI), Fiscal Year 2008 Report.
14. Population Representation in the Military Services, Fiscal Year 2008 Report.
15. Harvey M. Sapolsky et al., *U.S. Defense Politics* (New York: Routledge, 2009), 31.
16. Lawrence Kapp, "Reserve Component Personnel Issues: Questions and Answers," *CRS Report for Congress,* February 10, 2009; Michael Waterhouse and JoAnne O'Bryant, "National Guard Personnel and Deployments: Fact Sheet," *CRS Report for Congress,* January 17, 2008.
17. Col. Rickey L. Rife, "Defense Is From Mars, State Is From Venus," Army War College, 1998.
18. Meese & Wilson, 127–130.
19. Frederick C. Smith and Franklin C. Miller, "The Office of the Secretary of Defense: Civilian Masters?" in George & Rishikof, 109–111.
20. DOD FY 2011 Budget Presentation, 7–11.
21. Stevenson, *SecDef,* 190.

22. R. Chuck Mason, "Securing America's Borders: The Role of the Military," *CRS Report for Congress,* June 16, 2010.
23. See Charles A. Stevenson, *Congress at War* (Washington, DC: Potomac Books, 2007), 4.
24. Walter Pincus, "The Pentagon's New View of Warfare," *Washington Post,* February 6, 2012.
25. Richard A. Best, Jr., and Andrew Feickert, "Special Operations Forces (SOF) and CIA Paramilitary Operations: Issues for Congress," *CRS Report for Congress,* August 3, 2009.
26. U.S. Statistical Abstract, 2011, 338.
27. Gordon Adams and Cindy Williams, *Buying National Security* (New York: Routledge, 2010), 86–90.
28. Smith & Miller, 111–113.
29. David Rothkopf, *Running the World* (New York: Public Affairs, 2005), 419.

Chapter 9

1. James B. Steinberg, "The Policymaker's Perspective: Transparency and Partnership," in Roger Z. George and James B. Bruce, eds., *Analyzing Intelligence* (Washington, DC: Georgetown University Press, 2008), 83.
2. William J. Daugherty, "The Role of Covert Action," in Loch K. Johnson, ed., *Handbook of Intelligence Studies* (New York: Routledge, 2007), 279.
3. Dana Priest and William M. Arkin, *Top Secret America* (New York: Little, Brown, 2011), 18.
4. Robert M. Gates, *From the Shadows* (New York: Simon & Schuster, 1996), 33.
5. I Statutes at Large, 128–129, July 1, 1790. A similar provision allowing secret expenditures is still on the books (31 USC 3526 [e]).
6. Godfrey Hodgson, *The Colonel: The Life and Wars of Henry Stimson, 1867–1950* (New York: Knopf, 1990), 203.
7. Priest & Arkin, 100, 103. Their figure for the Office of the Director of National Intelligence (ODNI) staff also includes personnel attached to the National Counterterrorism Center (NCTC).
8. Public Law 108–458, sect. 1018, of the Intelligence Reform and Terrorism Prevention Act of 2004.
9. Thomas Fingar, "Office of the Director of National Intelligence: Promising Start Despite Ambiguity, Ambivalence, and Animosity," in Roger Z. George and Harvey Rishikof, *The National Security Enterprise: Navigating the Labyrinth* (Washington, DC: Georgetown University Press, 2011), 139, 149; Richard A. Best, Jr., "Intelligence Reform After Five Years: The Role of the Director of National Intelligence (DNI)," *CRS Report for Congress,* June 22, 2010.
10. Priest & Arkin, 97.

11. Fingar, 142.
12. Fingar, 148.
13. Roger Z. George, "Central Intelligence Agency: The President's Own," in George & Rishikof, 158.
14. Gates, 563–564.
15. Richard A. Clarke, *Against All Enemies* (New York: Free Press, 2004), 277; George, 161.
16. Gordon Adams and Cindy Williams, *Buying National Security* (New York: Routledge, 2010), 123.
17. George, 160.
18. Quoted in George, 159.
19. George, 164; Walter Pincus and Dana Priest, "Some Iraq Analysts Felt Pressure From Cheney Visits," *Washington Post*, June 5, 2003.
20. Adams & Williams, 124.
21. Adams & Williams, 123. Another recent source says NSA has "35,000+" personnel. Matthew Aid, *Intel Wars: The Secret History of the Fight Against Terror* (New York: Bloomsbury Press, 2012), 44, also has higher figures for other parts of the IC: CIA, 25,000; NRO, 4,500; NGIA, 16,000.
22. Adams & Williams, 124–125.
23. Adams & Williams, 125–126.
24. Adams & Williams, 127–128.
25. Adams & Williams, 126–129.
26. Greg Miller, "27% of U.S. Spy Work Is Outsourced," *Los Angeles Times,* August 28, 2008. Priest & Arkin, 181, say the figure is 29% of the workforce in the IC are contractors.
27. Mark M. Lowenthal, *Intelligence: From Secrets to Policy, Fourth Edition,* (Washington, DC: CQ Press, 2009), 66.
28. Lowenthal, 82–107.
29. Priest & Arkin, 77.
30. Presidential Policy Directive (PPD) 35 Intelligence Requirements, March 2, 1995, www.fas.org/irp/offdocs/pdd35.htm
31. Paul R. Pillar, "Adapting Intelligence to Changing Issues," in Johnson, *Handbook,* 151–152; Lowenthal, 59, 73–74.
32. See Paul R. Pillar, *Intelligence and U.S. Foreign Policy* (New York: Columbia University Press, 2011) and Joshua Rovner, *Fixing the Facts* (New York: Cornell University Press, 2011).
33. Quoted in Lowenthal, 111.
34. Lowenthal, 186.
35. Lowenthal, 120–121, 125–126.
36. Gates, 56.
37. Pillar, *Intelligence and U.S. Foreign Policy,* 139.
38. Lowenthal, 63.
39. George, 163, 159; Walter Pincus, "Measuring a President's Approach on Foreign Policy," *Washington Post*, January 17, 2012.
40. Priest & Arkin, 80, 81.

41. Pillar, 200.
42. George, 160.
43. Quoted in William J. Daugherty, *Executive Secrets* (Lexington: University Press of Kentucky, 2006) 13.
44. Daugherty, *Executive Secrets*, 14.
45. Daugherty, *Executive Secrets*, 71–89; Daugherty, *Handbook*, 280–283, 291.
46. Jeffrey T. Richelson, *The U.S. Intelligence Community, Fifth Edition*, (New York: Westview, 2008), 420–424; Yochi Dreazen and Marc Ambinder, "CIA Deploys to Libya as White House Authorizes Direct Assistance to Rebels," *National Journal*, March 30, 2011.
47. Jennifer D. Kibbe, "Covert Action, Pentagon Style," in Loch K. Johnson, ed., *The Oxford Handbook of National Security Intelligence* (New York: Oxford University Press, 2010), 571, 576.
48. Public Law 102-88.
49. Daugherty, *Executive Secrets*, 101–107.
50. Daugherty, *Executive Secrets*, 34.
51. Gates, 567–568.
52. Steinberg, 83–84.
53. John McLaughlin, "Serving the National Policymaker," in George & Bruce, 72.
54. Mark M. Lowenthal, "The Policymaker–Intelligence Relationship, in Johnson, *Oxford Handbook*, 439–440.
55. McLaughlin, 74–78.
56. David Ignatius, "Obama's Intelligence Retooling," *Washington Post*, June 9, 2010; Josh Gerstein, "Panel Found 'Distracted' DNI," *Politico*, June 2, 2010.
57. Pillar, 5.
58. Quotations are in David M. Barrett, *The CIA and Congress* (Lawrence: University Press of Kansas, 2005), 3, and Daugherty, *Executive Secrets*, 92.
59. Barrett, 458–460, 102–112.
60. Loch K, Johnson, "A Shock Theory of Congressional Accountability for Intelligence," in Johnson, *Handbook*, 343.
61. Daugherty, *Executive Secrets*, 95; L. Britt Snider, *The Agency and the Hill*, CIA Center for the Study of Intelligence, www.cia.gov/library/center-for-the-study-of-intelligence/csi-publications/books-and-monographs/agency-and-the-hill/index.html

Chapter 10

1. Hart–Rudman Commission, *New World Coming: American Security in the 21st Century*, September 15, 1999, i–vii.
2. Tom Ridge, *The Test of Our Times* (New York: St. Martin's Press, 2009), 277.
3. Richard H. Ward, Kathleen L. Kiernan, and Daniel Mabrey, *Homeland Security: An Introduction* (LexisNexis, 2006), 11.

4. Donald F. Kettl, *System Under Stress: Homeland Security and American Politics, Second Edition* (Washington, DC: CQ Press, 2007), 106–107; Ward et al., 246.
5. Kettl, 54–55.
6. Public Law 107–296, sect. 101.
7. Gordon Adams and Cindy Williams, *Buying National Security* (Routledge, 2010), 141–143; Office of Management and Budget, 2012 Budget, Analytical Perspectives, 403–410.
8. Ward et al., 110–111.
9. Department of Homeland Security, 2012 Budget in Brief, 95–97, www.dhs.gov/xlibrary/assets/budget-bib-fy2012.pdf
10. See www.nctc.gov/about_us/about_nctc.html
11. Project on National Security Reform (PNSR), Toward Integrating Complex National Missions Lessons From the National Counterterrorism Center's Directorate of Strategic Operational Planning, February 2010, www.pnsr.org/data/files/pnsr_nctc_dsop_report.pdf
12. Mark A. Randol, "The Department of Homeland Security Intelligence Enterprise: Operational Overview and Oversight Challenges for Congress," *CRS Report for Congress,* March 19, 2010.
13. Government Accountability Office, "High-Risk Series: An Update," Report to Congressional Committees, February 2011, 91–110, www.gao.gov/new.items/d11278.pdf
14. A list of the various sector plans can be found at www.dhs.gov/files/programs/gc_1179866197607.shtm
15. Ward et al., 118.
16. McAfee/CSIS Report, *In the Dark: Crucial Industries Confront Cyberattacks,* April 2011, http://www.mcafee.com/us/resources/reports/rp-critical-infrastructure-protection.pdf
17. Center for a New American Security, "America's Cyber Future: Security and Prosperity in the Information Age," vol. 1, June 2011, www.cnas.org/files/documents/publications/CNAS_Cyber_Volume0I_0.pdf
18. See White House Fact Sheet: "The Administration's Cybersecurity Accomplishments," May 12, 2011.
19. Dana Priest and William M. Arkin, *Top Secret America* (Little, Brown, 2011), 88.
20. Siobahn Gorman, "Chamber Critical of White House Cybersecurity Plan," *Wall Street Journal,* May 26, 2011.
21. Gary M. Shiffman and Jonathan Hoffman, "The Department of Homeland Security: Chief of Coordination," in Roger Z. George and Harvey Rishikof, eds., *The National Security Enterprise: Navigating the Labyrinth* (Washington, DC: Georgetown University Press, 2011), 216.
22. Shiffman & Hoffman, 209.
23. Statement for the Record, The Honorable Janet Napolitano, Secretary, U.S. Department of Homeland Security, Before the U.S. Sen-

ate Committee on Homeland Security and Governmental Affairs, February 17, 2011.
24. Ward et al., 142.
25. Ward et al., 234.
26. Kettl, 79; Shiffman & Hoffman, 217.
27. Shiffman & Hoffman, 204, 219.
28. Michael A. Sheehan, *Crush the Cell: How to Defeat Terrorism Without Terrorizing Ourselves* (New York: Crown, 2008), 7.
29. John Mueller and Mark G. Stewart, "Terror, Security, and Money: Balancing the Risks, Benefits, and Costs of Homeland Security," paper prepared for Annual Convention of the Midwest Political Science Association, Chicago, IL, April 1, 2011.
30. Public Law 107–296, sect. 903.
31. Statement by the president on the White House Organization for Homeland Security and Counterterrorism, May 26, 2009.
32. See GAO report at www.gao.gov/new.items/d11278.pdf
33. Project on National Security Reform (PNSR), *Forging a New Shield Executive Summary,* December 2008, 486.
34. See agency rankings at http://bestplacestowork.org/BPTW/rankings/overall/large
35. James A. Thomson, "DHS AWOL?" RAND Review, Spring 2007.
36. Stephen Flynn, "Recalibrating Homeland Security," *Foreign Affairs,* May–June 2011, 130–140.
37. Paul Rosenzweig, Jena Baker McNeill, and James Jay Califano, "Stopping the Chaos: A Proposal for Reorganization of Congressional Oversight of the Department of Homeland Security," WebMemo by the Heritage Foundation, November 4, 2010.
38. Timothy Balunis, Jr., and William Hemphill, "Escaping the Entanglement: Reversing Jurisdictional Fragmentation Over the Department of Homeland Security," *Journal of Homeland Security and Emergency Management,* vol. 6, is. 1 (2009), art. 58.
39. See DHS list at http://www.dhs.gov/files/international/counterterrorism.shtm
40. Presidential Policy Directive (PPD) 8, "National Preparedness," March 30, 2011.
41. Napolitano testimony, February 17, 2011.

Chapter 11

1. George W. Bush, *The National Security Strategy of the United States,* September 2002.
2. Barack Obama, *The National Security Strategy of the United States,* May 2010.
3. For more on these activities, see Paul B. Stares and Micah Zenko, "Partners in Preventive Action: The United States and International Institutions," Council on Foreign Relations, September 2011.

4. Margaret P. Karns and Karen A. Mingst, *International Organizations, Second Edition* (Boulder, CO: Kynne Rienner, 2010), 17, 26.
5. Karns & Mingst, 274–279.
6. Linda Fasulop, *An Insider's Guide to the UN, Second Edition*, (New Haven CT: Yale University Press, 2009), 96; the State Department voting report can be found at www.state.gov/documents/organization/139481.pdf
7. J. Samuel Barkin, *International Organizations* (New York: Palgrave Macmillan, 2006), 59.
8. Karns & Mingst, 111.
9. Karns & Mingst, 312–315.
10. Karns & Mingst, 329, 331; Fasulo, 114–118; Marjorie Ann Browne, "United Nations Peacekeeping: Issues for Congress," *CRS Report for Congress*, August 13, 2010.
11. Karns & Mingst, 319.
12. Barkin, 72.
13. Fasulo, 203–207.
14. Ellen Hallams, *The United States and NATO Since 9/11* (New York: Routledge, 2010), 58.
15. International Institute for Strategic Studies, *Strategic Survey 2010: The Annual Review of World Affairs* (London: Routledge, 2010), 77–80.
16. Karns & Mingst, 182–183.
17. Karns & Mingst, 189–190.
18. Karns & Mingst, 198.
19. Karns & Mingst, 200–201.
20. Barkin, 95.
21. Karns & Mingst, 403.
22. Karns & Mingst, 403–405; Barkin, 106.
23. James Raymond Vreeland, *The International Monetary Fund* (London: Routledge, 2007), 41–44.
24. 2009 Report to Congress by the National Advisory Council on International Monetary and Financial Policies, U.S. Treasury Department, August 5, 2010.
25. Barkin, 91–93; Karns & Mingst, 415; Kent Jones, *The Doha Blues* (New York: Oxford University Press, 2010), 51.
26. Raymond J. Ahearn and Ian F. Fergusson, "World Trade Organization (WTO): Issues in the Debate on Continued U.S. Participation," *CRS Report for Congress*, June 16, 2010.
27. Jeffrey L. Dunoff, "Does the United States Support International Tribunals? The Case of the Multilateral Trade System," in Cesare P. R. Romano, ed., *The Sword and the Scales: The United States and International Courts and Tribunals* (New York: Cambridge University Press, 2009), 354.
28. Romano, xiii.
29. John R. Crook, "The U.S. and International Claims and Compensation Bodies," in Romano, 297–321.

30. Sean D. Murphy, "The United States and the International Court of Justice: Coping With Antinomies," in Romano, 65–66.
31. Murphy, 78, 66–67; Romano, 429–430.
32. Steven Kull and Clay Ramsay, "American Public Opinion on International Courts and Tribunals," in Romano, 12–29.
33. John P. Cerone, "U.S. Attitudes Toward International Criminal Courts and Tribunals," in Romano, 150–156.
34. Cerone, 182.
35. Romano, 423.
36. Karns & Mingst, 222, 235.

Chapter 12

1. Thomas Knecht, *Paying Attention to Foreign Affairs: How Public Opinion Affects Presidential Decision Making* (Pennsylvania State University Press, 2010), 3.
2. Quoted in Timothy E. Cook, *Governing With the News: The News Media as a Political Institution* (University of Chicago Press, 1998), 131, and dated May 12, 1992.
3. Quoted in Gary J. Andres, *Lobbying Reconsidered* (New York: Pearson Longman, 2009), 192.
4. Knecht, 9.
5. Knecht, 205.
6. Douglas C. Foyle, *Counting the Public In: Presidents, Public Opinion, and Foreign Policy* (Columbia University Press, 1999), 267–268.
7. Foyle, 268.
8. Steven W. Hook, *U.S. Foreign Policy: The Paradox of World Power, Third Edition* (CQ Press, 2010), 214.
9. See www.worldpublicopinion.org/pipa/articles/brunitedstatescanadara/238.php?nid=&id=&pnt=238 and www.cbsnews.com/stories/2007/09/12/opinion/pollpositions/main3253552.shtml
10. First examples at www.publicagenda.org; Liberia examples in George F. Bishop, *The Illusion of Public Opinion* (Rowman & Littlefield, 2005), xiii–xiv.
11. Yankelovich's views are discussed in Jim Willis, *The Media Effect* (Praeger, 2007), 63.
12. See report at www.cfr.org/thinktank/iigg/pop/about.html
13. Bruce W. Jentleson and Rebecca L. Britton, "Still Pretty Prudent," *Journal of Conflict Resolution*, vol. 42, no. 4 (August 1998), 395–417.
14. Wolfowitz quote cited in *USA Today*, May 30, 2003; Shoon Kathleen Murray and Christopher Spinosa, "The Post-9/11 Shift in Public Opinion: How Long Will It Last?" in Eugene R. Wittkopf and James M. McCormick, eds., *The Domestic Sources of American Foreign Policy, Fourth Edition* (Lanham, MD: Rowman & Littlefield 2004), 103, 105; Hook, 230.

15. Foyle, 46–47.
16. Peter D. Feaver and Christopher Gelpi, *Choosing Your Battles* (Princeton University Press, 2004), 103–105, 134–140, 185–186; Feaver document quoted in Hook, 229.
17. Bob Woodward, *State of Denial* (New York: Simon & Schuster, 2006), 326.
18. Foyle, 208.
19. Knecht, 215.
20. Quoted in Brandon Rottinghaus, "Presidential Leadership on Foreign Policy, Opinion Polling, and the Possible Limits of 'Crafted Talk,'" *Political Communication*, 25 (2008), 139.
21. A point made in the 1960s by Douglass Cater, who called the press "the fourth branch of government." Cater is quoted and discussed in Cook, 1–2.
22. Doris A. Graber, *Mass Media and American Politics, Eighth Edition* (CQ Press, 2010), 228–230.
23. Graber, 305.
24. Morton Halperin, *Bureaucratic Politics and Foreign Policy, Second Edition*, (Brookings, 2006), 182–183.
25. Richard T. Cooper and Faye Fiore, "In Politics, Leaking Stories Is a Fine Art," *Los Angeles Times*, April 9, 2006.
26. Halperin, 185–188.
27. Graber, 307.
28. Alex Mintz and Karl DeRouen, Jr., *Understanding Foreign Policy Decision Making* (Cambridge University Press, 2010), 161.
29. Data are from Pew Center reports available at www.journalism.org
30. Pew report for 2011 at http://stateofthemedia.org/2011/overview-2/
31. Allan J. Cigler and Burdett A. Loomis, eds., *Interest Group Politics, Eighth Edition* (CQ Press, 2012), 3–4.
32. David M. Paul and Rachel Anderson Paul, *Ethnic Lobbies and U.S. Foreign Policy* (Lynne Rienner, 2009), 14.
33. Frank R. Baumgartner et al., *Lobbying and Policy Change* (University of Chicago Press, 2009), 239, 193.
34. Within government, stakeholders are those agencies and offices that have some authorities or responsibilities related to the issue under review, such as all the entities related to policy toward, say, China or export of warplanes to Saudi Arabia. Outside of government, stakeholders are those who believe their interests are already affected, or likely to be affected, by a policy being considered.
35. Paul & Paul, 24.
36. Thomas Ambrosio, ed., *Ethnic Identity Groups and U.S. Foreign Policy* (Westport, CT: Praeger, 2002), 10.
37. Quoted in Thomas, 151.
38. Thomas, 152–153.
39. Thomas, 177.
40. Data at www.opensecrets.org

41. Gerald Warburg, "Lobbyists: U.S. National Security and Special Interests," in Roger Z. George & Harvey Rishikof, *The National Security Enterprise: Navigating the Labyrinth* (Washington, DC: Georgetown University Press, 2011), 270; Kim Eisler, "Hired Guns: The City's 50 Top Lobbyists," *Washingtonian Magazine,* June 2007.
42. Lobbying and campaign contribution data are available at www.opensecrets.org
43. William D. Hartung, *Prophets of War: Lockheed Martin and the Making of the Military Industrial Complex* (New York: Nation Books, 2011), 29.
44. Lobbying and campaign contribution data are available at www.opensecrets.org
45. Thomas, 142–143; Anthony J. Nownes, *Total Lobbying* (Cambridge University Press, 2006), 28; Andres, 200.
46. Quoted in Nicholas W. Allard, "Lobbying Is an Honorable Profession: The Right to Petition and the Competition to Be Right," *Stanford Law and Policy Review,* vol. 19, 1 (2008), 48.
47. Baumgartner et al., 193.
48. Data at www.opensecrets.org
49. Matthew R. Kambrod, *Lobbying for Defense: An Insider's View* (Annapolis, MD: Naval Institute Press, 2008), 115; data at www.opensecrets.org
50. Thomas, 148–149.
51. James G. McGann, "The Global Go-To Think Tanks, 2010" The Think Tanks and Civil Societies Program, University of Pennsylvania; Ellen Laipson, "Think Tanks: Supporting Cast Players in the National Security Enterprise," in Roger Z. George & Harvey Rishikof, 290–291.
52. Eliot A. Cohen, "How Government Looks at Pundits" *Wall Street Journal,* January 23, 2009.
53. Laipson, 289.
54. Laipson, 293.

Chapter 13

1. Committee on Government Operations, U.S. Senate, "Organizing for National Security," vol. 3, Staff Reports and Recommendations, 1961, 4.
2. Hart–Rudman Commission, *Road Map for National Security: Imperative for Change,* March 15, 2001, xiii.
3. Reorganization authority lapsed in 1984. President Obama requested a renewal in 2012 in order to restructure the trade-related organizations in the executive branch.
4. Dean Acheson, *Present at the Creation* (New York: W. W. Norton, 1969), 243; Thomas D. Boettcher, *First Call: The Making of the Modern U.S. Military, 1945–1953* (Boston: Little, Brown, 1992), 176.

5. Acheson, 244–246.
6. See "Organizing for National Security," vol. 3; Cody M. Brown, *The National Security Council,* Project on National Security Reform (PNSR), 2008, 27.
7. Murphy Commission, "Commission on the Organization of the Government for the Conduct of Foreign Policy," Washington, 1975.
8. *The Tower Commission Report* (Bantam Book and Times Books, 1987).
9. Report of the National Defense Panel, *Transforming Defense: National Security in the 21st Century,* December 1997, i–vii.
10. Hart–Rudman Commission, 2001; *New World Coming: American Security in the 21st Century,* September 15, 1999.
11. Center for Strategic and International Studies (CSIS), *Beyond Goldwater–Nichols, Phase 2 Report,* July 2005, 1–8.
12. CSIS, *CSIS Commission on Smart Power,* 2007, 61–69.
13. PNSR, *Forging a New Shield,* November 2008, http://pnsr.org/data/files/pnsr%20forging%20a%20new%20shield.pdf
14. See Peter Feaver and William Inboden, "A Strategic Planning Cell on National Security at the White House," in Daniel W. Drezner, ed., *Avoiding Trivia: The Role of Strategic Planning in American Foreign Policy* (Brookings, 2009), 98–112.
15. See PNSR report on this at www.pnsr.org/data/images/pnsr_the_power_of_people_report.pdf
16. For a critique of DNI, see Amy Zegart, *Spying Blind* (Princeton University Press, 2007), and Richard A. Best, Jr., and Alfred Cumming, "Director of National Intelligence Statutory Authorities: Status and Proposals," *CRS Report for Congress,* January 12, 2011, http://assets.opencrs.com/rpts/RL34231_20110112.pdf; for Department of Homeland Security (DHS), see Government Accountability Office (GAO) high risk report, www.gao.gov/highrisk/agency/dhs/; for National Counterterrorism Center (NCTC), see PNSR, *Toward Integrating Complex National Missions: Lessons From the National Counterterrorism Center's Directorate of Strategic Operational Planning,* February 2010, www.pnsr.org/data/files/pnsr_nctc_dsop_report.pdf
17. A fuller description of these teams is at PNSR, *Forging a New Shield,* 442–459.
18. Public Law 112–81, sect. 1207.
19. See Andrew F. Krepinevich and Barry D. Watts, *Regaining Strategic Competence,* Center for Strategic and Budgetary Assessments, 2009, intro., chap. 4, and conc., www.csbaonline.org/4Publications/PubLibrary/R.20090901.Regaining_Strategi/R.20090901.Regaining_Strategi.pdf; Jones memo to NSC members is at www.fas.org/irp/offdocs/ppd/nsc031909.pdf
20. See www.fas.org/irp/offdocs/ppd/nsc031909.pdf

Index

Abrams, C., 215–216
Abu Ghraib prison, 103
Acheson, D., 325
Action channels, 3, 80
Adams, C. F., 37
Adams, G., 124
Adams, J., 30
Adams, J. Q., 31–32, 119, 308
Adams, S., 21
Advice and consent, 19, 54, 86, 92–93, 94
Advocacy and affinity groups, 302, 311–321
Afghanistan
 CIA in, 222
 foreign aid to, 181, 190, 191, 192
 military operations in, 134, 135, 214–215
 Obama's strategy for, 83–85
 reconstruction, 102–103, 160
 reservists in, 216
Air Force, 40, 206, 207
Alaska, 38
Albright, M., 60
Algiers, 29
Alien and Sedition Acts, 30
Al Qaeda, 1–2, 52, 83, 228
Ambassadors, 141–142, 151, 158, 159–160
American Israel Public Affairs Committee (AIPAC), 315, 318

Anti-Ballistic Missile Treaty (1972), 93, 208
Apartheid, 89, 115–117
Appropriations, 87, 91–92, 120, 122–123, 127–132, 134–136, 163, 165, 171–172, 227, 252–253
Appropriations committees, 98, 102, 122, 123, 126, 128, 129, 130, 135, 137, 165, 227, 269
Armed forces. *See* U.S. military
Armed Services Committees, 95, 97, 102–103, 126, 128, 226, 227
Arms control, 50, 51, 61, 70, 88, 106, 146–147, 158, 288, 306
Arms Control and Disarmament Agency, 88, 106
Arms Control and International Security Affairs, 148
Arms Export Control Act (1976), 188
Army, 33, 40, 43, 46, 207
Articles of Confederation, 7–10, 17
Asian financial crisis, 193
Asia–Pacific Economic Cooperation (APEC), 276, 278
Association of Southeast Asian Nations (ASEAN), 276
Atomic Energy Commission, 206

365

Baker, J., 166–167
Balance of power, 16–19, 27
Banking systems, 194
Barbary Coast, 29, 31
Bay of Pigs invasion, 64, 222, 310
Berger, S., 71
Betts, R., 213
Biden, J., 52, 73, 84, 338
Bill of Rights, 24
Bin Laden, O., 52, 65
Biological protection, 256
Black [classified] programs, 136
Border security, 21, 256
Bosnia, 100, 216
Botha, P.W., 115
Branches of government, 16–19
Bremer, P., 73
Bretton Woods system, 49, 192
Brinkmanship, 34
Britain
 and Articles of Confederation, 8, 10, 28, 31
 Civil War support, 37
 military aid to, 48
 Oregon treaty with, 34
 U.S. political party entanglement, 38
Brownlow Commission, 324–325
Bryan, W. J., 43, 59–60
Brzezinski, Z., 71
Buchanan, J., 35
Budgets
 congressional-presidential clashes, 136–140
 Congressional role, 120, 126–136
 dysfunction, 136–137
 as governing tool, 120–122
 presidential role in, 120, 124–126, 133
 process, 121–124, 130–133
 revenue and outlays, 121
Budget and Impoundment Control Act (1974), 123

Budget committees, 127–128
Budget Control Act (2011), 124, 132
Budget Enforcement Act (1990), 139
Bully pulpit, 74
Bundy, M., 62, 71
Burden sharing, 297
Bureau of Intelligence and Research, 238
Bush, G. H. W.
 and Iraq, 167
 meetings with advisors, 68
 National Security Council establishment, 51
 new tax endorsement, 139
 NSA/NSC relationship, 71
 and Pakistan, 89–90
 and Serbia, 59
 as vice president, 73
Bush, G. W.
 budget, 133, 138
 and free trade agreements, 197
 G-20 summit, 291
 intelligence briefing, 65
 limits on military actions, 221
 military doctrine, 208
 missile defense treaty, 256
 national building criticism, 59
 and National Security Council, 51–52
 NSA/NSC relationship, 71, 75
 process, 80
 September 11, 2001 response, 1–3
 "the Decider", 62
Byrd, R. C., 110

Cabinet, 23, 28
Calhoun, J. C., 31
Campaign contributors, 302, 318–321
Carter, J.
 China diplomatic relations, 90
 foreign policy, 51

Index 367

National Security Council meetings, 68
NSA/NSC relationship, 71
and South Africa, 115–117
Carter, R., 105
Cartwright, J., 84
Case Act, 93
Case studies
 Afghanistan, 83–84
 Budget Enforcement Act, 137–140
 Cuban independence, 112–114
 Gulf War Coalition, 166–168
 Iraq Invasion, 227–230
 Korean-U.S. Free Trade Agreement, 197–199
 NATO in Libya, 297–300
 South African apartheid, 115–117
 U.S.-Mexican security collaboration, 272–273
Center for Strategic and International Studies (CSIS), 327
Centers for Disease Control and Prevention (CDC), 182
Central America, 35, 43, 248
Central Command (CENTCOM), 212, 222, 228
Central Intelligence Agency (CIA)
 covert actions, 222, 231
 covert operations, 50, 106
 creation and purpose, 49, 88, 106, 206, 233
 criticism, 236
 functions, 236–237
 and Nicaragua, 248–249
 paramilitary forces, 222
 secret spending for, 136
 September 11, 2001 changes, 2
Chairman of the Joint Chiefs of Staff (CJCS), 68, 211–212, 228
Chemical Weapons Convention, 55
Cheney, D., 1, 51, 73, 80, 138, 167

Chile, 100, 252
China, 35, 59, 61, 165–166, 196
Chinese National Offshore Oil Corporation (CNOOC), 196
Church and Pike Committees, 98
Citizenship and Immigration Services (CIS), 265
Civilian Conservation Corps, 206
Civil War, 36–3733
Clausewitz, von, C., 202
Clifford, C., 60
Clinton, B.
 and advisors, 62
 budget requests, 133
 draft avoidance, 213
 foreign policy, 51
 limits on military actions, 221
 and National Security Council, 68
 NSA/NSC relationship, 71, 75
 process, 80
 and Serbia, 59
Clinton, H., 83, 103, 189
Coalition building in Gulf War, 166–168
Coalition support funds, 192
Cohen, E., 213
Cold War, 49, 207, 246, 283, 286
Colonialism by contract, 43
Colombia, 167
Commander's Emergency Response Program (CERP), 181, 192, 223
Commission on Smart Power, 327
Commissions and committees, 324–328
Committee on Foreign Investment in the United States (CFIUS), 91, 171, 179, 195–196
Comprehensive Anti-Apartheid Act (1986), 117
Confederation Congress, 10, 20, 22
Conflict diamonds, 100
Congo, 167

Congress
  advice and consent, 54
  appropriations. *See*
    Appropriations
  under Articles of Confederation, 8–13, 17
  budget role, 119–140
  committees, 91, 97, 102–103, 134–135, 191, 260, 269, 273
    See also individual committee names
  Confederation, 10, 20–22
  and Constitution, 16–20, 25
  Continental, 8, 10
  contingency funds, 133–134
  and Cuba, 41
  culture, 99–100, 103–104
  defense authorization, 31, 34–35, 37, 39–41, 44–45, 46, 47, 53, 55, 57, 107–111, 112–114
  and Department of Defense, 226–227
  executive oversight, 32
  export controls, 187
  First, 22–25, 27
  foreign assistance programs, 191
  foreign policy power, 4–5
  Harding administration, 46
  Homeland Security Council, 258
  House of Representatives. *See* House of Representatives
  and intelligence community, 251–252
  Jefferson administration, 31
  John Adams administration, 30
  LBJ administration, 50
  legislative process, 87–91
  McKinley administration, 41
  and National Security Council, 106
  national security influence, 12–13, 100
  9/11 attacks response, 2–3, 52
  Nixon administration, 50
  nominations, 94–95
  oversight, 97–98
  partisanship politics, 38, 99–100, 101, 117, 136–140
  and presidential power, 54–58, 99, 111, 112–114
  Reagan administration, 51
  Roosevelt administration, 47–48
  self-protection, 336–337
  Senate. *See* Senate
  shared powers, 18–19, 25
  and South Africa, 115–117
  and State Department, 163–166
  trade agreements, 47, 185–186, 197–199, 294–295
  treaties, 42–43, 45–46, 92–94
  Truman administration, 49
  Washington administration, 27–29, 92–93
  See also House of Representatives; Senate
Congressional Budget Office (CBO), 123, 129, 131
Congressional delegations (CODELs), 103
Congressional oversight, 97, 128, 179
Connally Reservation, 94
Consensus, 60, 62
Constitution. *See* U.S. Constitution
Constitutional Convention, 9, 12–20
Constitutional treasury, 34
Constructive engagement, 115
Consular officers, 33, 154, 159
Consular posts, 144, 145–146
Contingency funds, 133–134, 165, 191, 333
Coolidge, C., 46
Cooling off treaties, 43

Coordinating Committee for Multilateral Export Controls (COCOM), 100, 211–212, 221, 222
Corwin, E., 18, 112
Covert actions, 48, 51, 74, 106, 236–237, 246–253
Critical infrastructure, 256
Cuba
    acquisition attempts, 35
    Bay of Pigs invasion, 64, 222, 310
    hostility towards, 61
    independence, 39–41, 112–114
    sanctions against, 89, 164, 184
    use of force authorization, 108
Cuban missile crisis, 78
Currency, 174, 192, 194
Customs and Border Protection (CBP), 265
Cybersecurity, 256

Darman, R., 138
Declaration of Independence, 9, 13, 114
Declaration of war, 2–3, 16, 39–40, 41, 44–45, 107–111, 114
Defense Appropriations Bill, 252–253
Defense Intelligence Agency (DIA), 238
Defense Security Cooperation Agency (DSCA), 182
Defense spending, 138, 218. *See also* Department of Defense
Democrats
    and Cuban independence, 39, 112–113, 114
    and Korean-U.S. Free Trade Agreement, 197–198
    and slavery, 32–33
    and South Africa, 117
    and tariffs, 38
    and tax cuts, 138
Department of Agriculture (USDA), 176, 182
Department of Commerce, 176, 180
Department of Defense (DOD)
    agency rivalries, 162
    budget, 125–126, 127–128, 135–136, 147
    Congress and, 226–227
    contingency funds, 134
    culture, 219–220
    foreign assistance programs, 52, 174, 181–182, 190–191, 192
    functions, 176, 200
    interagency process, 225
    and Iraq War, 228
    leadership, 210–214
    and National Security Council, 106
    nominations, 95
    organization, 216–217
    oversight, 97
    planning and policy making, 223–224
    security assistance, 223
    tensions and rivalries, 224–225
Department of Energy, 182, 239
Department of Foreign Affairs, 24–25
Department of Health and Human Services (HHS), 182
Department of Homeland Security (DHS)
    authorizations, 127
    component agencies, 239
    creation, 2, 3, 106, 258–260
    international programs, 182
    mistakes, 335

Department of Justice, 182
Department of the Treasury, 176, 178–179, 239
Détente, 51
Developing countries, 174–175
Diplomacy
  bureaucratic rivalries, 162–166
  coalition building, 166–168
  funding, 164, 165
  negotiation, 158
  by non-State Department personnal, 156–157
  overview, 141–143
  and policy making, 160–162
  public, 142, 159
  State Department. *See* State Department
Director of National Intelligence (DNI), 234, 235–236, 327, 336
Direct tax, 30
Disarmament, 46, 106, 203. *See also* Arms control
Dissensus on foreign policy, 60, 61
Dollar diplomacy, 43
Dominican Republic, 38, 42
Don't Ask, Don't Tell law, 214
Drug Enforcement Administration (DEA), 239
Dulles, J. F., 60

Earmarks, 91, 123
Economic instruments
  Appropriations. *See* Appropriations
  military, 91–92
  Budgets. *See* Budgets
  agencies, 175–182
  institutions, 173–182
  international, 175–176
  overview, 170–174
  processes, 182–183
  sanctions, 183–185

Economic Support Fund (ESF), 192
Economy Act (1933), 135
Egypt, 51, 167, 190, 191, 192, 151, 293, 298
Eisenhower, D., 49–50, 57, 60, 78, 208
Embassies, 148–150, 155, 159–160
Emergency preparedness and response, 256, 266
Entitlements, 128
Environmental Protection Agency (EPA), 182
Ethiopia, 167, 281
Ethnic groups, 43, 302, 313–316
Executive agreements, 42, 50, 93
Executive departments, 23, 54, 86, 135, 143
Executive Office of the President (EOP), 47, 65, 88, 122–123
Executive orders, 42, 55, 56, 116, 177, 195, 234, 246, 271, 298, 329
Executive power
  budget process, 124–126
  changes, 55–58
  Congressional interplay, 86–88, 91, 94, 98–99, 106, 123, 136–140
  Constitutional, 15–17, 52, 54–56
  constraints, 58–60
  economic, 136, 194
  history, 27–45
  legal, 57–58
  personal diplomacy, 74
  post Cold War, 50–52
  unitary, 58.
  See also individual presidents
Exon–Florio amendment, 195
Expeditionary civilian forces, 331
Export Administration Act (1949), 187

Index

Export-Import Bank, 47, 186
Export policies, 186–188
External influences
   advocacy groups, 302, 311–321
   affinity groups, 313–316
   campaign contributors, 302, 318–321
   ethnic identity groups, 302, 313–316
   lobbyists, 302, 316–321
   media, 302, 306–311
   overview, 301–302
   public opinion, 302–306
   stakeholders, 302
   think tanks, 302, 321–323

Feaver, P., 213
Federal Bureau of Investigation (FBI), 1, 148, 182, 235, 256–257
Federal Emergency Management Agency (FEMA), 132, 134, 266, 327
Federalist Papers, 20
Federalists, 13, 20, 21, 22
Federal Reserve, 176, 178
Feed and Forage Act (1861), 134
Filibusters (military expeditions), 35
Filibusters (prolonged debates), 102, 127
Fire alarm hearings, 252
First Congress, 22, 23–25
Foley, T., 138
Food and Drug Administration (FDA), 182
Ford, G., 50–51
Foreign assistance, 174–175, 188–192
Foreign Assistance Act (1961), 134, 135, 163, 181
Foreign direct investment (FDI), 102, 171, 182–-183, 195
Foreign Intelligence, 262

Foreign Intelligence Advisory Board (PFIAB), 106
Foreign language proficiency, 331
Foreign Military Funding (FMF), 192
Foreign Military Sales (FMS), 192
Foreign Operations Appropriations Bill, 91, 132, 136
Foreign policy
   advocacy group influence, 311–321
   and Articles of Confederation, 8
   case studies. See Case studies
   Civil War, 36–38
   Cold War, 49–50
   Congressional influences. See Congress
   Constitutional influences, 7, 16, 18
   diplomatic influences, 141–145, 148–150
   economic instruments. See Economic instruments
   external influences, 301–323
   and First Congress, 24
   and foreign assistance, 189–192
   and foreign direct investment, 195
   homeland security instruments, 242–273
   informal influences, 98–99
   institutions, 176
   intelligence instruments, 231–254
   international organization instruments, 274–300
   Israel, 315–316
   and Joint Chiefs of Staff, 211
   legislation, 87–91, 163
   media influence, 302–306
   metaphors, 4–5

military instruments, 162, 182, 200–230
National Security Advisor, 71
and National Security Council, 65, 67, 69, 79, 81
9/11 attacks response. *See* September 11, 2001 attacks
Obama administration. *See* Obama, B.
oversight influence, 97–98
political influence, 111–112
and president, 82–85
presidential influence, 53–85, 135–136, 170, 242
presidential power, 27, 30
and private interests, 35
processes, 2–4
public influence, 104–105
public opinion influence, 302–306
reform. See Foreign policy reforms
and Roosevelt, 47
Foreign policy reforms
history, 339
Impediments to, 335–339
new proposals, 328–335
process, 339–341
proposal history, 324–328
Foreign Relations Committee. *See* Senate Foreign Relations Committee (SFRC)
Foreign service, 142, 153–155, 158
Formosa, 109
Forrestal, J., 66, 210
France, 23, 28, 30, 167
Franklin, B., 19
Franks, T., 212, 228–229
Freedom Support Act, 189
Free trade agreements (FTAs), 185–186, 188, 197–199, 295
Fulbright, J. W., 96, 97

G-7. *See* Group of Seven (G-7)
G-8. *See* Group of Eight (G-8)
G-20. *See* Group of Twenty (G-20)
Gates, R.
Bush, G. H. W. advisor, 77
on Director of National Intelligence position, 235
effectiveness, 213–214
export controls, 187
interagency cooperation, 225
job demands, 211
Obama, B. advisor, 83–84
on presidential knowledge of intelligence, 241, 249–250
processes, 218, 224–225
on secret intelligence, 232
General Agreement on Tariffs and Trade (GATT), 49, 294
Generalized System of Preferences (GSP), 185
Genocide Convention, 94
George, A., 62
Geospatial intelligence (GEOINT), 239
Germaneness rule, 102
Germany, 44, 46, 102, 108, 111
Gingrich, N., 139, 156
Globalization, 194
Global Security Contingency Fund, 191, 333
Global War on Terror (GWOT), 2, 80, 228
Goldwater-Nichols Department of Defense Reorganization Act (1986), 89, 106, 208, 211, 225, 331, 338–339
Good neighbor policy, 46
Gore, A., 73, 96
Government Accountability Office (GAO), 98
Government Operations Committee, 325

Government Sponsored Enterprises (GSEs), 133
Gramm–Rudman–Hollings Amendment (1985), 123, 132
Grant, U. S., 37, 38
Great Britain. *See* Britain
Grenada, 208
Group of Eight (G-8), 158, 194, 275, 276, 278, 292
Group of Seven (G-7), 194, 291
Group of Twenty (G-20), 158, 174, 194, 278, 291–293
Gulf War (1990–1991), 51, 134, 166–168, 208, 215–216

Hadley, S., 71
Haig, A., 59, 60
Haiti, 110, 134
Hamilton, A. 12, 20, 22, 25, 28, 29, 30
Hamilton, L., 97, 101, 103–104, 110
Hamre, J., 210
Hancock, J., 21
Harding, W., 46
Hart–Rudman Commission, 257, 327, 328, 334
Henning, G., 45
Henry, P. 19–20, 22
HIV/AIDS, 88, 121, 164, 189, 284
Holbrooke, R., 73, 80, 83, 157
Homeland security
　budget, 260
　history, 255–257
　mission, 260–267
　presidential choices, 271–272
　secret service, 267
　September 11, 2001 attacks response, 261, 267
　system creation, 257–258. *See also* Department of Homeland Security (DHS)
　U.S.-Mexican collaboration, 272–273
　See also Department of Homeland Security (DHS)
Homeland Security Council (HSC), 52, 106, 258. *See also* Department of Homeland Security (DHS)
Hoover Commission, 325
Hopkins, H., 73
House Appropriations Committee, 98. *See also* Appropriations committees
House Foreign Affairs Committee, 102–103
House of Representatives
　J. Q. Adams election, 32
　budget process, 127, 132, 138
　Cheney in, 73
　Confederation Congress, 22
　and Constitution, 18
　culture, 101
　A. Jackson impeachment, 38
　Russian treaty, 43
　and South Africa 116
　Washington administration, 29
House Permanent Select Committee on Intelligence (HPSCI), 252
House Ways and Means Committee, 122, 129, 165, 179
Hughes, C. E., 46
Hughes–Ryan amendment (1974), 106, 252
Hull, C., 47
Human intelligence (HUMINT), 236, 239
Human rights, 100
Hussein, S., 100, 166, 228, 245–246

Imagery intelligence (IMINT), 238
Immigration, 43
Immigration and Customs
    Enforcement (ICE), 265
Imperial power, 42
Import policies, 188–189
Information technology (IT), 332
Intelligence community (IC)
    analysis, 240–244
    components, 231–232,
        234–239, 265
    congressional oversight,
        251–254
    covert actions, 251–253
    Director of National
        Intelligence (DNI), 234,
        327, 336
    history, 233–234
    judgments, 245–249
    missions, 258, 260–267
    operations, 232–233, 244–249
    presidential needs, 249–251
    processes, 239–249
    secrecy, 232–233
Interagency Policy
    Committees (IPCs), 71, 75, 77
International Atomic Energy
    Agency (IAEA), 276
International Court of Justice, 94
International courts, 276
International Emergency Economic
    Powers Act (IEEPA), 183,
    187, 194
International Military Education
    and Training (IMET), 182
International Monetary Fund (IMF),
    49, 133, 174, 275, 284,
    292–293
International organizations
    courts, 295–296
    defined, 277
    economic, 174, 290–295
    major, 276–277
    non-state, 296–297.
        See also Nongovernmental
        organizations (NGOs)
    overview, 274–275
    regional, 285–291
    role, 275–277
    United Nations. *See* United
        Nations (UN)
    U.S. involvement with, 297
International Trade
    Commission (ITC), 91, 186
Iran, 50, 51, 61, 208
Iran-Contra scandal, 51, 71, 74,
    98, 326
Iraq, 93–94, 100, 102–103, 128,
    135, 166–168
Iraq War, 108, 209, 214, 216,
    227–230
Irish Republican Army, 100
Iron triangle, 98
Israel
    aid to, 164, 190, 192
    AIPAC, 315, 318
    and Budget Enforcement
        Act, 51
    Nixon and, 50
    OSCE partnership, 288
    support for, 60, 104
    trade agreements with, 186
    U.N. and, 279, 281
    U.S. Jews and, 314, 321
Ivory Coast, 167

Jackson, A., 33
Jackson, H. M., 325
Jackson Subcommittee, 328
Jackson–Vanik amendment
    (1974), 183
Japan, 35
Javits, J., 96
Jay, J., 28–29
Jefferson, T., 30–31
Jentleson, B., 105

Jews, 43, 88, 99, 104, 183, 314, 321
Johnson, A., 37–38
Johnson, L. B., 50, 57, 60, 68
Joint Board of the Army and Navy, 47–48
Joint Chiefs of Staff (JCS)
  advantages and disadvantages, 201
  chairman, 68, 211–212, 228
  creation, 48, 66
  role, 229
  statutory standing, 88, 106
Joint Committee on National Security, 326
Jointness, 208
Joint Select Committee on Deficit Reduction, 124
Jones, J., 71–72, 75, 83, 334
Justice Department, 238–239

Kellogg–Briand Pact, 46
Kennedy, J. F., 50, 71, 78, 156, 208
Killer amendments, 94
King George III, 9
Kissinger, H., 50, 63, 71, 328
Knox, H., 9, 12, 25, 28, 205
Korean–U.S. free trade agreement (KORUS FTA), 173, 197–199
Korean War, 202
Kosovo, 110, 216
Kuwait, 111, 139, 166

Laird, M., 210
Lake, T., 71, 80
Laos, 111, 132, 221, 222, 247
Latin America, 39
Lawmakers, 4
Law of anticipated reactions, 99
Leading from behind, 297
Lebanon, 109, 111
Lee, R. E., 37

Legislative branch
  appropriations, 135
  and balance of power, 27, 55
  committee roles, 331
  Constitutional provision, 16
  foreign policy deficiencies, 103
  lobbyist influence, 316
  and procedural legislation, 91
  trade authorization, 185
Legislative process, 86-89, 101, 320
Libya, 61, 110, 297–300
Limited national emergency, 47
Lincoln, A., 36–37
Lobbyists, 302, 316–321
Lodge, H. C., 45
Louisiana Purchase, 32
Lowenthal, M., 250
Lugar, R., 104

MacArthur, D., 98
Macon, N., 101
Madison, J., 13, 14, 18, 31
Malaysia, 167
Mandela, N., 117
Marcy, C., 96
Marine Corps, 30, 40, 207
Marshall, G. C., 48, 206, 210
Marshall Plan, 88
Mayhew, D., 104
McChrystal, S., 83–84
McConnell, M., 115
McDonough, D., 80
McKinley, W., 39–41, 112–114, 221
McLaughlin, J., 250
McNamara, R., 50, 208, 210, 338
Measurement and signatures intelligence (MASINT), 239
Media, 302, 306–311
Mexico, 33, 34–35, 37, 44, 107, 108, 110, 133, 190, 205, 215, 221, 270, 272–273

Middle East
  economic aid, 164, 190, 192
  force authorization, 108, 109
  peace, 104, 157
Militarization, 328. See also Use of force
Military. See U.S. military
Military aid, 190, 191–192
Military Operations Other Than War (MOOTW), 202
Military personnel. See U.S. military
Millennium Challenge Corporation (MCC), 88, 174, 189, 190, 191
Miller, F. C., 225
Mine-resistant, ambush-protected (MRAP), 213–214
Missouri Compromise, 32
Mitchell, G., 73
Mitterand, F., 167
Mock mark-up sessions, 198
Mondale, W., 73
Money laundering, 194
Monroe Doctrine, 32, 42
Monroe, J., 20, 31, 32
Morris, G, 24
Mullen, M., 211
Multilateralism, 277–278
Multinational corporations, 174
Multiple advocacy, 62
Murphy Commission, 328
Murphy, R., 326
Myers, R., 228

National Counterterrorism Center (NCTC), 261, 332
National Defense Panel (NDP), 326, 328
National Economic Council (NEC), 51, 74, 106, 176, 177
National emergency, 47
National Export Initiative (NEI), 187
National Geospatial-Intelligence Agency (NGA), 238, 239
National Guard Bureau, 216
National Institutes of Health (NIH), 182
National Intelligence Estimate (NIE), 240, 245, 252
National Intelligence Program (NIP), 234, 235, 237
National Reconnaissance Office (NRO), 238
National Security Act (1947), 48, 66, 206
National Security Agency (NSA), 70–72, 75, 238, 239, 330
National Security Council (NSC)
  agency rivalries, 162
  changes to, 325–326, 328, 333
  congressional inputs, 106
  creation, 47, 65–72, 206
  crisis management, 78, 79
  critiques, 82, 337
  culture, 76
  Obama's use of, 83–85
  presidential changes, 49–52
  processes, 76–78, 80–81
  Scowcroft Model, 74–75
  staff, 67–71
National security staff, 70–71. See also National Security Council (NSC)
Natural disasters, 223, 266
Navy, 11, 25, 29, 31, 40, 42–43, 207
Negotiations, 142, 158
Neustadt, R., 57
Neutrality Acts, 48
New organizations, 329–332
New processes, 332–335
New Strategic Arms Reduction Treaty (START), 94, 158
Nicaragua, 89, 134, 248
9/11 Commission, 252–253

Index   377

911 force, 223
Nixon, R.
  and China, 50, 61
  Congressional disagreements, 123
  diplomatic success, 50
  financial policies, 192
  and Kissinger, H., 50
  limits on military actions, 221
  military doctrine, 208
  missile defense treaty, 256
  National Security Council
    relationship, 68, 71
  process, 78
  and State Department, 156
Nominations, 94–95
Nongovernmental organizations
  (NGOs), 170, 190, 276, 277
Nonproliferation and
  International Security
  Program, 182
Nonstate actors, 276. *See also*
  Nongovernmental
  organizations (NGOs)
North American Air Defense
  Command (NORAD),
  260–261
North American free trade agreement (NAFTA), 177, 197, 272
North Atlantic Treaty Organization
  (NATO), 60–61, 100, 143,
  251, 275–276, 286, 297–300
Northern Command
  (NORTHCOM), 261, 272
Nation-building, 213
Nuclear Non-Proliferation Act
  (1978), 89
Nuclear weapons, 49, 89–90,
  107–108, 206–208, 256
Nunn–Lugar program, 189

Obama, B.
  Afghanistan strategy, 83–85
  and intelligence community, 251
  and Libya, 297–298
  National Security Council
    relationship, 52, 71–72, 75,
    68–69
  process, 80
  reorganization of economic
    agencies, 174
  and signing statements, 58,
  trade agreements, 187, 198
Office of Foreign Assets Control
  (OFAC), 171, 179
Office of Global Security Risk, 195
Office of Intelligence and
  Analysis (OIA), 239
Office of International Affairs
  (OIA), 179
Office of Management and Budget
  (OMB), 122–123, 124–125,
  133, 260, 332, 333
Office of Strategic Services (OSS),
  48, 233
Office of Terrorism and Financial
  Intelligence (OTFI), 179
Office of the Director of National
  Intelligence (ODNI),
  235–236
Oil
  1970s shocks, 194
  Iraqi, 167, 168
  Kuwait, 138
  offshore drilling, 95
Oil companies, 196
Operation Desert Fox, 228
Operation Desert Shield, 167
Operation Desert Storm, 51, 167
Operation Enduring Freedom
  (Afghanistan), 286
Operation Jump Start, 221
Operation Provide Comfort,
  245–246
Organization for Security and
  Co-operation in Europe
  (OSCE), 276

Organization of American States (OAS), 276
Overseas Private Investment Corporation (OPIC), 173
Oversight, 97–98
Oversight investigations, 24

Pakistan, 89–90, 191
Panama, 38, 42, 51, 94
Panetta, L., 224, 225
Paraguay, 35
Partisan politics, 38, 111–112, 116–117, 138–139
Party control, 38
Pass back, 125
Patrician tutelage, 41
Pay-as-you-go (PAYGO), 132
Peace Corps, 100
Peace dividend, 51
Peace treaties, 42
Pearl Harbor, 66
Pentagon. *See* Department of Defense (DOD)
Percy, C., 104
Perry, W., 210
Philippines, 41
Pillar, P., 241
Pirates, 29, 31
Pocketbook nerve, 326
Policy Coordinating Committees, 75
Political dissent, 111–112
Political parties, 28, 100
Polk, J., 34–35
Posse Comitatus Act (1878), 220, 260
Powell, C., 80, 212
Presidential Policy Directive (PPD), 240
Presidential power. *See* Executive power
Presidents
  decision making style, 61–63
  foreign policy advisors, 65–74
  information sources, 62–65
  management and decision making, 61–65
  personal diplomacy, 74
  See also Executive power; individual presidents
President's Daily Brief (PDB), 236, 241–244
President's Emergency Plan for AIDS Relief (PEPFAR), 189, 192
Preston, T., 62
Principals Committee (PC), 74–75
Private assistance, 174–175
Private foreign policy initiatives, 35
Procedural legislation, 90–91
Project on National Security Reform (PNSR), 327–328, 332
Provincial reconstruction teams (PRTs), 160, 181
Public diplomacy, 142, 159
Public opinion, 43, 63, 105, 302–306
Purple suiters, 208

Qaddafi, M., 298–300
Quadrennial Defense Review (QDR), 106, 223–224, 326
Quadrennial Diplomacy and Development Review (QDDR), 189–190, 333, 334
Quadrennial National Security Review, 327

Randolph, E., 14
Ratification of treaties, 29
Reagan, R.
  advisors, 68
  Central America policies, 89
  foreign policy, 51
  Lebanon troup withdrawal, 111
  military doctrine, 208
  and National Security Agency, 78
  and National Security Council, 74

and South Africa, 115, 117
Soviet Union criticism, 59
strategic defense initiative, 256
Reed, T., 113
Reforms, 339
Reports required by Congress, 98
Reprogramming, 134–136
Republicans
and Budget Enforcement
Act, 138–139
and budget tactics, 132
and Cuban independence, 39, 112–113
expansionist platform, 39
first political party, 28
and South Africa, 116–117
and tariffs, 38
and use of force, 46
Rice, C., 71, 74, 160
Rogers, W., 101
Romania, 167
Roosevelt Corollary, 42
Roosevelt, F. D., 47–49, 57, 65–66
blocked by congress, 111
Brownlow Commission
appointment, 324–325
limits on military actions, 221
and secret funding, 136
weapons production
increase, 206
Roosevelt, T., 42
Root, E., 41, 42
Rosy Scenario, 138
Rubin, R., 133, 193
Rules of Engagement, 224
Rule XXII, 102
Rumsfeld, D.
Department of Defense changes, 326–327
disputes, 51–52,
Global War on Terror, 228
interagency dfficulties, 225
Iraq War, 211–212, 228–229
management style, 213,

security policy dominance, 157,
Quadrennial Defense Review
use, 223–224
September 11, 2001 response
Russia, 37, 42, 43, 94
Russo-Japanese War, 42

Scott, J., 105
Scowcroft, B., 71, 74, 75
Secretary of defense, 49, 60, 66,
201, 206, 209–211, 227,
270, 325
Secretary of state, 150–153
Secret spending, 135
Securities and Exchange
Commission (SEC), 174, 195
Security assistance, 223
Senate
advice and consent, 19, 54, 86, 92–93, 94
appropriations, 127. *See also*
Appropriations; Senate
Finance Committee
budget decisions, 131, 132, 136
campaigns, 319, 320
committees. *See* individual
committee names
confirmation, 95, 151, 177,
220, 258, 282–283, 329,
330, 332
and Constitutional Convention, 14–17
and Cuba, 114
and Federal Reserve, 178
filibusters, 102. *See also*
Filibusters
First Congress, 23–24
homeland security jurisdiction, 270, 273
and Libya, 299
and military issues, 226
national security advisor
confirmation, 82
oversight, 253

partisanship, 102
and presidential power, 56
rules, 101–102, 105
South African decision, 116–117
trade decisions, 198
treaties, 38, 41, 45, 92–94
treaty powers, 112
Washington administration, 28–29, 92–93
Wilson administration, 44, 45
Senate Appropriations Committee, 130. *See also* Appropriations committees
Senate Banking Committee, 187
Senate Finance Committee, 122, 129, 165, 179
Senate Foreign Relations Committee (SFRC), 94, 96, 97, 103, 104, 116, 152
Senate Select Committee on Intelligence (SSCI), 252
September 11, 2001 attacks, 1–2, 52, 88, 106, 111, 209, 222, 252–253
Serbia, 59, 110
Seward, W. H., 36–37
Shays' Rebellion, 12
Shevardnadze, E., 166
Ship construction authorization, 29
Shultz, G., 156
Signals intelligence (SIGINT), 238
Signing statements, 58
Situation Room, 64
Slavery, 14, 19, 32
Smith, F. C., 225
Snapback provisions, 198
Snowflakes, 213
Solarz, S., 105
Somalia, 80, 110
South Africa, 89, 115–117
Southeast Asia, 111, 132, 222
Soviet Jews, 43, 88, 99, 183

Soviet Union, 49–51, 61, 207
Spain, 40–41, 100, 111, 112–114
Spanish-American War, 40–41, 112–114
Special envoys, 158
Special Operations Command (SOCOM), 88, 106, 208, 221, 340
Special operations forces (SOF), 121, 201, 222, 247
Spending bills, 127, 131
Stability operations, 202
Stakeholders, 302
Standing Liaison Committee, 47–48
Star Wars, 256
Stassen, H., 101
State Department
    Bush, G. W. administration, 157
    and Congress, 163–166
    culture, 142, 155–156
    foreign assistance programs, 190
    growth of, 35–36
    history, 24–25, 42, 144–145
    leadership, 143–153
    operations, 156
    organization, 145–150
    personnel, 153–157. *See also* Foreign service officers (FSOs)
    processes, 157–159
    role in foreign economic policy, 176, 180
State War Navy Coordinating Committee, 48
Steinberg, J., 250
Stennis, J., 251
Stimson Doctrine, 46
Stimson, H., 65
Strategic Offensive Reductions Treaty (SORT), 93
Strengthening officials and organizations, 329
Substantive legislation, 89–90

Index 381

Suitcase bombs, 261
Summit diplomacy, 49–50, 158
Support for Eastern European Democracies (SEED), 189
Support to Military Operations (SMO), 240
Supreme Court decisions, 109
Symington, S., 96

Taft, W. H., 43
Taiwan, 90, 109
Taliban, 83, 228
Tariffs
  Congressional role, 185
  Constitutional provisions, 19
  Cuban products, 41, 114
  as economic incentive, 173
  and federal revenues, 129
  and import restrictions, 188, 198
  political controversy, 38–39
  punitive, 294
  and trade agreements, 171, 185
  and trade committees, 165
Teller, H., 114
Tenet, G., 80, 249
Terrorism, 57, 184
Texas annexation, 33–34
Thailand, 111, 132, 193, 221
302(b) allocations, 127
Think tanks, 302, 321–323
Tocqueville, de, A., 103–104
Tonkin Gulf Resolution, 109
Tower Commission, 326, 328
Track One, 142
Trade Adjustment Assistance (TAA), 198
Trade agreements, 47, 185–186, 197–199, 294–295
Trade Promotion Authority (TPA), 47, 185, 197
Trading With the Enemy Act (1917), 183

Train-and-equip programs, 192
Transfers, 134–136
Transportation security, 256
Treasury Department, 25, 179
Treaties, 42–43, 45–46, 92–94
Treaty of Versailles, 45–46
Truman, H. S., 49, 60, 66, 233
Turkey, 167
Tyler, J., 34

Unanimous consent, 102
Understandings, 94
Unilateralism, 277–278
Unitary executive, 58
United Nations, 49, 278–285
United Nations Educational, Scientific and Cultural Organization (UNESCO), 284, 297
United Nations Security Council (UNSC), 143, 167, 168, 184, 275
United Nations (UN), 80, 228, 274–276
  See also United Nations Security Council (UNSC)
United States Agency for International Development (USAID), 160, 170, 174, 176, 190, 191, 327, 336
United States Trade Representative (USTR), 185–186
Unocal, 196
USA PATRIOT Act, 2–3, 184, 194, 257
U.S. Coast Guard (USCG), 239, 258, 261
U.S. colonialism, 39, 41, 43
U.S. Constitution, 7–10, 14, 16–19, 20–22
U.S. consular and diplomatic posts, 35–36
U.S. expansion, 31–35, 38, 39

U.S. government agencies, 175–182
U.S.–Mexican border, 21
U.S.–Mexican War, 110
U.S. military
  911 force, 223
  consolidation, 206
  forces, 207
  growth of, 205–206
  international deployments, 222–223
  nuclear weapons, 206–208
  operations, 203, 204
  overview, 200
  personnel, 214–216
  planning and policy making, 223–224
  reservists, 215–216
  security assistance, 223
  tensions and rivalries, 224–225
  warfighting, 221–222
U.S. security assistance, 223
U.S.-Soviet arms race, 49–50
U.S.-Soviet cooperation, 166
U.S. Trade and Development Agency, 174
U.S. Trade Representative (USTR), 88, 173, 176, 179–180
U.S. wars, 202
Use of force, 2–3, 107–108, 201–204, 213, 221–222, 224

Vanderberg, A., 101
Vice presidents, 72–73
Vietnam War
  as analogy, 78
  and civilian-military relations, 213
  Congressional actions, 97, 109, 110, 111, 132
  contingency funds use, 134
  diplomatic efforts, 50
  military doctrine, 208
  popular support loss, 202
  president's daily brief on, 242–243
Virginia Plan, 14, 15

War council, 1
War Department, 25, 30
War powers, 16, 58, 107–111
War Powers Resolution (1973), 50, 55, 58, 90, 108, 109, 110 110, 164–165, 300
Warfighting, 221–222
Warner, J., 103
Warning fatigue, 250
Washington Armament Conference, 46
Washington, G., 7, 12, 16, 23, 27–29, 65, 92
Washington Monument cuts, 133
Weapons of mass destruction (WMD), 228, 252, 260, 336
Weinberger, C., 60
West Point Military Academy, 31
Whigs, 32–35
Whiskey Rebellion, 29
Wilmot Proviso, 34
Wilson, W., 43–45, 59–60
Wolfowitz, P., 228
World Bank, 49, 174, 275, 284, 292–293
World Trade Organization (WTO), 196, 275, 276, 294–295
World War I, 44–45, 206
World War II, 48–49, 111, 202, 260
Worldwide Intelligence Review (WIRe), 241
Wotton, H., 141

Zaire, 167
Zinni, T., 228